FLIGHT
TO THE **TOP** OF THE
WORLD

The Adventures of Walter Wellman

◀ ▶

DAVID L. BRISTOW

UNIVERSITY OF NEBRASKA PRESS | LINCOLN

Library of Congress Cataloging-in-Publication Data
Names: Bristow, David (David L.), author.
Title: Flight to the Top of the World: The Adventures of
Walter Wellman / David L. Bristow.
Description: Lincoln: University of Nebraska Press, [2018] |
Includes bibliographical references and index.
Identifiers: LCCN 2017045452
ISBN 9780803296787 (cloth: alk. paper)
ISBN 9781496207043 (epub)
ISBN 9781496207050 (mobi)
ISBN 9781496207067 (pdf)
Subjects: LCSH: Wellman, Walter, 1858–1934. |
Explorers—Arctic regions—Biography. | Arctic
regions—Discovery and exploration. | Adventure and
adventurers—United States—Biography.
Classification: LCC G635.W33 B75 2018 | DDC 910.92
[B]—dc23 LC record available at https://lccn.loc.
gov/2017045452

Set in Minion Pro by Mikala R Kolander.

For my big brother, Mark,
for introducing me to history, and for
my big sister, Sandy,
for introducing me to reading

It is not the critic who counts; not the man who points out how the strong man stumbles, or where the doer of deeds could have done them better. The credit belongs to the man who is actually in the arena, whose face is marred by dust and sweat and blood; who strives valiantly; who errs, and comes short again and again, because there is no effort without error and shortcoming; but who does actually strive to do the deeds; who knows the great enthusiasms, the great devotions; who spends himself in a worthy cause.

—THEODORE ROOSEVELT

CONTENTS

Part 1. Newsman in the Far North, 1891–1899

Part 2. The Insider, 1900–1904

Part 3. The Polar Airship, 1905–1909

Part 4. The Atlantic Ocean, 1910–1912

ILLUSTRATIONS

ACKNOWLEDGMENTS

I thank my wife, Danette, for her patience and encouragement as she listened to one discovery or half-baked idea and read one rough draft after another; Bridget Barry, Emily Wendell, and Elizabeth Zaleski of the University of Nebraska Press; copyeditor Vicki Chamlee; the anonymous readers whose comments challenged and improved the manuscript; my agent, Susie Cohen; Elizabeth Borja, Heidi Stover, and Kate Igoe of the Smithsonian Institution; Tomeka Myers and Georgia Zola of the Library of Congress; Heidi Voss-Nilsen of Norsk Folkemuseum in Olso; Hans Aas of Vågemot Miniforlag in Skien, Norway; and the staff of the Lincoln (Nebraska) City Libraries for handling all those interlibrary loan requests.

PROLOGUE

Atlantic City, New Jersey, October 15, 1910

The Boardwalk lay under heavy fog when Melvin Vaniman arrived at the airship hangar at 4:45 a.m. In the gloom, wrote the *New York Times* reporter who accompanied him, the wooden hangar rose like a "big black blotch in the night that was hardly less black with fog, two small lights glimmering through an open door being the only guides to its location."[1]

The hangar's ceiling stood eighty feet above the floor. In the semidarkness of this cavernous space, a 228-foot-long airship swayed gently on its moorings, straining against a web of ropes tied to hundreds of green burlap sandbags. Two crewmen were already aboard the narrow car that doubled as a keel for the cigar-shaped gasbag. While they worked on the engines, Vaniman talked with Murray Simon, an Englishman and the only sailor on the six-man airship crew.

Vaniman and Simon agreed. Today was the day. The lack of wind was perfect for the delicate operation of maneuvering the airship out of its hangar. The forecast for the North Atlantic was favorable. And the hurricane working its way north from the Caribbean would arrive too late to do anything but give them a push on their way to Europe. Simon had already phoned the Hotel Chalfonte across town. The captain approved and was on his way.

Stepping outside into the predawn chill, Vaniman raised a blue-and-white flag as a signal that the long-awaited launch was under way. But the flag was useless until there was more light, so he went back inside to the telephone, looking at phone numbers he had written on the back of an oil company ad card. The police and fire chiefs had promised thirty to forty men each to serve as a ground crew.

Simon, meanwhile, was at the big canvas doors through which the airship must pass. Vaniman had designed them to withstand a strong wind.

The double doors were secured by twenty-five steel anchors buried in the sand outside and tied with ropes to fifty stress points on the doors, which were also laced together down the center. Simon slashed through the lashings with his sailor's knife. The doors swung open, and the mist rolled in.

Headlights pierced the darkness as automobiles began to arrive: a patrol wagon with uniformed police, a hose cart and a hook and ladder truck from the fire department, and a speeding auto driven by a young woman. It screeched to a halt by the door, and out climbed a tall, bespectacled man with a graying mustache. He wore an aviator's cap and goggles, a khaki uniform, and knee breeches. He walked with a noticeable limp and used a cane. His name was Walter Wellman, and he was one of the most famous men in the world—and, lately, one of the most ridiculed.

Although his contemporaries first compared his life to a Jules Verne novel, few people today have heard of Walter Wellman (1858–1934). He led five expeditions in search of the North Pole, two by dog sled and three by dirigible airship. He was the first person to bring airships and wireless telegraphy to the Arctic and was the first to attempt to cross the Atlantic Ocean by air. He endured hardships, cheated death on more than one occasion, and surrounded himself with a team of assistants as eccentric and daring as he was.

All this would be noteworthy by itself, but Wellman managed to complete these ventures while he was a nationally known political reporter and consummate Washington insider. Although he was not the first newspaper-sponsored adventurer, more than any of his predecessors he turned exploration into a real-time media event, and his reputation both flourished and suffered because of it.

Even apart from his expeditions, Wellman sometimes did as much to shape events as to report them, such as during the great 1902 anthracite coal strike when he stepped in as a back-channel conduit between President Theodore Roosevelt, union leader John Mitchell, and financier J. P. Morgan. As a journalist Wellman cultivated high-ranking sources whom he could quote anonymously. In an age in which presidents did not usually grant on-the-record interviews, he was alternately quoted and resented by other journalists for his almost unequaled access to the William McKinley and Roosevelt administrations. He played the now-familiar media game of

trading loyalty for access, yet as a progressive Republican he was capable of infuriating either party, playing the roles of muckraker and sycophant with equal enthusiasm.

For one who seemed to be constantly planning and fund-raising for his next expedition, Wellman remained a prolific writer, churning out articles that ranged from political analysis to gossip to exposés. As he grew older, the man who left school at age twelve began presenting himself as a self-styled expert on an array of topics including banking, labor, international relations, public transportation, and aerial warfare. He was an optimist and technophile, sometimes brilliantly prescient and sometimes little more than a visionary crank. His contemporaries lacked the benefit of hindsight to tell which was which.

Wellman's story, in other words, isn't just about his adventures. It is also a story of mass media and public opinion in a time of rapid social and technological change. He lived in a time when explorers were racing to fill in the last remaining blank spots on the map, a time when aviation promised to fulfill humanity's greatest hopes and darkest fears, a time of industrial transformation that pitted labor against capital and raised questions about who was to own this new technological world and for whose benefit it would be managed, and a time of nationalism, imperialism, and the emergence of one of the most dynamic presidents in U.S. history.

And Walter Wellman was in the middle of it all, participating, commenting, manipulating, and generally embodying the ambitions and contradictions of his age. It's true that he attempted more than he achieved, but he accomplished more than he is usually given credit for. Whatever else you can say about him, he was never dull.

Dawn arrived chilly and gray, and a crowd of dozens, then hundreds, then more than a thousand people began to gather along the waterfront as word about the airship's launch spread through the city. Drawn by its ant army of handlers, the airship emerged slowly from its wooden house. Larger than any aerial craft except a German zeppelin (which none of the crowd had probably ever seen), the airship had two motors, four propellers, and a theoretical range greater than any man-made device that had yet flown. Wellman had named it the *America*.

Wellman embraced his wife and daughters, then climbed aboard to the cheers of the crowd. Vaniman's wife carried aboard the ship's mascot, a gray kitten. "We won't come back until we have had a try at Europe," Van said.[2]

People had talked of a flight across the Atlantic Ocean for years, but until that day no one had ever staked his life on the idea. Back in 1844 Edgar Allan Poe had fooled thousands of *New York Sun* readers with a hoax about a transatlantic balloon flight. Aeronauts seriously discussed the possibility for years afterward. A few even raised money and built large balloons for it, but the plans were always dropped before the day of departure. It was too much like suicide.

Now the world had aeroplanes, but no one would even think of crossing an ocean in a flimsy craft of such limited range. A motor balloon stood a chance but only if its gasoline motors and large propellers were strong enough to buck the wind and if its hydrogen-filled gasbag was large enough to lift four and a half tons of fuel and stay aloft for three thousand miles.[3] Everything about the *America* was designed for range and endurance. Wellman and Vaniman believed it was the first and only machine capable of spanning the distance. The airship also carried a twenty-seven-foot lifeboat stocked with thirty days' provisions in case they were wrong.[4]

The *America* rose into the air, and within minutes disappeared into the fog. So began what the *Washington Times* called "the most daring, perilous, and spectacular trip in the history of aviation."[5]

For the rest of the day, people crowded around the wireless telegraph station at the pier, for among its other modern marvels the airship carried a Marconi transmitter and a "wireless man" named Jack Irwin, who was on loan from the White Star Line, a British shipping company. The idea of a seagoing aircraft communicating with those on shore—something wholly unprecedented—enthralled the public almost as much as the flight itself. At 11:00 a.m. a wireless operator picked up the *America* "somewhere out in the dull gray mists," heading northeast by east. The airship would soon be out of range of shore stations. Respecting the gravity of the moment, the wireless man wryly sent the *America* off with the following farewell:

SO LONG TO YOU JACK IRWIN DEAR BROTHER. JONAH'S WHALE WILL NEVER COUGH YOU UP DEAR BROTHER. YOU'RE A GONER.[6]

FLIGHT TO THE TOP OF THE WORLD

PART 1

Newsman in the Far North,
1891–1899

1

In Search of Christopher Columbus

The Bahamas, June 1891

"Landsman that I am, making my first sea voyage in June," wrote Walter Wellman, "I never believed the stories I had heard of the calmness of the great ocean. 'As smooth as glass' had to me always seemed more than a poet's license, which is generally a polite synonym for lie."[1]

But to Wellman's delight, he found it so. Looking down from the deck railing, he gazed upon a surface without so much as a ripple, "till a cork could float hour after hour with its uppermost end as dry as tinder."[2] Only the gentle, eternal swell of the sea remained.

"What could be more delightful than four or five days like these?"[3] Wellman asked his readers, for he was writing no diary or private letter but a newspaper article for the *Chicago Herald* that would then be syndicated to other papers across the United States. And this was no pleasure cruise but a journey of exploration. Wellman had come to the Bahamas to locate the exact spot where Christopher Columbus had first landed in the New World nearly four hundred years earlier, to raise a monument there on behalf of Wellman's employer, and to celebrate the deed in newspaper columns.

As voyages go, this was a mild one. Wellman explained for his readers the importance of bringing a deck chair because the ship may not have enough on board, warned of losing your money in card games (though he was an avid hearts player), and recommended a visit to the hold, where you could "see the poor stokers feed the fires while the fat is being tried out of themselves in a temperature of 125 degs. Fahrenheit."[4]

Arriving at Nassau, Wellman and his companions chartered a smaller vessel to cruise the islands. He carried a translation of Columbus's logbook, intending to visit various sites and compare them to the explorer's own description of his landfall.

"If successful in locating the spot," said the *Herald*, "the location of which has hitherto been a matter of great doubt and endless dispute," Wellman would "erect a monument commemorative of Columbus' great achievement."[5]

If successful. But naturally the *Herald* was counting on the publicity of a successful identification. Wellman's ship carried materials for the monument. Was there really any chance that he would fail to mark a spot and proclaim it genuine?

From the beginning of his career as an explorer, Wellman radiated confidence that he could solve problems that had even eluded the experts. The price of Wellman's admission to this world of discovery was a sponsor's expectation of immediate and unqualified success. Wellman probably didn't think much of either of these points while in the Bahamas. Why would he? The water was glassy smooth, the task straightforward. If anything, it all seemed too easy.

Walter Wellman was born November 3, 1858, near Mentor, Ohio, the youngest of four brothers.[6] Though he would reach age thirty-two before taking his first sea voyage, three of his uncles became captains of Lake Erie vessels, and his father, Alonzo, had been a ship's carpenter as a young man before moving to Ohio.[7] During the Civil War, from 1862 to 1864, Alonzo served as a private in the 105th Ohio Infantry before transferring to the Mississippi Naval Squadron for the final thirteen months of the war. Alonzo was a seaman aboard Commodore Andrew Foote's flagship the USS *Black Hawk*, a 902-ton "tinclad" (lightly armored) side-wheel riverboat assigned to gunship duty on the Mississippi River and its tributaries. On April 22, 1865, as the war was drawing to a close, the *Black Hawk* accidentally burned and sank near Cairo, Illinois. Alonzo survived and was discharged in June.[8] Returning home to Ohio, he was a stranger to little Walter, now six years old.

The following year Alonzo moved the family to the backwoods of Michigan, where they lived for five years and where Walter received his only formal schooling.[9] In 1871 the Wellmans hitched up a team and headed west to the frontier, settling in a prairie dugout near York, Nebraska.[10] Walter's older brothers Rinaldo, Frank, and Arthur went into printing and journalism, and Frank and Arthur founded the *York Monitor* in 1872. It

was the town's first newspaper, but it soon had rivals. The Wellman brothers found themselves in a newspaper war full of dirty deeds and personal invective. The earliest newspapers are no longer extant, but one quotation achieved immortality in a county history. One of the Wellman boys tried to prevent the county board from paying a printing bill to rival newspaperman W. E. Dayton, who then wrote, "We challenge the paltry wretch to do his dirtiest. The cleanest thing he can do is dirty beyond expression and the nastier he becomes the sooner he will die of his own rottenness."[11]

Walter, meanwhile, left home at age twelve to clerk at a country store where Pawnee Indians from a nearby reservation were among his main customers.[12] But he returned to follow his brothers into the printing trade, serving as their apprentice until—at age fourteen—he and a partner founded a weekly paper in Sutton, Nebraska.

Like York, Sutton was a frontier town. Walter's *Sutton Times* was its first paper. Republican in politics like his brothers' paper, the *Times* had a "patent inside," meaning that Walter received sheets of newsprint with syndicated national news printed on one side, with the other side left blank for local content and advertising. The first issue on June 20, 1873, included an article about the history of Sutton (the town was barely two years old) and nine columns of advertisements from "twenty-three different branches of business and profession."[13]

In addition to serving as editor and publisher, Walter could set type and do most of his own mechanical work.[14] Many years later, when he was a well-known Washington reporter, his typesetting skills remained impressive. In 1894 the Washington Press Club needed a printed notice in a hurry, and Congressman Amos J. Cummings of New York—a proud former printer—volunteered to do the work. Wellman, probably sensing an opportunity for publicity, boasted that he could do the job faster and more accurately. The bet was on, and club members appointed referees and timekeepers and headed for a print shop. Wellman set up the 111-word notice in twenty-four minutes, or four and a half minutes faster than the congressman, who made four errors while Wellman "pulled a clean proof."[15]

Walter returned to Ohio in 1878, when he was nineteen, and soon became editor of the *Canton Repository*. Among the local residents, he came to know a blonde, blue-eyed young woman named Laura McCann

and a young congressman named William McKinley. Walter married Laura on Christmas Eve 1879, when he was twenty-one and she was eighteen. And McKinley, already a rising star in the Republican Party, even then seemed a good man to know.[16]

As in Nebraska, times were always lively in the Ohio newspaper business, where rivalries were hot and tempers short. In the summer of 1879 a rival paper, the *Critic*, printed an accusation that an unnamed minister of an East Tuscarawas Street church "had too well loved his maid servant and strayed from the paths of virtue." The writer was a Pittsburgh correspondent who used the pen name Montgomery. Soon the local clergy was in an uproar, demanding a retraction and the name of the writer's source. Wellman joined the fray by calling the accusation "all bosh" and suggesting that the next time Montgomery visited Canton, "he will find all the Tuscarawas Street preachers and one or two landlords waiting to receive him when he lands, and he can go back to Pittsburgh singing, 'Oh, the tar, the tar, the feathers and the tar.'" Montgomery responded by claiming that Wellman himself had been his source for the story and that Montgomery had merely published it "in good faith word for word" (without, of course, bothering to investigate the matter himself). Montgomery concluded by leaving "Mr. Wellman and the injured ministers to fight it out among themselves."[17]

Montgomery may have been lying, but controversy and scandal followed Wellman as he continued working in the newspaper business. In 1881 Walter took Laura and their baby daughter, Ruth, to Cincinnati, where he and his brother Frank founded the *Penny Paper*, which was said to be the only penny daily between Lake Erie and the Gulf of Mexico.[18] Penny newspapers were not new in the 1880s—the first was the *New York Sun* in 1833—but they were uncommon at a time when most papers sold for two or three cents an issue. Penny papers tended to be small and sensational (to appeal to a working-class readership), and they were mostly sold by newsboys on the street rather than by subscription.

Starting out with only a few hundred dollars between them, the Wellmans soon ran short of capital and nearly had to close the paper, but Walter found willing investors in brothers James Scripps and E. W. Scripps. Later that year, Walter found himself in a different kind of trouble. He used his paper to attack a Cincinnati gambling boss and con man known

as "Policy Bill Smith" and lambasted police and local officials for allowing the swindling to continue. In October 1881 Smith hired a Pinkerton detective to entrap Wellman, who was then arrested on charges of blackmail and criminal libel.[19]

Wellman's and the detective's public statements agreed on certain points. The detective had approached Wellman claiming to be a Chicago journalist named J. A. Corwin. Saying that he had damaging information about Smith, Corwin sought Wellman's help in a blackmail scheme. Corwin wrote an article that he asked Wellman to have set in type. Corwin requested a proof sheet, with the understanding that he would show this single printed copy to Smith's people and threaten that Wellman was ready to publish it if they didn't pay up. Wellman acknowledged printing the proof sheet and receiving $100 for it.[20]

Wellman, however, insisted that he knew he was being swindled and that Smith was probably behind it. He said he decided to beat "Policy Bill" by taking his money without incriminating himself. Wellman insisted that he handed over the proof sheet and pocketed the money only after making Corwin sign a receipt acknowledging that the *Penny Paper* would not publish the article and that Wellman did not know what Corwin was going to do with it.[21]

In November Wellman was convicted, fined $100 and court costs, and sentenced to thirty days in jail. On appeal, however, the case against him was dismissed. "The prosecution failed to show up, they having no case," said the *Canton Repository*, Wellman's former paper. By then Wellman had resigned from the *Penny Paper*, and he and Frank had sold their remaining shares to E. W. Scripps.[22] Scripps went on to found the press conglomerates E. W. Scripps Company and the United Press news service. The *Penny Paper* eventually became the *Cincinnati Post* and remained in publication until 2007.

Scripps made two statements about the case—one in an 1883 article in the *Post* and the other in an unpublished early twentieth-century manuscript. The article appeared when two of Scripps's employees were facing criminal libel charges brought by another of Wellman's old enemies. Scripps seemed eager to distance himself from the former editor. He wrote that after Wellman's arrest, Scripps met with him "and learned that he was guilty. Wellman at that time told me a sad story of his temptation and fall."

Scripps added that Wellman willingly left the company and that Scripps "secured him a much higher price for his stock than it was really worth" because "he was entitled to a fair defense against the rascals who had led him into crime for the purpose of wreaking vengeance."[23]

In Scripps's unpublished memoir, however, he said only that "Wellman had been made the victim of a 'frame up.' This was the first instance that I had known when a detective agency had been used to perpetrate a crime."[24] Scripps said he hired a lawyer, but Walter and Frank had been eager to settle, apologize, close the paper, and leave town. Walter had been promised immunity if he did so, and legal threats may have been the least of the Wellmans' dangers from an angry underworld boss. Scripps considered Walter "a very capable young journalist" but was clearly disappointed that he was willing to give up so quickly. He said Walter and Frank fled across the Ohio River into Kentucky.[25]

The brothers were soon back in Ohio, where in March 1882 they founded another penny paper, the *Akron Daily News*, promising it would be an independent Republican paper that would avoid intense partisanship.[26] But it did not escape controversy. Its columns were soon aflame, charging local utility companies of rate fixing. Circulation soared; the utilities lowered their rates. Emboldened Wellman demonstrated his lack of partisanship by lambasting Akron's Republican congressman A. S. McClure and endorsing his Democratic opponent, David R. Paige, in that year's election. Paige won, but Wellman found himself in a bitter editorial war with both the Republican-backed *Akron Daily Beacon* and the *Sunday Gazette*.

Again the Wellmans sold out, but Walter soon returned to work as the *Akron Daily News* editor and resumed his attacks on *Sunday Gazette* editor Carson Lake. The war of words became something of a local legend. According to a local historian, Wellman "vilified Lake in scandalous fashion. Lake promptly filed suit for libel and Wellman, knowing he had stepped out of bounds, prepared to leave town." In a farewell issue Wellman "tore Lake limb from limb, picturing him as the worst scoundrel that ever drew breath. Then, while the sheriff was rattling the front door, he passed out the still wet newspapers to newsboys, grabbed his valise and hastened out the back door and out of Akron."[27]

This sounds like an exaggeration, but there is at least some truth to the story. Lake and his *Gazette* had made many enemies. Ohio Democratic

papers referred to him variously as "a man without political or personal character" who "propagates falsehoods" and as one of the "Republican hirelings on the Republican treadmill of slander and falsification."[28] In May 1883 Wellman had Lake arrested for libel after the *Gazette* told its readers about Wellman's blackmail conviction without mentioning Wellman's successful appeal. A grand jury failed to indict Lake, who within weeks filed his own unsuccessful libel suit against Wellman and the *Daily News*, seeking $5,000 in damages for an article titled "The Nameless," which was widely believed to be about Lake. (Later that year, Lake sued another Akron paper, seeking $10,000 in damages, but was awarded a judgment of only five cents.) Whether it was the pressure of Wellman's legal troubles or a simple "lack of business," as the *Gazette* claimed, the *Daily News* closed its doors in July 1883.[29]

Such was the world in which Walter Wellman came of age as a journalist. It was sensationalist, litigious, quick to speak, and quick to anger. Wellman himself was described by a local historian as a "swaggering reformer of a journalist."[30] He was young, cocky, and out of work, with a wife and now two small daughters, Ruth and Rose, to feed. Within weeks he was back in the news as a partner in the Akron Toy Company, which manufactured a "toy safe bank."[31] By early 1884 he had returned to Canton, where he represented a local electric company and tried to convince the city council to allow the running of wires so that twenty-five businesses could light their offices with newfangled incandescent bulbs.[32]

Wellman didn't stay in the electric business for long, though his interest in technology would endure. His days as a publisher, however, were over. Later that year he took a job as a journalist with the *Chicago Herald*, trading his independence for the relative stability and larger audience of a big city paper.[33]

At last Wellman thrived. Although bylines were rare at the time, Wellman signed his early pieces "Mentor" after his hometown. He was a popular writer and began cultivating an affable persona in print—not folksy but upbeat, intelligent, and rarely confrontational. As the *Herald*'s Washington DC correspondent, now writing under his own name, Wellman delighted in providing his growing readership with an insiders' view of the nation's capital.

Fig. 1. Walter Wellman, ca. 1885. The *Chicago Herald*'s new reporter would soon rise to national prominence at the paper's Washington DC bureau. Smithsonian National Air and Space Museum (NASM 9A10729).

In the early years of writing for the paper, he wrote mostly lightweight stuff: glowing personality profiles, minor anecdotes, and mild gossip that didn't truly scandalize but made readers feel they were in the know. When a convention of schoolteachers visited the capital in 1891, for example, Wellman wrote with amusement (and apparent approval) of the hundreds of ladies who descended on the White House and "browbeat the watchmen at the gates into giving them admittance," who strolled past distracted guards onto the floor of the House of Representatives, and who threw snowballs by moonlight at the big equestrian statue of Andrew Jackson.[34] The women felt entitled to go where they pleased and to speak their mind.

People such as the curious schoolteachers weren't just Wellman's subjects; they were also his natural audience. Through him, readers could enter the White House or the back rooms of the Capitol and listen in on the conversations and the gossip. Wellman's access to the powerful grew as his sources learned, first, that he wouldn't embarrass them and, second, that his syndicated articles had tremendous reach and could sway public opinion. He may have been writing a lot of fluff in 1891 when he first made plans for his Bahamas trip, but he was laying the groundwork for more substantial reporting later.

Historians and geographers had variously identified five different Bahaman islands as Columbus's San Salvador, his first point of contact with the New World. By Wellman's time, opinion had narrowed to two islands—Samana and Watlings. Wellman cruised the coast of Samana and Cat Islands (the latter favored by Washington Irving as the landing site), but he didn't think they matched the explorer's description. Columbus had written of San Salvador: "This island is very large and very level, and has very green trees and many streams of water and a very large lagoon in the middle without any mountain, and is covered with verdure most pleasing to the eye."[35]

Watlings, Wellman noted, was the only island in the Bahamas with a lagoon in the middle. Furthermore, Columbus's entry of October 14 seemed to describe Graham's Harbor on Watlings; entering the harbor, Wellman found the hill and headland just where they should be. This was the spot, he decided, and gave the order to go ashore.

Only 770 people, all but one of whom were black, lived on Watlings Island. The island's native inhabitants had not long survived in the presence

of the brutal Spaniards and their imported diseases. Wellman acknowledged, "It is painful to add that the people are badly afflicted with leprosy."[36] The islanders Wellman saw were the descendants of enslaved Africans who had been brought over to work sugar plantations for the benefit of European investors, but Wellman hadn't come to write about the Bahamian people. He had come to celebrate a feat of exploration. Supplies were unloaded and hauled to a little headland overlooking the beach on the island's northeastern shore. There Wellman and his companions erected a grotto of native stone and slabs of Italian marble. A marble globe formed the centerpiece. Just below it they placed a marble plaque inscribed with the words:

ON THIS SPOT
CHRISTOPHER COLUMBUS
FIRST SET FOOT ON THE SOIL OF
THE NEW WORLD.
ERECTED BY
THE CHICAGO HERALD
JUNE 15, 1891.[37]

Jagged and weather-beaten, the monument remains to this day. That it marks Columbus's actual landing site is uncertain. Wellman himself said that he expected "to become involved in a lively controversy."[38] A few years later British geographer Jacques Redway, a Fellow of the Royal Geographical Society, wrote an article for *National Geographic Magazine* in which he dismissed the lagoon on Watlings Island as an ephemeral feature and did not consider it decisive. He argued instead for Samana Island. Redway acknowledged, however, that Columbus wrote poorly and ambiguously in Spanish, that his instruments were imprecise, and that the closest thing in existence to Columbus's original log is a later abridgment with interpolations—all of which undermine confidence in any claim.[39]

Other experts, however, reached the same conclusion that Wellman did. In 1925 Watlings was officially renamed San Salvador, whose name had been transferred from Cat Island, one of the other contenders.

Though Wellman had already achieved some prominence as a journalist, the Bahamas trip was often cited in later years as the moment when

he first gained national attention. At the time of his departure, he was promoted as "a young man of indomitable spirit, great experience as a newspaper worker and writer in all fields of journalism, and the physical strength and endurance of an athlete."[40]

It was a short step from celebrating another man's conquest to dreaming of a conquest of one's own. And why not? Who was Columbus, after all, before his first great voyage? He was a skilled mariner, but other mariners could—and soon did—make that same voyage. What set Columbus apart was that he recognized the possibility and convinced the king and queen of Spain to finance it.

To become an explorer, one needs only two things—a dream and access to power. Wellman soon realized that he had both.

2

Arctic Enthusiasm Is an Intermittent Fever

Washington DC, February 1894

By the winter of 1894, the United States was mired in a severe economic depression. Hundreds of banks and thousands of businesses had failed. Unemployment reached levels not seen again until the 1930s, and many Americans found themselves reduced to hunger and beggary. Labor and capital fought each other in bloody strikes, while the nation argued about the causes of the troubles, blaming the railroads, the gold standard, the speculators, the immigrants, and the Democrats.

Wellman's thoughts were mostly turned elsewhere. In January he warned his readers that foreign ministers in Washington were predicting a major war between Europe's vast and growing armies. Norway wanted independence from Sweden, and in this Russia saw an opportunity to gain year-round access to the Atlantic Ocean. Warmed by the Gulf Stream, even Norway's northernmost ports, such as Tromsø, remained ice free through the long Arctic winter. If Russia should back Norwegian independence in exchange for Atlantic ports, both Germany and Britain would surely object—even to the point of war—and then France would be drawn in as well.

"All through the old world every fifth man is a soldier," Wellman added, quoting an anonymous diplomat. "Enormous taxes are levied for the support of these vast troops. . . . It is becoming an axiom in the diplomatic world of Europe that some day, and not a distant day at that, excuse must be given the people for this levy upon them. If they are to be continually asked for tribute to military rule, they must be afforded proof that military rule is a necessity."[1]

It is unclear how much of Wellman's intelligence came from foreign diplomats and how much from Wellman's imagination. Either way it was a thought-provoking scenario: start with an insignificant local conflict,

add an alliance with a larger nation that threatens the delicate balance of European power, and soon the whole thing escalates into a destructive world war.

Norway and its ice-free Arctic port of Tromsø were very much on Wellman's mind that winter, though for a different reason. In February he announced his intention to lead an expedition to the North Pole.

Wellman was financing the project mostly from his own pocket. He admitted to his family that he would be "financially ruined" if the expedition failed.[2] The *Evening Star* of Washington DC bought exclusive rights to a series of articles, boasting that the expedition was "a Washington enterprise": "[Wellman] has planned to keep up a line of communication with home until the party is well advanced into the ice fields, and so readers of *The Star* will be able to keep the little band of bold explorers in sight, so to speak, until they disappear into the mysterious region around the pole."[3]

Newspaper-sponsored exploration was not new, but Wellman was the first journalist to lead a polar expedition. And more than any previous Arctic explorer, he planned to turn his adventure into a public event. Rather than waiting to publish a full account of the journey upon his return, Wellman would take his readers along in real time—or as close to it as steamship communication would allow. He had already learned how to entice readers with an insider's view of life in the nation's capital. Now he would do the same for life on an Arctic voyage.

Explorers of that era were fond of portraying the discovery of the North Pole as the dream of the ages. It wasn't. The obsession with that invisible and, practically speaking, useless point did not become a nationalistic quest until the nineteenth century. Even then, for decades the primary object of desire wasn't the pole itself but the Northwest Passage.

Long before anyone knew if the passage existed, sailors sought a navigable water route connecting the Atlantic and Pacific Oceans across the top of the North American continent. Was there really a way through the maze of uncharted islands, bays, and inlets of the Far North? No one knew. And even if a sea route existed, was it ever free of ice? Or might the passage be even farther north, across the Arctic Ocean itself? Some people believed that they'd find an open polar sea if they could only penetrate far enough into the pack ice.

Fig. 2. Laura McCann Wellman, October 9, 1893, less than six months after the birth of her fifth child, Rebekah. Walter was planning to depart the next spring for his first polar expedition. Smithsonian National Air and Space Museum (NASM 9A10734).

But the most remarkable thing about the Northwest Passage is how it remained a highly prized goal—even growing in desirability—long after everyone knew it would be useless for commerce. The season for navigation was simply too short and too unpredictable at high latitudes.[4]

Britain was the first nation to realize that sailing the passage would be nothing more than a great adventure. Following the Napoleonic Wars, the Royal Navy found itself for the first time in many years without suitable enemies. By 1817 90 percent of British naval officers were unemployed, which at that time meant living in poverty on half pay, and with no chance of promotion.[5] So the navy began sending ships northward in search of the two great Arctic prizes—the passage and, to a lesser extent, the pole itself.

The history of the quest for the Northwest Passage is too long and rich in stories to tell here, but two objects will suffice for our purposes. One is a sledge. The other is a book.

The sledge, built of oak and iron and with a twenty-eight-foot boat rigged for river travel lashed to its top, stood abandoned on the barren northwest shore of King William Island, some two hundred miles above the Arctic Circle. The boat contained two skeletons, and on the ground nearby lay the remains of several more men.

Together the sledge and the boat weighed at least thirteen hundred pounds—or would have had the sledge not been loaded. "But it *was* loaded," writes Pierre Berton in *The Arctic Grail*,

> with an incredible accumulation of unnecessary articles: books (*The Vicar of Wakefield* was one), every kind of footgear from sea boots to strong shoes, towels and toothbrushes, gun covers and twine, soap and sheet lead, dinner knives, crested silver plate, pocket watches and tools, a bead purse, a cigar case—everything, in short, that civilized nineteenth-century travelers considered necessary for their comfort and well-being.[6]

In 1859 a team of men discovered this sledge by following a debris trail southward along the island's western shore. They had come in the ship *Fox* under the command of Capt. Francis L. McClintock of the Royal Navy, though the ship was owned and the expedition sponsored by Lady Jane Franklin. Lady Franklin had a quest of her own: not to find the passage

but to find her husband, Sir John Franklin, who had sailed off to seek the passage in 1845 and hadn't been heard from since.

Franklin's ships, the HMS *Erebus* and HMS *Terror*, were three-masted bomb vessels built to carry heavy mortars. Together their crews totaled 129 officers and men. By the spring of 1848, the mighty ships had been trapped in the ice for a year and a half. Twenty-four men had died, including Franklin. In desperation the survivors had abandoned their ships and begun walking south toward the Canadian mainland. No one made it home alive.

As McClintock's men examined the bizarre contents of the sledge, they recognized how poorly prepared Franklin and his men had been for their ordeal. By then the men of the *Fox* had already found other bodies, artifacts, and a few terse written records—enough to piece together a rough outline of Franklin's story.

Like the story of every other Arctic expedition, Franklin's was a tale of adaptation to one of the world's harshest environments. In addition to the obvious threats—deadly cold and the danger of starvation, plus maddening months of darkness in winter—the Arctic imposed years of isolation resulting from the combination of ice and great distances. If anything went wrong, you and your shipmates were on your own.

Through the years, explorers tried three main survival strategies. The first—the Royal Navy's preferred method—was to bring everything, or as much of Victorian civilization as you could pack into a warship.[7] In their standard woolen uniforms and with a diet of tinned rations, a typical Royal Navy expedition needed nothing from the land or its native people. Usually the men would do well enough until the second year when scurvy began to set in. And if a ship was trapped or crushed by ice, the sailors man-hauled their heavy sledges and starved once their rations were gone.

The second strategy was to learn from the Inuit (Eskimos). Gradually some Arctic explorers began not only employing native guides and hunters but also adopting native clothing, food, shelter, and transportation. The English may have considered Inuits ignorant savages, but those "savages" never got scurvy and rarely starved.

The third strategy was to use new technology. Even the *Erebus* and *Terror* had been fitted with steam engines for polar travel. While some explorers went primitive, others tried the latest machines and materials

in the hope of gaining an advantage over the elements and their competitors. For the remainder of the pre–World War I era of exploration, most expeditions adopted some combination of these three strategies. Few were more daring in their use of technology than Walter Wellman.

As for Franklin, his disappearance provoked the largest search and rescue effort in history, with more than fifty expeditions in all.[8] Franklin became a national hero, a martyr to science and progress. Evidence of his utter failure was slow to be accepted. Years before McClintock and the *Fox* expedition, a Scottish captain named John Rae returned with news of the party's demise. Rae said Inuits had told him of finding bodies that showed evidence of cannibalism, the desperate act of starving men. The public was shocked, and Rae was vilified in the press for believing the obvious lies of savages—but physical evidence later confirmed the story.[9]

When it was all over, Franklin and his men were still dead, but a 70,000-square-mile blank spot on the North American map had been filled in with the barren and ice-girded islands of the Canadian archipelago.[10] The mysterious Northwest Passage was now drawn in ink for all to see, though no one had managed to sail a ship through it from one ocean to the other. But the British were at last satiated with glory and martyrdom, and they withdrew from the Arctic for a generation. When the passage was finally navigated in 1903–6, the feat was accomplished not by a Royal Navy warship but by a Norwegian fishing vessel with a six-man crew led by Roald Amundsen, arguably the greatest polar explorer of them all.

The second object in the history of the quest for the Northwest Passage is a book titled *Arctic Explorations in Search of Sir John Franklin* by Elisha Kent Kane, an American. Though little read today, the two-volume work was a best seller in 1856 and remained influential for a generation. When Kane died the following year at age thirty-six, he was one of the most famous and admired men in America, and he was mourned with a funeral cortege that would be exceeded in size only by that of Abraham Lincoln.[11]

Kane rose to fame as the medical officer on the Grinnell Arctic expedition of 1850–51, which discovered Franklin's first winter camp but did not solve the mystery of the lost men. Henry Grinnell, a merchant and philanthropist who had become obsessed with Franklin and the Arctic, sponsored the expedition (but did not go along) in hopes of drawing the U.S. Navy into the Franklin search. With this in mind, Grinnell encouraged

Kane's writings and lectures after the expedition returned. The navy was not persuaded, but Kane proved to be a popular writer and speaker. Grinnell put him in charge of a second expedition in 1853.[12]

Kane was ill suited to leadership, and the expedition was a nightmare of scurvy, frostbite, hunger, and dissension among the crew. With his ship trapped in the ice for two winters, half the crew departed (with Kane's reluctant acquiescence) and headed south on foot. When they returned after running low on supplies, he forced them to mess separately from the other men. Another desertion followed in which Kane tried to shoot a man returning to the ship. Finally in 1855 Kane gave the order to abandon ship and led a desperate eighty-three-day journey, with the party dragging whaleboats over the pack ice to Melville Bay and proceeding by water five hundred miles south to an Inuit village and eventual rescue.[13]

Kane's unexpected return after three years created a sensation in the United States. Though the expedition had been a failure by every measure except the bare survival of most of the crew, Kane papered over the feuds and shortcomings in his best-selling book.[14] More important, he crafted a better narrative than the dispassionate reports of his British contemporaries; his was more vivid and with a greater sense of drama. The public responded by lauding Kane as a hero, a self-made man of great character who overcame physical weakness and willed himself to endure hardships that would have killed a lesser man. More than anyone else he created a passion for the Arctic among Americans and inspired a generation of explorers, all of whom hoped to match the public reverence and awe that surrounded him. What more could a man wish for than to have his name ring through the ages like that of the immortal Elisha Kent Kane?[15]

"Arctic enthusiasm is an intermittent fever, returning in almost epidemic form after intervals of normal indifference," wrote Hugh Robert Mill in the July 1893 issue of *McClure's Magazine*.[16] A year before Wellman's departure, the fever was again burning hot. Robert E. Peary, a young American naval engineer, had returned to Greenland for a second multiyear exploration of the island's northernmost reaches. Frederick Jackson, an Englishman, was on his way to the barely explored Franz Josef Land east of Spitsbergen. And in a most unconventional journey (many experts called it suicidal), a Norwegian scientist named Fridtjof Nansen had sailed a specially built

wooden schooner into the polar ice pack with the intention of being frozen in. Assuming the ship was not crushed to matchsticks, Nansen intended to ride the slow drift across the North Pole and out the other side. His ship, the *Fram* (Forward), was provisioned for five years.[17]

"It is refreshing, in this prosaic time, to recognize the power of pure sentiment in the quest for glory," Mill wrote. "Polar research is a survival, or rather an evolution, of knight-errantry, and our Childe Rolands challenge the 'Dark Tower of the North' as dauntlessly as ever their forbears wound slug-horn at gate of enchanted castle."[18]

Wellman almost certainly agreed but couched his own argument not in terms of myth but in science, which "runs against a great blank space beyond the eightieth parallel of north latitude. Until we know what exists beyond that line these sciences must remain incomplete, unsatisfactory," he wrote in the *Evening Star* of February 24, 1894.[19]

This was a common argument, though not a universally accepted one. And was it even an honest statement of purpose? Unlike most of his peers, Wellman openly acknowledged the uncertainty of his own motives:

> Kindly critics will say of us, no doubt, that love of adventure is a stronger incentive than pursuit of knowledge. Possibly this is true. It is useless to argue the point. The main thing is not the ambition which impels us, but what we accomplish, how much of a contribution we make to the world's knowledge.[20]

Wellman's plan borrowed from an earlier expedition, updating it with modern technology. In the summer of 1827 Capt. William Parry of the Royal Navy set out from Spitsbergen of the Svalbard archipelago in one of the earliest attempts to reach the North Pole.[21] His crew man-hauled two seventy-foot, three-quarter-ton boat sleds on steel runners; a dozen men pulled each boat. With those big boats, Parry probably expected to find the Open Polar Sea and continue northward by water. He certainly anticipated smoother ice than what he encountered. Spring was too far advanced by the time Parry departed Spitsbergen on June 21; with the pack warming and shifting, his party set out across an endless boulder field of broken ice piled up from its grinding pressure.[22]

Conditions were torturous. Sharp ice crystals tore at the men's boots. At other times they waded through knee-deep slush or became disoriented in blinding fog. The heavy boats were useless in the shallow meltwater ponds around which the men had to make countless detours. Parry kept them on scanty rations—only a pound and a quarter of meat a day—and in addition to hunger they began to show signs of scurvy. While they marched north ten hours a day, a relentless wind kept pushing the pack south, erasing much of their progress. On the worst days the drift took all of their progress and then some. Parry kept that information to himself.[23]

At last he gave up. The men finally stumbled back to their ship after sixty-one days of unimaginable toil. Every day they had hauled their giant boat sleds across a tortured yet featureless icescape, similar to Sisyphus in Hades forever pushing his boulder up the same hill. The men had covered 978 miles to reach a latitude only 178 miles north of their starting point. Their farthest north, 82°45', was still more than 500 miles from the pole.[24]

Still Parry had set a farthest north record that would stand for nearly fifty years, and he had done it with common sailors and without wintering in the Arctic. It says something about Wellman that in reading Parry's account, what struck him was not the hardships the men endured but the opportunity their example presented. If Parry could accomplish such a thing while hauling those god-awful wooden boats, how much more could Wellman do with lightweight modern equipment?

Wellman's plan called for a hundred-day journey using a mostly Norwegian crew. In 1893 he had written a series of reports from the World's Columbian Exposition in Chicago. Among the exhibits was one highlighting the prowess of Norway's Arctic fishermen and sealing crews.[25] This proved to be a turning point for Wellman; within weeks he traveled to Norway to begin planning a polar expedition.[26] With such men to help the less-experienced Americans, he would start across the pack earlier in the season than Parry had, by May 10 to May 15, before the sun softened the ice too much and before the worst of the southern drift began. Wellman would use dogsleds pulled by Belgian dogs—said to the be the world's best for hauling—and he would reduce the sleds' weight by carrying "scientifically concentrated foods" and by using a lightweight metal only recently made available. Wellman commissioned what he said were

the first aluminum boats built in America, plus aluminum sledges and other devices. Use of the metal, he proclaimed, would be his expedition's distinguishing feature.[27]

Aluminum, the dream of chemists! Though it is earth's most abundant metal, it combines so easily with minerals that it is rarely found in pure form. Scientists learned to isolate it in the nineteenth century, but for years it was so difficult to produce that aluminum was for a time more valuable than gold. In the popular imagination it became a wonder metal, said to be "strong as steel and but little heavier than wood." It was widely believed that if aluminum could be manufactured economically, it would usher in a futuristic world of lightweight ships and guns and of super-durable trains and railroad tracks, and would even facilitate aerial navigation.[28]

Then in 1888 an electrolytic process allowed for large-scale production, and the metal finally entered manufacturing. By the early twentieth century it was apparent that while useful, aluminum wasn't the super metal it had been made out to be. But in 1894 it still retained enough mystique for Wellman to invoke it as a symbol of his approach to exploration. And as every fisherman knows, the aluminum boat was indeed an idea with a bright future.[29]

Thus Wellman had his edge in the northward race. By his reckoning, the Gulf Stream gave him an advantage over his competitors, for although Spitsbergen did not extend as far north as Greenland or Franz Josef Land did, he could get there early in the season and not have to overwinter. And Belgian dogs and aluminum equipment would allow him to do what Parry could not—even though Parry was a legendary Arctic explorer, the most successful of his generation, and Wellman was a novice whose only previous expedition had been a relaxing cruise in the Bahamas.

"We believe we are about to reduce the art of sledging to a greater state of perfection than was ever before known," Wellman boasted. But he made no promises. Rather than speak of the pole itself, he set his sights on breaking the farthest north record, acknowledging that of the expeditions in the field, the public would expect the least of "we the amateurs." The ice pack could be traveled; he was sure of that. "Whether or not it can be traveled at a significant rate of speed to enable us to do in a single summer what others have failed to do in years, remains to be seen."[30]

3

A Dog Show and the Seven Islands

Belgium, Norway, and Spitsbergen, April–May 1894

The early morning streets of Liege, Belgium, "looked like a dog show," Wellman wrote. "The butchers, the bakers, the coal dealers, the milk peddlers, the grocers, every conceivable sort of light delivery wagon was drawn by dogs."[1] He estimated that two-thirds of the city's light traffic used dogs rather than horses for motive power.

And this was why he had come. Of all of Europe's countless draft dogs, Belgians were said to be the best. A good dog could draw a thousand pounds over rough pavement. Why not over rough ice?

Wellman and his assistants set up shop at a local dog market, hoping to buy fifty animals in three days. He'd been warned it would take longer, but Wellman was in a hurry. The icy sea lanes north from Norway to Spitsbergen would open soon.

After hiring local dog dealers and placing newspaper ads, word spread that a wealthy American was looking for dogs. Soon a parade of working-class locals arrived with dogs of questionable quality for which they demanded outrageous sums, asking two hundred francs and being offered thirty. Now and then one of Wellman's American helpers lost his temper and told somebody to go to hell. It was "a perfectly safe bit of advice," Wellman observed, "when given in the English tongue."[2]

Testing dogs by hitching them to loaded carts, Wellman departed three days later with fifty-three burly and tractable dogs of no identifiable breed. Some sellers, obviously in need of money, said goodbye to a beloved pet with a kiss on the nose. Other dogs were of uncertain provenance. "How many of them were stolen from their rightful owners we never will know," Wellman admitted.[3]

In Greenland Robert Peary was hiring Inuit men to drive teams of Inuit dogs, but Wellman was bound for a land with no native population, dog

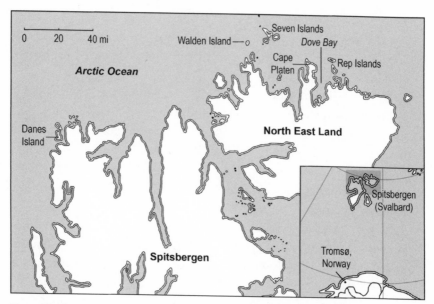

Fig. 3. Northern Svalbard, showing place names of Wellman's 1894 expedition. Map by author.

or human. Europe was his jumping-off place, and he recruited men and dogs there. Wellman said Belgian dogs were stronger than Siberian or Inuit dogs (though he had yet to work with either kind), and he praised Norwegians for their courage and polar expertise.[4] According to some sources, he shared the common view that Europeans were racially superior to indigenous peoples.[5] As for the dogs, he knew that other expeditions had used European dogs in the Arctic and that it would not be especially cold during his summer journey. The dogs would be fine, if only he could get them there.[6]

Located along Norway's rugged west coast, the town of Ålesund sits across a close-linked chain of little islands shaped like a fish hook, as if to honor the town's main industry. April brought unseasonably warm weather during which Wellman sat in shirtsleeves on his hotel veranda overlooking the harbor.

Here Wellman was to meet his Arctic ship, the *Ragnvald Jarl*, and load his cargo and polar team. But Norway had banned foreign dogs to control the spread of distemper. Wellman secured permission to transport his

Belgian dogs provided they weren't brought ashore. He landed them on a rocky islet in a fjord near town, and many of Ålesund's nine thousand inhabitants soon turned out in every manner of sailboat and rowboat to visit the dog pound island.[7]

At last Wellman met the *Ragnvald Jarl*, calling it "the best ice craft in the Norwegian waters." Although not fast or large, only 400 tons and 110 feet long, it had "a hull as strong as a hull can be made, her fore-hold being literally filled with strengthening timbers." The *Jarl* had made many a voyage to Spitsbergen in pursuit of seal or bottle-nosed whale. Wellman described its skipper, Capt. Johan Bottelfsen, as "one of the best ice pilots in the world."[8]

Though some Norwegians were inclined to see Wellman as an unwanted rival to their countryman Nansen, Wellman soothed national jealousies by promising to carry both the American and Norwegian flags. As the *Ragnvald Jarl* prepared to steam out of the harbor on April 24, 1894, a crowd gathered at the custom house quay to cheer the crew and wave handkerchiefs while a band played "The Star-Spangled Banner" and guns from a nearby fort fired in salute.[9]

From there the ship moved up the rugged coast to Tromsø and then out into the Arctic Ocean to the Spitsbergen archipelago, enjoying a surprisingly fast and easy voyage through mostly ice-free water. At Danes Island (known today by its Norwegian name, Danskøya), the expedition's men stocked their base camp with supplies in case they failed to make it home before winter. On May 10 they sailed for the Seven Islands (Sjuøyane) at the northernmost reach of the archipelago.[10] Here, or at some point nearby, Wellman and the sledging team would leave the ship at the edge of the ice pack and drive their Belgian dogs north.

That is what the public knew of Wellman as spring turned to summer in America. Mostly the nation's attention was turned inward toward its own problems. In April thousands of unemployed workers known as Coxey's Army staged a cross-country protest march to Washington DC. They demanded public works spending to create jobs; instead, authorities arrested their leaders. In May four thousand factory workers in Pullman, Illinois, went on strike. Wellman in 1886 had written a glowing profile of the town, which the Pullman Palace Car Company owned and operated.

George Pullman, he said, sought to "build a town with better health, morality and happiness than usually enjoyed by workers."[11]

But in 1894 Pullman laid off workers and slashed wages without reducing rents for his profitable company houses. The strike went nationwide in June when the American Railway Union began refusing to service Pullman cars. By the time it was over, President Cleveland had mobilized the U.S. Army, dozens of people were dead, strikers were blacklisted, and union president Eugene Debs was sentenced to six months in federal prison—from which he would emerge an ardent socialist.

Meanwhile, in Cripple Creek, Colorado, the Western Federation of Miners won a bloody strike against mine owners, earning a reputation as a "fighting" union. Wellman had rarely covered labor disputes, and now he was isolated from current events. No further word was expected from him until his ship returned to base camp and relayed news that the sledging team had been deposited safely on the ice pack.

But the *Jarl* did not return, and by mid-July rumors spread that all was not well with the expedition.[12] A ship's crew found Wellman's base camp on Danes Island. One of the Norwegian members of Wellman's team, a geologist named Peter Øyen, had been left behind to guard the supplies. The sailors reportedly found Øyen badly provisioned and "in an almost dying condition." With no companion but a dog, he "had given up all hope of ever seeing the face of a human being again" and bitterly accused Wellman of reneging on a promise to leave a second man on the island.[13]

It soon appeared that Øyen might be the lucky one. On July 24 the Washington DC *Evening Star* reported that Arctic skippers "believe that the *Ragnvald Jarl* has been crushed in the ice," leaving only "a remote chance that the members of the Wellman expedition have been saved by managing to get upon an ice floe."[14] A ship went to look for the *Jarl*, but north of Spitsbergen the ice had become unseasonably dense, and all routes were blocked.

Two days after leaving Danes Island on May 10, the *Ragnvald Jarl* approached the Seven Islands, the northernmost part of Spitsbergen. The ice pack lay somewhere to the north. Here was mostly young ice, barely thick enough to walk on but dense enough to slow the ship. In

areas of heavier ice, Captain Bottelfsen ordered the engines run astern to back the ship and then full ahead to plow through. They kept this up all day, backing and ramming. If that didn't work, the men anchored a line to the ice and pulled the ship ahead with a steam winch, or they dropped heavy timbers overboard to break up the surface, or they used the old whalers' trick of having all hands on deck run back and forth from gunwale to gunwale, rocking the ship as it wormed its way through the ice. If all else failed, the captain ordered the men overboard to cut a channel with axes. One sailor broke through and was saved only because he had tied a rope around his body. Wellman was amazed at the Norwegians, who were "afraid of nothing, glorying in exposure and as strong as young giants."[15]

Despite the ice, they reached the Seven Islands in just two days, a remarkable feat. Only half a dozen polar expeditions had traveled this far north, and the world record latitude was merely a hundred miles farther. They were three to four weeks ahead of schedule and six weeks ahead of where Parry had been in 1827.[16]

Wellman saw it all with a newcomer's eyes. At Table Island (Tavleøya), he marveled as the *Jarl* ran its prow "into the most beautiful pressed up ice, full of ultramarine tints and the most rugged and fantastic shapes. Here the pack, in grinding by with terrific force, had pressed its own debris high on shore, producing a mass of indescribable confusion, hopeless as a road, but attractive as a spectacle."[17]

The ever-shifting pack had retreated to the north, but here was evidence of its power to build impenetrable walls of icy debris and to crush anything in its way. This could happen with little warning. Wellman went to bed that night under a bright midnight sun, but by morning the sky was heavy with snow. A northwest wind swept thick ice down upon them, and within hours the *Jarl* was frozen in—for hours or weeks, they couldn't know. They lay awake in their bunks the next night, listening nervously to the "wrenchings, grindings and groanings" of ice pressure on the hull.[18] The next day, a gale opened the sea, and the men chopped a two-hundred-foot channel to free the ship. They continued their journey north.

Despite Wellman's earlier lavish praise of the *Ragnvald Jarl*, he now admitted, in a narrative that would run later in the *Evening Star*, that the ship was too small. In Tromsø the crew had loaded all the coal it could

carry, but the backing and ramming through the ice had left it short. The *Jarl* might not take them as far as he had hoped. Wellman also revealed that the *Jarl* was rumored in Tromsø to be old and worthless.[19]

Though Wellman had earlier praised Bottelfsen as "carefulness and conservatism personified," in reality he had guaranteed the captain cash rewards for reaching target latitudes by given dates.[20] Wellman insisted that his offer reflected no lack of confidence, but he clearly felt the cautious mariner needed a boost.

Later Wellman narratives follow a similar pattern of boastful hype followed by excuse making—or, more generously, an inclination to praise and a disinclination to openly criticize his comrades in print. Had Wellman been looking solely to boost his own reputation, he would have omitted mention of the cash rewards from his published report, for by then Captain Bottelfsen's caution had proved well justified.

As for Wellman's overall reliability as a narrator, he shapes events into pleasing narratives because that is his job. An entertaining narrative isn't necessarily a false one, but it's well to remember that most of his record of events was written with the expectation that it would be of interest to the public. He was also often motivated by the need to raise money for the next expedition or to defend himself from public criticism. As a result, he usually omits or downplays errors and interpersonal conflict, gives failures a positive spin, and sometimes leaves out or alters details for this purpose. And like most people, his recollections become more favorable to himself after the passage of years. But when his account can be checked against a companion's, he tells basically the same story. He writes with his own perspective and agenda, but unlike some of his more famous contemporaries, he is not guilty of any wholesale invention of accomplishments. His expedition narratives are the work of a flawed and complicated man, but they are not fiction.[21]

In the meantime, Wellman found ample reason to praise another man, a sailor named Paul Bjørvig. Two years older than Wellman, the thirty-seven-year-old was an experienced sailor, hunter, and *ishavsfarer*, or "Arctic sailor," with Ishavet (ice sea) being the Norwegian name for the Arctic Ocean. Son of a Tromsø skipper, Bjørvig was only thirteen when he began accompanying his father on annual hunting expeditions to islands of the high Arctic, and at fourteen he survived a shipwreck.[22]

While the *Jarl* waited at Walden Island (Waldenøya) for the ice to clear, several men left the ship to hunt reindeer and polar bear. They killed a female bear, but her cub escaped. Ignoring his comrades' warnings, Bjørvig, unarmed, "set out to drive the supposed cub nearer to the dead body of its mother and the rifles of her slayers."[23]

More than one explorer has remarked upon the oddities of Arctic light and the way it can distort size and distance. Bjørvig was too close to run away by the time he realized that his cub was a full-grown bear, "so the wild Norwegian, as we often call our fair-haired daredevil of a sailor, ran at the bear, shouting with all his might and waving his arms."[24]

This is actually what Arctic hunters of that day said to do, and it often worked. Just not this time. The bear came at Bjørvig, who took "a long slide down the side of a ridge, landing up to the neck in a pocket of snow."[25]

While the bear hesitated at the top of the ridge, the other men ran to within rifle range. As the bear descended, a shot rang out. The bear fell, it was said, only ten feet from Bjørvig.

Twelve miles is a long way to haul a bear's carcass, but that is how far the men had come from the ship. Lacking water, they ate snow to quench their great thirst, but it only made their throats burn. Bjørvig instead scooped up the bear's blood with both hands and drank his fill.[26] Over the years Wellman praised none of his men more lavishly than this mighty Norwegian.

By May 22 the *Jarl* could go no farther, and a mountaintop view revealed bad ice to the north. If Wellman started for the pole in that direction, he'd have to cross at least forty to fifty miles of jagged and jumbled ice before reaching the (presumably) smoother main pack. But the ice was better along the coast of North East Land, and Wellman decided to go east in search of a better way north.[27]

At last he was out on the ice with his men and dogs. He wrote nothing about his first days of sledging, but the mileage says it all—only twenty miles in three and a half days.

It got worse. On May 30 two sailors from the ship caught up to Wellman's party. Staggering and snow-blind, they reported that the *Ragnvald Jarl* had been crushed by ice. Wellman and three others hurried back to Walden Island, where they found the *Jarl* still pinned in place by ice driven

through its hull. The ship's one remaining mast jutted at an angle from the ice-strewn deck, and its sides "had been pressed inward, causing the deck to swell up and burst in the center."[28]

Captain Bottelfsen's men had hauled most of the cargo ashore. Everyone was alive, Wellman wrote, but the disaster had "cut off our line of retreat, left us stranded in the sea of ice."[29]

So Wellman did the only thing he could do under the circumstances. He returned to his sledge team and pressed on for the North Pole.

4

Shipwrecked at the Hotel White Bear

Spitsbergen, May–July 1894

Before proceeding to the North Pole, Wellman sent one of the aluminum boats back to Walden Island so Captain Bottelfsen could send men south to find a ship. Wellman figured he had ninety days to go north and get back to the islands by September 1. If he returned much later, the last ships would flee the coming winter ice, and then his survival would depend upon making it all the way back to Danes Island before winter darkness.[1]

There was no guarantee of finding a ship or that some further mishap wouldn't strand the men far from base camp. But one didn't go to the Arctic looking for guarantees, nor did a worthy commander allow himself to be turned back by so trivial an obstacle as a shipwreck. Wellman may have been a novice, but he had read widely. He knew how it was done.

He expected physical hardships, and here they began. One of the men nearly died of dysentery, which they believed was caused by drinking too much water, a constant temptation in the dry air. Wellman credited Dr. Thomas B. Mohun with saving the man's life. Like Wellman, Mohun tried to solve old problems with new methods of his own devising, such as treating snow blindness by dripping liquid cocaine into the eyes, a practice later adopted by other polar explorers.[2]

Wellman experimented with food. One of the biggest challenges for a sledging expedition was the weight of rations. Game would be scarce on the ice pack, so they had to carry everything with them. Anything that would reduce the sledges' weight would make the grueling journey easier and extend the men's range. Wellman began issuing the men (and himself) a "scientifically demonstrated" daily ration of less than one and a half pounds of food, sometimes more when their diet could be supplemented with bear meat.[3]

Breakfast consisted of "three small amebis crackers, weighing an ounce each." Wellman said they were "almost a perfect food, containing sixteen percent of nitrogenous matter," and he boasted of living on ten crackers a day for several days. The trick was to nibble them slowly so as to gain all their "nutriment," and he noted with annoyance that the Norwegians gobbled their food down all at once. Still, the men were holding up well, "though the majority of them are more or less hungry all the time."[4]

Worse for the men, perhaps, was the coffee shortage. Wellman had listened to expert advice that tea was "the true Arctic drink," with superior warming power. Tea he brought aplenty, but the Norwegians "down their portion of coffee as if it were nectar. They even boil the grounds the second time and drink the brackish concoction, then eat the dregs out of the bottom of the pot."[5] This only strengthened Wellman's skepticism of expert advice and Arctic tradition.

He wouldn't admit it, but one of Wellman's prized innovations—his mighty Belgian dogs—quickly proved to be a mistake. They didn't understand the languages of their new masters, shivered in the wind, and left bloody trails from their ice-torn paws. And when the party reached open seas on June 6, Wellman faced a new dilemma. The boats were meant for ferrying loads across small leads in the ice pack, but he hadn't planned on crossing such a large body of open water. The boats weren't big enough to carry both the dogs and the men.[6]

Wellman ordered the dogs shot. They had "served us faithfully and had suffered more than their share of the hardships" and "looked up with friendly eyes at the men who held the deadly rifles over them. But the necessities of arctic work know no such thing as pity where dogs are concerned."[7] Wellman could publish this news with little fear of public outcry. Other expeditions planned on a high mortality rate for their dogs, which were beaten, kept on short rations, and sometimes shot and fed to other dogs or to the men themselves as needs arose. Years later, after a second Arctic journey, Wellman would describe the killing of dogs as "the bitterest of all the bitter things we had to do."[8]

Raising the sails on the aluminum boats, they followed the coast of North East Land. "The arctic summer is upon us," Wellman wrote on June 23. "The sky is more deeply blue than even Italy can boast. It is so still that

one can hear the gurgling of the little streams of water falling down the hillside, four miles away."[9] Maps were inaccurate in this barely explored land. Reindeer walked innocently into camp. Eider ducks sat quietly as the men walked up and shot them.[10] Fresh meat roasted on roaring fires of driftwood, and for a change everyone ate his fill.

But the jagged ice to the north didn't move, and they saw no way around it. If they were to get any nearer the pole, "it must be by literally crawling over the rough ice and through the pools of slush."[11]

We have only Wellman's word about what happened next. Writing for the *Evening Star* (Washington DC), he described once again dividing his crew and heading north with eight men, one boat, and seventy days' provisions. They sailed the last stretch of open water until ice piled in broken slabs twenty to thirty feet high brought them to a halt. Without dogs, they man-hauled their twenty-three hundred pounds of gear and provisions. Between the hummocks lay pools of icy sludge too thick to push the boat through and yet too soft to walk upon.[12]

"For three days we worked as we had never worked before," Wellman wrote. "No words of mine will serve to give you an adequate conception of the nature of that hopeless struggle."[13]

In three days they advanced less than three miles. Climbing a headland on North Rep Island, Wellman and one of his men looked north over an endless sea of jumbled ice with "not a piece of level surface larger than a bedchamber."[14]

It was the Fourth of July. Back home people were celebrating with parades and fireworks. Wellman had no ship, no dogs, and no hope of advancing more than a trivial distance nearer the pole. His one successful innovation, the three aluminum boats, were now many miles apart with the scattered members of his expedition. And base camp, with supplies to get them through the winter if need be, was two hundred agonizing miles away. "We have run against a stone wall and are not foolish enough to beat our brains out against it," he wrote.[15]

Writing privately to his relatives on August 20 of the "impassible ice" and the loss of the ship, Wellman said that to "have started north over it might have ended in all our deaths. I was tempted—much tempted—to try it, but am glad I did not. When July 4th came and no change in the impassible ice, I saw we were beaten, as nothing could be done for weeks,

if at all. We turned back to Walden Is., but were ready to move northward any moment if a change came. None came."[16] In this letter he says nothing about a three-day northward push, and at least one historian concludes that Wellman never pushed north into the pack—that he simply turned around after the eastward journey proved futile.[17] Wellman himself gave two different turnaround points: in 1894, he said it was North Rep Island; in 1911, he wrote of pushing north from Platen Island, not as far east as his earlier claim, giving one the sense that he didn't quite know where he was.[18] On one point he had no doubt, and it served as the headline for one of his *Evening Star* dispatches: THE ICE KING WINS.

Joining up with the men he'd left behind, Wellman and company struggled back toward Walden Island through deteriorating ice conditions. It took three days to cross Dove Bay, where the summer heat cracked and weakened the ice without entirely melting it. On July 8 a young meteorologist named Alme broke a bone in his foot while leaping across a tidal crack. That evening the men camped on an ice floe in a driving rain while the wind drifted them away from home. The doctor gave Alme opiates, but later Wellman "found the poor fellow lying in his boat crying bitterly." Wellman writes:

> When I asked him if he was suffering so much, he replied: "My foot is easier, but the doctor says I can't walk for a month. That means I can't help pull the boat."
> "Don't worry about that. We'll get along all right."
> "But—but you won't leave me out here in the ice, will you?"
> The secret was out. The brave boy knew we would have to drag him in the boat, making our work so much the harder. And he had actually feared we would abandon him to perish out there in the wilderness of ice![19]

The next day the men hauled their boats through heavy fog and "ice that was neither soup nor flesh." With Alme lying in one boat, they rushed it from one floe to another, trudging through one to three feet of water as the ice broke under their feet.[20]

Eventually they reached Nelson Island, only eight miles from Walden Island. The sight of a distant flag told them that at least some of Bottelfsen's

men were still there. One more day would do it, but the ice was as rotten as anything they'd crossed so far. Then a north wind began blowing the jumbled pack down toward them. Once that filled the sea between the islands, they would be in real danger of being cut off. Wellman described the final dash to Walden as a "race for life." Soaked and exhausted, they reached the island on July 22, after two months on the ice. Captain Bottelfsen and four of his men had started for base camp at Danes Island a month earlier, and nothing more had been heard from them. The seven men remaining on the island were living in a hut made of timbers salvaged from the *Ragnvald Jarl.*[21]

Dubbed the Hotel White Bear, the hut seemed luxurious to Wellman and the polar group, but nobody was safe. Despite the advancing summer, jagged ice now blocked the way to the mainland. They waited for the wind to sweep the strait clear, but the wind came and the ice didn't move. They had food for only sixty more days and no winter gear. "If we stay here," Wellman wrote, "we will starve to death by Christmas, and escaping that will freeze to death by New Year."[22]

After two weeks of anxious waiting, they set out in the boats into a strait still half full of drifting ice. Four days later they reached open sea and met a few Norwegian hunting ships, one of which bore a letter from Bottelfsen. The captain had already made it back to Tromsø and promised to send a ship. Wellman didn't wait. Hiring one of the hunting ships, he and the men returned to Tromsø by way of Danes Island, thus ending his first Arctic adventure.

For a journalist experienced in scandalmongering, Wellman seemed strangely puzzled by press coverage of his expedition. "I have here my obituary in all languages," he told a reporter. "It would be amusing but for the pain caused my wife and family." He also complained about public criticism he received for leaving Professor Øyen alone on Danes Island at the start of the expedition. Nearly two months later the crew of an English ship found Øyen lonely, despondent, angry at Wellman, and, according to one report, inadequately supplied. Wellman insisted that Øyen had been left in camp "with 12,000 pounds of the best provisions."[23]

The lonely professor remained a sore point even as the story evolved in Wellman's memory. Wellman's initial report said that Øyen was left to

guard the base camp with the understanding that he would be alone until the summer hunting ships began to arrive. Wellman had planned to leave a second man but couldn't spare anyone else. This matches Øyen's story. Wellman, who insisted that Øyen had stayed voluntarily, also revealed that the dog who was his sole companion was left only because it had gotten loose and no one could catch it. Wellman didn't seem to understand what prolonged isolation could do to a person.[24]

In Wellman's 1911 memoir, *The Aerial Age*, the scene is transformed into Øyen's spurning Wellman's offer to leave a second man. The dog is simply Øyen's companion, and the professor himself, in Wellman's words, "was not likely to be lonesome" because summer hunting parties would come to the islands in a month or two. Wellman couldn't resist adding that Øyen's English visitors left him with "a case of Scotch whiskey, not a drop of which was left by the time we were able to get back to the depot."[25]

Wellman's activities upon his return to Europe received relatively little attention at the time. Instead of returning directly home from Norway, he visited Germany and France to investigate the possibility of using a balloon in his next expedition.[26] Later he said the idea came to him during the endless hours of toil on the ice, though it went back further than that. In 1887 he had written favorably about Adolphe de Bausset, a Chicago physician who had proposed flying to the North Pole in a metal airship with all the air pumped out to create a vacuum. Wellman had praised the proposal as "an excellent opportunity," but the idea had proved impractical.[27]

The more conventional balloon Wellman had in mind would have to be enormous, large enough to lift "three or four men, sledges, dogs, provisions" and carry them on a south wind from Spitsbergen to somewhere near the pole. Even if he had to sledge all the way back, the balloon would shorten the round-trip and reduce the amount of provisions he would need to carry.[28]

Such a balloon would cost about $100,000, Wellman figured, and he was already thousands of dollars in debt from his recent expedition.[29] But while he was in Paris looking at balloons, a man with that kind of money was in Paris looking for him. Newspaper publisher H. H. Kohlsaat had recently sold a newspaper, was flush with cash, and was said to be interested in funding Wellman's next expedition—but the two men missed each other.

By the time he learned of Kohlsaat's interest, Wellman had cooled to the ballooning idea. Even to his optimistic mind, floating away into one of the world's harshest environments in "a mere toy of the winds" began to seem like madness.[30]

Had he met Kohlsaat in Paris, Wellman believed he'd have gotten the money and proceeded with the balloon flight. Instead, another man—a Swede named S. A. Andrée—launched a balloon from Danes Island in 1897 and became an Arctic legend. Andrée's legacy would haunt Wellman in ways that he perhaps never fully understood.[31]

5

The President Cannot Be Stampeded

Washington DC, February–May 1898

Wellman set a busy agenda in the early months of 1898—first, keep the United States out of a war and, second, launch a new expedition to the North Pole. War was raging between the Cubans and their Spanish colonial overlords, and for months Wellman had been predicting Spain's peaceful withdrawal "upon terms which save her pride." The separation of the colony from the mother country was inevitable, Wellman believed, as a result of natural forces. Further, Wellman added, President William McKinley understood this and would wait until the right moment to step in with statesmanship and diplomacy, "without adding any new calamities to the world's store."[1]

Wellman's critics thought he underestimated Spanish pride and stubbornness, but his columns were considered a reflection of the president's own views. Other newspapers referred to Wellman's employer, the *Chicago Times-Herald*, as a "court journal" and to Wellman himself as "the consistent mouthpiece" of the McKinley administration.[2]

In some ways McKinley was a surprisingly modern president, especially in his relationship with the press. By tradition, it was considered improper to interview the president as if he were a common politician. The dignity of the office required the president to remain, at least in appearance, above the fray of day-to-day politics. But the world was changing. Improved printing technology and soaring advertising revenues allowed for larger, cheaper, and more widely read newspapers. McKinley recognized the growing power of the press and sought to shape the news narrative. He began holding informal press briefings—the forerunner of the modern press conference—and, perhaps more important, cultivated relationships with selected reporters. This inner circle was privy to inside information from cabinet officials and even from the president himself,

with the understanding that everything would be attributed to unnamed sources. Favored reporters thus gained a substantial advantage over their rivals, and in return they refrained from embarrassing the administration or criticizing it too bluntly. Today it's taken for granted that Washington manipulates the media by trading access for loyalty. McKinley and Wellman were among the earliest modern players.[3]

Wellman was an obvious choice for McKinley's inner circle. He and the president had known each other since Wellman was an editor and McKinley a congressman in Canton, Ohio, and Wellman was now one of the nation's most widely read Washington correspondents. His columns were a blend of sober analysis and gossipy sensationalism. To read Wellman was to feel privy to whispers in the corridors of power.

Wellman promoted McKinley's agenda of peaceful resolution, but this became difficult after February 15, 1898, when the uss *Maine* exploded in Havana Harbor, killing 266 of 355 men aboard. Some newspapers called for immediate war. Others, such as the *Chicago Post*, blasted "the freak journals and jingo editors" of the sensationalist Hearst and Pulitzer papers and "the cardinal-colored falsehoods daily cabled to or concocted by the yellow journals of New York and their Chicago imitators. . . . Sated with the round of crime, they clamor for war that, like the jackal and the vulture, they may fatten in the trail of its horrors."[4]

Wellman and the *Chicago Times-Herald* remained cautious. Was the explosion accidental or sabotage? Wellman acknowledged that if Spain were found to have ordered the attack, war "would be instantly declared, and . . . Spain would be destroyed as a nation." But this possibility was so remote that "it needs no serious consideration."[5] He also reported, however, that the U.S. Navy Department is "settling down to a conviction that the Maine was not destroyed by an accident within the vessel."[6] If the perpetrator was unconnected with the government, Spain would be expected to execute the guilty party and pay for the ship plus punitive damages; war would follow if Spain refused. Still, Wellman insisted "upon the best authority" that the president did not expect a war.[7]

The mixed messages continued. "The president has already shown that he cannot be stampeded, despite all the clamor of yellow journalism," an unnamed cabinet official told Wellman according to a February 27 account, but the same day papers were reporting "heavy shipments

of guns from the Washington navy yard and other warlike measures."[8] Navy Department secretary John Davis Long canceled a planned leave of absence but assured the public that the shipments were just ordinary dispositions; there was no need for alarm.[9] What wasn't reported was that Long's subordinate, Theodore Roosevelt, had been taking advantage of Long's frequent absences to prepare the navy for the war that Roosevelt (among others) so eagerly desired.

On March 2 Wellman reported that he had "actual knowledge" that the United States would soon intervene in Cuba and that Spain would not oppose it.[10] Meanwhile, Americans awaited the report of a naval board of inquiry as to the causes of the *Maine* explosion, even as the United States bought two new cruisers from Brazil and awarded large contracts for munitions. Wellman said McKinley was "building for peace when he prepares for war," seeking to discourage Spain from fighting.[11]

As public opinion shifted strongly in favor of war, Wellman wrote on March 26 that Spain had consented to McKinley's plan to deliver much-needed food to Cuba: "In other words, the United States will feed the starving first and fight afterward if necessary." Wellman attributed U.S. motives to "Christian charity . . . a lesson in tolerance, generosity and patience."[12] By mid-April even Wellman was preparing his readers for war, talking down fears of yellow fever and insisting that America would fight "not a war of revenge or of conquest" but a war whose duty is "one of humanity." America would win, naturally, and with victory would come responsibility. While earlier Wellman had written that Cuba would throw off its colonial shackles as a matter of natural progression, now he spoke of a growing feeling "that after all the Cubans cannot be trusted to set up and manage a stable, permanent government. . . . It may be necessary for the United States to keep Cuba as a suzerainty or colony managed in trust for at least a time." Spanish merchants felt that even annexation by the United States would be preferable to native rule.[13]

After months of escalation, Spain and the United States at last declared war on each other and, as April drew to a close, prepared for battle. For years afterward, historians often portrayed McKinley as a weak president dragged into war against his will, but it's not clear that this was so.[14] Wellman said from the start that Spain would have to leave Cuba; the question was a matter of how. McKinley seems to have preferred to accomplish this

without fighting, but in the end the belligerent "yellow" papers and the cautious Wellman—the latter channeling McKinley—had led two temperamentally different sets of readers to precisely the same conclusion. Wellman had said to wait for the naval commission report, and when it was published on March 28 with the opinion that an external explosion under the *Maine*'s hull had ignited the ship's powder magazines, the following sequence of events seemed all but inevitable.[15]

Wellman was indeed McKinley's mouthpiece regarding Cuba, but in other areas he retained the youthful progressive streak that sometimes put him at odds with the Republican Party. As the war got under way, he wrote an exposé of how the railroads were grossly overcharging the Post Office Department for shipping, even running thousands of tons of "dummy mail" over the lines to pump up the fees. "Considering the effective support given by the railroads to the present administration in the campaign resulting in its selection," Wellman wrote, "can any one hope that it will abolish this robbery?"[16]

After months of carrying water for the administration, Wellman apparently felt he had earned the leverage to push for something on his own agenda. Being near the center of power wasn't enough; he wanted to wield power of his own. And he didn't want merely to report the news; most of all he wanted to *be* the news. That is why in the early weeks of war, he stuck to the plans he'd been making since the previous summer to leave the country for a year's stay in the mysterious Arctic islands of Franz Josef Land, one of the most isolated places on earth. One editorialist warned that Wellman "is going rapidly in the opposite direction from where the glory lies," while another observed wryly that his departure showed "that he possesses an unsuspected confidence in the ability of the American people to manage affairs in his absence."[17]

6

Like Opening a Grave

Northbrook Island, Franz Josef Land, July 28, 1898

Just twelve miles of water separated Wellman's ship, the *Frithjof*, from land-fall on one of the southernmost islands of Franz Josef Land. It was three o'clock in the morning, and Wellman was still awake, peering through worsening fog and hoping for a first glimpse of Cape Flora. At the cape stood a house, and inside that house, Wellman hoped, was a man he wanted very much to meet.

Four weeks had passed since Lt. Col. Theodore Roosevelt had led his Rough Riders in a charge up San Juan Hill in Cuba, and more than three weeks had passed since the Spanish Caribbean Squadron was destroyed at the Battle of Santiago de Cuba. Wellman had other things on his mind. As was by now his habit, he had offered the *Frithjof*'s skipper a cash prize for beating all other ships to Cape Flora. Wellman was sure others were looking for the same man he was, and he wanted to reach him first. As with the pole itself, no one would remember who got there second. So great was his urgency—plus his usual optimism that things would work out—that he had departed without arranging for a ship to pick him up the next year. His agent in Norway and his brother Arthur Wellman were working on that, though it wasn't clear that they would have enough money. Despite contributions from various powerful men, including President McKinley himself, Wellman had once again gone into debt to finance his expedition.[1]

The fog grew so thick that Wellman could see no more than a ship's length ahead of the *Frithjof*, and through the murk he heard the bellow of walruses. "Every few moments, as we groped along," he wrote, "a white mass rose out of the gloom dead ahead, and we were compelled to run the propeller full speed astern" to avoid a collision. Here lay flat-topped icebergs "covering an area great as Madison Square. . . . Prudence finally compelled us to lie to."[2]

Fig. 4. The crew of the 1898–99 expedition aboard the ship *Frithjof* before debarking at remote Franz Josef Land for a yearlong stay. *Left to right:* Daniel Johansen, Olaf Ellefsen, Bernt Bentsen, Paul Bjørvig, Edward Hofma, Evelyn B. Baldwin, and Walter Wellman. Working from a photo, the magazine artist made the facial expressions warmer and the scene less gloomy. Wellman did something similar in his accompanying narrative. From *The Century* 57, no. 4 (February 1899): 532.

Lying even farther north than Spitsbergen and touching 81°51' north latitude, the archipelago known as Franz Josef Land had been known to the public only since 1874, and parts of it were still unexplored in 1898. It lies 160 miles east of Spitsbergen, and its northernmost cape is a little more than 600 miles from the North Pole. Unlike Spitsbergen it is not warmed by the Gulf Stream, leaving it ice bound and accessible only for a brief window in late summer. Some years the sea ice clogged the channels between the islands all year round and even clung to the outer coast, posing a constant threat to ships that braved its waters.[3]

Wellman had said in 1894 that Franz Josef Land might be better than Spitsbergen as a jumping-off place for a North Polar expedition but only if you could get there and only if you were willing to spend a year or

more.[4] This time he was willing and had bid goodbye to his wife and five daughters until late summer 1899 at the earliest.

But Wellman had another reason for choosing Franz Josef Land. Back in 1893 he had read with interest about Norwegian explorer Fridtjof Nansen, who that year sailed his ship into the Arctic ice pack with the intention of getting frozen in for several years. Nansen's schooner, the *Fram*, was specially built to withstand the ice pressure. His plan was to ride the northwesterly drift until the pack spit him back out again, perhaps after carrying him across the North Pole itself.

To the surprise of many skeptics, the *Fram* returned home safely three years later—but without Nansen, who with another man had left the ship to make a dash for the North Pole. The two men set a farthest north record before turning back. Knowing they'd never find their ship on the drifting ice, they returned south by way of Franz Josef Land and survived an Arctic winter in a tiny hut that was little more than a hole in the ground. In the summer of 1896 Nansen crossed paths with an English explorer named Frederick Jackson. This unlikely meeting in one of the remotest spots on earth became an international sensation when Nansen and his partner returned home after being all but given up for dead.[5] Wellman met with Nansen, now an international hero, before finalizing his own plans.[6] And as he arrived in Franz Josef Land himself, Wellman had in mind a meeting similar to Nansen's famous encounter with Jackson. On his way to the North Pole, Wellman wanted to become the man who rescued S. A. Andrée.

In August 1895 a Swedish engineer named Salomon August Andrée stood before the International Geographical Union's congress in London, describing to a skeptical audience of scientists and explorers his plan to fly a balloon to the North Pole. "I believe it is possible to venture further into the Arctic in a few days' balloon flight than during a century of exploration on foot," Andrée said.[7]

Some in the London audience thought Andrée's idea was intriguing, but most probably agreed with the man who stood and pronounced the idea "foolhardy, and not one to be seriously discussed at a meeting of this character."[8]

Such is the reception Wellman would likely have received had he gotten further with his own polar balloon plans. Andrée and Wellman came to

the idea independently of each other: Andrée was already thinking along these lines before Wellman's 1894 polar balloon research in Europe, and Wellman made and abandoned his plans before Andrée went public with his.[9] Multiple proposals for polar ballooning had appeared in the 1870s, though none had come to fruition.[10]

Though Andrée was little known to most of the audience members, the forty-year-old Swede was already experienced in ballooning and in Arctic work. He had wintered in Spitsbergen as a junior member of a scientific expedition, and his interest in ballooning went back at least to 1876, when he visited the United States and studied briefly under American aeronaut John Wise, a longtime proponent of using regular air currents for long-distance travel. In 1859 Wise had participated in a balloon flight that launched in St. Louis and ended with a crash landing in New York State; it was a test flight for a proposed (but later abandoned) transatlantic attempt. Wise suggested polar ballooning in an 1879 letter to the *New York Times*, though Andrée may not have known about it.[11]

Serious aeronauts used gas balloons, not hot air. The modern hot-air balloon with its portable propane tanks had not been invented yet. Nineteenth-century hot-air balloons were usually little more than cloth bags inflated over bonfires and used for quick ascents at county fairs.[12] To go far, one needed a varnished silk balloon that held coal gas or, better, pure hydrogen. Such a balloon carried sandbags for ballast and had a rope-controlled trapdoor valve at the top of the envelope to release gas. The aeronaut threw out sand to rise and opened the valve to descend.[13]

This wasn't as easy as it sounds. Slight changes in temperature affected buoyancy, and it was easy to overcorrect and send the balloon shooting upward or plummeting downward. Long-distance travel required a delicate hand to conserve gas and ballast.[14]

By the mid-nineteenth century, some balloonists—including John Wise—were hanging a long, heavy rope to trail on the ground or water below. If the balloon rose, it would bear more of the rope's weight; if it descended, it would bear less. The rope thus became a sort of self-regulating ballast. (Wellman would further develop this idea in his airships.)[15]

Andrée learned to use a guide rope, but for him it had a second purpose. From the beginning of manned ballooning in the 1780s, aeronauts sought to do with ships of the air what sailors had long done with ships

of the sea—navigate against the wind. Mariners did this by steering their ships into the wind at an angle, with sails set at a different angle to get a push from the wind. While unable to sail directly against the wind, they could make headway by following a zigzag course, or "tacking."[16]

Early balloonists tried and failed to do the same thing, not realizing that steering with sails only works if a ship is moving slower than the wind so that some of the air pushes it and some blows past it. But as their balloons traveled as part of the wind, any sails they carried hung limp and useless.[17]

A guide rope seemed to solve this problem. Andrée learned that by slowing the balloon down, he could use sails to alter the balloon's course, though not as much as on a sailing ship; he would still have to sail more or less with the wind. Andrée wasn't the first to think of this, but he claimed to have had more success than his predecessors had. If the wind blew toward twelve o'clock, he said he could navigate between eleven and one o'clock. Although it was a narrow range, it would be significant on a journey of hundreds of miles.[18]

Andrée's North Pole plan was straightforward. He would use a very large hydrogen balloon capable of staying aloft for thirty days if necessary. Starting at Danes Island in Spitsbergen—the site of Wellman's old base camp and known for its good harbor—Andrée would build a temporary hangar to shelter his balloon from the wind while it was inflated. Then he would wait for a good wind from the south and set out with a crew of two other men plus sledges and provisions in case they had to return on foot. Navigation would depend on a steady wind in generally the right direction. If all went well, the wind would carry them over the pole and on to the Bering Strait "in not more than six days."[19]

Andrée laid out this plan at the London conference, and one expert after another rose to criticize it. American explorer Adolphus Greely advised against endorsing the expedition, warning that Andrée could find himself stranded in the middle of the ice pack, facing the prospect of man-hauling sledges home across hundreds of miles of rugged sea ice. When Andrée stood to make his reply, he asked the explorers in the room, "When something happened to your ships, how did *you* get back?"

Everyone knew the answer: sometimes you didn't. Greely himself had nearly starved to death in the Canadian Arctic; eighteen of his twenty-five men had perished.

"I risk three lives in what you call a 'foolhardy' attempt," Andrée said, "and you risked how many? A shipload."[20] Wiping his brow, Andrée sat down as the hall echoed with cheering.

Like Wellman, Andrée's financial backers were not scientific societies but wealthy and powerful men, including Alfred Nobel and the king of Sweden. Andrée came to London seeking respect, not cash.[21]

The following year, 1896, Andrée sailed north with a team of laborers and an enormous French-built balloon he named *Örnen*, or "Eagle" in Swedish. Various delays and weeks of steady north winds led him to postpone the attempt until 1897. The press began to pick him apart. All had not been well in Spitsbergen. The balloon was leaky, and Nils Ekholm, one of Andrée's two crew members, had warned that it would only stay aloft for a week or two at most. "It would be mad to take off," Ekholm told Andrée.[22]

The tumult became public knowledge when Ekholm announced his resignation to the press. Public skepticism grew, and many people dismissed Andrée as a fool or a fraud. By the following summer, he returned to Danes Island determined to prove his critics wrong. And yet, on July 11, 1897, when the balloon stood ready and the wind blew from the south, Andrée was strangely hesitant. Rather than giving the order to proceed, he asked his two companions, "Shall we try it or not?"

They said yes. Then Andrée told one of the ground crew, "My companions insist on starting, and as I have no absolutely valid reasons against it I shall agree to it, although with reluctance."[23]

They departed, but shortly after launch three of the balloon's heavy drag lines—necessary for navigation—came loose and fell off. With that, the *Örnen* became an ordinary free balloon, entirely at the mercy of the winds.

Despite his earlier reluctance, Andrée kept going. Soon, in the words of a man on shore, the *Örnen*, "a grey speck over the sea, . . . finally disappears. Our friends are now shrouded in mystery."[24] Two days later Andrée sent a message by pigeon that all was well, and he was making "good speed" to the north.[25]

The world heard nothing more.

By early 1898 as Wellman made final preparations for his own expedition, he held out hope that Andrée and his two companions were still alive.

Writing for the March issue of *McClure's Magazine*, Wellman laid out three possibilities based on the weather at the time of the *Örnen's* launch: One was that the balloon went down in the ocean southeast of Spitsbergen and the men drowned. A second was that the winds carried them far to the east or north of Franz Josef Land. In that case they were probably lost, having only eight weeks to get back to land and hunt a winter's worth of food before the bears and seals disappeared. Wellman knew from experience how difficult such travel could be, and August and September were the worst months for sledging because of rotten ice.

But the third possibility was that the balloon came down in or near Franz Josef Land and that the men were now safe at Frederick Jackson's abandoned house at Cape Flora. Jackson had left the house stocked with supplies for this very reason, and Andrée knew it. Aboard the *Frithjof*, Wellman and his men talked about Andrée while awake and dreamed of him while asleep.[26]

But as they waited in the fog two or three tantalizing miles off Cape Flora, other news was surely on Wellman's mind. As in 1894 Paul Bjørvig, the bear-defying "wild Norwegian," was on the crew. Bjørvig had been at Danes Island when Andrée launched his balloon, and he told the story of what he'd seen and heard that day. He said when the men cut the ropes to launch the balloon, one of the sailors cut his hand and swore: "Hell!"

"Hell!" Andrée had repeated. "Yes, that's where we are going."

Such were the last words anyone on the ground heard Andrée say.[27]

Before landing at Cape Flora, then, Wellman knew that Andrée had not been sanguine about his chances of survival. When the fog lifted and Wellman climbed into the crow's nest "eager with hope," he gazed at last at the cape's black mountain and at a log house and smaller structures standing on a high plateau "bathed in sunlight."[28]

"In an instant my heart sank," Wellman wrote. "There was the house, but its door was barred, its window-boards were up." The party landed and dug away the ice, but inside the house "damp and mold were rife upon furniture, books, walls, utensils, everything. It was like opening a grave."[29]

Time and events in Wellman's own life would sharpen his impressions of Andrée. Wellman said in his 1911 memoir that Andrée knew not only that his balloon was unfit but also that "if he failed to start, the yellow press would hound him into his grave, and he preferred death in the Arctics. I

know from men who were with him that Andree said, just before he sailed, in July, 1897, that he was committing suicide. He did not dare abandon his effort and go home to face the newspapers."[30]

Wellman, journalist and explorer, was adamant on this point. He blasted

the cowards who love to throw printer's ink and other nasty stuff at a man who tries to do something and doesn't do it quickly enough to suit the mob—the mob that always howls to have the gladiator kill the beast or the beast eat the gladiator the first half hour or damns it as a poor show—he [Andrée] at last fell victim to their goadings.[31]

But that was written in 1911. In 1898 Wellman still saw the press as the explorer's natural partner and public medium. As the *Frithjof* resumed its cruise, Wellman was sure of two things: Andrée and his companions were dead, and Wellman had a chance to accomplish by sledge what the Swedes had failed to do by air.

7

Tell Them What It Was Like for Us Here

Franz Josef Land, August–December 1898

Wellman and his men stood on shore amid piles of gear and provisions on August 3, watching the black smoke of the *Frithjof* fade away to the south. They had spent their final day aboard writing letters home, the last communication they would send or receive for a year or more. Even the ever-optimistic Wellman admitted that it was "not exactly a joyful moment."[1]

Yet the day's beauty was striking. The world was "bathed in the most brilliant sunlight, glistening upon sea and icebergs and glaciers, and illumining the somber cliffs of the mountains." The cliffs of Cape Tegetthoff showed black where the snow had fallen away, and glaciers gurgled their meltwater streams down to the sea. Fifteen miles west across a sound, the top of the glacier covering most of McClintock Island stood 2,000 feet above sea level, and away toward the northeast lay a series of capes rising "darkly from the marble-sheeted land."[2]

"Already we were under the influence of the Arctic spell," Wellman wrote. "Its glamour was in our eyes, its fever in our blood." They all knew this would be no summer outing. Ahead lay endless weeks of cold and darkness, physical hardship, danger, and possibly death.[3] In return was a chance for an adventure most men could only dream of and the honor, fame, and wealth that comes with it. A year earlier Wellman had discussed this expedition with Fridtjof Nansen, and as with the rest of the world, Wellman knew how the Norwegian had become a figure of international respect and known as a great man.[4] Now Nansen's farthest north record was within Wellman's reach, but he was torn between thoughts of glory and thoughts of home.

"It's true I never loved you so much before in my life," he wrote in one of his final letters to his family before the ship departed. "At night I lie awake and think what a great fool I was to leave you—think of the

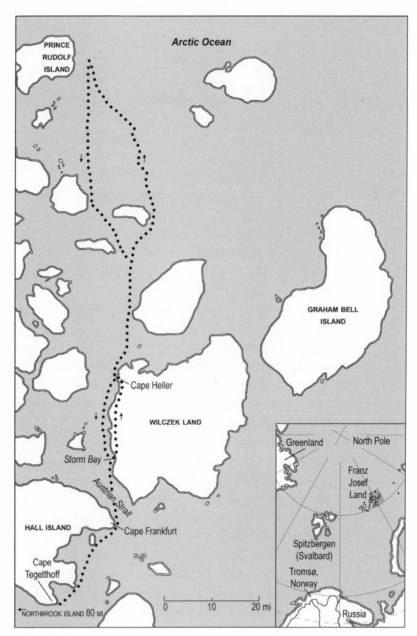

Fig. 5. Eastern Franz Josef Land, showing Wellman's 1898–99 polar journey.
Map by author.

delightful home we had, of dear girls, and of their sweet, sweet, mother."[5] Thinking of the daughters who would be at least a year older upon his return, he promised to bring pets for the three youngest: a bear cub for twelve-year-old Rae, a dog for seven-year-old Rita, and an Arctic fox for five-year-old Rebekah. "There never were five sweeter girls in the world," he said, "even if you do fight a little."[6]

There had been no letters from home waiting for him at his last port, he had complained to his brother on July 1. "Not one of my girls has taken the trouble to send me a letter here, though I am sure they would do it but for their mother's interference."[7] Laura was furious with him. Arthur apparently already knew why, for Walter did not explain further. He was more hopeful by August 2 when he wrote Arthur again. A letter from Laura had caught up with him in the meantime, and "she has forgiven me, & written me sweetly, & if the fates spare me to get back to her I will make full amends for all my wrong-doing."[8] Polar expeditions were mostly about waiting, and as later letters would reveal, Wellman had many quiet hours ahead in which to ponder his wrongdoing.

In the meantime, everything was leading up to a dash for the pole. The good season for travel on the ice pack began when daylight returned in early spring and ended, as Wellman now knew, when the ice grew too soft in the summer's warmth, a period of about 100–125 days. During that time the sledging party would try to get to the pole and back while hauling everything they would need, for it would be useless to leave supply caches on the ever-shifting sea ice.

Wellman had spent countless hours going over the figures. A man needed at least two pounds of food per day (no more experiments with tiny portions of "scientific" foods); a dog required one pound. A dog could haul effectively no more than sixty pounds; a man, no more than two hundred. This, then, was the dilemma: the lighter the load, the faster one travels; the heavier the load, the longer one can survive on the ice. The trick was to find the happy medium to maximize the men's range.

They needed one other thing: to shorten the "dash," they must get as far north on land as possible before winter. Cape Tegetthoff was not Wellman's first choice for a base camp. He had hoped the *Frithjof* could take them farther north, ideally to Prince Rudolf Island at the archipelago's northernmost reach, but sea ice had blocked every route. The Arctic

was like that. Some years it gave you clear sailing; some years it didn't. But it could have been worse. The cape had been named for the Austro-Hungarian ship *Tegetthoff*, which had been abandoned near this spot a quarter century earlier after having been icebound for more than a year. The *Frithjof* found open water at the same location.[9]

Still, Wellman faced more than a hundred miles of difficult sledging before he even got out of the islands. If he was to have a fighting chance of reaching the pole the following spring, he had to get farther north before winter. And that meant summer travel. Wellman knew from his 1894 experience how difficult it could be, but this time he would be sledging from island to island and not trying to force his way into the Arctic Ocean ice pack. He had plenty of dogs—eighty-three Siberians this time, not Belgians—and figured he could make headway without having to re-travel routes to move supplies in stages.[10]

"It is a great temptation to winter here, because we have so many supplies here, and could make ourselves reasonably comfortable," he wrote to his family. "But I fear if we do we shall have to stay out two years in order to make a success, and I cannot endure the thought of two years' absence from you all." He was determined to make it back in one year, "but not unless I have a success behind me."[11] To his brother he wrote that if the expedition ran to two years, Arthur would have to "borrow money on life insurance; finance the thing some way; beg money from everybody. You can get it. I did. People who have money can be worked if you go at them in the right way."[12]

With a one-year expedition in mind, Wellman planned to send a reconnaissance party north to find a site for a winter hut. This group would then spend the rest of the summer hunting, laying in meat for the dogs and men. He and the rest of the men would follow more slowly, hauling the heavy equipment. Then the whole group would winter in the northern hut. Wellman and a few select men would set out for the pole in early "spring" (actually the coldest part of winter) when daylight returned.[13]

Thus, success on the pack ice in 1899 would depend on success in the islands in 1898. And much of that would depend on the man who would lead the reconnaissance party, Wellman's second-in-command, Evelyn Briggs Baldwin.

Born in Naperville, Illinois, in 1862, the thirty-seven-year-old Baldwin grew up on a Kansas farm, went to college, and worked five years as a high school principal before starting a new career as an assistant observer for the U.S. Weather Bureau. In 1893 he signed on as meteorologist for Robert Peary's second Greenland expedition. Upon his return Baldwin enraged Peary with published remarks deeming the expedition a "partial failure" and blaming the inadequate provisions and equipment. Baldwin soon learned that Peary neither tolerated nor forgave criticism.[14]

Baldwin next wrote a book, *The Search for the North Pole* (1896), a history of polar exploration in which he reserved special praise for wealthy individuals and corporations that sponsored expeditions, hoping to attract sponsors for an expedition of his own. The following year he traveled to Spitsbergen, hoping to talk his way onto Andrée's balloon, but arrived after it had departed.[15]

Baldwin then met Wellman. The circumstances are unknown, but Baldwin must have made an impression.[16] Willa Cather, not yet a famous novelist, had spent time with Baldwin in Washington DC in 1901. She described him as "having much the manner of a sailor ashore, and the presence of many women visibly disconcerts him. He is a short, swarthy man, ill at ease in drawing rooms. . . . Although his appearance does not convey the impression of great physical strength it is well known that he once made a journey of eighty miles over the ice hummocks north of Greenland in the teeth of the Arctic winter alone with his dogs and sledge." In spite of his social awkwardness, Baldwin exuded self-confidence, though Cather wondered "whether these Pole seekers really feel the confidence they express."[17]

Wellman approved of Baldwin's manner and experience, making him the expedition's second in command before ever having worked with him in the field. Baldwin and the reconnaissance party set out from Cape Tegetthoff on August 5, two days after the *Frithjof* departed. Wellman planned to follow with the second group about five days later. He sent Baldwin off with a letter of instructions and three Norwegian sailors: Paul Bjørvig, Bernt Bentsen, and Emil Ellefsen.[18]

"They're such strong, strapping fellows—and I so small and weak, physically, when compared with them," Baldwin wrote in his diary. They soon needed all their strength. The ice was smooth but very wet, and the men found they could make headway only by leaving most of their gear behind,

going back and forth three times to move everything to the next camp. Soon they were breaking through rotten ice, just as Wellman had in 1894.[19]

Then on August 9 the ice began to undulate beneath them. A great sea swell began breaking up the ice, and they were suddenly in danger of being swept out to sea. A mile of rotten ice lay between them and the shore. They made it with little time to spare.[20]

Baldwin and Wellman kept in touch by couriers who traveled on foot between Cape Tegetthoff and the slow-moving sledge team. Baldwin began to express his concerns in his diary and in letters to Wellman. On August 9 he warned Wellman of bad ice conditions. Already the German silver sledge runners were falling apart; when the runners got wet, the water froze and sprung the tacks loose. If things were still this bad by the time they reached Cape Frankfurt at the northeastern tip of Hall Island, Baldwin felt it would be better to wait for colder weather rather than "tempt *sure* fate beyond that point."[21]

Travel along the ice-jumbled shores was out of the question. Leads of open water lay ahead, but the Norwegian sailors didn't trust their boats. Despite Wellman's 1894 praise of aluminum boats, he had brought none this time; the Navy Department had tested his boats in 1895 and found they had already deteriorated badly.[22] Baldwin needed boats not only for transportation but also to hunt walruses to feed the dogs. The best he had was the one they called the "Lapp boat"; also known as a sewn boat, the Scandinavian clinker-built wooden craft was held together with roots or willow branches or some other flexible wood. This was ancient technology, but such boats were still in use to save the cost of metal fasteners.[23] With "a continuous black line of open water" ahead, Baldwin lamented that Wellman had not brought a whaleboat or a steam launch.[24]

By the middle of August, Wellman sent Baldwin two more men for the advance party. In a letter for all the men to read, Wellman explained that the breakup of the ice made it impractical for the heavily laden second group to come north. Baldwin, therefore, was to advance as far north as possible, build a winter hut, and leave two men there with dogs and supplies for the spring journey. So as not to eat up more of the advance provisions than necessary, Baldwin and the others were to return to Cape Tegetthoff for the winter.[25]

Wellman also sent a private letter to Baldwin, admitting that "we are handicapped by lack of boats. Now I know I should have brought a whaleboat. . . . Have lain awake nights cursing myself and chewing the bitter rag because I didn't."

As a result, "my dear fellow, you see I have really placed the success of the expedition in your hands. Unless you succeed this fall we shall either fail or have to stay two years—and I think you agree with me that must be avoided if possible."[26]

Wellman then said that one reason he was not coming north this summer "is that I know you will do better work and get better work out of the men if you are alone than you will if I am with you. Next spring I shall probably turn the whole thing over to you and simply go as a passenger. If you make a success of this your honors will be great. And you may depend upon it that there will be no Peary business this time."[27]

Whether Wellman was entirely sincere or not, he understood that Baldwin needed encouragement. On August 21 Baldwin wrote in his diary that "the men know our success is doubtful with our very small boats and especially unless we can soon find walruses for the dogs."[28] On August 25 Baldwin wrote to Wellman that they probably wouldn't get much farther north till the sound froze over again and that he had only ten days' worth of food left for the dogs. They'd have to turn back unless game appeared soon.[29]

Wellman replied on August 27, encouraging Baldwin and praising him for his progress. "To the contrary, I feel confident that all things are working out well. *I* see, as you will later, that even some of our mistakes are, as luck will have it, turning to our advantage."[30] In a private letter Wellman added, "You are having a pretty tough time of it, old fellow, but you have the pluck and you will win. . . . Frankly, dear Baldwin, you have as much courage and nerve as any man I ever knew, but you are too prone to look on the dark side of things. You *act* like a hero, but talk like a man who is nervous. . . . I am not scolding or lecturing, but I wish you would write more cheerfully."[31]

With that, Baldwin was on his own, pressing northward beyond the range of couriers. By late August he was encamped on the west coast of Wilczek Land at a place he soon dubbed Storm Bay. Bjørvig led two other men to Cape Heller on the island's northwest coast on September 1. Here, at last, the hunting was good, but with ice too thin to walk on and too

thick to row a boat through, the men found themselves trapped on the water. "If we could not get out we would freeze to death in the boats before the ice got thick enough for us to walk on," Bjørvig said.[32] With one man sitting astride the bow and breaking the ice with his feet, another would pole the boat forward with a seal hook. Exhausted, they made it back to shore but were unable to cross the sound to the next island or even to take their boat back to Storm Bay.[33]

Even though they were on the same island as Baldwin and the others, getting back by land required a risky crossing of a glacier. Crossing sea ice was bad enough—one could break through into icy water—but on a glacier one could fall into a snow-covered crevasse and plunge hundreds of feet to certain death. Back at Cape Tegetthoff, Wellman himself nearly came to grief during such a crossing. Breaking through an ice bridge and sinking up to his armpits, his feet dangled over empty space until his companions pulled him free.[34]

Bjørvig and his companions safely crossed the glacier and reached Storm Bay on September 16. Two days later, Baldwin led the entire group by dog team north and back across that same glacier to Cape Heller, a grueling journey of nearly twenty-four hours through blowing snow and darkness. They moved from sea level up to 1,130 feet elevation and back down again, letting the sledges down steep slopes by hand. Along the way the dogs received a final half ration of meat. The men were now completely out of meat for the dogs until they reached the cape.[35]

They would advance no farther. Cape Heller would be the winter camp for the dogs and two men yet to be named. In hindsight, had Baldwin investigated the glacier, they could have arrived four weeks earlier, but there was nothing to be done about that now.[36] The men hunted walrus and bear, and they gathered rocks and moss with which to build a hut under Baldwin's direction. The resulting structure, dubbed Fort McKinley, was a crude house with stone walls topped by a roof of ten walrus hides supported by two driftwood ridge poles. The men chinked the walls with moss, then lined them with bearskins inside, and banked them with dirt and gravel outside. Bjørvig chinked gaps in the roof with partly thawed blubber.[37]

With the successful hunting and house construction, Baldwin began feeling better about the success of this crucial part of the expedition. But tempers were wearing thin. Anxious to preserve supplies for spring,

Baldwin limited the men's tobacco ration. The men complained about this and about the poor condition of their boots and the lack of replacements.

In his diary Baldwin's attitude toward his men alternated between praise and faultfinding. He wrote of reprimanding Bjørvig "roundly" for failing to keep his harpoon sharpened, resulting in the loss of a shot walrus. This confrontation "stirred the men up considerably." Baldwin lamented that "the majority of these men are careless and need constant watching . . . or else everything will soon go to ruin."[38]

Baldwin took to heart Wellman's advice from an August 15 letter: to succeed, "*make your men hustle*. They will have all winter to rest . . . take it easy yourself, and send the rest out to make things hum."[39] Bjørvig complained in his diary that throughout the journey Baldwin did little work and "treated us like animals."[40] Baldwin, he said, "was all for looking after himself . . . was the last type of man you could want, and the fact that we did not thump him was a little strange. He was not so big that any one of us could not have given him a thump."[41]

Baldwin kept the men on short rations, feeding them little but walrus and bear meat. Purportedly he wanted to conserve supplies for the polar dash in the spring, but Bjørvig said that at night "that rascal was lying there and eating away in the dark, we did not see him but he could not hide the empty tin cans."[42]

Of all the men, Bentsen became the most sullen as the days grew darker and colder. A Tromsø schoolmate of Bjørvig's, Bentsen was an Arctic sailor of long experience. In 1893 he had talked his way aboard Nansen's *Fram* only hours before the ship set sail on its three-year journey into the polar ice. Afterward Nansen wrote warmly of Bentsen, praising him as a jokester and raconteur who was a pleasure to have as a shipmate. Baldwin, however, concluded that life aboard the well-stocked *Fram* had spoiled Bentsen. "I have always considered him the peace-breaker in the party," Baldwin wrote.[43]

Baldwin began lecturing the men to raise morale. During a "general good humored talk" in early October, he remarked that they "were no longer school-boys out for a picnic."[44] A few days later when snow drifted in through the winter hut's supposedly snow-proof bearskin door, Bentsen had had enough. He complained loudly in Norwegian, then switched to German so that Baldwin could understand: "Mr. Baldwin, you say we are

not school boys any longer, but I say any school boy could build a better hut than this."⁴⁵ Baldwin didn't reply.

Then Emil Ellefsen spoke up and said the work should be more evenly distributed. Baldwin assumed that Emil meant that the Americans back at Cape Tegetthoff should also be in the field, and he explained that the Norwegians were the only ones being paid. Bentsen brooded on this as well. A few days later, he was heard to mutter that despite its American leadership, this was a "Norwegian expedition, at three kroner and fifty ore a day."⁴⁶

The grumbling continued over the next few days as the men built a snow wall enclosure for their twenty-seven dogs. Emil was heard to say that the men might as well have gone "out on the ice-cap and lie down to die."⁴⁷ Baldwin bided his time. On October 11 when the men were in a better mood, he delivered another lecture in which he argued that the men's earlier criticism "not only reflected upon me, but also upon the organizers of the Expedition"—meaning Wellman—and he asked that each man think matters over and "do what he considered to be the proper thing to do."⁴⁸

Baldwin thought his talk had helped, but Bentsen remained surly. By October 16 the ice was still too thin for travel, but Baldwin at last raised the question of which two men were to stay in the winter hut. He called for volunteers, and, not surprising, each of the five men stated his willingness. To do otherwise would have violated an unwritten code.⁴⁹

Wellman had left the choice to Baldwin, though he had privately suggested Bjørvig and Bentsen. Baldwin announced his decision four days later, on October 20: Bjørvig and Bentsen would stay; Baldwin and the others would head south the day after next.⁵⁰

"God knows if we will see them again some time," Bjørvig wrote. "It is in God's hands."⁵¹ The situation looked bleak. They had plenty of meat and blubber and enough coffee, if they were careful, but little of anything else. Baldwin allowed them only four candles for the entire winter, so they gathered moss to use in a blubber lamp that would provide a tiny bit of light through the long weeks of darkness. The stores reserved for the spring journey were not to be opened except in an emergency. All this was on behalf of the Americans, who would spend the winter in comfort at Cape Tegetthoff. Baldwin even took the best rifle.⁵²

The ice was still dangerously thin for the return trip. Baldwin knew that taking even one boat for safety would require ten dogs to haul it,

and taking dogs and boats south only to bring them north again in the spring would negate the labors of this past summer. But waiting for the ice to thicken would mean worse weather and greater darkness. As it was, they'd have to pitch camp by two thirty in the afternoon.

Baldwin and his companions spent eight days picking their way across treacherous ice and fending off bear attacks before arriving at Cape Teget-thoff on October 30.[53] Bjørvig and Bentsen, meanwhile, made themselves as comfortable as possible in their dark and primitive home. To conserve fuel, they cooked only two meals per day, mostly bear meat and coffee. "Warming up the shelter is not even to be considered," Bjørvig wrote.[54] They stayed outdoors as much as possible. It was hardly any colder, and even with the sun below the horizon there was more light outside. They cared for the dogs and defended the "fort" from bears, and back inside they read their one newspaper by the flickering light of their moss lamp.

Bentsen fell ill after only a week. It began as a sore throat, but by November 7, he was passing blood. He stopped eating—all he wanted was coffee—and suffered great pain that Bjørvig had no medicines to relieve. "I am healthy enough and hope that God does not abandon us here, for that is how things are beginning to look," he wrote.[55]

As the sunless weeks dragged on, Bentsen began hallucinating. At times he was normal; at times he was surrounded with companions only he could see. Often at bedtime Bentsen would tell Bjørvig to leave room in the sleeping bag for a man named Hans.

"I have a hard enough job keeping myself in touch with reality," Bjørvig wrote. He had his jobs, being the "dog handler, snow shoveller and not least nurse, though without medicines. . . . But I manage it all, and even have a good time overall." When the weather was clear, the moon circled the horizon, shining even clearer than it did back home in Norway.[56]

They both knew Bentsen was dying. As the year drew to a close, he lost feeling from the waist down, and his body turned white as snow. Bjørvig asked his friend "if there was anything he wanted me to say to those at home if I got back."

"Tell them what it was like for us here, that is all," Bentsen replied.[57]

In those dark days, Bjørvig's mind wandered far over the icy hills. "I am building castles in the air that are splendid, indeed I am so overwhelmed that I have talked out loud about them. But the naked truth is that they

are just castles in the air. This is what I do to keep my courage up, because once your courage fails, you will not make it out alive."[58]

Bernt Bentsen died on January 2, 1899. "It is pretty miserable to lie together with a dead man," Bjørvig wrote of their shared sleeping bag.[59] Beside him lay his dead friend, and before him loomed nearly two months of dark solitude before he could hope to see another human being, two months during which Paul Bjørvig was the northernmost living man on earth.

8

The Strenuous Life

Franz Josef Land, February–July 1899

Baldwin sat on a packing box in a corner of Harmsworth House, writing a letter to Wellman. The topic was Olaf Ellefsen and his responsibility for a missing blanket. Care of equipment was a serious matter for men so isolated. "I will most gladly confront him in the manner indicated by you and agree with you that there must be no open quarreling in the expedition," Baldwin wrote.[1]

Wellman sat on another packing box just a few feet away. He and Baldwin were exchanging letters because it was impossible to have a private conversation in a one-room house occupied by seven men.[2]

They called it Harmsworth House in honor of a financial supporter. Built near the shore of Cape Tegetthoff, the wood-framed, canvas-covered house was decagonal in shape, about fifteen feet in diameter, and heated by an iron stove in the center. "Our beds were reindeer-skin sleeping-bags spread out upon the floor," Wellman told his readers. "Our dining table was the top of a biscuit box, and our dishes a plate and mug for each man."[3] Buried in deep snow, the little house was visible only by "the little stovepipe at the apex of the roof, pouring forth its cherry sparks, and a small, black hole at the entrance to the shed, through which we crawled. . . . We had good beds, good food, including plenty of fresh bear meat, and American oatmeal, bacon, and flapjacks were not forgotten."[4] That was putting a good face on it. Years later Wellman remembered this same house as a "damp, freezing den."[5]

Most important, Wellman emphasized, was that they had harmony and good friendship through 127 consecutive sunless days, during the darkest of which it was "just possible to distinguish midday from midnight."[6]

Wellman was eager to show that his first Arctic winter had not been marred by the bickering so common to polar exploration, leading to bitter

tales upon which the press loved to feast. But speaking privately when he began his polar airship expeditions several years later, he warned a crew member that while the Arctic winter was "one of life's great experiences," it was also an ordeal full of "dangers to the mind, more than anything else. The depression of the dark, months of it, and no companionship other than a few men."[7]

In *Collier's* magazine in 1902, Wellman wrote generally about men's experiences being "shut up together" in a hut. "After a few weeks they know every scrap of one another's history. After a few months they know every thought of which any one of them is capable concerning any possible subject. . . . Men who at home are companionable and genial become morose, morbidly sensitive, childish in their proneness to take offense and sulk." Their leader might suggest "games or other diversions, such as storytelling or literary exercises, but they decline or participate half-heartedly. Men permit animosities to be roused by trifles, and ridiculous grudges they nurture as the most serious affair of their isolated, lonely life."[8]

Wellman's instructions to Baldwin in the matter of the missing blanket are lost, but clearly he was trying to keep the peace in a volatile environment. Just as clearly he was disinclined to confront Ellefsen himself. Unlike most expedition commanders, Wellman was not a naval officer; rather, his leadership was that of a political player. He seems content to let Baldwin be the bad guy while Wellman remained the affable and well-loved leader who worked behind the scenes to enforce his will.

He knew how Baldwin irritated the men. Writing to his brother Arthur on February 15 (in a letter that would not be delivered till late summer), Wellman said Baldwin was off the North Pole team. He was ill and "is not fit for the field. Besides he has not behaved very well, and is a very timid, gloomy, despairing, apprehensive man. He weighs down the spirits of his associates—a most undesirable thing when the battle is severe enough at best." But Wellman added, "I don't want a single word of this breathed to any one unless it should be necessary to defend me—and I do not think it will be."[9]

When Baldwin recovered, he was to lead a team that would map Wilczek Land and any as-yet-undiscovered islands nearby. Wellman also elevated Dr. Edward Hofma to command of the base camp at Cape Tegetthoff,

effectively making him Baldwin's equal.[10] Wellman would head north with only Norwegian companions.

"Our one weak point is dog-power," he told Arthur. Fewer than half of their 83 dogs survived; the others were victims of disease and fighting. Of the survivors "many of these are worthless. . . . If I had 15 of the 40 dogs we have lost I should feel sure of success—and believe we shall beat the record as it is."[11]

One other matter had been weighing on Wellman's mind during the dark months of winter.

"I also wish you to know how carefully I have analyzed myself up here," he wrote to his brother Arthur and sister-in-law Emma on December 31, 1898. His thoughts, he said, "are *wholly* centered in my home at Washington, without any mental reservation or the slightest trace of the old spirit of adventurous wanderings. You know what I mean, and you may know I write with full deliberation and conviction."[12]

They knew about his mistress, a Miss Willard, who was now living in Hanover, Germany, as far as he knew. All we know today is what Wellman wrote about her in his February 15 letter to Arthur:

She shall be treated justly, generously. I left an assignment of $3,500 life insurance to her, for the child's benefit, and I want her to have it without any questioning or caviling.

If I return I shall provide for the child and help her as a man of justice would treat a divorced wife, but I should *never* go to her, or be with her, or even see her if I could avoid it. I respect her, and admire her, and have no word of complaint of her to utter. She is a magnificent, noble girl and I wish her happiness and contentment. But my *love* henceforth is all for my wife. . . . If I get back I shall attend to Miss W's future, so far as I have anything to do with it, and that is wholly financial and helpful. If I do not return I ask you to see to it, and without hurting her by revealing what I have here written. If I die that settles everything.[13]

Wellman clearly didn't want to die, telling Emma and Arthur that "I feel that I have been 'born again' up here."[14] He didn't seem to mean this

in a religious sense; rather, as he wrote to Arthur, "I have too much to live for, and I want to get home to make my dear wife happy—I *never* loved her as much as I do now—and I have the courage to fail and live."[15]

Wellman and three Norwegians headed north on February 18, starting a month earlier than previous expeditions at this latitude. Wellman wanted as much time as possible to head north before the ice turned mushy in the summer sun. "The sun had not yet risen," he wrote, "but in the middle of the day the sun was near enough to the horizon to give us a gray, hazy dawn-light." The men sank to their knees in the soft snow, stumbling over hard ridges hidden below. Storms were frequent, and temperatures plunged to −50°F. Sometimes the wind was too strong to pitch the tent; they could only peg down the corners and crawl under it.[16]

Arriving at Fort McKinley on February 27, the fort's dogs "set up a shout of welcome," and Wellman's dogs ran to meet them, "dragging sledges, men, and all after them."[17] He recognized an overturned boat and spotted a pile of empty food tins. Beyond that he could see nothing that indicated human habitation. Other than the chained-up dogs, the place seemed strangely deserted.

Suddenly a black-faced man burst from a hole in the snow, dressed in furs and holding a rifle. It was a soot-faced Paul Bjørvig, ready to shoot the polar bear he expected to find.

"Hello, Paul, how are you?" Wellman said uneasily. Something didn't seem right. Fearing Bjørvig had gone mad, and wary of the rifle he was holding, Wellman embraced him mainly to lock his arms.[18]

"I am well, sir, but—but poor Bentsen is dead."

Wellman let go of Bjørvig's arms. He listened quietly as Bjørvig told him of Bentsen's illness and death. Bjørvig "talked and laughed and cried by turns," and a tear froze on his cheek.[19]

He soon invited Wellman into the hut for coffee. He crouched into the mouth of the tunnel, pulling Wellman after him. A dog nursed her pups near the entrance. She licked Bjørvig's hand and growled at Wellman, who crawled under the flap of the bearskin door on his hands and knees.

Wellman stood and bumped his head on the ice-covered ceiling. It was too dark to see. Bjørvig led him to a seat.

"Sit down, sir, sit down and rest yourself, and I'll have the coffee ready in a moment."

A tiny fire was smoldering in a niche in the wall. Bjørvig stoked it with driftwood and a hunk of blubber. Wellman saw the flames rise but felt no heat. If anything, it seemed colder inside than it was outside. Walls and ceiling were covered with frost, glittering "like a bed of diamonds."[20]

"Where did you bury Bentsen, Paul?" Wellman asked.

"I have not buried him, sir. He lies in there."[21]

Bjørvig pointed to the dark end of the hut and continued tending the fire. Wellman considered this: Bjørvig had spent two months alone with no companion but a friend's frozen corpse.

"Why did you not bury him, Paul?"

"Because, sir, I promised him I wouldn't."[22]

Wellman lit an oil lamp and walked the few feet to the hut's dark end. There he found the shared sleeping bag, but Bentsen's face was covered by the top flap.[23] Bjørvig explained that he and Bentsen had agreed in autumn that if one of them were to die, the other would leave the body in the hut to keep it safe from bears and wolves until a proper burial was possible.[24]

After Bentsen died, Bjørvig had passed the weeks alone, tending to the dogs, living on bear meat, singing to himself, and reciting poetry from his prodigious memory. At first he doubted his own ability to survive in his freezing den. "I believe that this is as bad as any man has had it," he wrote, but somehow he found courage and even beauty in his circum- stances, sleeping with five dogs to stay warm and going outside to watch the landscape change as the moon endlessly circled the sky.[25] Believing "something supernatural" was helping him, his courage grew with the returning sunlight. Sunlight on the clouds on February 22, "revealing so many and such fine colours that I can barely describe them," was "the most beautiful sight I have ever seen."[26]

Five days after this enchanting sight, Wellman "marveled that Paul Bjør- vig was still sane." The tough sailor seemed nervous but cheerful, almost normal.[27] For once Wellman had no words. Overcome by the thought of what Bjørvig had endured, Wellman and the other men simply shook his hand, one after the other, with everyone awkward and helpless in the silence of the moment.

Bjørvig did not sleep that night. He sat up, smoking his pipe and watching the flames in the niche in the wall. They buried Bentsen the next day. Though it was −44°F and the other men stayed inside as much as they could, Bjørvig spent hours chinking the gaps of the burial cairn.

"I want to make sure the bears and foxes don't get him," he said.[28]

Wellman seems unaware of an inconsistency in his published accounts of the expedition. His description of the bleak and primitive conditions he found at Fort McKinley is mostly consistent with Bjørvig's diary. But just a few paragraphs earlier, in describing the selection of the men who would stay there, Wellman emphasized not only that all five Norwegians had volunteered but also that Bjørvig and Bentsen had been "delighted" to be chosen, while the others had been "grievously disappointed."[29] Wellman said that spending a winter in a "little hut well stocked with food and tobacco . . . was to be the realization of their dream."[30]

Wellman wasn't present for the selection, and by the time he wrote his magazine articles he knew full well that the winter hut had been neither well stocked nor the fulfillment of any dream but a nightmare. As shown in his letters to Baldwin, even before it was built Wellman guessed it would be a delicate matter to order two men to stay there. His published narratives reveal a political writer's sleight of hand, highlighting or diminishing hardships as needed to give Bjørvig his due while protecting Wellman's own reputation as a leader.

Bjørvig held no bitterness toward Wellman. Privately he blamed Baldwin for everything. He felt certain that if Wellman had seen their living conditions in October, he would not have let them stay there alone.[31] Wellman returned the loyalty, praising Bjørvig lavishly in print and calling the lonely winter "one of the finest deeds of human courage ever recorded."[32]

The following weeks were among the happiest of Wellman's life. Departing Fort McKinley with the extra dogs and supplies, he was at last on his way to the North Pole, and among his three Norwegian companions was Paul Bjørvig. They spent their first eleven days marching through temperatures of −40° to −48°F, and the wind was worse than the cold. Each day they hauled exhausting loads, and each night they slept spooned together in a frost-filled sleeping bag, "which in an hour or two becomes puddly and soggy from the thawing produced by the heat of the body."[33]

Afterward Wellman delighted in sharing with readers other little details of winter camping, such as how, when pitching a tent, you should not leave your mittens off for more than a few seconds. Not only will you freeze your fingers, but your mittens will freeze so hard that you won't be able to get them on again. Instead, keep them warm by stuffing them inside your jacket.[34]

Discomfort did not mean misery. Wellman wrote, "It was glorious to feel one's strength, to fear nothing in the way of hardship or exertion, to carry a consciousness of superiority to all the obstacles which nature had placed in our path."[35]

They made good progress despite the cold and frequent storms. The Norwegians were pleased with Wellman, who worked alongside them and shared the same rations.[36] The days quickly grew longer, and by March 20, they camped off the coast of Prince Rudolf Land, Franz Josef Land's northernmost island.

"Our prospects were bright," Wellman wrote afterward, and this was literally true as soon they would have constant daylight. More important, they "had traveled one-fifth of the way to the Pole, and had yet at our command for northerly advance six or seven weeks of the most favorable season."[37] But it was actually one-sixth of the way; they had come 100 nautical miles north from Cape Tegetthoff and had 500 more to go. In 270 nautical miles, they'd match Nansen's farthest north record of 86°14'.

That day, for probably the thousandth time during the journey, Wellman's five-hundred-pound sledge became stuck in a rough spot. He called to his dogs and "threw my weight into the harness. A lunge forward, and down into a little crack in the ice—a tiny little crack such as we had crossed every day by the scores—went my right leg." He fell facedown with the ice scraping the shin of his pinned leg.[38]

The pain was so intense that at first Wellman thought he had broken his leg in two or three places. As the pain subsided, he dismissed the injury as merely a bruise and a sprain. He kept going the next day and the day after that.

Then a storm arose on March 22 that was so strong the dogs couldn't be made to face into the wind. This was nothing out of the ordinary, and the wind calmed by evening. At midnight, though, they awakened to the sound of ice crashing against ice. They felt a tremor. Men went out

to investigate and found that the ice was breaking up. Wellman remembered the crack opening "directly under our sleeping bags, and in its black depths we could hear the waters rushing and seething."[39]

They ran out into the darkness. One of the men stepped by accident into the crack and pulled his wet foot out just before the edges closed again like a vice. Nearby one of the dogs was decapitated by the ice opening and closing. All around the ice heaved and the dogs howled. Sledges began toppling into the water, and the ice shook and broke underfoot, spouting water from the openings. The ice on which the men stood began to tilt, and their tent, cooking gear, and sleeping bags all began to slip toward the rushing, watery sludge.

Working quickly, they cut the dogs' harnesses and secured what they could of their gear, but they had to find a safe place to move everything. Paul Bjørvig and Emil Ellefsen found a stable ice floe about 150 yards away. The men had time for three round-trips across a widening chasm before a river of ice blocked the way to their former campsite, which was soon transformed into a "swirling maelstrom of ice and water" from which "came the doleful howling of a number of dogs whose fastenings we had been unable to cut." The cries of the dogs grew fainter. Then they heard only a single dog and, finally, only the roar of ice, which sounded strangely like a large fire.[40]

The men were all still alive. They inventoried their losses. Gone were a third of the dogs—the ice was stained red with their blood—and all the dog food, hundreds of pounds of food for the men, their spare clothing and footwear, their skis and canvas canoe, and their navigational instruments.[41]

The polar dash was over. "The bitterest hours of my life were these which immediately followed realization of the fact that our journey was at an end," Wellman wrote years later. He tried to conceal his tears from the others, but "there is not much privacy in a sleeping-bag occupied by four men."[42]

The journey then became a retreat for survival. Heading south Wellman said he stumbled on for several more days on his now badly swollen leg, proudly ignoring advice that he should ride in a sledge. Finally he collapsed. His men placed him in a sleeping bag, loaded him on the sledge, and—as he told it cheerfully in his 1911 book, *The Aerial Age*—"calmly informed me that if I dared to climb out they would put me back again. A nice bit of mutiny!"[43]

Fig. 6. A storm broke up the ice underneath Wellman's camp off the coast of Prince Rudolf Land, Franz Josef Land's northernmost island, on March 22, 1899. A magazine artist enjoyed imagining a scene that needed no exaggeration. The men lost a third of their dogs and most of their food and felt lucky to escape with their lives. From *McClure's Magazine* 14, no. 5 (March 1900): 408.

Bjørvig's notebook says nothing about Wellman's trying to walk home, but he and the others worried that Wellman would not survive the agonizing sledge journey.[44] The tent became a makeshift hospital, where they heated water and bandaged his injured leg in temperatures of −40°F. Through days of forced marches the Norwegians were, Wellman wrote fondly, "as brave as lions and as tender as women."[45] By the time they arrived back at Fort McKinley, Wellman's circulation had become so poor that he felt his leg freezing. The men cut open his trousers and spent hours rubbing the leg with their frost-nipped hands. When they finally reached Harmsworth House at Cape Tegetthoff on April 9, Wellman's leg was still inflamed, and he suffered from a constant low fever.[46]

Here they would wait for their ship to arrive in late summer. Baldwin and his men explored the eastern reaches of Franz Josef Land, adding a new island to the map that—per Wellman's instructions—they named Graham Bell Land in honor of the National Geographic Society president (and telephone inventor) Alexander Graham Bell. Thus Baldwin, for all his faults, led the only successful portion of the expedition.[47]

Wellman could do nothing. "Nearly four months I lay flat on my back on the floor of the hut, tormented with the most agonizing itching, weak, feverish, despondent, sleepless."[48]

As Wellman lay suffering the day after his return to Cape Tegetthoff, Theodore Roosevelt gave a speech in Chicago titled "The Strenuous Life." In Wellman's absence, the former assistant secretary of the navy had become first a war hero and then the governor of New York.

In his speech Roosevelt dismissed "the man who desires mere easy peace" and praised "the man who does not shrink from danger, from hardship or from bitter toil. . . . It is only through strife, through hard and dangerous endeavor, that we shall ultimately win the goal of true national greatness." And just as a man must cultivate physical hardship to build his character, so must a nation seek great challenges—such as the vastly expanded international role that Roosevelt envisioned for the United States. This effort was one and the same for both men and nations, he believed.[49]

Roosevelt was far from alone in his ideals. He and Wellman (who were the same age) were part of a generation that was redefining American middle-class manhood, celebrating man's "animal instincts," and

placing a new emphasis on what earlier generations had dismissed as boyish behavior, such as competitive sports and physical culture. This was partly a response to fears that men were becoming overly urbanized, civilized, and effeminate, but it also fit nicely with America's burgeoning imperial ambitions.[50]

In an 1896 speech Oliver Wendell Holmes Jr., future U.S. Supreme Court justice, told of a man killed in a stunt going over Niagara Falls. Holmes praised the act as "a perfect expression of the male contribution to our common stock of morality." He said this with the understanding that the act was, in itself, useless. That didn't matter. He invoked the slang expression "doing a stump," which referred to boys showing off for each other with dangerous stunts. "Why do we send expeditions to the North Pole?" Holmes asked. "It is nothing but nations doing stumps to one another."[51]

The relief ship arrived at Cape Tegetthoff on July 27, 1899, and Wellman—thin, pale, and unable to walk—and the surviving members of his team disembarked in Tromsø on August 17.[52]

Wellman had done his stump, and his countrymen either appreciated that or didn't, depending on their acceptance of the ideals of the new manhood. One newspaper lamented that Wellman had started north "a magnificent specimen of American strength and manhood" but returned "a nervous and physical wreck, hobbling around on crutches. And what did he accomplish? Nothing, except to find out for himself that the reports of very cold weather in the arctic regions are perfectly true."[53] In contrast, another paper noted that Robert Peary had also been injured the previous winter, losing seven toes to frostbite in northern Greenland. He and Wellman were two of a kind. "Whether this type of heroism is prompted by an unselfish desire to benefit the world or by a selfish desire for fame does not matter. The heroism of the explorer remains a factor in all the world's development." Though the cost in life and money may seem out of proportion, such men who add to humanity's knowledge "are the world's benefactors."[54]

As for Wellman's suffering, circumstance had both harmed and saved him. He knew what had caused the icequake and how unlikely it had been. The day after that fearful storm, he and his men had seen a huge grounded iceberg at the head of the great gash in the ice pack. It was obvious what had happened. When the storm set the ice field in motion, it

Fig. 7. Walter Wellman in August 1899, five months after his injury on the ice and with little to do but wait at Harmsworth House for a ship to take him home. Forty years old, he would walk with a cane for the rest of his life. From *McClure's Magazine* 14, no. 4 (February 1900): 321.

had driven the ice down upon the great berg just as a sawyer moves his board against the saw. . . . And our camp had been right in the line of the cut! All other spots for miles and miles were just as they had been. Start an ant crawling across a newspaper. Take a pair of shears, shut your eyes, make a random clip, and cut the insect in two.[55]

It was terrible luck, and it was brilliant luck. If not for that icequake, Wellman was sure that he could have ignored his aching leg and continued day after day with the North Pole in his eyes until he collapsed; then he would have faced an even longer homeward journey and worse odds of survival. "We were the ant creeping across the surface of this great ice-sheet," he wrote, "and that is what chance did for us—the one out of millions that saved at least one human life."[56]

Badly injured and deeply in debt, it was in Wellman's nature to find the silver lining. Upon his return to the United States in October, he told reporters that "I live in the hope that I am not permanently crippled."[57] His leg healed, but he walked with a cane for the rest of his life. As far as he knew, his days of adventure were over.

But he could still write. He was still Walter Wellman, the famous journalist. He would return to Washington and work off his debts, redouble his efforts to be the man in the know in the nation's capital. This was the only path left open to him, but it didn't take much of an optimist to see that this path had its charms.

PART 2

The Insider, 1900–1904

9

The People Are Barely Able to Exist

Washington DC, Pennsylvania, and West Virginia,
April–August 1902

Just months into his presidency, Theodore Roosevelt blundered into a public relations disaster and needed an ally to shape the press narrative. In December 1901 he began feuding with Nelson A. Miles, commanding general of the U.S. Army. To no one's surprise but Roosevelt's, the press and public sided with the popular general over the upstart president. Worse, Miles was a Democrat with presidential ambitions, while Roosevelt was an "accidental" president elevated by an assassin's bullet. Four previous vice presidents had completed a dead president's term; none had gone on to win his own.

The feud began when Roosevelt, taking offense at some remarks Miles made to the press, loudly reprimanded the general at an open reception. "I will have no criticism of my Administration from you, or any other officer in the Army," Roosevelt said in his shrill voice, jabbing his forefinger at the general. "Your conduct is worthy of censure, sir."[1]

Infuriated, Miles leaked embarrassing information about the administration's management of the war in the Philippines, and then he dropped hints about the existence of a secret report. It was well known that Miles was courting the anti-imperialist wing of the Democratic Party with an eye on the 1904 presidential election. Roosevelt wanted him out of the way, but he had to move carefully.[2]

Roosevelt had discovered the power of the press as a young New York assemblyman in the 1880s. Circumventing his party's conservative leadership, he learned to cultivate friendships among the press corps to help sway public opinion toward his progressive agenda. As president he expanded upon McKinley's informal policy of trading access for loyalty. With press

briefings and working space for reporters inside the White House, the Roosevelt administration functioned much as a modern presidency does.[3]

As he had been with McKinley, Wellman was a natural for Roosevelt's inner circle of reporters. They had known each other since 1889, when Wellman had introduced (and praised) the young U.S. Civil Service Commission member to his nationally syndicated audience.[4] These days Wellman's connections were such that in May, when former Democratic presidential nominee William Jennings Bryan wanted a presidential letter of introduction for a visit to Cuba, he didn't contact the White House directly. He asked Wellman.[5] And later that summer, when a boorish but unnamed "high government official" got drunk at a social gathering and hugged a congressman's wife against her will, it was Wellman who fired the rhetorical shot across his bow. "Not a few public men owe a large debt of gratitude to the press for its silence," Wellman told his readers, leaving little doubt that as a leader of the Washington press corps, he was issuing a warning.[6]

Wellman had influence, and as a progressive Republican and explorer who had lived "the strenuous life," he was just the sort of man for whom Roosevelt would feel affinity. On April 5, 1902, Roosevelt invited Wellman to dinner, "partly because I want to talk the Miles matter over with you" and partly to talk about polar bears.[7] Wellman gladly accepted and soon publicly took Roosevelt's side in the Miles affair. In Wellman's telling, the president was the "deeply wounded and highly incensed" leader whose forbearance was nearing an end. Despite the political risks, "this episode is understood to be the last straw." Miles had been warned.[8]

Access and loyalty worked both ways, or so Wellman thought. Like many Western men, Wellman favored free trade and opposed the high import tariffs that shielded U.S. industries from foreign competition and raised consumer prices. A few weeks after the dinner invitation, he wrote the president about it, enclosing one of his recent columns. "The tariff must be revised," Wellman insisted, "for it is barbarous, extortionate, damnable. I want to see you take the lead. It is the biggest work to be done in the country today."[9]

Though Wellman warned that there would be "hell . . . to pay" in the 1904 elections, a high tariff was sacrosanct to eastern Republicans, and Roosevelt feared splitting the party. Growing impatient, Wellman told his readers that "President Roosevelt's sincerity in his anti-trust crusade

will largely be judged" by his willingness to support tariff reductions in industries controlled by trusts. In the end, party unity won. Roosevelt did not press for a tariff reduction, and Wellman moved on to other topics. He might push the president but would never condemn him. Nothing was worth jeopardizing his White House access.[10]

Roosevelt and Wellman soon had a bigger issue to worry about. In 1902 a major strike pitted the nation's largest labor union, the United Mine Workers of America (UMWA), against a coalition of railroad companies that monopolized anthracite coal, the main heating fuel in the northern states. Before it was over, Roosevelt would define a new role for the federal government in labor disputes, and Wellman would reach the peak of his political influence. Both of these results depended on the leadership of the United Mine Workers' thirty-two-year-old president, a man Wellman soon came to admire. His name was John Mitchell.

John Mitchell had known poverty and hardship from earliest childhood. Born in 1870 in the coal-mining town of Braidwood, Illinois, he was two years old when his mother died and six when his father was crushed to death by a runaway team of horses. He spent most of his unhappy childhood in the care of his stepmother, ran away at age ten and worked on a farm, and returned home at age twelve and began working in the mines.[11]

Mitchell never felt at ease underground. In the light from his miner's hat, he saw rats scurrying underfoot and came to welcome them as a sign that the air was (relatively) safe to breathe. At age thirteen he helped recover bodies of miners who drowned when surface water broke through and filled a passage. He ran away again at age fourteen but returned home after failing to find work.[12]

Mitchell always resented his childhood poverty and lack of education. He felt sure he'd have been a taller and more handsome man had he not spent his youth stooped over in low-ceilinged passages. But as an adult he was an affable, curious, and deeply ambitious joiner and a natural leader. Fired in 1894 for his role in a strike, he became an unpaid United Mine Workers subdistrict organizer, traveling from camp to camp, sometimes sleeping outdoors, and living on contributions from the miners.[13]

Rising quickly through union ranks, Mitchell was elected to the union's vice presidency at age twenty-eight and to the presidency itself a year

later. An avid reader of newspapers, he proved adept at press relations and began cultivating friendships with reporters.[14]

Mitchell understood power. He was both a skilled negotiator and a master of dirty politics. Gaining control of the union's journal, he used it to boost his own reputation while undercutting those of his rivals. He used national union funds for his campaigns and pressed union staff into service as his personal spies and campaigners. He undermined the power of the locals while centralizing control in the national office.[15] He did all this, he believed, for the miners' own good, because only a tightly controlled union could stand up to the coal companies.

But Mitchell was no radical. He knew that many coal operators wanted a strong national union to prevent the incessant local strikes plaguing the industry. Progressives praised Mitchell for advocating the joint conference system, which involved region-wide agreements between the union and mine owners. Despite the bloody history of labor relations, such a "scientific" solution created hope that a viable middle ground existed between the robber barons and the Marxists.[16]

Mitchell and the UMWA had done well in the bituminous, or soft coal, fields, but anthracite was another matter. Hard coal burned cleaner than soft coal and was the preferred heating fuel across the eastern United States, but it was mined almost exclusively in five counties of Pennsylvania. A handful of railroad companies had gained control of the anthracite mines and forced out smaller operators. Then they imported workers from southern and eastern Europe not only to undercut wages but also to stoke ethnic divisions and pit groups of miners against each other so that they would never stand together as a union.[17]

No labor leader had succeeded against a monopolized industry until Mitchell did so in 1900. That year a presidential election gave him leverage. President McKinley faced Democrat William Jennings Bryan, and Republican leaders feared that a prolonged strike would hand the presidency to the populist firebrand. They made sure the mine owners feared it too.

"It made no difference to us who won or lost," Mitchell said of the election.[18] But with Republican assistance, he won a 10 percent raise for his men and emerged as one of the country's most respected labor leaders.

Though Mitchell knew it was only a temporary truce, he had learned an important lesson: a strong union was necessary but insufficient. To win a major strike, one needed the support of powerful men.[19]

Wellman shared Mitchell's view. The second anthracite strike began on May 15, 1902, and a few weeks later, Wellman headed for Mitchell's strike headquarters in Wilkes-Barre, Pennsylvania, although he knew the real power lay elsewhere. Within days of his arrival, Wellman expressed hope that the strike would soon be over, and he based his hopes, as usual, on behind-the-scenes knowledge. Men of influence, including George W. Perkins of J. P. Morgan's banking house, were planning to meet at Ohio senator Mark Hanna's house in Washington DC. The railroad magnates who owned the anthracite mines were part of Morgan's vast financial empire; although they were not his employees, they were not immune to his power, either. Such was Morgan's reputation that a meeting involving his deputy, but none of the actual mine owners, was thought to herald a settlement.[20]

Instead, the strike deepened. By late spring not only the miners but also the maintenance crews were on strike, or 147,000 men in all.[21] In New York and Washington, men of power had no idea how to force a resolution to what was slowly becoming a national fuel crisis.

In truth, Mitchell had not wanted the strike, had done everything possible (short of jeopardizing his presidency) to prevent it, and doubted his chances of winning it. Days before a UMWA convention voted to strike, he had written to union organizer Mary Harris "Mother" Jones and predicted, "It will be a fight to the end, and our organization will either achieve a great triumph or it will be completely annihilated."[22]

The outcome was in doubt, but the issues were clear. "The people are barely able to exist," a Catholic parish priest later testified. In cases of sickness, miners were "unable to secure bare necessities," and one mine had "a burial fund, because their people can not save enough money to insure them burial. . . . The children have to leave their homes and get work. The average age when the miners' children leave school is a little over eleven years."[23]

The railroad magnates had begun undermining the 1900 settlement almost from the start, raising prices in company stores to compensate for

the 10 percent pay raise. Miners complained about the ten-hour work-days, the frequent layoffs, and the ways in which they were systematically cheated at the weighing of their coal. Mitchell initially demanded a 20 percent pay raise and a reduction in the workday from ten hours to eight; then he reduced them to a 10 percent raise and a nine-hour day. The owners produced figures showing they couldn't afford it, using creative bookkeeping to move mining profits to the railroad ledgers.[24]

The larger issue was control. The mine owners stated openly that they would reject even reasonable demands to deny the union any power. George Baer, one of the railroad presidents, explained this in a letter to Mitchell before the strike: "There can not be two masters in the management of business. The objection to your proposition is not alone the impracticability of forming a uniform scale of wages, but it is to the divided allegiance it creates. Discipline is essential in the conduct of all business."[25]

The big questions of the era were, who owned this new industrial civilization, and for whose benefit would it be managed? In the minds of conservative men, every bit of it was private property. They weren't thinking only of the means of production. Their attitude toward mine workers also was of a piece with their attitude toward Cubans and Filipinos or toward Negroes and Indians. The world was a giant schoolyard, and some boys were simply stronger and more suited to leadership than others. Technology, geography, social status, wealth—even the glory of discovering the North Pole—all were forms of property to be conquered and owned by the worthiest individuals. This, they believed, was for the good of all. As George Baer said in an interview later that year: "We are working for the future of an industry which if it yields to public clamor at this time is irretrievably ruined."[26]

Wellman soon revealed which side of the strike he was on, even as he positioned himself as a defender of capitalism. A group of corporations, he wrote, controlled "the entire output and the selling prices in an industry to which the public pays more than $250,000,000 a year. They destroy all competition, choke individual initiative, suppress as far as possible the laws of supply and demand, nullify the great principle upon which all industrialism is founded—rivalry between men engaged in the same business as to which shall produce and sell the cheapest that which the public has to buy."[27]

Even worse were their private armies:

Pennsylvania, politically the most rotten state in the union, has a disgraceful law. By it, mine owners go to the big cities, hire bums, ex-convicts, discharged policemen, drunken sailors, the riff-raff of the streets. . . . The operators put badges on their Hessians, place weapons in their hands, and thus the coal and iron police are created. . . . They act under the orders of their employers; they are a private standing army—and such an army! It is not surprising that these Hessians shoot and kill boys in wantonness and plunge a community into paroxysms of anger.[28]

Conservative newspapers also reported that anthracite mines had become armed camps. "Men working in them are hounded with insult, hanged in effigy, threatened with death," as the *New York Sun* put it.[29] There was truth in both stories; the papers emphasized one or the other based on their ideological commitments. In fact, Mitchell tried to discourage violence among the miners, knowing it could shift public opinion against the union.

Mitchell soon found himself fighting on a second front. West Virginia was not part of anthracite country, but it threatened to undermine the UMWA's multistate agreements in bituminous coal, the soft brown coal still widely used in industry. The state's nonunion mines were undercutting the prices of mines affiliated with the UMWA. Even while managing the anthracite strike, Mitchell heightened his efforts to organize West Virginia. By August he still had little to show for it.[30] Wellman went there to find out why. Soon he proclaimed that he had found a solution not only to the anthracite strike but also to the entire "labor question."

By 1902 Mary Harris Jones was already a legendary labor organizer, a woman who had suffered such great personal losses that threats of prison held no power over her. Born in 1837 she fled Ireland with her family during the potato famine. In America her husband and four children died during a yellow fever epidemic in 1867, and four years later her dress shop burned in the Great Chicago Fire. She became a labor organizer and one of the movement's most powerful speakers. In time she was known simply as

Mother Jones and called working men "my boys." In the summer of 1902 she was arrested while giving a speech in Clarksburg, West Virginia. A federal judge had already issued an injunction against her before she had said a word. At her trial the prosecuting attorney called her "the most dangerous woman in the country today."

"Don't surrender!" she told the miners at the time of her arrest. "Pay no attention to the injunction machine at Parkersburg. The Federal judge is a scab anyhow. While you starve he plays golf. While you serve humanity, he serves injunctions for the money powers."[31]

John Jay Jackson Jr., the federal circuit court judge, handed out sixty- to ninety-day jail sentences to Jones and her coconspirators for the crime of encouraging men to join a union and strike.[32] His habit of criminalizing speech had made him, at least among labor circles, the most reviled judge in America. Wellman was eager to meet him. In August Wellman visited the Fairmont region of West Virginia and wrote a series of articles that was also published as a small book. In it he expresses both his idealism and his ambivalence toward men of power.[33]

The judge's "wise, white old head is not bothered by Jeffersonian theories of the rights of man," Wellman began dismissively, but he followed this with a glowing biographical sketch, for Jackson was an Abraham Lincoln appointee who had spoken out fearlessly against secession. Wellman then asked pointed questions ("Would you regard mere efforts to incite men to quit work by argument, persuasion, and moral pressure as a violation of the law?") and reported Jackson's replies without comment. (Jackson "replied emphatically in the affirmative.")[34] Wellman apparently irritated the nearly eighty-year-old judge:

> Some wretched critic had said he was too old and decrepit to sit on the bench. Suddenly, during one interview, the judge bethought himself of this falsehood. Without a word of warning he seized me and threw me to the other side of the room. The minute I landed there he had me again and tossed me back to the place I had started from. "There!" he exclaimed, with a smile of exultation, "do you think I am so old and feeble?"[35]

Wellman seemed more amused than affronted. "His views he came by through inheritance," Wellman wrote, noting that Jackson's father had been a wealthy man and a slave owner. "But he is a great old judge and a picturesque character for all that."[36]

Overall, Wellman handled Jackson gently, leavening his implied criticisms with open praise. Two days later he wrote that labor men would say "the courts here are all in the hands of the rich corporations, and that the State of West Virginia is 'run' by wealthy men and their tools, the judges. Such an indictment from such a source may not carry much weight. It is too much prejudiced."

Wellman then showed how corporations usually got any injunction they wanted. Without naming names, he noted that most of the judges were "descendants of aristocrats, with cavalier blood in their veins." He speculated that they may have "inherited a dislike for the hoi polloi."[37]

This was Wellman's usual method when writing about powerful men with whom he disagreed: he initially showed deference and followed by offering an impersonal critique of their arguments, spiced with just enough innuendo to keep it lively without seeming strident. He liked to style himself as a conservative before making a progressive case.

This wasn't necessarily insincere. In some ways Wellman seemed genuinely charmed by the cantankerous old judge. Throughout his career Wellman was drawn to men of strength and power, and as both a journalist and an explorer establishing such connections was simply good business. Neither Wellman nor Mitchell sought to destroy the powerful. Rather, they wanted to join them—to enlighten and correct the great men when needed, of course, as well as to have their advice accepted as the gentle rebuke of a peer and not the impudence of an underling.

And in the Fairmont region Wellman believed he found a way to enlighten the mine owners. He would come alongside as a friend who could show them how to defeat the unions in a way that just happened to be progressive.

Wellman argued that unions had failed to organize Fairmont not because of court injunctions but simply because the miners here, unlike the rest of West Virginia and Pennsylvania, were content. "It is our policy to treat our men so well they will not want to join the union," the managers told

him. Wellman said local miners confirmed this. Good wages, aid to sick and injured miners, the employment of "trouble men" who listened to complaints and settled disputes—all made for an enlightened and humane workplace.[38]

"Of course the aim of the company is a selfish one," Wellman wrote. "It wants to keep the men at work. But it appears to me like an intelligent and wholesome selfishness."

Enlightened self-interest was the solution, Wellman believed, in much the same way that Mitchell believed in the power of trade agreements to highlight common interests shared by capital and labor. Neither Wellman nor Mitchell had to choose whether to side with powerful capitalists or with poor miners. In their minds there was no inherent class struggle, only shortsightedness.

THE MINERS ARE CONTENT, boasted a Wellman headline in the *Chicago Record-Herald*. THE LABOR PROBLEM IS SOLVED.[39]

But were the anthracite bosses even listening?

10

With Johnny D'Mitch and the Coal Barons

Washington DC and Wilkes-Barre, Pennsylvania,
August–October 1902

By August Wellman was growing frustrated with Roosevelt's inaction. "There is a coal trust," he told his readers. "It has created a monopoly in the anthracite business. It is operating in restraint of interstate commerce. It is violating federal law. . . . The president and the attorney general have further said they could not move against the coal trust in the absence of complaints. Let this serve as a complaint. I file it at the White House and the department of justice."[1]

Roosevelt had ordered his labor commissioner, Carroll D. Wright, to investigate, but Wright's June 20 report was withheld from publication. Roosevelt angrily denied rumors that he had "pigeonholed" the report because it was favorable to the miners, but he still didn't release it. Wellman protested on August 15 that the document "belongs of right to the public. . . . What has become of it?"[2]

Wright's report was finally released on September 3 and strengthened the miners' case.[3] Wright found many management practices "which appear to be unwise, unfair, and calculated to work hardship" and recommended, among other things, a nine-hour day for a six-month trial period, a joint committee to handle grievances, and collective bargaining "whenever practicable."[4]

The railroad presidents were having none of it. A Maysville, Kentucky, man wrote to President George Baer of the Philadelphia and Reading Railroad, appealing to him to settle the strike. Baer replied that the interests of working men would be "protected and cared for, not by labor agitators, but by the Christian men to whom God in his infinite wisdom has given control of the property interests of the country." The correspondence

appeared in the August 21 *Maysville Evening Bulletin* under the sarcastic headline THE LORD GOD REIGNS.

Baer's remarks were widely ridiculed, but the mine owners seemed immune to public outrage. And the outrage was unprecedented. Never before had strikers tied up a major industry without being widely condemned as dangerous radicals.[5]

Mitchell was no radical, but he warned Republicans of a rising tide of socialism should the strike fail. *The Independent*, a popular magazine, said the mine owners "have unwittingly done more in five months to promote in the United States that State socialism which they abhor than could without this help have been accomplished in a decade by all the avowed advocates and teachers of it."[6]

Roosevelt was growing alarmed. Though he believed he had no constitutional power to intervene, he feared that winter would bring a "coal famine" and with it, "the certainty of riots which might develop into social war."[7] With coal prices soaring, at the end of September he made plans to summon Mitchell and the mine owners for a face-to-face discussion, with the president himself mediating. This was unprecedented. Years later Roosevelt wrote of his desire to "save the great coal operators and all of the class of big propertied men, of which they were members, from the dreadful punishment which their own folly would have brought on them if I had not acted."[8]

Enter Walter Wellman. Lacking legal standing in the matter, Roosevelt wanted to avoid a clash with financier J. P. Morgan, considered the power behind the mine owners. Roosevelt sent Wellman to New York to inform Morgan of his plans, giving Wellman a major scoop.

"That is right," Morgan told Wellman. "The president is doing just the right thing in the right way. Tell him so for me."[9]

Wellman did, and he told the nation as well, while highlighting his own role as "the messenger who brought Mr. Morgan's approval to Washington." Wellman further emphasized that Morgan had been trying unsuccessfully for weeks to convince the railroad presidents to come to the bargaining table. It was commonly believed that Morgan possessed near-absolute control over the mine-owning railroads and that he had thus far refused to end the strike partly out of spite for Roosevelt, who earlier that year had filed an antitrust lawsuit against Morgan's Northern Securities holding company.

"Mr. Morgan rose above any such narrow consideration," Wellman insisted. "He stands ready to co-operate with the president."[10]

With that, the mine owners were put on notice that the strike was no longer a private affair but one in which the people—and their government—had a compelling interest.

With the White House closed for renovation and the addition of the West Wing, the meeting was held at the temporary White House at 22 Lafayette Place. Wellman set the stage for his readers:

> The railway presidents came to town in a gorgeous special train. While here they lived in their private cars. They drove to and from the White House in carriages. John Mitchell and his lieutenants arrived in the smoking car of a night train. They walked down Pennsylvania avenue to a cheap but tidy hotel, carrying their grips in their hands. They rode to the White House in the street cars.[11]

The meeting was a disaster. Reporters weren't invited, but Wellman pieced the story together afterward. "More amazing effrontery I have never seen come from mortal man," one of Roosevelt's advisers said of the mine owners, adding that he had feared more than once that the president would lose his temper.

Recently injured in a carriage accident, Roosevelt came to the meeting in his pajamas and sat with one leg propped on pillows. The mine owners reminded the president that he had no legal right to intervene, except to send in federal troops on the owners' behalf, and they insisted he do so.

When Mitchell proposed arbitration, the mine owners replied with "so much personal abuse of that gentleman and his organization that on several occasions President Roosevelt found it necessary to interfere."[12] The coal barons seemed to be trying to provoke an angry outburst, which they could cite as proof of their opponents' unreasonableness. Roosevelt could be prickly (as General Miles well knew), and Mitchell, in their eyes, was just a troublemaker from some brawling coal-mining town.[13]

Mitchell remained calm. The president did his best.

"There was only one man in that conference who behaved like a gentleman," Roosevelt said later in praise of Mitchell, "and that man was not I."[14]

Nothing was accomplished. "Well, I have tried and failed," Roosevelt wrote to Senator Mark Hanna, who shared his worries. Hanna had recently told reporters that the mine owners "do not know what sort of a volcano they are living over." He added that 90 percent of Americans now sympathized with the strikers and that he knew of businessmen "who are willing to contribute large checks rather than see the men starved into submission."[15]

Even so, Wellman reported that Roosevelt would take no further official action for the time being. And Wellman would know, for he was continuing to act as an unofficial back channel between Roosevelt, Mitchell, and Morgan.[16] Roosevelt's growing desperation could be seen in his request to Mitchell to have the miners return to work immediately while Roosevelt appointed a commission to investigate their grievances. Wellman noted that Mitchell did not accept this call for "full surrender. No one with more than a theorist's knowledge of the situation ever supposed he would."[17]

Mitchell was gaining the upper hand, and he knew it. Morale was high among the strikers, financial support from sympathizers was keeping families from going hungry, and Mitchell himself was regarded by his men as a "Napoleon of labor." Wellman wrote that immigrant miners "have a dim idea that there is such a man as Theodore Roosevelt. But ask the first Hun or Polander you meet on the street who is President of the United States and the odds are about even that he will reply: 'Johnny D'Mitch.'"[18]

Johnny D'Mitch could afford to hold out, but with cold weather coming, Roosevelt began to seriously consider sending in the army to dispossess the mine owners until the strike was settled.[19] In the meantime he pressured Pennsylvania governor William Alexis Stone to send in the state militia to guard the mines and their few remaining workers. The railroad presidents claimed that thousands of men stood ready to work if only they were guaranteed safety from union men. This claim would now be put to the test.[20]

"Outwardly it looks like a fight to the bitter end," Wellman wrote on October 11, "but inside information of a trustworthy character indicates that underneath the surface forces are at work" that would soon end the strike in the miners' favor. "It will be ended because Morgan and [Pennsylvania Railroad president Alexander] Cassatt have willed it."[21]

This was vintage Wellman, touting with equal enthusiasm both the prediction and his possession of the inside knowledge supporting it. The

crisis was drawing rapidly to a conclusion. The mine owners provoked another round of public derision by requesting that Roosevelt begin federal antitrust proceedings, not against their own monopoly, but against the United Mine Workers.[22] Morgan, meanwhile, learning of Roosevelt's contemplated military intervention, finally convinced the mine owners to sign a document agreeing to arbitration—the very thing Mitchell had been calling for all along. It was delivered to Washington on October 13.[23]

There was a catch. The owners specified the professions of the men whom Roosevelt would appoint to the arbitration board: a military officer, a mining engineer, a Pennsylvania federal judge, a man who'd mined and sold anthracite, and even a "man of prominence, eminent as a sociologist." Not one seat was reserved for a union man.[24] At Mitchell's request, Roosevelt met with two representatives of the mine owners, but after a tense two-hour meeting, they refused to grant the union a seat at the bargaining table.

But when an exasperated Roosevelt suggested that he might appoint a labor man as the "eminent sociologist," to his astonishment the men agreed. Roosevelt marveled that "the mighty brains of these captains of industry would rather have anarchy than Tweedledum, but that if I called it Tweedledee they would accept it with rapture."[25]

It wasn't clear that the union would accept the deal. Writing from strike headquarters at Wilkes-Barre, Wellman thought the plan would have to be modified further. He said the rank and file were against arbitration and wanted to hold out for full recognition of the union. And ultimately union delegates, and not Mitchell, held the power to end the strike.[26]

When Wellman and Mitchell were spotted together at the Wilkes-Barre railroad depot at three o'clock in the morning on October 15, it was widely assumed that Roosevelt had summoned them to Washington. That was, in fact, where they were heading, and Wellman was continuing to keep the White House apprised of developments and to relay messages and offer advice.[27] Approached by reporters, Mitchell let Wellman do the talking, and Wellman was coy.

"I expect to see President Roosevelt while I am in Washington," he said. "If he asks me for any information concerning the situation here, I will give it to him, as a matter of course." But beyond that Wellman was evasive, except to admit that "Mr. Mitchell and I have been working in

concert to a certain extent."[28] Arriving in Washington, Wellman immediately telephoned the White House while Mitchell again declined to make a public statement. Uncharacteristically, Wellman told reporters that he was "as much in the dark as every one else."[29]

Wellman and Mitchell were back in Pennsylvania the next day as the nation continued to hold its collective breath. That evening Wellman placed a long-distance telephone call to the White House with good news: Mitchell had persuaded the union's governing board to recommend accepting the plan and to put it to a union-wide delegate vote at an October 20 convention. "Of course all the probabilities are that the convention will follow the wishes of President Mitchell and his advisers," Wellman added.[30]

The celebration began even before the convention. "Joy reigned throughout the coal region yesterday," Wellman wrote on October 17. "Bells were rung on the schoolhouses and churches, locomotive engineers tooted their whistles, small boys paraded with drums and improvised banners." The miners were mostly satisfied with Roosevelt's appointments to the arbitration board. Better yet, the mine owners were said to be unhappy and were already blaming Morgan and Roosevelt.[31]

So the union delegates ended the strike, and the arbitration board awarded the miners a 10 percent pay increase and a nine-hour day but stopped short of requiring the coal operators to recognize the union or make a formal trade agreement.[32] Failing to resolve the issue of union recognition did not bode well for the future, Wellman feared; nevertheless, the strike stood as labor's lone victory against a trust-controlled industry until the 1930s.[33]

For both Mitchell and Wellman, the 1902 strike was a victory not only for the miners but more importantly for progressive capitalism. Wellman, in a Roosevelt-approved interpretation of events, considered Mitchell the ideal labor leader, one who presided over a "pure democracy" and whose attitude and performance "were at all times reasonable and public-spirited." Likewise, Wellman held that J. P. Morgan was "not a dictator" but a leader who worked for peace and who could have done more "only at the expense of a rupture between the great [financial] interests."[34]

The resolution was also a great personal triumph for Roosevelt. Wellman called it the "greatest event affecting the relations of capital and labor in

the history of America" and thought it was "likely to go very far toward making great and prolonged strikes well-nigh impossible in the future."[35]

As for the railroad presidents, Wellman blasted their "pride of opinion, obstinacy, arrogance, childishness, inability to sympathize with the interests of other people, or even to comprehend how their own were to be best served."[36] The problem had been personal, not systemic. Neither Wellman nor Mitchell criticized capitalism itself or acknowledged such a thing as "class struggle."

But Mother Jones did. She felt Mitchell had blundered away a larger victory. "The strike was won," she wrote. "Absolutely no anthracite coal was being dug. The operators could have been made to deal with the union if Mr. Mitchell had stood firm. . . . Flattery and homage did its work with John Mitchell."[37]

The 1902 coal strike changed John Mitchell. By the time it was over he was acquiring a taste for expensive clothes and fine living, making new friends, and moving up, just as Wellman had already done. In their own ways, both men had become insiders, but how much power did either of them really wield? And between them and their new high-ranking friends, who was using whom?

Several years later the *Chicago Daily Socialist* took Wellman to task for his praise of the selfishly enlightened coal operators in Fairmont, West Virginia: "Those same benevolent mine owners are now begging for funds to care for the widows and orphans they made. . . . So long as the profit-taking class rules, lives will be made secondary to profits."[38]

In Colorado in 1904 Wellman met a labor leader who believed this statement wholeheartedly and who fought to overthrow the rule of capital. He was known as "Big Bill" Haywood, and he threatened everything that Wellman, Mitchell, and their powerful allies held dear.

11

This Crime against Organized Labor

Colorado and Washington DC, June–December 1904

Thirty-two men stood on the platform of Independence Depot, waiting for the train to take them home. It was two o'clock in the morning, June 4, and they had emerged from eight hours in the close-quartered darkness of the Findley Gold Mine into the spacious darkness of the Colorado night. At more than nine thousand feet above sea level, the air was cool and thin and echoed with the chug-chug of the train in the distance. Latecomers rushed down the hill toward the depot, not wanting to miss their ride.[1]

Suddenly the platform burst upward with an earsplitting concussion. "The timbers and planks were driven up through the bodies of the unfortunate men," Wellman wrote. "Shoes were found with the leg bones sticking through the leathern heels. Bodies and legs and heads and arms went flying through the air and were afterward gathered up from the surrounding acre."[2]

Across the nation, newspapers printed the gruesome toll: thirteen men killed and six seriously injured, including one man who lost a leg and two men who lost both legs. The dead men left behind six widows and eleven children. All but one man were nonunion. They were "scabs," or strikebreakers, who kept the mines of Victor and Cripple Creek open when the Western Federation of Miners (WFM) wanted them closed.[3]

Wellman was not in Colorado when it happened. He arrived in July, during a working vacation for he and his wife while their daughters spent the summer at the fashionable seaside resort of Cape May, New Jersey—so reported the society columns of the Washington DC *Evening Star*, which by now regularly tracked the family's doings. The Wellmans may have been new money, but in Washington society, pedigree was less important than power.[4]

But while Mr. and Mrs. Wellman were coasting down a mountainside on a railroad handcar, the nation was wondering whether a new civil war had broken out. What historians call the Colorado Labor Wars involved multiple strikes in the mining industry in 1903 and 1904. "Wars" is hardly an exaggeration, for the conflict involved the National Guard and vigilante groups, mob violence, beatings and assassinations, acts of terrorism, military despotism, and the suppression of civil rights. Atrocities were committed on behalf of corporations, state government, and unions alike and to a degree that shocked a nation already jaded by decades of violent labor troubles.[5]

Some of the violence involved the suppression of a strike led by John Mitchell and the United Mine Workers of America in Colorado's northern and southern coal fields.[6] The main struggle, however, was not in coal but in hard rock mining, mainly for gold and silver. Here the union was not Mitchell's UMWA but the more radical Western Federation of Miners.

The 1903–4 troubles began with a strike in the smelting mills of Colorado City. Company owners had hired Pinkerton detectives to identify union members, who were then fired. The workers struck peacefully, but Colorado governor James H. Peabody sent six companies of National Guardsmen to harass them. WFM miners in Cripple Creek then launched a "sympathetic" strike to force mine owners to stop doing business with the offending mills. Within a few weeks they forced the mill owners to the bargaining table, but a reneged agreement soon led to a second strike. And the war was on.[7]

Behind the union struggle was a larger conflict between Colorado voters and the state legislature. In November 1902 Coloradans voted overwhelmingly to amend the state's constitution to require eight-hour workdays in mining and related industries. The amendment directed the legislature to codify the eight-hour day with appropriate legislation. In 1903 both the state house and senate passed bills, but then—under heavy lobbying from the mining industry—the legislators failed to reconcile the different versions in conference committee. The eight-hour law died when the legislature adjourned in April.[8]

The legislature's defiance of the people's will radicalized many Coloradans, who saw that even the state constitution was powerless against the political might of the mine owners.

"What is the use of your ballots anyway?" WFM president Charles Moyer asked a crowd in Pueblo. "You might as well tear them up and throw them in the gutter."[9]

By the summer of 1904 the conflict had dragged on for a year, during which time President Roosevelt had declined to intervene. It was a presidential election year, and Roosevelt, still an accidental president, was hoping to win a term of his own. Wellman had already spent the early months of the year attacking one of Roosevelt's potential rivals, newspaper publisher William Randolph Hearst. Though Hearst would later be known as a staunchly conservative anti-communist, in the early twentieth century he was a Democrat who was seen as friendly to labor. Wellman derided him personally and without his usual circumspection, calling Hearst's campaign "the scandal of a deliberate, brazen, persistent and possibly successful effort to buy the democratic presidential nomination and the presidency itself."[10]

Some labor-oriented papers spread a rumor that Wellman had privately admitted to writing the articles "under orders" and that they didn't reflect his actual high opinion of Hearst.[11] This is unlikely. Week after week Wellman's columns cast the president and his advisers in a favorable light; it would have been more plausible to accuse Wellman of simple partisanship.

Roosevelt was attacked from both ends of the political spectrum. He was despised by big business and much of his own party for intervening in the 1902 coal strike and yet condemned by many labor leaders (John Mitchell excepted) for not doing enough. Speaking in New York that summer, Mother Jones said that Colorado proved that the working class "might as well tell your troubles to the moon" as ask the president for help, and she called on union men to let Roosevelt know "he won't get a labor vote in New York City." More ominously, she warned that the Colorado strikers "are just such men as brought on the French Revolution, and that's what we are going to have in this country soon unless the ruling classes take steps to prevent it by giving the laboring men their rights."[12]

Roosevelt hoped the public would see him as occupying the reasonable middle ground. The Hearst campaign eventually collapsed, and Democrats nominated Alton B. Parker, a New York judge who was thought to be sympathetic to labor but who had given few specifics. Roosevelt worried

that Parker's perceived neutrality might give him an advantage.[13] Parker could be whatever the voters hoped he would be, whereas Roosevelt was tied to his record. As one Democratic paper claimed, "The history of this administration has been one of labor strikes. At no time has there been so much trouble in labor circles as during Roosevelt's presidential incumbency. All over the country labor has been in one continual warfare."[14]

As Wellman looked at the shattered Independence Depot, which stood, "after a fashion, windowless, doorless, shattered, bits of glass and stains of blood covering its floors," he may have wondered what could have led to such vindictiveness.[15] Or perhaps his mind was made up before he left Washington. All we know is that he investigated the events of the previous year and wrote a series of articles that culminated in one of the strongest and most partisan statements he ever made on a major issue. In his narrative, the war story became a tale of two generals—William "Big Bill" Haywood, the powerful secretary-treasurer of the WFM, and Gen. Sherman Bell, commander of the Colorado National Guard.

"He is one of the smartest men I ever met in or out of the labor world," Wellman wrote of Big Bill Haywood. The thirty-five-old had been born exactly one year before John Mitchell and, like both Mitchell and Wellman, had little formal schooling. Wellman said Haywood always carried a dictionary, a Bible, and the works of Shakespeare with him on his travels. Unlike Mitchell, Haywood was not a union president, though it hardly seemed to matter. The WFM's secretary-treasurer was its most dynamic personality and often seemed to wield more power than President Charles Moyer. Nearly six feet tall, Haywood's stocky and muscular build gave the impression of a greater stature than he actually possessed. A childhood accident had blinded his right eye, which was concealed beneath a sunken eyelid. "He looks a fighter," Wellman wrote, "and is a fighter—too much of a fighter, perhaps, for the good of the thousands of miners who follow him."[16]

In one of their interviews Wellman sought to clarify the purpose of the Cripple Creek strike. Haywood confirmed that the miners had not objected to their wages, hours, or working conditions. They struck to support the smelters in Colorado City.

"One of our principles is that an injury to one is the concern of all," Haywood explained. "Besides, we knew a war was coming, that it was inevitable, and we were ready for it."[17]

Wellman knew John Mitchell would never have supported such a strike. Mitchell believed that unions would only gain leverage with employers by fulfilling contracts. Haywood, however, told Wellman that one of the WFM's main goals was to "obtain possession of the government through political action . . . that we may improve the condition of the working people generally."[18]

He showed Wellman a union card with the WFM's creed printed on the back: "Labor Produces All Wealth: Wealth Belongs to the Producer Thereof." Unlike Wellman and Mitchell, Haywood did not want a better place within capitalism. He wanted a new economic system.

Haywood told of being a young miner in Idaho, climbing every day up a thirty-foot ladder to reach the level on which he worked. One day two of the owners came by, and one challenged the other to climb up to where Haywood was working.

"I wouldn't climb that ladder for ten thousand dollars," the second man said. Haywood climbed it for three dollars a day.

"He was not made of finer clay than I," Haywood told Wellman. "He was no more fond of his wife and children. Life was no sweeter to him. I was risking my life every day to make money for that man. So I was set thinking, and in time I became a socialist."[19]

If Haywood had his way, then the owners would be dispossessed, and the state would operate the mines for the benefit of the workers. Ultimately that's what all these strikes were about. Who really owned all that gold and silver, and for whose benefit was it being mined? Haywood was certain that his was the righteous cause, and he believed that the WFM would already have won in Colorado if not for "the high-handed tyrannical course of the State militia and that insane man in gold lace, General Sherman M. Bell."[20]

Sherman Bell loved military finery. His custom-made National Guard uniform was gaudy with epaulets, gold lace, tassels, and yards of cordage. Bell had been one of Theodore Roosevelt's Rough Riders during the Spanish-American War, and Roosevelt called him the "gamest man in a regiment of game men."[21] While campaigning for the vice presidency

in 1900, Roosevelt was harassed by a group of rock-throwing miners in Cripple Creek, and Sherman Bell led a company of Rough Riders that surrounded Roosevelt and assaulted the protesters.[22]

By 1903 the thirty-two-year-old Bell was adjutant general of the Colorado National Guard. In addition to his guard pay, he received the princely annual salary of thirty-two hundred dollars from the Colorado mine owners.[23] Bell left no doubt as to where his loyalties lay. Once ordered into strike zones, he disregarded civil law, searching homes and arresting men without warrants. He said his goal was to destroy the union, and he told Wellman that he didn't "care a damn" what anyone thought. And "anyone" included judges. Bell and his men imprisoned strikers, certain local officials, and the entire staff of a pro-union newspaper in a makeshift prison called a bullpen, holding them for weeks and months without charges.

"Well, then they started up that habeas corpus business," Bell said, "and I told 'em that wasn't any good—that what they needed was not habeas corpus, but post-mortems."[24]

In response to a judge's writ, Bell surrounded the Teller County Courthouse with armed men, trained a Gatling gun on the building, planted sharpshooters on nearby rooftops, and marched troopers with fixed bayonets into the courtroom itself. Only then did he deliver the prisoners. And when the judge defied this show of force by ordering the men released, Bell simply ignored the ruling and marched the prisoners back to the bullpen. He told the judge that he would "shoot him and every damned man that tries to take my prisoners away from me."[25]

For Wellman and other reporters, the bombastic Bell was a fountain of good copy, more quotable even than Haywood was. But the best and most oft-repeated quotation from the Colorado Labor Wars came not from Bell but from one of his subordinates, Maj. Thomas McClelland, who summed up his commander's legal philosophy in two pithy sentences: "To hell with the Constitution. We aren't going by the Constitution."[26]

The war was won (or lost) by the time Wellman published his articles. Though the WFM denied involvement, the bombing of Independence Depot turned public opinion against the union. The strike was broken and the WFM all but purged from Colorado.[27] What remained was the interpretation of events and the laying of blame. Which man, Haywood

or Bell, posed the greater threat to American society? And had President Roosevelt been correct in allowing events to run their course?

Both sides stated their case. Bell, of course, did not try to reason with Wellman. That wasn't his style. But Governor Peabody argued that the WFM's intimidation of strikebreakers had required a strong response. The union, he said, had a long history of violence. He gave examples, noting especially that three years earlier a previous WFM president had advised local unions to exercise their Second Amendment rights and form rifle clubs. "What can we expect," Peabody asked Wellman, "of an organization whose head openly advises its membership to arm themselves for the purpose of resisting the government and its agents?"[28]

Haywood likewise believed that the opposition posed an existential threat to civil society. During the military occupation, he designed a poster featuring an American flag whose stripes listed the state's crimes against democracy. Among them were "Martial Law Declared in Colorado! Habeas Corpus Suspended in Colorado! Free Press Throttled in Colorado!" A banner headline asked, IS COLORADO IN AMERICA?

In reply the state charged Haywood and Moyer with flag desecration.[29]

In May 1904, before the Independence Depot bombing, *McClure's Magazine* published an article titled "The Reign of Lawlessness: Anarchy and Despotism in Colorado" by Ray Stannard Baker. Like Wellman, Baker was a progressive who sometimes aimed his pen at capital and sometimes at labor. Baker blamed all sides, not only the union and the mine owners, but also the governor and state legislature, the National Guard, the press, and the citizenry as well. All parties, he argued, had countenanced lawless behavior when it suited their interests and condemned it when used by others.[30]

Wellman, however—writing in August after public opinion had hardened against the WFM—took sides. "I have never known a labor war in which the guilt and responsibility of one side stood out so clearly and unmistakably," he wrote. He summarized the WFM's involvement as "this crime against organized labor, this offense against our civilization."[31] Wellman's final article appeared on August 14 and was reprinted by the Colorado Republican Party as a pamphlet titled *Walter Wellman's Indictment of Moyer, Haywood, and the Western Federation of Miners*.

Reading Baker's and Wellman's articles together, it's remarkable how two journalists could agree on so many facts and write from similar

ideological viewpoints but reach such different conclusions. One major difference had to do with the Colorado legislature's failure to pass the eight-hour law. Baker said it was a major grievance among strikers, but Wellman said it was merely a justification after the fact. He pointed out that the Cripple Creek strike began while the legislature was still in session and still expected to pass the law. This was correct, but Wellman ignored the eight-hour law's growing importance later that year as strikes spread to other Colorado cities.[32]

Neither Baker nor Wellman fully understood how the legislature's betrayal had embittered Haywood. Big Bill had spent two years campaigning for the law only to discover that the "sniffling old profligate at the head of the Rockefeller interests wielded more power with his golf sticks than the people of Colorado with their ballots." Never again would Haywood rely on the ballot as means of change. From then on, first through the Western Federation of Miners and later as head of the Industrial Workers of the World, he urged only direct action "at the point of production."[33]

Whatever one thinks of Haywood and his ideology, one can easily understand how ordinary Coloradans might have lost faith in the democratic process. Such nuance is absent from Wellman's final article. Instead, his rhetorical skill is employed in a sober acknowledgment of wrongdoing on all sides while arguing that only one side bore responsibility. "The Federation had appealed to force and terrorism," he wrote, "and were met with like weapons."[34] Baker made a similar point, showing how the union denied sanctioning violence even as it shielded violent members from prosecution in union-majority counties. ("Scab-beating is not a crime in Teller County," Baker wrote.[35]) But Wellman went further, blasting the WFM's involvement in the smelters' strike as a "plot of desperate, power-hungry men to extend their authority over another industry by fair means or foul."[36]

Wellman acknowledged that Sherman Bell's military dictatorship was marked by serious injustices, but he echoed Governor Peabody in stating that union violence justified the intervention. Wellman even claimed that Bell's bloody rhetoric was mostly for show and that the general in gold lace had actually prevented more violence than he committed.[37]

Baker, ironically, in describing WFM violence before the troops arrived, said it was serious but "not to be compared in extent with that of the

anthracite coal strike in 1902."[38] Baker had already written a long article for *McClure's* documenting widespread violence and intimidation by John Mitchell's UMWA in Pennsylvania, a situation Wellman had ignored at the time.[39]

Although Baker and Wellman were both Progressives, they reasoned from different starting points. Baker's analysis reflects his opposition to monopoly in any form. He opposed trusts because they monopolized industries and opposed labor unions to the degree that they sought a closed shop, which Baker called "the trust idea applied to unionism."[40]

Wellman held similar views, but for him something else was more fundamental. During the Haywood interview, Big Bill earned Wellman's enmity when he said his union sought to "obtain possession of the government through political action" and dispossess the mine owners. That goal was the unpardonable sin. It trumped all crimes by all other parties in Colorado. Wellman found himself in the awkward position of defending Sherman Bell, who was even more of a strutting caricature of authoritarianism than West Virginia's Judge Jackson. But in spite of Bell's contempt for the niceties of civil law and human rights, Wellman trusted him over Haywood. One need not respect the written law to respect America's power structure and work within it. Bell posed no threat to capital and was deferential to men of wealth and status, the same type of men to whom Wellman had earned privileged access.

Labor newspapers roundly criticized Wellman for his Colorado series, but in the nation as a whole he was on the winning side.[41] And so, it turned out, was Roosevelt. Wellman made no mention of the president in his Colorado articles. Unlike in 1902, he did not even suggest that the president might have a role to play in the crisis; instead, Wellman called on labor men to repudiate the Western Federation of Miners as "unclean."[42] He did not need to add that a president who declined to intervene on behalf of such an organization was no enemy of labor.

On November 8 Roosevelt defeated Alton Parker by an even greater margin than Wellman had forecast.[43] Wellman soon began calling in favors. He had a new project in mind, one that would require a lot of money. He wrote to his boss, publisher Victor Lawson, and around the same time

President Roosevelt invited Lawson to lunch to talk about Wellman's plan, "in which I am greatly interested."[44]

"I recognize that his interest in your plans would, of course, be exceedingly valuable," Lawson wrote to Wellman on December 20. Nevertheless, he expressed regrets that other financial commitments prevented him from funding it at present, though he was hopeful for the future. Wellman's plan, Lawson said, "has made a strong appeal to my imagination and to my newspaper inclination to try to do important things."[45]

Wellman would have to wait, but he had the attention of at least two of the nation's most powerful men for a project that would require both futuristic technological prowess and breathtaking audacity. Once again, Walter Wellman had his eyes on the North Pole.

PART 3

The Polar Airship, 1905–1909

12

Motor Sledges and Airships

Washington DC, 1903–1906

Even after his crippling injury in Franz Josef Land, Wellman had never entirely given up on the North Pole. Instead, he was "determined to watch the progress of the arts and mechanics" to find a means of travel "better than the barbaric employment of sheer brute strength."[1] Though making a virtue of necessity, his love of technology was genuine and represented a natural continuation of his earlier experiments with aluminum boats and "scientific" rations. The superior type of man, he believed, used his mind to transcend physical limitations. That's what the new scientific age was all about.

By late 1903 Wellman believed he had found a way. On December 12 in New York City, as the guest of honor at the annual dinner of the Arctic Club, he proposed that the club organize a new expedition based on a plan that was "morally certain" of success: "With present methods a [sledging] party can make at the most an average of ten miles a day. By my plan there is no doubt at all that twenty miles a day can be made on an average. The method which I propose is perfectly simple and feasible, and will mark as great an advance in sledging as the electric car marked over the horse car."[2]

Wellman wanted a wealthy citizen willing to fund the expedition—$100,000 would do it—and then he would reveal his secret.[3] He did not wish to receive the money himself or even go on the expedition. He simply felt it should be done.

Such a vague proposal would have gotten a less famous man dismissed as a crank, but Wellman knew it would make good news copy and, more to the point, would ensure that he received partial credit for such an expedition even if he never left the United States. But no sponsor came

forward, and within a year Wellman decided to raise the money and lead the expedition himself, bad leg and all. So he contacted Roosevelt and Victor Lawson.

What we know about Wellman's 1903–4 plan comes from his 1911 book *The Aerial Age*, in which he says he "looked to the then rapidly developing automobile" and sought to modify it for polar travel.[4]

The type of machine he had in mind was not entirely new and went by many names. In 1836 two inventors in Galena, Illinois, tested a "steam sleigh" intended for passenger and freight traffic on the frozen Mississippi River. It proved underpowered and impractical, and eventually it was made irrelevant by the coming of the railroad.[5] The nineteenth century saw other steam sleighs, some successful, that were built for heavy-duty, short-run hauling. The boiler alone of an 1889 steam logging sleigh in Lewis County, New York, weighed 8,000 pounds.[6]

By the end of the century, internal combustion engines and electric motors made it practical to build smaller vehicles. An 1896 letter to the editor of *Scientific American* mentioned the horseless carriage and suggested, "Why not take the sleigh in hand and move that with a similar motor?" The writer recommended adding a "driving wheel back of the seat and midway between the two runners." The wheel would be studded with "little projecting spars."[7] Whether the idea started here or people developed it independently, "motor sleighs" or "automobile sleighs" of this description soon began appearing in North America and Europe.[8]

In 1897 an electric motor sledge was prominent in "The Great Stone of Sardis," a science fiction story serialized in *Harper's New Monthly Magazine*. With aluminum runners and enough charge to last a week, the imaginary sledge was "far superior to any drawn by dogs or reindeer."[9]

In 1900 three Frenchmen and Mary Hitchcock, a New York society woman turned adventurer and author, announced plans for a journey to the Yukon gold region by means of a 5-horsepower automobile sleigh. The machine was said to be large enough to haul fuel and camping gear but small enough to power a paddle wheel canoe.[10] Nothing apparently came of the plan, but a more ambitious proposal by Canadian mariner captain Joseph-Elzéar Bernier received wide publicity in the fall of 1902. Bernier planned to reach the North Pole by drifting with the ice pack, as Nansen had done. Then he wanted to set up a chain of supply depots

at fifty-mile intervals on the pack ice, stock them with the automobile sleigh, and keep them in communication with each other by means of wireless telegraph.[11] Nothing came of this either. The Canadian government eventually provided Bernier with a steamship for other missions but never for the pole.[12]

By 1901 even Santa Claus was said to be trading his sleigh for an automobile (though not necessarily an auto sleigh). Starting in about 1902 motor sleighs became a wintertime fad in various northern cities, though they remained obscure enough that for several years each report regards them as a new invention.[13]

Thus, by the time of Wellman's secret plan, the idea of a motor sled was not new but still remained a source of wonder. More important, it was tied to a growing awareness that automobiles were not simply a fad but also a transformational technology poised to change the world in profound ways. By combining this with the international politics of the North Pole quest, Wellman wanted to show the United States how to do a stump on the Old World in a modern and thoroughly American way.

Because his idea was untested in polar conditions, Wellman had to be careful to distinguish his plan from crackpot proposals such as that of Peter Nissen of Chicago, who experimented with an inflated canvas bag in which he hoped to roll to the pole. The "air-bag" had a doughnut hole in which Nissen suspended a boat on a steel axle and planned to ride in the boat while the wind rolled the bag "as a thistle is blown across a field."[14] What set Wellman apart from the cranks, the amateurs, and the old-fashioned dog mushers, he believed, was his adaptation of new technology based on firsthand knowledge of polar sea conditions, plus his boldness and wherewithal to actually launch the expedition.[15] That, presumably, is what he pitched to prospective donors.

Wellman knew that existing motor sleighs were useless for travel on rough sea ice, but "a light vehicle, weighing only 150 or 200 pounds, or less than a loaded sledge, would be different." It had to be light enough for two men to lift it over hummocks and ridges. Thus, it would not carry loads but tow them, acting as a "little locomotive" that could move quickly and effortlessly on smooth stretches and give the men a rest between obstacles. Despite his stated confidence, Wellman didn't trust the machines entirely; he would supplement them with traditional dog sledges.[16]

Fig. 8. "One of the 'Mechanical Dogs'" is a fairly accurate sketch of one of Wellman's motor sledges. The sketch illustrated a syndicated article, "The Accessories of the Wellman Polar Expedition," which appeared in numerous papers during the summer of 1906. The large front wheel doubled as a fuel tank, while the motor was under the driver's seat. The machine proved unsuited to rough Arctic conditions. *Rice Belt Journal* (Welsh LA), August 3, 1906.

Wellman had also designed a heated tent made of three layers of silk with insulating airspaces between the layers. Even with a stove, he explained, the interiors of ordinary tents were hardly warmer than outside, but his triple-tent could be warmed by thirty or forty degrees with a small amount of fuel, thus saving the men's "physical strength and effectiveness."[17]

This, apparently, was the plan with which Wellman enticed Lawson and Roosevelt in 1904, and no doubt he supplemented it with mechanical drawings and detailed tables of expected weights, mileage, and fuel consumption. At this time Wellman was becoming more broadly interested in modern transportation; in 1904 he published a pamphlet titled *Municipal Transport Problems* in which he addressed the logistical challenges of creating a practical subway system in New York City.[18] Whether moving city dwellers or polar provisions, he was watching for any new

advancement that might be useful, and in 1905 he learned of yet another major development in transportation. He soon demoted the motor sledge to a secondary role in an even more daring plan.

In early July 1905 reports reached the United States of a new dirigible airship being tested by the French military. On July 9 the Washington DC *Evening Star* reported on the "sensational trip of M[onsieur] Lebaudy's airship this week from Nantes to Meaux, sixty miles, more or less, against the wind, followed by a second trip of fifteen miles dead against a strong headwind."[19] The significance may not be apparent to the modern reader. Airships were not new in 1905, especially in France. An engineer named Henri Giffard invented a steam-powered airship in 1852; it proved navigable but too underpowered to fly against the wind. Other French engineers developed the electric-powered *La France*, which in 1884 became the first airship to return in flight to its starting point, and in Paris in 1901 a young Brazilian named Alberto Santos-Dumont won an aeronautical prize and became world-famous by making a seven-mile round-trip flight in less than thirty minutes. Thousands cheered as his airship rounded the Eiffel Tower under perfect control.

But none of these airships had navigated against more than a light breeze. In a strong wind they were all, as Wellman liked to say of Andrée's balloon, "a mere toy of the winds."[20] Even Santos-Dumont likened propelling a dirigible through the air to pushing a candle through a brick wall.[21]

Historians often credit the *Lebaudy* as being the world's first practical airship. That distinction depends upon one's definition of practicality. The ship was 185 feet long, 32½ feet at its greatest diameter, and held more than 104,000 cubic feet of hydrogen. An impressive sight, it was still too small to lift the payloads necessary for a voyage of exploration. The *Lebaudy* was meant only for demonstrations; its owners hoped to sell airships to the French military.[22]

Although the *Lebaudy* was soon wrecked in a storm, in October a rebuilt airship made an impressive reconnaissance of military works near the German frontier. Officers photographed forts from the air and dropped dummy bombs.[23] The Hague Convention of 1899 had banned aerial bombardment by balloons "or by other new methods of a similar nature," but this provision had expired after five years.[24]

Now it was clear that airships could deliver bombs with reasonable accuracy, but how vulnerable were they to ground fire?[25] In further tests, the *Lebaudy* dropped dummy bombs while being chased by automobiles with mounted machine guns. It was "like a glance into the future by a Verne or a Wells," said the *Washington Times*.[26] To minimize risks to the airship, the crew let out small balloons at which the automobile gunners could shoot. While shooting from a moving automobile 4,000 feet below was not an easy task, they hit several.

Further reports discounted the vulnerability of airships to ground fire. "It is so protected by cells that two hundred bullets would have to perforate it before reducing its ascensional powers," reported the *New-York Tribune* on October 29. It would take artillery fire to bring down an airship, and "owing to the difficulty of discharging an explosive projectile at an almost vertical axis there is really no danger of being hit by a shell."[27] And in November the *Lebaudy* crew captured aerial reconnaissance photos from 4,400 feet, or "quite beyond the range of any projectiles."[28]

It appeared that the world had a new superweapon. For the time being France and the *Lebaudy* stood alone at the pinnacle of aeronautics. In Germany Count Ferdinand von Zeppelin's enormous but underpowered aluminum-framed *LZ1*—nearly four times the size of the *Lebaudy*—had been dismantled five years earlier after a few test flights left potential investors unconvinced of its worth; a second Zeppelin airship was still under construction.

Heavier-than-air flight, meanwhile, was still in the experimental glider stage for everyone but two secretive brothers from Dayton, Ohio. Even by 1905 few people knew that Wilbur Wright and Orville Wright had been making powered flights since December 17, 1903. Of those who did know, few considered their aircraft anything more than a stunt, a thrill machine that was capable only of short hops. On October 5, 1905, a week before the *Lebaudy* bombing tests, Wilbur Wright culminated a series of unpublicized test flights near Dayton with a flight of nearly forty minutes. Far more than a stunt, it was the world's first "practical" airplane, and although the Wright brothers did nothing at this point to encourage it, at last news of their work began to spread.[29]

Although their attitudes toward publicity were different, the Wright brothers and the owners of the *Lebaudy* were all hoping to secure lucrative

military contracts. Walter Wellman, meanwhile, looked to the airship not as a weapon of war but as a tool of exploration. It was not lost on him that the *Lebaudy* was said to have lost less than 2 percent of its hydrogen per day. Such a ship could stay aloft for a long time if need be, maybe even long enough to cross the polar sea.[30]

Wellman's announcement on the last day of 1905 was almost too far-fetched to be real: What was officially called the Wellman Chicago Record-Herald Polar Expedition was set for the summer of 1906. "Build an airship, go find the North Pole," *Chicago Record-Herald* editor in chief Frank Noyes had ordered Wellman, "and report by wireless telegraph and submarine cables the progress of your efforts." The airship would be built in France that winter and assembled in Spitsbergen in June. As soon as the weather allowed, Wellman and a crew of five would fly north, where they would send daily reports by wireless and, if all went well, arrive at the pole in less than a week.[31]

Despite the pretense of this being an assignment, the idea was Wellman's. Inspired by the *Lebaudy*, he may have begun planning as early as June or as late as October, probably adapting some of the logistics of his motor-sledge proposal.[32] His plans were far along by the time of the announcement, which accurately describes the airship's specifications and names its builder, Louis Godard of Paris.

This sudden turn of events was in keeping with Wellman's long-held interest in aerial navigation that dated to Adolphe de Bausset's proposed North Pole vacuum airship in 1887. Reporting from the World's Columbian Exposition in 1893, he had predicted that aerial navigation would "solve the mystery of the north pole" within twenty-five years.[33] He investigated ballooning to the pole after his 1894 expedition, and his interest in ballooning was rekindled in 1901 when he reported on an international balloon race from Paris. The winning balloon traveled deep into Russia, covering 1,193 miles in less than thirty-six hours. "If Andrée had only had such a fair wind!" he wrote, pointing out that Spitsbergen lay only 800 miles from the North Pole. "And is there anything unreasonable in the hope of the Parisian enthusiasts that . . . some day we shall have great international balloon races, with Chicago as the starting-point and Paris for the goal?"[34]

All this had primed Wellman to see greater possibilities in the *Lebau-dy*'s success, but press reaction to his announcement was mixed, ranging from "the most spectacular undertaking in the history of Arctic exploration" to a suggestion that his news would have been more appropriate to April Fools' Day.[35] Wellman received greater support in the French press, probably because the airship's builder, Louis Godard (whom Wellman had met during the 1901 Paris balloon race), was a well-known aeronaut. Even better, Santos-Dumont, the world's most famous aeronaut, was going to supervise its construction and accompany Wellman as the ship's pilot. In the end the Brazilian provided advice but did not join the expedition.[36]

What made Wellman's announcement so startling was not only the extreme danger of the enterprise but also the status of the man who would risk it. Wellman wasn't some crank on the margins of society or even a little-known engineer as Andrée had been. He was a nationally known figure who stood at the top of his profession. In the months before his announcement, in addition to his behind-the-scenes reporting on the Portsmouth Peace Treaty between Japan and Russia (for which Theodore Roosevelt would win the Nobel Peace Prize), Wellman also published a major exposé on the life insurance industry and even raised eyebrows by predicting that Secretary of War William Howard Taft was the certain Republican presidential nominee for 1908 and would face the equally certain Democratic nominee William Jennings Bryan. (Taft quickly responded that he had "no intention whatever" of seeking the presidency.)[37]

Now Wellman was about to walk away from everything and risk Andrée's fate. "Some of our best friends may question our sanity," he acknowledged.[38] In March the magazine *The World To-Day* published a revealing profile apparently based, like so much of Wellman's own reporting, on anonymous sources. The author, Charles W. Arthur, said that no one who knew Wellman doubted his sincerity. "It is a daring, audacious thing he is preparing to do, but he has done daring and audacious things before." What drove Wellman was less clear; he was "unknown even to many of his colleagues," was seldom seen in press galleries, and was not a "'mixer,' or, for that matter, a generally popular man. His temperament and his personality" did not win him friends "indiscriminately" beyond a circle of close friends.[39]

This is a different picture from that of reports in the 1890s, when Wellman was president of the Washington Press Club and at the center of the press corps's social life.[40] Now as "the most widely known and quoted Washington correspondent," Wellman was said to deal "only with important men" and to write "only on big subjects."[41]

He seemed older than his forty-seven years, having more gray hair and a more deeply lined face than most men his age, and still walked with a limp. One contemporary report observes that despite his prolific output of newspaper and magazine articles, "Mr. Wellman himself thinks he is rather lazy, and not infrequently expresses regret because of that self-attributed shortcoming. His favorite diversion is billiards, and almost any afternoon when he is in Washington he may be found playing that game in the old hotel across the street from his office."[42] That Wellman loved a game of geometrical precision seems of a piece with his preparation of elaborate tables of data for his expeditions, with his passion for solitaire, and with his reputed habit of keeping a written record of each game.[43]

None of this explains why he would take such a risk at this stage of life, knowing how unforgiving both the polar environment and the press could be. Whenever he justified the risks of exploration, he usually wrote about "scientific progress for the good of mankind and the advancement of knowledge."[44] He may have revealed something more personal when writing about Theodore Roosevelt in 1903. In a brief biographical sketch in which he called Roosevelt "the luckiest man we have ever had in public life," Wellman wrote that when the president was assistant secretary of the navy in 1898, he "had no following and if things had been permitted to continue the way they were going, it was pretty sure that he could not hope to rise much higher." Then came the war with Spain, with Roosevelt charging headlong into it even though "he could not afford to leave his wife and children unprotected in case of accident. No matter. He gave up his place in civil life, where he had won some distinction, and went into war, of which he knew nothing. He literally risked everything he had upon a single cast of the die and won."[45]

A second Roosevelt story provides another clue. Secretary of State Elihu Root had taken offense at mild teasing by a young reporter and apparently complained to the president. On October 20, 1905, Wellman complained in the *Chicago Record-Herald* that the president had ordered his cabinet

officials not to speak to the press—including, presumably, Wellman. "Mr. Roosevelt is greatly impressed by single incidents," Wellman wrote with uncharacteristic bitterness, "and often argues from incident to principle in somewhat arbitrary and hasty fashion."[46] Wellman's tone throughout the article betrayed the indignation of a man who had been reminded of the gap in status between himself and the men he had begun to think of as his peers. After all he had accomplished, he was still just a reporter. The doors could be closed against him at any time.

But it was possible to become regarded more than a simple reporter. Graying and crippled, it still wasn't too late. His life could change with a single cast of the die.

13

The Scheme Was Crazy Enough to Seem Workable

Paris, France, and Tromsø, Norway, January–June 1906

Wellman sailed for Paris on January 3, 1906, accompanied by two of his five daughters—Rose, age twenty-two, and Rae, age twenty and known to society columns as a contralto singer who had spent the past year at the New England Conservatory of Music. The two young women would stay in the City of Light while their famous father made arrangements to build his polar airship.[1]

Without ever having flown in an airship, Wellman now had to sort out conflicting expert advice before construction began.[2] It would be a *Lebaudy*-style ship, that much was clear: semirigid in construction (a pressure airship similar to a modern blimp but with a solid keel); with multilayered, rubberized fabric to contain the hydrogen; and one or more gasoline-powered motors to turn the propellers. But would it be a fast ship or a slow ship?[3]

One school of thought held that a polar airship should be built for range and not speed. No airship had ever been designed to cover the distances Wellman required. Even the *Lebaudy*, the world's most advanced airship, had been making two- to three-hour trips and had a range of no more than about six hours, or 120 miles.[4] To go from Spitsbergen to the pole and back, Wellman needed to fly twelve times that distance.

Long-distance ballooning held the closest precedent. As Wellman knew from his own reporting, the winner of the 1901 Paris race had traveled 1,193 miles in less than thirty-six hours.[5] A steady wind made the journey possible, but it wasn't all luck. As Andrée did, competitive balloonists used gas, not hot air, in their balloons. Success depended upon the balloon not leaking much hydrogen (airtight was not good enough) and upon the pilot's ability to conserve gas and ballast by maintaining a steady altitude.

A long-range airship, some argued, should therefore stay close to the surface, as low as a few hundred feet, and drag a heavy guide rope to regulate altitude. During the summer, the Arctic Ocean was in some ways a surprisingly ideal environment for this sort of travel. In normal circumstances a balloon or airship would have to drop ballast and valve gas to compensate for dramatic changes in buoyancy from day to night and during fluctuations in the weather. Over the polar ice, however, the ship would have constant daylight, with temperatures hovering around the freezing point.[6]

The airship need not cruise at more than 12–15 miles per hour. It only needed enough horsepower to overcome *most* of the expected headwinds. If a contrary wind exceeded or even approached the airship's top speed, the crew could simply drop anchor and wait out the wind. In studying three years' worth of weather data from Nansen's ship, the *Fram*, Wellman calculated that during a ten-day journey he could expect winds that would allow a ship with a top speed of only 17 miles per hour to make headway about 90 percent of the time.[7]

Wellman had already described such a low-and-slow airship in his December 31 press release before his well-publicized trip to seek expert advice in France.[8] While in France he said that an aeronautic expert warned him that this method would surely fail, insisting that he needed a ship capable of achieving speeds of at least 34 miles per hour.[9] The problem, Wellman knew, was that higher speed meant more resistance, which required higher horsepower, vastly more fuel, and a much larger airship to lift it all. Wellman figured that such a big and fast ship would require 400 horsepower instead of 75 and would burn an additional eighty-five hundred pounds of fuel. He'd need a ship five times larger than what he was planning on, and it would cost about $1 million. It was a lovely idea, but even Wellman couldn't raise that kind of money. His unnamed critic worked with paper and pencil and, in Wellman's telling, soon reached the same conclusion: "You are right, and I was wrong."[10]

The Frenchman may have been wrong about the fast airship, but whether Wellman was right about the slow airship remained to be seen. None of this had been done before. Wellman expended a great many words and data to convince donors and skeptics that his proposed ship would have

sufficient range in various hypothetical scenarios. With enough fuel for 140 hours of motoring at an average of 12 miles per hour, the airship had a theoretical range of 1,680 miles in still air, and that was more than enough for the round-trip.[11]

Wind could either help or hurt, but the option to drop anchor would minimize the effects of the worst headwinds.[12] Wellman compiled logs for a number of hypothetical voyages, arbitrarily using wind speeds and directions from the *Fram*'s logs. In the best scenario he would arrive at the pole in 28 hours; in the worst it would take 152 hours—68 of which would be spent motoring and the rest on waiting out strong headwinds.[13]

One can imagine Wellman's readers and potential donors looking at all this and concluding that, however crazy the idea sounded when stated bluntly—"fly an airship to the North Pole"—Wellman made it look as though it could actually be done, albeit with considerable risk. The numbers were based on data from previous airships, engines, and weather, but if the new ship performed as expected, if Wellman didn't wreck, if he avoided a fiery explosion of his 225,000 cubic feet of hydrogen, if his navigation was true, if there wasn't some deadly unknown problem missing from all those drawings and tables—all big *ifs*—then maybe the trip was possible.[14]

Opinions were divided, but Wellman had the support of the National Geographic Society, which appointed a man to his airship crew. Returning to the United States, he gave a speech to the New York Motor Club on March 23 in which he said he had "no desire to reach the North Pole without a return ticket and a chance to use it." Though he insisted that he would have more than enough fuel for the round-trip, he was also bringing sledges and a metal boat in case the airship failed to make it home. At first he had said he would bring seventy-five dogs, but now he was having motor sledges built both in the United States and in France.[15]

Overall, Wellman was hedging his bets, powering his airship with two smaller motors rather than one large one, thus trading some efficiency for greater safety. Rather than trust one contractor or one design for his motor sledges, he hired companies to build prototypes of at least three different designs of "gasolene dog." He would take along three or four of the best, and if none were satisfactory he'd take dogs instead.[16]

On one point he saw no flexibility. If he ended up on land he would "head for the nearest settlement. . . . We make no preparations for spending the winter in the cold regions. If we are left up there it is forever."[17]

With these high stakes in mind, Wellman said that if the airship failed its preliminary tests, he would delay launch until 1907 and rebuild the entire ship if necessary.[18] That said, he was eager for a 1906 launch, and he knew that if he was to build the ship, test it, and get it to Spitsbergen in time for the brief Arctic summer, he would have to hurry.

Felix Riesenberg was a twenty-six-year-old deck officer in the merchant marine who saw Wellman's announcement in the *Chicago Record-Herald*. "The scheme was crazy enough to seem workable," he recalled, and being in Chicago at the time, he visited the *Record-Herald*'s offices. Luck was with him. Wellman himself was in town and had not yet hired a navigator. Riesenberg soon received orders to report to Tromsø in June. Being hired for an internationally famous voyage "had an influence on my mind," he recalled. "I became dangerously enthusiastic."[19]

In Tromsø Riesenberg worked under the command of Maj. Henry Hersey of the U.S. Weather Bureau. Hersey, a former Rough Rider, had been appointed to the expedition by the National Geographic Society, and Wellman had placed him in charge of the first supply trip to Danes Island. The group was to depart Tromsø once the sea was reasonably clear of ice. On the island they were to set up base camp and, most important, erect the giant hangar in which the airship would be inflated. Wellman, meanwhile, returned to Paris to oversee completion of the French-built airship he had named *America*.[20]

Because of Riesenberg's merchant marine experience, Hersey put him in charge of loading the ship. Lumber was stacked at the end of the stone quay, and a nearby warehouse was filled with huge rolls of canvas for the hangar, crated parts of a hydrogen-generating apparatus, and boxes and barrels full of provisions and Arctic clothing. Many tons of supplies were to be put aboard the three-masted bark anchored in the harbor. The *Frithjof* was a sealer turned expedition ship that had taken Wellman to Franz Josef Land in 1898. As an ice ship, it was equipped with a steam engine and a meter-thick, heavily braced wooden hull, and it seemed to Riesenberg "as though we were trying to wedge a mountain of material into a small hole."[21]

He ordered the men to cram items into every nook and cranny. The port wardens grew uneasy with how low the *Frithjof* was sitting in the water and ordered him to stop. By then the ship was loaded to the main hatch, but the lumber still sat on the quay. If Wellman was to have any chance this year, they had to get base camp built right away. Spitsbergen, of course, was treeless except for inch-tall Arctic willows. The lumber absolutely had to come on board.

Riesenberg took the wardens out for drinks and then more drinks. They agreed to let him chain the lumber on deck "but not an ounce more," though stacks of equipment remained in the warehouse.[22]

A dinner in the expedition's honor was held the evening before the June 15 departure. All the local dignitaries were there, including the port wardens. After countless cries of *Skaal!* (Cheers!), Riesenberg remained barely clearheaded enough to stumble out into the sunshine at one o'clock in the morning and rally the crew and carpenters. With Paul Bjørvig leading the sailors, they loaded everything that remained in the warehouse and took on twenty tons of coal besides. By the time the rest of the party staggered out of the hotel, the *Frithjof* was waiting with steam up and anchor atrip. The ship got under way the moment the captain was aboard. As it left the harbor, Riesenberg, steadied by a mug of black coffee, watched through the glass as the drunken port wardens made their way along the dock toward the now-empty warehouse.[23]

In later years Riesenberg would write the textbook *Standard Seamanship for the Merchant Service* for his profession. The "Riesenberg Saying" is still taught to cadets at the State University of New York's Maritime College: "The sea is selective, slow at recognition of effort and aptitude but fast in the sinking of the unfit."[24] The saying's author owed his life to the fact that it did not hold true on his horrific passage to Spitsbergen in June 1906. The overloaded *Frithjof* wallowed through heavy seas, breached constantly by waves. With its decks awash and cabin doors battened down, its interior reeked of vomit from the many landlubbers aboard. "Why she did not sink, God only knows," Riesenberg wrote.[25]

On the same day the *Frithjof* left Tromsø harbor, a Parisian crowd cheered and presented bouquets as Wellman departed in a chartered freight train loaded with fifty tons of airship materials.[26] The engines had been tested

only four days earlier; the airship itself was complete but untested. Hurrying north Wellman would take the *America* straight to the Arctic for its maiden flight.

Wellman had long since told reporters that test flights couldn't be done in France because "atmospheric conditions are so different" or that no building in Paris was "large enough to hold such a monstrous airship."[27] Neither statement was accurate, but both sounded better than the real reasons—the twin pressures of time and publicity. Wellman had given Godard four months to build an airship twice the size of anything previously built in France, and Godard, in Wellman's words, soon "found it necessary to prepare his working drawings at the same time he was assembling his material and starting the actual construction."[28] Labor strikes prevented Godard from receiving the motors on time, and when he finished his work Wellman publicly praised the balloon itself but said the mechanical parts were "good, but not perfect, requiring slight changes at Spitzbergen, where we shall complete the machine."[29]

Back in the States, newspapers reported how Wellman had bid his mother goodbye before leaving for France, with "her arms around his neck, her gray head upon his breast and tears flowing down her cheeks."[30]

"There is no other human enterprise as hopeless as that on which Wellman will set out within a few days," said the *Arizona Republican*. "When the months have extended into years and all that has been heard of the aerial explorer will be rumors that parts of his equipment have been picked up on the shores of frozen seas, men will repeat the old inquiry, Is the north pole worth so much?"[31]

Wellman was no stranger to this style of writing and surely understood what it meant. It wasn't just that some papers wrote with respect and others with disapproval. The important thing was that after all the buildup, the press and the public expected a grand resolution to this drama. Whether the star of the show was a hero or a corpse mattered less than whether he delivered a satisfying closing act or not.

14

The Airship Station on Virgo Bay

Danes Island, Spitsbergen, July–August 1906

Indented in the north shore of Danes Island, Virgo Bay lay sheltered among barren mountains whose peaks glowed pink in the midnight sun and where the air screeched with flocks of eider ducks. Normally uninhabited the island had seen human activity before. It was here in 1894 that Dr. Øyen spent a lonely summer cursing Walter Wellman, and here three years later Andrée and his companions were last seen alive. The wreckage of Andrée's balloon house still lay on shore; a stone monument stood nearby in his memory. Silent film footage exists of Wellman paying his respects at the monument in 1906. Ever the reporter, he appears to copy down the stone's inscription. Then he is back in the boat and tips his cap to the camera.[1]

There were other reminders of the dead. Just across the bay, parts of Amsterdam Island were strewn with the bones of seventeenth-century Dutch and Danish whalemen whose shallow graves had been raided by bears and wolves, just as Bernt Bentsen had once feared. Associated also were the names and stories of famous men who had passed this way: Henry Hudson, Horatio Nelson as a young midshipman, Captain Parry, Adolf Nordenskiöld, and Otto Sverdrup and the *Fram* when they had escaped from three years in the polar ice, asking everyone they met for news of their departed shipmates Fridtjof Nansen and Hjalmar Johansen. "North-west Spitsbergen is rich in minor echoes," Felix Riesenberg wrote, "like rare music audible to the very few."[2]

On the shore of Virgo Bay, Camp Wellman looked as busy as a mining camp when its namesake arrived on July 9. Wellman was disappointed by what he didn't see—a completed airship hangar. The ground wasn't even cleared yet. This wasn't the men's fault. Finding a level piece of ground was not easy, and the most promising spot was occupied by a volcanic boulder as big as a small house.[3]

Fig. 9. Camp Wellman, Danes Island, summer 1906. Shown here are the original five-arch frame of the hangar, the first version of the airship car with its large canvas-covered propellers on either end, and the wicker basket to hold the fuel tanks. Anders Beer Wilse/Norsk Folkemuseum, Olso, Norway.

Wellman had brought a case of dynamite, "direct from the Nobel works in Sweden," but no one in his small army of men had any blasting experience. Wellman gave Riesenberg the assignment, advising him to "use at least a kilo" to break the boulder into small pieces for easy removal. "He was growing tense," Riesenberg remembered. "We all were, unshaven, grey. Time was slipping."[4]

Riesenberg ordered the men to drill three holes under the rock, placed a two-and-a-half-kilo carton of pink dynamite sticks in each, and warned everyone to stand back at least five hundred feet.

A rigid shock, a frightful, ripping, roaring detonation, shook the small valley. Rocks seemed to poise in the air, but amid a sudden plume of blue-grey smoke, ice and sand, the great boulder, fully twenty feet across, lifted from its age-old bed, rose like a baseball, split into two parts, the whirling jagged edges whistling. One part rose inland, tossed into the mountains. The larger part, screaming like a mad ripsaw, soared over

the heads of our group—up, up, up—it curved gracefully and plunged, a cold black meteor. A grisly fear froze me and held me as if we were about to see an ancient mastodon slaughtered by Jove, for that rock was plunging directly at the *Frithjof*. Some closed their eyes when it hit. I was stiff, sweat oozing from every pore. The rock missed the old bark by fifty feet, throwing a cascade of water over her decks. She rolled in the heavy surge, her masts shaking. Some of the crew, seeing death descending, dropped to their knees in prayer.

As waves washed on the beach, a crescendo of tremendous salutes followed the explosion—a clapping of mighty, magnifying sounds. A vast amphitheatre, many miles across, was full of applauding mountains. Rocks, dislodged by the shock, were tumbling from cliffsides. Birds rose in their thousands, screeching in fright; dogs howled, and from far off Smeerenburg Sound, glacier after glacier calved and flung back shots, the echoing thunders like the salvos of a fleet of Jupiterian battleships. This lasted for minutes while dimming echoes were exchanged and re-exchanged; thousands upon thousands of tons of glacier ice tumbled into the sea. I have never witnessed a more magnificent explosion.[5]

From this anecdote and from the one about the *Frithjof*'s overloaded departure from Tromsø, clearly Riesenberg is a lively (if occasionally over-the-top) narrator who provides material not found in Wellman's published accounts. Writing three decades after the events he describes, however, might his memories be enhanced by the passage of time or by the tradition of old sailors spinning yarns? Wellman doesn't mention this incident, though perhaps that's because it didn't qualify as a proper polar adventure and made his crew look like amateurs.

Riesenberg sometimes mixes up dates or sequences of events, but I haven't caught him inventing stories out of whole cloth. His style, however, is that of a man who believes that telling a story properly means telling it big and filling the whole room with its grandeur. Whenever Riesenberg's version of events can be compared to that of Wellman or engineer Melvin Vaniman, his story is always similar but bigger. Next to him, even Wellman seems subdued. I suggest listening to him the way you do to a friend from whose stories you automatically subtract a third to a half for storyteller's license.

Part of it, too, is the perspective of an older, more cautious man looking back on the recklessness of his youth. Throughout the Wellman chapters of Riesenberg's memoir runs one underlying theme—foolish risk and the willingness of enthusiastic men to ignore it. In this, he indicts not only himself but also his comrades and commander.

Continuing his narrative, Riesenberg describes the men standing around the hole left by the great boulder. Wellman said nothing about the close call with the ship. One more obstacle between him and the North Pole had just been removed.

"Felix, you certainly lifted that rock," he said.[6]

Despite its remote location, Virgo Bay was a busy place that summer and not only with Wellman's men. The bay was full of chartered steamers and private yachts. Two motion picture companies sent camera crews, and wealthy tourists came not only to watch the airship depart but also to spend time with its busy commander. Reporters came in search of interviews, news, sensational stories, and, apparently, military intelligence.[7] When Wellman arrived on July 9, he was surprised to see a German flag flying above a tent on shore. It belonged to the journalist Otto von Gottberg of the Berlin *Lokal Anzeiger*. Wellman knew him from the Portsmouth Peace Conference and was happy to have him at camp, perhaps flattered that the expedition was drawing international attention.

Some years later—in 1917, by which time the ongoing world war had poisoned views regarding Germans—Wellman's former chief engineer on this expedition, Alexandre Liwentaal of Geneva, Switzerland, wrote an article in which he said the Germans had come with another agenda, one to which Wellman had been blind. Gottberg, Liwentaal said, was a retired military officer who had been sent by the German General Staff "to watch our proceedings." Pleasant and multilingual, Gottberg had only one weakness for a spy—he liked to get drunk and boast of Germany's military prowess. Once when Liwentaal "treated his boastfulness some-what lightly he broke out furiously: 'Yes. We will make war when we think the moment has arrived. We shall over-run Belgium and jump on France unawares. We shall get to Paris in a fortnight, and settle France in a month. Then we shall take the French Navy and destroy Britain.'"[8]

As later events make clear, Liwentaal is probably not a reliable informant, but in this case he could be reporting a real conversation. Other than the final sentence, Gottberg had given a fair summary of the Schlieffen Plan, developed in 1905–6. Germany's operational plan for a general European war called for a quick, sweeping envelopment of the French so that Germany could then turn about and concentrate its forces against the slow-mobilizing Russians. It is conceivable that Gottberg could have said something like this in a moment of boozy indiscretion. Liwentaal already knew something of German militarism, having worked for Count Zeppelin, who made no secret that his giant experimental airships were meant as weapons of war.[9]

The point Liwentaal missed—or concealed—in his 1917 article was that Germany's militarism had been no secret. A 1906 photo from Virgo Harbor shows German military officers examining a Wellman motor sledge. The following year the Germans returned and even helped tow Wellman's airship into the harbor, and Zeppelin himself later investigated the area and in 1909 announced (but did not launch) a polar airship journey of his own. Everyone, including Wellman, knew the Germans had come in hopes of learning something they could use in their next war against France or Britain. Liwentaal said Wellman just laughed at Gottberg's patriotic braggadocio.[10] Maybe he did. In 1906 it didn't seem to have anything to do with America.

Wellman had long seen the polar race as an arena of international cooperation and peaceful competition. The development of long-range aeronautics not only heightened the competition but also gave it a militaristic overtone that Wellman may not have yet fully understood.

In an increasingly technological world, polar exploration had become a way for the modern public to participate vicariously in a primitive quest and thrill to tales of fur-clad men traveling by dog sledge across one of the final uncharted wildernesses. They were the last heroes of a passing heroic age. Back in Sir John Franklin's time, polar explorers had worn military uniforms, traveled in warships, and disdained native ways as unworthy of civilized men, but by the early twentieth century the studio portrait of the explorer in his fur-trimmed Eskimo hood was a standard part of a proper expedition's press kit.[11]

In such times Wellman stood as an anomaly among pole seekers, being an ardent futurist who made a point of bringing the latest technology into the Arctic as if to show that no spot on earth was beyond the reach of the new scientific man. So eager was he to use new methods that in addition to the airship and motor sledge, in 1906 Wellman introduced a third experimental technology to the Arctic—wireless telegraphy.

A Chicago newspaper had suggested its use several years earlier. In September 1899 when Guglielmo Marconi was experimenting with his first transatlantic transmissions, and when an injured Wellman had recently returned home from Franz Josef Land, the *Chicago Record* (not yet merged with Wellman's *Times-Herald*) observed that "if Sig. Marconi's confidence is well founded Walter Wellman could have been in communication with London or New York during his entire journey. The lost Andrée might have kept the world advised of his movements."[12] The following year the English balloonist Rev. J. M. Bacon experimented with wireless telegraphy from a balloon. While receiving signals from twenty miles away, he lacked a strong enough transmitter to send them.[13]

To the people of the early twentieth century, the notion of wireless communication was as startling and epoch making as aeronautics or polar conquest. As Ray Stannard Baker wrote in *McClure's* in February 1902, Marconi's invention

was of a nature to balk human credulity. Think for a moment of sitting here on the edge of North America and listening to communications sent *through space* across nearly 2,000 miles of ocean from the edge of Europe! A cable, marvelous as it is, maintains a tangible and material connection between speaker and hearer: one can grasp its meaning. But here is nothing but space, a pole with a pendent wire on one side of a broad, curving ocean, an uncertain kite struggling in the air on the other—and thought passing between.[14]

Not only would wireless communication give Wellman an added measure of safety—and its advantages for the newsman were obvious—but it also would reinforce the futuristic nature of his expedition. The North Pole had never been important except as a trophy of national manhood.

Wellman sought to redefine the quest as a technological achievement rather than a physical ordeal; it was more of a moon landing than a marathon, to put it in the terms of a later generation.

Wellman had contracted with the American DeForest Wireless Telegraph Company of St. Louis to provide three wireless stations as links to the outside world: one at Hammerfest, Norway; one on Danes Island; and one aboard the *America* itself.[15]

On July 23 President Roosevelt received a dispatch:

ROOSEVELT, WASHINGTON:

GREETINGS, BEST WISHES, BY FIRST WIRELESS MESSAGE EVER SENT FROM ARCTIC REGIONS.

WELLMAN[16]

Wellman later complained that the DeForest company had failed to complete its contract and that the "number of messages we were able to get through in nowise compensated us for the outlay of money, labor and annoyance."[17] Riesenberg remembered it as worse than that. Wellman "filed many pages of copy" for transmission, he recalled, but became suspicious when he received only vague congratulatory messages in reply. It turned out that the equipment didn't work, and the messages were fraudulent. The wireless operators at Hammerfest and Danes Island had "fixed up a number of exchange messages in advance, and this childish scheme had been foisted on Walter Wellman," who angrily sent the men and their equipment home on the next ship.[18] Within months American DeForest was exposed for defrauding investors.[19]

Delays and failures mounted as the brief Arctic summer passed. Even after the ground was cleared for the airship hangar, it took longer to build than Wellman had planned. The hangar was Liwentaal's design, a clever piece of work in the face of peculiar engineering challenges. Not only did the hangar need to enclose an enormous area and protect it from the wind, but also Liwentaal was limited to using those materials that Riesenberg crammed into the overloaded *Frithjof*. The design called for nine latticed wooden arches of eighty-two feet high to be joined with latticed spans,

covered with nearly an acre of canvas, and anchored with wire stays. Setting it up was no easy task, and Wellman finally reduced the number of the arches to five so they could get it done.[20]

The motor sledges, the first such machines in the polar regions, were another source of disappointment. Wellman had commissioned different designs with the intention of taking the best on the airship. One was a modified Indian motorcycle, with a pair of skis in place of the front wheel.[21] Motorcycles at this time were little more than bicycles with single-cylinder putt-putt motors, and apparently Wellman didn't take this flimsy craft to Danes Island. The design on which Wellman pinned his hopes had a large wheel in front and sled runners in back. The runners bore the weight of the engine and driver; the hollow metal wheel had herringbone treads and doubled as a fuel tank. The contraption may have been fine for a pleasure outing on a smooth frozen lake, but it proved wholly unsuited for its role as "gasolene dog" on the ice pack. Underpowered and overweight, its leaky drive wheel gradually became lighter until, in Riesenberg's words, "it was nothing more than an empty drum that pounded itself to pieces on the ice, moving nothing."[22]

Even this setback wasn't fatal to the expedition. Wellman, apparently realizing how reckless it was to use an experimental vehicle as a backup for another experimental vehicle, had brought a pack of Siberian dogs just in case.[23] He was already on record as saying he didn't think it was possible to reach the North Pole with dogs, which in his experience were too slow and sulky.[24] Of course the dogs would just be noisy passengers as long as the airship stayed aloft, but no less of an explorer than Fridtjof Nansen had written in 1898 (when there was still hope for Andrée's return) that one could reasonably use a balloon to carry dogs and sledges north, then abandon the balloon, and head south over the ice, thus avoiding the need to cover the same area by sledge twice. It was hauling provisions for the round-trip that made sledging to the pole so difficult.[25]

Despite the setbacks, by late August Wellman had his hangar, his dogs, and his airship gasbag, which he would trust with his life. All he needed now was for the "good, but not perfect" mechanical parts of the ship to work. From the beginning he had emphasized that *America* would be no mere balloon with a flimsy wicker basket but a strong ship with a car "made

entirely of steel tubing."[26] In his articles Wellman stuck to this story even after he had possession of Godard's car, which was made of wood sheathed with metal and carried a large wicker basket to hold the fuel tanks.[27]

Once inflated, the airship would be shaped like a fat pickle, 164 feet long and 53½ feet in diameter. Enclosing 225,000 cubic feet of hydrogen, it would start out with eight tons of lift. Wellman was determined that his airship would not be as leaky as Andrée's was said to have been, and Godard's crew made the new gasbag out of three layers of fabric—two of cotton and one of silk—coated with alternating layers of rubber.[28]

Godard's metal-sheathed airship car was 52½ feet long, a little less than 6 feet wide, and tapered toward the huge, slow-turning, fabric-covered propellers at either end. Before launch the car would be covered with fabric to give the aeronauts some protection from the elements. Two motors of 55 and 25 horsepower were installed just aft of center, and the fuel tanks were to be carried in the big wicker basket that would hang beneath the car.[29] Though the motors had been tested in France, they had not been tested while attached to the car and fitted with propellers. When this was finally done at Danes Island, Wellman wrote, "The motors could not be made to work right, the driving gear went to pieces, and the propellers could not stand even half of the strain which it was designed to put upon them."[30] To the degree that the motors did run, the flimsy car couldn't take the vibration, and other tests showed that the wicker basket would collapse under the weight of the fuel tanks it would need to carry.[31]

Wellman had been saying all along that he might have to delay the North Pole flight until 1907, but that didn't stop a portion of the press from suggesting that maybe he hadn't intended to fly at all and that the whole thing was just an advertising scheme to help the *Record-Herald* sell newspapers. Like Andrée, Wellman now heard a chorus of critics question not only his judgment but also his integrity.[32]

He would try again. That was a given. But he would no longer work with Godard, a competent balloon maker who had been out of his depth when building a powered airship. The gasbag could be salvaged, but otherwise the *America* needed to be completely redesigned. Wellman was beginning to see himself as an engineer, but he knew he couldn't solve these problems alone.

If there was one thing Walter Wellman could always count on, it was that he knew the people who mattered. Before the end of 1906, two new names would be associated with Wellman's in the nation's newspapers. One would become his most important collaborator; the other, his most famous rival.

15

Wellman vs. Peary

Washington DC, November 1906–May 1907

Unlike Wellman, Robert E. Peary was a man for whom the North Pole was not one interest among many but a singular obsession. Two years older than Wellman, as a boy Peary had been inspired by the writings of Elisha Kane but, as boys will do, moved on to other things. As a civil engineer in the U.S. Navy, he helped survey a route in Nicaragua for the proposed isthmian canal (later built through Panama). A respectable career lay ahead of him, but for Peary it wasn't enough.[1]

The young engineer was browsing a secondhand bookstore when he came across a report on the barely explored Greenland ice sheet. At once his boyhood passion was rekindled. He began reading everything he could find about the Arctic. In 1886 the thirty-year-old Peary and a Danish companion man-hauled toboggan sleds in an attempt to cross Greenland on foot. They turned back after no more than a hundred miles, but the interior was so little known that Peary's article about the journey got him elected to the American Association for the Advancement of Science.[2]

Peary was hooked. Planning a second expedition, he wrote to his mother:

My last trip has brought my name before the world my next will give me a standing in the world. . . . Remember Mother I *must* have fame & I cannot reconcile myself to years of commonplace drudgery & a name late in life when I see an opportunity to gain it now & sip the delicious draught while yet I have youth & strength & capacity to enjoy it to the utmost.[3]

Like Roosevelt and Wellman, Peary was in a hurry and would risk everything upon a single cast of the die. Or so he imagined. From all his

reading, he surely knew how an Arctic quest could torment a man year after year with the great prize that it dangled just out of reach, goading him with the fear of failure and obscurity, and enticing him back again and again to try just once more until he was either dead or broken by hardship. Every expedition leader knew the bleak stories of his predecessors, but no one ever went north thinking their fate would happen to him.

In 1892 Peary was lauded for proving the insularity of Greenland with his discovery of Independence Bay, which—so he claimed—separated the main island from an archipelago to the north. Between 1893 and 1902 he turned his attention to the North Pole itself, making several attempts, but, like Wellman, he was quickly stymied by the condition of the sea ice. He reported the discovery of new islands, even insisting that he had seen Axel Heiberg Land in the distance two years before Otto Sverdrup sailed there and claimed discovery.[4]

Jealousy of Sverdrup cost Peary eight toes. In 1898 Sverdrup captained the *Fram* on what he promised would be a purely scientific expedition to the west coast of Greenland and not to the North Pole.[5] This would place Sverdrup in Peary's territory, among the Inuit villages with their skilled mushers and sled dogs that Peary had claimed for his exclusive use. He found it inconceivable that the Norwegians did not share his polar ambition, and he and his allies blasted Sverdrup in the American press, accusing him of stealing Peary's methods and polar route.[6] And when by chance he met Sverdrup on Ellesmere Island in January 1899, Peary felt that all his fears were confirmed. He was sure that the Norwegians were secretly heading north toward Adolphus Greely's old camp at Fort Conger, a site that Peary wanted for himself as a northern base. Determined to claim it first, he set out immediately in −50°F weather, stumbling to his destination on frost-numbed feet. His frozen toes soon began snapping off, but he had won possession of the dilapidated "fort" made of wood and tar paper. Sverdrup was nowhere nearby, for his rivalry with Peary existed only in the latter's imagination.[7]

Peary's frostbite, which impaired his ability to wear snowshoes or even walk normally, should have ended his exploring career, but it did not. He stayed in the Arctic, making little progress in his polar attempts of 1900 and 1901.

"Soon they will call me a fake, say I am just hoarding what I can mint from the public's credulity," he wrote privately in early 1902. "Yet, would it profit me to confess that all my savings, all my wife's savings, all that I can beg, borrow or steal, have gone into the quite inadequate equipment I have gathered for the next attempt?"[8]

The 1902 dash ended fifteen days after it began, with Peary looking out from a pinnacle of ice at the tortured frozen sea ahead. "My dream of sixteen years is ended," he wrote. "I cannot accomplish the impossible."[9]

Both Wellman and Peary were out of the North Pole game by the early twentieth century. Both had multiple failures to their credit. Both were in their mid-forties and, even aside from their crippling injuries, were past their physical prime in a highly athletic profession. But within a few years, both were suddenly back in the headlines, buoyed by technology. For Wellman it was the airship *America*; for Peary it was his new $100,000 steamship, the *Roosevelt*. Paid for by the wealthy members of the Peary Arctic Club and named for the president, the new ship was designed to plow its way through the ice (though it was a wooden ship and not a modern icebreaker) and take Peary farther north than his previous starting points.[10]

Peary departed on what he said would be his last polar expedition in the summer of 1905. By early July 1906—while Wellman was racing north with his airship—newspapers began expressing fears for Peary's safety, suggesting that during an unusually severe spring in Greenland, Peary's new ship "may have been ground to pieces by the drifting ice."[11] Some papers went so far as to proclaim, PEARY IS LOST.[12]

When Peary and his battered ship finally returned in November, he again had not reached the North Pole, but this time he claimed to have beaten the world's farthest north record by reaching 87°6' north latitude, or about 200 miles from the pole. While his return was not quite that of a conquering hero—by now the public was becoming jaded with "farthest north" records—Peary won a sustaining dose of praise and respect. While not enough to satisfy his thirsty ego, it still enabled his fund-raising for yet another expedition.[13]

Like a funhouse mirror, polar fame was usually a distorted reflection of achievement. Elisha Kane, the ineffective leader of a failed expedition, became an American hero by writing a best-selling book. Otto Sverdrup, during the same 1898–1902 period when Peary was floundering in northern Greenland, led a brilliant expedition that charted 1,750 miles of new coastline and produced nearly three dozen scientific papers, but he remained little known to the public outside Norway.[14]

If polar fame had been strictly about achievement, even in 1906 Peary would have been overshadowed by the Norwegian Roald Amundsen, who had just fulfilled the dream of three centuries by navigating the Northwest Passage along with discovering the exact location of the North Magnetic Pole. Amundsen was on his way to becoming the most accomplished of the big-prize polar explorers, but he lacked the media savvy of Wellman or Peary. Not wanting to brag about deeds before he accomplished them, Amundsen did little to cultivate press interest before setting out in 1903 with a six-man crew in the seventy-foot sloop *Gjøa*. Two years later he wintered on the Yukon coast with the most difficult part of the east–west journey behind him. Now he told the world.[15]

Amundsen skied 500 miles south to an Alaskan telegraph station and wired an exclusive press release to a national syndicate. However, a Seattle newspaper leaked the news, which spread like gossip from paper to paper instead of reaching the public all at once as a major media event. Worse, even though the journey's final stage through the Bering Strait would be easy once the ice broke in the spring, the press failed to understand the significance of Amundsen's location. Concluding that he still had many miles to go, the papers instead focused on the North Magnetic Pole, which was of relatively minor public interest. By the time Amundsen reached San Francisco in October 1906, his story was considered old news. Six men in a fishing boat had just accomplished what the Royal Navy and a generation of its best warships and sailors had not, but outside Norway, public reaction was respectful but restrained. Amundsen's own matter-of-fact speeches and writing did little to excite the public. Thus, he failed the modern explorer's first duty—to give the people an epic story. Amundsen had mistakenly assumed that the deed itself would be enough.[16]

Wellman, meanwhile, faced growing criticism and a false but widely repeated accusation that his polar plan was a hoax "filched bodily from one of Jules Verne's most weird tales; and the details of Verne's plan were copied with almost painful exactness."[17] Arriving back in the United States on November 17, Wellman had promised to continue his airship work. "Peary's experience demonstrates the impossibility of a voyage to the pole by either land or sea," he said. "The only way in which it can ever be reached is with a balloon."[18] When asked about Wellman, Peary told reporters that present-day airships were still too fragile for Arctic exploration.[19]

By coincidence both Wellman and Peary called at the White House on December 1. Newspapers differed as to which man was with the president when the other arrived.[20] The *National Tribune* noted the two men's physical similarities, being of nearly the same age, height, and build. Wellman's mustache was gray; Peary's was red. Wellman wore his usual tall silk hat; Peary, a Southern-style slouch. They shook hands cordially and parted ways, Wellman with a limp and the nearly toeless Peary walking "as firmly as a giant."[21]

They began sniping at each other in the press within a week. Responding to Peary's comment that he had no faith in airships for Arctic exploration, Wellman again predicted failure for Peary and told the *New York Times*, "All the things that Peary may say will make no difference to me. I believe that the airship is the only solution of the problem."[22] The following April, when Peary remarked that the needle-like Arctic snow would surely destroy a balloon, Wellman replied, "I want to say Peary has no idea at all about ballooning." He explained that his airship had a "tensile strength of 500 pounds to the square foot. I would like to see the snow which could harm that."[23]

Thanks to Roosevelt, Peary secured yet another three-year leave of absence from his naval duties and set about raising money to repair his ship and head north. With both Wellman and Peary promising a 1907 departure, the public could now enjoy an increasingly bitter rivalry for the North Pole.[24]

"Commander Peary regards Wellman as a mere interloper in the 'science' of Arctic exploration," wrote Ira E. Bennett of the *Washington Post* on May 4, 1907. He continued:

GO IT, PEARY! GO IT, WELLMAN!

Fig. 10. In 1907 America's big polar rivalry was not Peary vs. Cook but Peary vs. Wellman. *Des Moines Register*, April 16, 1907.

He talked a little along that line in his club while here a few weeks ago. Wellman belongs to the same club and mutual friends lost no time in fanning the flames of rivalry and jealousy. When Wellman heard that Peary regarded him as a "charlatan" and a "hot air voyager" he indicated that his faith in dog teams on floating ice was mighty little and that the man who'd keep hammering away with dogs was little more intelligent than an Eskimo.[25]

The race was set. Both men planned to head north as soon as the ice cleared. Wellman would try for the pole that summer; Peary was determined to get as far north as he could before winter and prepare for a dash over the ice pack in early 1908. In this polar duel, Wellman would have the first shot.

16

Balloons, Aeroplanes, and the
Acrobatic Photographer

Hawaii, New Zealand, Australia, and France, 1901–1907

Melvin Vaniman climbed slowly up the rigging of the tallest mast aboard the bark *Gerard C. Tobey*, which sat at anchor at Honolulu, Hawaii, on February 25, 1901. It was slow work for a landlubber and slower still because under one arm he carried an enormous camera nearly three feet long and more than a foot thick. The camera was his own design, built to capture a panoramic view with as much detail as possible. The ship rocked in winds gusting to thirty-five miles per hour, and the crew had a non-negligible chance of witnessing a poetic tragedy in which a man would get himself killed for the sake of his art.[1]

The captain had tried unsuccessfully to talk him out of it, but now, having granted Vaniman permission, he felt some responsibility for the outcome. Scrambling up into the rigging, the captain took the bulky camera and climbed up to the royal yard. When Vaniman arrived, the two men sat together on this highest spar while the sailors hoisted it as far as it would go. Then the captain climbed down. Vaniman was on his own.[2]

Standing at last above the rigging with an unobstructed bird's-eye view of Honolulu Harbor, Vaniman lashed himself and his camera to the mast just as the sky clouded over. Dull lighting would not do. For two and a half hours he stood swaying on that wobbly spar ninety feet above deck, listening to the flapping of loose ropes and the whistling of taut ones. His hat was gone and lens cap too. He improvised by covering the lens with a piece of paper from his pocket. He was about to give up when the sun came out at last.[3]

Now it was a matter of timing. As the mast swayed, Vaniman tried to release the shutter at the moment when the camera was level. He took three shots to be certain. Thus, twice he had to replace the glass plate negative;

while one arm hugged the mast and secured the camera, the other hand was free to handle the plates. Then he allowed himself to climb down, arriving on deck "in a half-fainting condition."[4]

The first two photos were crooked, but the third was perfect and well composed. With rich tonal range and striking detail, it was "undoubtedly the best ever secured of a harbour-city view," according to the *Pacific Commercial Advertiser*, but "he will climb no more masts for all the pictures in Christendom."[5]

It was a long way to the top of that ship's mast from the Illinois farm where Vaniman had been born thirty-four years earlier. The oldest of four boys, he came from a family of German Baptist Brethren (Dunkards) in the Virden district near Springfield. The brethren emphasized simplicity in living and opposed modernization, but young Melvin was a born tinkerer who found work in engine shops and studied electrical engineering, in addition to earning a reputation as an agricultural expert.

It was music, however, that made a traveler of him. He studied and taught music at Valparaiso University, then taught music at a normal school in Iowa before joining an opera company in 1887, when he was still only twenty years old. For the next eleven years he toured the country as an opera singer until a plague scare in Hawaii closed the theaters and bankrupted the touring company.[6]

There are worse places in the world to be stranded. Vaniman found work as an electrician before making a career of photography, a hobby he had picked up during his opera travels. His panoramic bird's-eye views drew the attention of a steamship company, which hired him to take promotional photos of its port cities. With his new bride, Ida Loud of Virden, Illinois, Vaniman spent the next few years in New Zealand and Australia as the "acrobatic photographer" who ascended tall buildings, ships' masts, scaffolding, or a special ninety-foot pole to take his stunning panoramic views. In time he purchased a gas balloon and, in May 1904, after months of experimentation and camera design, captured a now-famous aerial photo of Sydney, Australia. Large-scale artistic panoramas already had a long history by the early twentieth century, but Vaniman's platinum prints—up to fifteen feet long—brought an astonishing degree of sharpness and detail to their subjects.[7]

Perhaps it was circumstance or perhaps it wasn't in Vaniman's nature to stick to one thing beyond a few years of intense focus. In 1904 he traveled to Europe to work as a photographer but found less success than in the clear skies of Australia and New Zealand. Tired of shooting from the unstable platform of a tethered balloon (which bobbed and rotated in the wind), Vaniman began designing a dirigible airship while he and Ida lived outside Paris in a little shed that doubled as a home and a workshop.[8] He soon had the good fortune to meet another American expatriate and aeronautics enthusiast named Frank S. Lahm.[9]

Son of an Ohio congressman, Lahm was thought to be a living testimony to the benefits of travel and outdoor activity. Declining health had forced him to give up business soon after he married at age twenty-nine. Five years later, when his wife died after giving birth to their third child, Lahm was too ill even to attend her funeral. In the spirit of the times, his doctor recommended travel for health, but Lahm was in such bad shape when he departed for Europe that his friends thought they had seen the last of him.[10]

Once overseas, however, Lahm made an astonishing recovery, took up mountain climbing, and scaled the Matterhorn merely ten months after missing his wife's funeral. No one seems to have thought this at all suspicious. A friend of the family's described Mrs. Lahm as a "ray of sunshine," and perhaps the timing of her demise and Lahm's recovery were coincidental. He thrived in France while his children grew up with relatives in the United States and knew their father through visits and correspondence.[11]

Lahm took up ballooning in the early 1900s and became a fixture in Parisian aeronautical circles.[12] It was inevitable that Vaniman would make his acquaintance once in France. The two of them collaborated on an unsuccessful aeroplane, and Vaniman soon built a triplane of his own design that was also unsuccessful. In early 1906 Walter Wellman took ballooning lessons from Lahm while his airship was being built, and later that year when Wellman was looking for a new engineer to rebuild the *America*, Lahm referred his friend Vaniman. Thus began the most consequential partnership in either Wellman's or Vaniman's career.[13]

The year 1906 was an exciting time for aeronautics. The *Lebaudy*'s flights had already put the world on notice that the future of warfare would

involve airpower, and in December the French government received its first official military airship, the Lebaudy *Patrie* (Fatherland). This potentially destabilizing technology was of growing concern in Germany. While the German military was watching Wellman, in April Kaiser Wilhelm, who was unable to get more money from the Reichstag, reportedly "appealed to the patriotism" of four Jewish millionaires in Berlin and raised $200,000 for *luftschiff* (airship) experiments.[14] At Lake Constance near Switzerland, meanwhile, Count Zeppelin went from failure in January—when his airship *LZ2* was damaged beyond repair after its only flight—to success in October with a two-hour flight of the *LZ3*. The count's mighty new luftschiff was twice as long and had more than double the horsepower of the *America*. All year Wellman had been boasting that his was "the world's largest practical airship" (the word "practical" disqualifying Zeppelin's first two efforts), but now the *LZ3* had flown whereas the *America* had not.[15]

Frank Lahm was involved at the periphery of an even more exciting development, if rumors were true. French aeronauts were experimenting with gliders and even with powered aeroplanes, though none of the latter had been successful. In 1905 word reached Lahm in Paris that two brothers from Ohio not only had made brief powered flights as early as 1903 but also now were quietly making prolonged flights outside of Dayton. That December Lahm asked a relative to visit Dayton and investigate. The man met the Wrights and interviewed eyewitnesses, and though the secretive brothers declined to fly for him, he was convinced—and soon Lahm was too—that the former bicycle mechanics had solved the problem of powered heavier-than-air flight. Lahm explained all this in a letter published in the Paris edition of the *New York Herald* in February 1906. The paper's editors, reflecting the skepticism of the French aeronautical community, responded with an editorial titled "Fliers or Liars?"[16]

Back in Ohio, the Wrights ignored the press. Unlike Wellman they cared little for public opinion, wanting only to perfect their invention and to secure both a patent and a military contract. The American press gradually embraced the Wright brothers in 1905–6, but even then the public knew more about Wellman's airship, which had not yet flown, than it did about the Wright flyer, which had. On July 1, 1906, the *Washington Times* ran a full-page story titled "Balloon or Aeroplane: In Which Will Man Navigate the Air?" The article, despite leaning toward aeroplanes as the

most likely "final solution of aerial navigation, if the problem is ever to be solved," did not mention the Wrights and claimed that "no man has yet managed to sustain himself in the air with the aeroplane." Though not typical, it was still possible in the summer of 1906 for such an omission to get past the editors of a newspaper in the nation's capital.[17]

Public perception of heavier-than-air flight changed dramatically that fall when Alberto Santos-Dumont astonished Parisians with Europe's first powered flights in his aeroplane *14-bis*.[18] With a boxy canard in front and equally boxy wings in back, the ungainly craft looks to a modern eye as though it was flying backward. Although Santos-Dumont soon added ailerons, the *Bird of Prey* lacked full three-axis control (pitch, yaw, and roll). The Wrights had long ago realized that this—and not just getting airborne—was the real problem of powered flight, and they alone had solved it.[19]

Nevertheless, the dapper Brazilian now had something the Wrights lacked—visibility. Large crowds of people had seen him fly. He made powered aviation real for the European public. As far as they were concerned, he was the aeroplane's true inventor.

Such was the new world of aeronautics in which Wellman and Vaniman found themselves in early 1907, a world of expanded possibilities and, consequently, heightened expectations. Like his new boss, Vaniman was not lacking in self-confidence. Wellman often referred to him as his chief mechanic, but it soon became clear that the former opera singer was much more than that.[20]

This year's effort would be more focused, without motor sledges or wireless telegraphy this time. All energy would go into the airship itself. Vaniman suggested replacing Godard's flat-bottomed car with a much stronger V-shaped car made of steel tubing and wire stays. Enclosed in oiled silk and 115 feet long, it would be wider at the top and narrow to a walkway of 1½ feet wide at the bottom. Wellman added the idea of "making the backbone" of the ship a long steel cylinder underneath the walkway. This cylinder would serve as the ship's fuel tank, which would be subdivided into sections so that the crew could draw fuel from different sections as needed to adjust the balance of weight. To trim the ship in a hurry, Vaniman also designed a sliding platform to ride atop the car,

Fig. 11. The 1907 crew of the airship *America*. *Front, left to right:* Melvin Vaniman, Felix Riesenberg, and Henry Hersey. *Back:* Walter Wellman. Hersey was ill at the time of launch and did not make the flight. Anders Beer Wilse/Norsk Folkemuseum, Olso, Norway.

so the crew could slide it forward or aft as needed. The sliding platform would carry 600 pounds of food—for as much as possible all weight was to be useful weight. Though the *America* still had few control surfaces compared with later airships, Vaniman enlarged the rudder and added new movable planes for vertical control.[21]

All this was done under the direction of Wellman, who was obviously pleased with his new mechanic's clever innovations. Vaniman added protective metal scales to the exterior of the provision-stuffed leather tube that served as the ship's altitude-regulating "Sausage Guide-Rope."[22] He also apparently devised the ship's low-altitude warning device, which was a steel bottle hanging on a hundred-foot cord. If it dragged on the ice, the bottle would tilt, and the mercury at the bottom would make contact with wires, closing an electrical circuit and ringing an alarm bell in the car.[23] To prevent the accumulation of snow and ice on the airship, Vaniman also invented a system to use the engine's exhaust to warm the hydrogen-filled gasbag. Inside the gasbag were air-filled ballonets that the crew would pump up as needed to maintain the airship's shape despite fluctuations in atmospheric pressure. Vaniman's new device heated air in a chamber surrounding the exhaust pipe, then pumped the warm air into the ballonets. Radiating through the entire ship, the heat would raise its temperature by a few degrees, which would be enough, he believed, to make a difference in the Arctic summer.[24]

The 1907 ship would rely on a single motor, a 750-pounder that Wellman described as heavy but fuel efficient. It would produce 70 to 80 horsepower and turn two 11½-foot steel propellers on either side of the car. The motor sledges were absent this year; instead, the ship would carry traditional sledges, a dozen dogs, and enough provisions to last the winter if need be. To carry the extra weight, Wellman had the gasbag cut in two and added a 20-foot section, increasing *America*'s lift by nearly a ton.[25]

Thanks to Vaniman and to the lessons of the previous year, by the summer of 1907 Wellman felt he at last had an airship worthy of the North Pole. Only one Vaniman innovation gave him pause, but he would sort that out—along with everything else—on Danes Island. Once again Wellman did not have time for a test flight in France. Once again he was in a race against the season.

17

Go? Of Course. What Else Are We Here For?

Danes Island, Spitsbergen, July–September 1907

Melvin Vaniman liked to sing while he worked. His trained voice carried from the airship hangar out over the rocky shore of Danes Island while he tinkered with the motor that was to propel the *America* to the North Pole. The motor was bolted onto the metal tube car Vaniman had designed, and its twin propellers jutted out on booms from either side. The car itself sat on blocks, for the giant gasbag was not yet inflated.[1]

One morning Wellman entered and noticed a fifty-foot piece of yellow silk tube lying on the floor. About a foot in diameter, the tube was part of the feeder line that would connect the hydrogen-generating apparatus to the gasbag. Since the gasbag wasn't even unpacked yet, it struck Wellman as odd to see this silk tube obviously bloated with hydrogen and weighed down to keep it from rising.

"What's this?" he said.

"Trying out my hydrogen carburettor!" Vaniman replied. Felix Riesenberg stood ready beside the motor and started it when Vaniman gave the signal. It roared to life with an unmuffled clatter.

The hydrogen carburetor (often spelled with two Ts in those days) was another of Vaniman's inventions that Wellman had already described enthusiastically in print. The idea was that the airship would grow lighter as it burned gasoline, requiring the crew to valve hydrogen to maintain a steady altitude. That seemed like a waste. Why not extend the ship's range by piping excess hydrogen into the engine to be burned as a secondary fuel? Vaniman's special carburetor would allow him to alternate the fuel intake from gasoline to hydrogen with the flip of a switch. But like most things on the *America*, it had not yet been tested.

Vaniman pointed to the hydrogen tube to show he was ready to turn on the gas. Wellman waved the other workmen back. Vaniman turned

a lever, and flames flashed from the carburetor along the intake pipe to the bloated yellow silk tube.

"Both of us were knocked flat by the resulting explosion," Riesenberg recalled, "clinging to the narrow deck of the nacelle, our ears humming, our heads splitting."

Vaniman thought it over for the rest of the morning.

"I know what was the matter," he said at last.

"Then forget it," Wellman snapped. "We can take off that extra mileage. No more hydrogen for me!"[2]

Vaniman tried to explain, but this was one technological innovation that Wellman could do without. They soon had other worries. On July 4 the airship hangar was partly wrecked by a gale; Wellman's time-saving decision to reduce the number of arches from nine to five had come back to haunt him. They spent four precious weeks repairing the damage. The weather remained unusually stormy during this time, and the hangar was in constant danger. Wellman slept poorly. Beside his bed he kept an electrical device connected to the anemometer outside; the speed of its ticking indicated the wind speed. When the ticks came too fast, he wrote, "out of bed I jumped, and ran to see if the precious balloon house was still standing, often finding it necessary to summon the entire force to renew the fight."[3]

At last the hangar was rebuilt (with nine arches this time) and the airship inflated. Though mostly protected from the wind, the interior was drafty enough that the *America* bobbed and swayed in the swirling air, straining at the cables that held the ship down. Like the men's nerves, at times the cables seemed to be strained nearly to the snapping point. Working as many as eighteen hours a day, the men had the ship ready by mid-August. As soon as the weather cleared, they could take the *America* out for a test flight.[4]

Vaniman and Riesenberg were working on the engine one morning when Wellman entered the hangar, stood on a box, and peered into the now closed-in car. He noticed a telltale yellow silk tube running down from the gasbag to the motor.[5]

"What's that?" he demanded.

Vaniman was nonchalant. "That? That's my hydrogen supply pipe. Got it hooked up again."

The airship hadn't exploded yet, but Wellman did. "Dammit, Van! I told you to forget it. God! We can't take any chances—*now*!"

Fig. 12. The uncovered airship hangar at Camp Wellman, Virgo Bay, Danes Island, Spitsbergen (Svalbard), 1907 or 1909. One of the challenges of navigating out of the oftenwindy islands was that the airship's heavy equilibrator held it to within a few hundred feet of the water, too low to fly over the mountains. From Wellman, *Aerial Age*, 184.

"It's okay, Walter. Absolutely right—*now*," Vaniman said. "I knew what was wrong before." And he told Riesenberg to start the motor.

As Riesenberg remembered it, he hadn't known that Van had hooked up the hydrogen tube until Wellman pointed it out, and then he was terrified. He remembered what had happened when the motor was hooked up to fifty cubic feet of "gaseous dynamite." Now it was connected to a quarter of a million.

Vaniman was about to turn the lever. Over the roar of the motor, "Wellman shook his fists, stamped on the box, shouted in pantomime," and then turned and waved the other men out of the hangar. As soon as they understood what was about to happen, they ran. Vaniman grinned.

But Wellman came back. Riesenberg, who by now was "on the point of mutiny" himself, wondered if the expedition commander would try to stop his reckless engineer by force. Riesenberg held a wrench and stood ready to "crack the bald dome of the chief" if Wellman told him to do it.

Wellman, calmer now, came close enough to be heard and nodded at Vaniman. "Go ahead," he said.

Van threw the switch . . . and the engine purred, running smoother than ever on its gaseous fuel.

Later that day Wellman got out a bottle of fifty-year-old rye for a toast. As the men raised their glasses, he said, "To Melvin Vaniman—he may shiver up here in the North, but he's not got cold feet!"[6]

Back in the United States, Robert Peary struggled to get his own expedition under way and was infuriated, no doubt, that Wellman had secured funding while he was still begging for money.[7] It wasn't a matter of public opinion. While both men generally had the good wishes of the American people, Peary's many unverified claims were still taken on faith, but Wellman's airship had yet to fly. Not surprising, the public felt Peary was more likely to succeed and Wellman was more likely to go the way of Andrée.[8]

The public, however, didn't determine who was able to go north. Wealthy donors did, and by the end of April 1907, Peary was still $60,000 short.

"The money will come; somehow I feel certain of that," Peary said, but he was nearly bankrupt, with his home heavily mortgaged and his latest book, *Nearest the Pole*, selling poorly.[9] By late June, when Wellman was already in Spitsbergen, Peary was spotted in the fashionable summer resort of Lenox, Massachusetts, courting Morris K. Jesup, a wealthy banker who was one of Peary's most generous patrons.[10]

By July Peary was saying he was almost ready to begin what he promised would be his final polar attempt, win or lose.[11] But on August 11 he announced that he would have to wait until the next year. In a press release that Wellman surely could have empathized with, Peary blamed the delay on the failure of contractors to complete repairs on the *Roosevelt*'s boilers. The "question of funds," he insisted, "does not and has not entered into this unfortunate situation."[12]

Peary's announcement came right around the time when Wellman's airship was ready for its first test flight—if only the wind would drop. Day after day the north wind blew too strongly for the *America* to even safely exit the hangar. Wellman thought he knew what to expect from other explorers' weather data; variable winds during the summer had blown in any one direction no more than a week to ten days at a stretch.[13] But data from a few expeditions didn't convey to this optimist that in the Arctic one should plan for any experience, including an abnormal season or year.

Wellman knew he would be savaged in the press if he failed to start for the pole, but summer was slipping away. The sun set briefly on August 31 for the first time since April 15; from now on the days would grow rapidly shorter until the four-month-long polar night began on Danes Island on October 23.[14] At the pole, the sun would set on the autumnal equinox and not rise until spring. Even now it was spiraling lower and lower in its long polar evening. This was important not only because the men needed to see where they were going but also because they could only know their latitude by measuring the angle of the noontime sun above the horizon. In late August Wellman asked Riesenberg to calculate the latest date on which he could make reasonably accurate observations of the sun at the North Pole. September 5 was the date; a polar attempt would be pointless after that.[15]

Everyone was on edge as the deadline approached. The men fueled the ship, loaded dogs into their kennels, and topped up the gasbag with hydrogen. For reasons that are now unclear, rumors of sabotage spread through the camp. Wellman set a twenty-four-hour guard in the hangar and began carrying a loaded pistol.

"Let anyone try anything, and I'll kill him," he told Riesenberg.[16]

They set a lookout on the mountain overlooking the bay. From here one could see northeast beyond Amsterdam Island to where the *Frithjof* steamed back and forth in the northernmost open water of the Arctic Ocean. Its crew was looking for the first sign of a change of wind. Back in Camp Wellman, men used kites for weather observations; on the evening of September 1 they thought a change of wind was coming.[17] At 2:00 a.m., around sunrise, the *Frithjof* cockbilled its yards to signal the mountaintop lookout that the wind was calming to the north. The signal was relayed to the men below, setting the camp in motion.[18]

Officially, they were still conducting only a test flight. September "was too late in the season to start for the Pole, as winter was approaching," Wellman acknowledged later, "and yet we were determined to start."[19] If anything went wrong, the coming darkness would force them to winter on the ice until the sun returned.

With Major Hersey ill, the planned four-man polar team was reduced to three: Wellman in command, Vaniman as engineer, and Riesenberg as navigator.[20] They ate a quick breakfast in silence, and then Wellman called

them outside where they could speak privately. Near this spot ten years earlier, Andrée had had a similar conversation with his two companions, asking them, "Shall we try it or not?" But Wellman, at least in Riesenberg's memory, chose stronger wording—perhaps a conscious choice. After they stood quietly for a few minutes he said, "I am determined to go. How about you, Melvin?"

"Go? Of course. What else are we here for?"

"And you, Felix?"

Riesenberg was scared. At breakfast he had sensed that the rest of the staff were "thankful not to be among the heroes." But there was only one way the sailor was going to answer such a question: "It's what I've been waiting for. I'm ready, sir."[21]

In the semidarkness of the hangar, Van tested the motor one final time, and the men drew apart the enormous canvas doors. Riesenberg jumped up into the car, but Wellman, with his bad leg, had to be helped aboard. He went forward while Riesenberg took his place at the wheel and compass, and Vaniman stayed amidships in the engine room. Wellman asked if they were ready and gave the order: "Walk her out!"[22]

Forty men held the ropes—an inadequate and untrained ground crew for such a large airship, Riesenberg believed—but by now the air was so calm that it didn't matter. Perfectly balanced, the ship hovered over the rocky beach. It was time to swing the compass, just as they would do for a nautical vessel. A ship's metal parts and electrical fields could distort the compass readings, so a new ship was swung through all points of the compass to check the readings against known directions. Then the navigator could compensate for any anomalies.

Navigation, Wellman had already told *McClure's* readers, "is not going to be a simple thing." If the skies were relatively clear, they could steer roughly by the sun, but mostly they would rely on the compass. In these latitudes that was a complicated matter. A compass doesn't point north; it points toward the North Magnetic Pole. The magnetic pole's location drifts over time, but in 1907 it was in the Boothia Peninsula of northern Canada. This meant that the correct compass heading would change during the journey. At Danes Island, true north was between fourteen and fifteen degrees west of magnetic north. The compass needle would swing around farther as they proceeded, pointing south by the time they reached the pole.[23]

Fig. 13. Launch of the *America* from Danes Island, September 2, 1907. Although the three-man crew had ballooning experience, no one had flown a powered airship before, nor had the *America* been given a test flight before its first North Pole attempt. Library of Congress Prints and Photographs Division, George Grantham Bain Collection, LC-DIG-ggbain-03344.

It was even more complicated than that. The compass doesn't always point directly at the magnetic pole but instead follows local magnetic fields. Today charts have lines of magnetic declination for the entire globe. In 1907 charts for the north polar region showed only theoretical lines; after all, Wellman was going where no one had ever been.

Assuming the theoretical lines were more or less correct, Riesenberg would still need to know the ship's current location to find the correct compass heading. For this he would mostly rely on dead reckoning, calculating his position based on his speed and the direction from his last known point. From ancient times sailors had estimated a ship's speed by throwing a board called a chip log off the stern. The log, which was attached to the ship by a rope that was knotted at regular intervals, would remain more or less stationary in the water while the ship moved away from it. The sailor then would count how many knots passed through his hands in a given amount of time. Likewise, the *America* had a "log" that

every few minutes would be lowered by cable to the surface of the ice; once down, the log would stay in place while the navigator measured the rate at which the cable played out.

Once a day, at best—if visibility allowed—Riesenberg would check his dead reckoning against a sextant reading. The angle of the sun above the horizon at its highest point (local noon) would give him their latitude, and by comparing local noon with a chronometer set to Greenwich time, he could calculate their longitude as well, though this would become less important as the meridians converged at the pole.[24]

There would be plenty for all three men to do, perhaps too much. Wellman had planned on four men working eighteen-hour days. Besides the continual tasks of navigation and tending to the motor, they would need to keep an eye on instruments such as the barograph (showing altitude), statoscope (showing whether they were rising or falling), and various manometers (showing gas pressure in the gasbag and ballonets). They must test the valves frequently, because overpressure could burst the airship and send them plummeting to earth. They must pump gasoline from different sections not only to keep the motor running but also to keep the ship in trim. They must raise or lower the retarder and guide rope serpents as needed, feed themselves and the dogs, and rest a little when they could. And they must do it all without having any previous in-flight airship experience.[25]

After the compass checked out, they took the end of a tow rope to the *Express*, a small steamer in the harbor. The *Express* had been chartered by German military officers who had come to observe and then offered to tow the *America* clear of the land. For the next hour the *America* floated five hundred feet above the water at the end of its leash.

They rounded the headland into Smeerenburg Sound (Smeerenburg-fjorden). From here, mountainous islands lay in all directions but one—due north, where nothing but a deep-blue lane of water was between the airship and the hazy white edge of the ice pack. Wellman gave the order to start the motor for the first time in the air.

Vaniman recalled with pride how the *America* "forged ahead, passing the *Express* as though the latter were standing still," and how it "became apparent that instead of the *Express* towing us we were towing the steamer."

The airship shuddered with a series of jerks, straining at the leash like an eager dog.

"Let go!" Wellman said.

Riesenberg cast off the line and watched it snake down to the water below. They felt the airship rise with the loss of weight, but the heavy guide serpent trailing in the water kept them from rising too high. At last the *America* was flying on its own, with the Stars and Stripes waving proudly from the stern.

18

Lost in a Snowstorm above the Polar Sea

Spitsbergen, September 2, 1907

The *America* had hardly begun moving ahead at half throttle when suddenly "a frightful racking jarred us," Riesenberg wrote. Vaniman shut off the motor.[1]

"What's up?" Wellman cried from his place in the forward cockpit. One of the handling lines had gotten tangled in the port propeller.

"I'll clear it!" Vaniman yelled from the engine room. It was a good thing the former "acrobatic photographer" wasn't afraid of heights. Exiting through a side door and out onto the propeller strut, he calmly untangled the rope and climbed back inside.

Wellman ordered full speed ahead. Even over the roar of the motor, they heard faint cheering from the *Express* as it fell away astern. Riesenberg reckoned they were making upward of fifteen miles per hour, about what Wellman had predicted. Snow began falling, and banks of heavy fog lay to the west. The sky grew dim, and as the sea faded below them, the *Express* vanished into the murk. The *America* was truly on its own.

Riesenberg could see below barely well enough to make out ripple marks on the water's surface. They told him the wind was out of the northwest and growing stronger. "To have attempted the bucking of polar winds with anything as puny as this would seem madness," he wrote. "It was madness then; it would be considered certain suicide now."

Smeerenburg Sound is only about two miles wide for most of its length and lined with mountains on both sides. Its east side is especially rugged, with a wall of glaciers and jagged peaks rising from sea level to more than two thousand feet in places. It was toward this wall that the wind now drove the *America*. In the engine room, Vaniman had his first inkling of trouble when through the starboard window he saw rocks and ice where

Fig. 14. Approximate route of Wellman's 1907 polar flight. Map by author.

sky should have been. Having slowed the motor down, he opened the throttle, and, in Wellman's words, "there ensued a hard fight between the storm and the motor."

Everything now depended on Vaniman. With the serpent holding them at about five hundred feet, they couldn't rise to clear the mountains. If the engine balked or gave anything less than full power, they'd be swept against a steep mountainside that would destroy the airship and send them tumbling to their deaths.

Here was the first hole in Wellman's plan. He had expected strong headwinds now and then; that was the point of the ice anchor, or retardateur. What he hadn't expected was getting hit by a change of weather before

reaching the ice pack. Of the many tables of figures he had prepared before the journey, none addressed the dangers of flying an underpowered motor balloon at low altitude through a fjord on a windy day.

"Inch by inch we fought our way past the mountains, one after another, clearing the last by only a few rods," Wellman wrote. And here, in his telling, ended the test flight: the airship having proved itself, he now gave the order to start for the North Pole. Such an order is absent from the narratives of Vaniman and Riesenberg, either never having been given or not worth remembering. As far as they were concerned, the *America* was on its way to the pole from the moment it left the hangar. But wherever the trip began officially, this was the most audacious aerial voyage yet attempted—even aside from the fact that it was being done by a green-horn crew on their ship's maiden flight.

As the headland receded and vanished behind them, Vaniman again slowed the motor. Apparently the wind had slackened, for he said they now had easy flying "under perfect conditions." It wasn't long before the wind picked up again and the snow thickened, reducing visibility to less than a quarter of a mile. Riesenberg remembered "Wellman, his face tense, peering ahead" through the storm.

Riesenberg was steering north, but the wind grew so strong that the ship began moving backward, drifting south–southeast. Through the blowing snow, they suddenly saw rising before them the distinctive gray bulk of a small island called Cloven Cliff (Klovningen), so named because a cleft through the center looked as if it had been made by a giant's ax. Like everything else, it was too tall for the *America* to miss, and this time, apparently, Vaniman's motor had no more to give. They would smash tail-first into the rocks unless Riesenberg could turn the airship away.

"I tried to throw the ship's head to port; it answered slowly," he wrote. "The compass, affected by some strange magnetic disturbance, began to spin; the *America* turned, missed Cloven Cliff by a scant cable's length and, caught in a swift current of air amid squalls of snow, raced backward."

Riesenberg struggled to point the ship north again, with no guidance from the erratic compass needle. At some point Vaniman came forward to ask what was the matter. Later he wrote: "They informed me that the compass was not working properly, and they had not the remotest idea

of their bearings. The only course was to again get into communication with the *Express*, but where was she?"

Wellman still believed that if they could only find the ship, they could somehow "rectify our compass and start again." The problem, as he described it later, was that they "were completely lost in a snowstorm above the Polar Sea and threatened with destruction." He wasn't exaggerating the danger of their position. They had drifted into the midst of several small mountainous islands off the main island's northwest coast. Rocky obstacles lay in almost every direction, but they could see nothing until they were almost upon them.

The gusting wind made it impossible to keep in one direction for long. As Riesenberg tried to hold the ship, with its small rudder and low-powered engines, into the wind, they made three complete turns. According to Wellman, "Three times we came up so near the mountains, looming suddenly ahead out of the thick air, that we thought all was over, but each time the motor and propeller brought us round to temporary safety, with the helm thrown hard over."

Unable to see the *Express*, they knew they must attempt a landing. Wellman said they decided to land on a glacier; his companions remembered having no choice. Riesenberg reported wind gusts of up to forty-five miles an hour; if true they would have blown the *America* backward at thirty miles per hour even at full throttle. The sky cleared just enough to see that they were closing rapidly with a wide amphitheater of ice at the end of a fjord between mist-covered, barely visible mountains. Even Vaniman, who tended to downplay risks, felt they were "in imminent danger."

"Stop the motor!" Wellman ordered. Vaniman did so and joined his companions at the wheel. After more than two hours of engine noise, the car was eerily quiet. As Wellman had often said of Andrée's balloon, the *America* was now "a mere toy of the winds," and as such they heard no breeze or even the slightest rustle of fabric.

Balloonists had learned long ago that among their profession's greatest dangers was the prospect of landing in a strong wind with no ground crew to catch the rope. Unlucky aeronauts were sometimes dragged hundreds of yards, even miles, bouncing and smashing through tree branches and stone walls while their deflating balloon caught the wind like a sail. As the

America approached the mile-wide, hundred-foot-tall glacier terminus—the jagged blue-white cliff from which icebergs calved into the fjord—Wellman gave the order to valve the gas. The airship floated a hundred feet above the ice, but the heavy serpent hung down to water level. Wellman also released the anchoring drag, which hit the ice cliff with a heavy *whang* and spun the airship sideways.

"The stern drag at one end and the anchor drag at the other held her broadside to the wall of ice," Riesenberg wrote, "but we were going so fast, riding over the white glacier top with such speed, nothing but a fine, white, tablelike spread of snow appeared below us. The two 'snakes' jumped the front, snapping in the air like whipping tails." These two tails dragged along on the ice, falling into and climbing out of the deep crevasses that scored the glacier's surface. The airship was still moving quickly a few feet above the ice and bounced twice off the surface.

By now Vaniman had pulled the wires to raise his razor-sharp "ripping knife" into position alongside the now-sagging gasbag.

"Rip! Rip!" Wellman shouted. Vaniman tugged at the wire to slice the crescent-shaped blade through the rubberized fabric. Nothing happened. With the mountains rushing toward them, Riesenberg ran aft and looked up through an observation window into the gasbag's hazy yellow interior. The blade had penetrated but was stuck on a seam.

"Give her a jerk!" he shouted. Vaniman threw his weight into it. At once the balloon collapsed with a rush of escaping gas. And depending on whose story you believe, the car either settled gently on the ice or struck hard.

Both Wellman and Vaniman told of a gentle landing: the deflated envelope falling clear of the metal-framed car, the car itself coming to a stop with only some bent tubes and broken wires, and the men still standing on deck. Riesenberg said he was thrown as the car struck. Grabbing a rope, he recalled that "[my] arms almost jerked from their sockets. My body turned a complete backward somersault, and I lay face up in the snow." Wellman, he said, landed in a snowbank, and Vaniman was thrown through a silk wall onto the motor but was unhurt.

"I got dropped into the saddle," Vaniman said, laughing, his face blackened with grease.

Wellman wrote that when they stepped out of the car, "we saw that the *America* lay across two crevasses." Riesenberg said that after landing he

discovered that they sat on the edge of a "gigantic crevasse" a hundred feet deep and large enough that it "could have swallowed a dozen *Americas*. No one would have looked for us there."

Recent aerial photos of the glacier reveal anything but a smooth surface.[2] The *America* landed half a mile inland from Fowl Bay in northwestern Albert I Land, or only about eight miles in a straight-line distance from Camp Wellman, though they had flown perhaps thirty-five miles to get here.[3] Approaching its terminus, the glacier's surface becomes increasingly fractured, crisscrossed by intersecting crevasses. Even narrow crevasses can be deep, and they can become bridged and hidden by snow. Crossing a glacier was always dangerous; men and dogs sometimes broke through snow bridges and fell to their deaths, as Wellman himself nearly did in Franz Josef Land in 1898.

It's plausible, then, that Riesenberg could have seen such a car-swallowing crevasse, and it's just possible that in their crowded narratives neither Wellman nor Vaniman thought to mention this unrealized danger, which they only discovered after their safe landing. Either way, by all accounts the world's first polar airship flight had been a wild two or three hours.[4]

Unflappable as always, Vaniman made coffee by putting a kettle on the still-hot exhaust pipe. Wellman, bitter but uncomplaining, checked the flight instruments, and Riesenberg tended to the dogs—apparently the world's first canine airship passengers—who had thrown up their preflight meals.

The weather cleared, and they signaled the *Express* with a smudge fire. For the next three days the airship crew lived on the glacier while parties of men came and went along precarious trails, roped together for safety. They took the *America* apart and hauled everything back down to the ship in the fjord.

"After the successful attempt we are convinced that the America in normal summer weather can make her way to the pole," Wellman wrote, using the word "successful" in the limited sense that the airship flew and proved steerable, and with "normal summer weather" being the crucial qualifier. "We all regard this plan as rational, doable and feasible. The thing can be done, and what can be done shall be done."[5]

It would cost money, of course; that was always the problem. Speaking to the *New York Times*, Frank Noyes of the *Chicago Record-Herald*

refused to say whether his paper would support another expedition.[6] In fact, the paper's owner, Victor Lawson, wanted nothing more to do with polar airships. A presidential campaign would soon be under way, and Lawson wanted Wellman back in Washington to do what he did best.[7]

Few newspapers reported on the flight in much detail. Most readers learned only that Wellman had abandoned his North Pole flight due to high winds; others read truncated reports of the flight that conveyed little sense of the danger.[8] As a result, many Americans saw no reason to credit Wellman even with a courageous failure. Thus, he returned home to face a growing chorus of press criticism in which his aborted polar flight was covered as "a 'joke,' as 'no surprise,' and as 'a justification of his critics.'"[9] *Success* magazine, for which Wellman had written several articles, sarcastically credited him with the invention of the "stationary airship":

> The aeronaut of the future will spend his summer sitting upon the Arctic Circle beside his airship reading the latest novel. Now and then he will have to stand up to be photographed. . . . But our enterprising American journalist has made a still greater discovery—the literary Arctic expedition. From camp Wellman in Spitsbergen he flew upon the wings of fancy straight to the North pole, upon which he posted an advertisement for a Chicago newspaper. . . . No man has ever done so much to popularize Arctic exploration. With writing material so cheap, such expeditions are within the reach of all; a fountain pen and wandering imagination are all the equipment necessary. How proud we should be that the first flight to the pole was made by an American— and in the language we love.[10]

The negative press was bad enough that on August 31, only days before the flight, the *Los Angeles Herald* cited "the interests of fair play" in calling "a halt on the ridicule and abuse heaped on Walter Wellman."[11] A second editorial on September 15 stated, "The Herald is not a champion of polar exploration, and certainly not of the Wellman proposition." Nevertheless, it continued:

> it cannot be denied that Wellman has shown a persistency and determination worthy of his cause. Assailed bitterly from the very sources

to which other men on similar undertakings look for sympathy and support; handicapped with a method wholly untried and prematurely condemned in the public mind; cut off by stinging ridicule from that great stay of other men, the sentiment of national pride in his work; lacking the support of scientific or corporate scholarship in any form, he has stood at his post awaiting the one chance of fair weather to make an attempt, the while fully conscious that failure—either in going or staying—would bring additional ridicule on his name and undertaking, and never answered a word to his detractors; and this means true grit and courage.[12]

Wellman acknowledged later that due to weather at least, they "had no chance at all; and we were pretty lucky to get out of it as well as we did."[13] In October he may have felt luckier still when he learned that the *Frithjof*, which Riesenberg remembered as an "old tub" with rotten sails, had been damaged by ice before sinking in a storm off the coast of Iceland. The dead included its captain and all but one of the sixteen-man crew. The lone survivor made it to shore on a piece of planking.[14]

So great was Riesenberg's disappointment at the expedition's failure that it took him years before he could write about it. "My feeling, deep and determined, had been: 'To the North Pole, or death.'"[15] But after more than a year in the Arctic, he was neither a living hero nor a dead one. He enrolled at Columbia University and got on with his life.

Of *America*'s three-man crew, only one seems to have left the glacier truly happy. Within weeks Vaniman was in London, telling everyone who would listen about his great adventure. At last the jack-of-all-trades had found his true calling. Van was now a veteran airshipman. He couldn't wait to try again.[16]

19

Campaigns and Dollars

Washington DC and Various Locations, 1908–1909

For the first time in three years Wellman did not sail north to the Arctic. He spent 1908 in the United States with little to do except infuriate fellow Republicans with his reporting on the presidential election, raise money for a new expedition, attempt to reform the American banking system, fend off accusations of fraud by a former employee, and file multiple lawsuits against newspapers that reported the accusation.

The accusation of fraud first appeared in the French "sporting" paper *La Vie au Grand Air* (The Outdoor Life) in an interview with Alexander Liwentaal, who in 1906 had designed Wellman's balloon hangar and accompanied Wellman to Danes Island. Liwentaal now denounced the whole affair as a "farce" and an "arctic bluff." He said Wellman had told him that he would not make a real attempt to reach the North Pole. Instead, Wellman had planned to bring the airship down on a nearby glacier and said that "we must have something that can be cinematographed," because he had already arranged for a series of lectures in the United States. The story crossed the Atlantic on May 10, 1908, when the *Washington Post* and *Seattle Times* printed Liwentaal's words in English.[1]

Wellman made no public statement, but over the next several months he filed libel lawsuits against the *Post* (seeking $50,000 in damages), the *Seattle Times* (seeking $50,000), and against *La Vie au Grand Air* (seeking $100,000). Considering that Wellman stood accused of trying to profit from a fake expedition, these large damage claims did little to improve his public image. Unsuccessful in court, they only further spread Liwentaal's story.[2]

More effective than legal action were the words of Wellman's former second-in-command, Maj. Henry Hersey. Liwentaal had called Hersey the "only serious member of the expedition."[3] Thus endorsed by the accuser,

Hersey told the *Milwaukee Sentinel* that Liwentaal had been fired after the 1906 season and had threatened at that time to go to the press. "What he says is the purest nonsense, of course. . . . He is a scientific fellow in an erratic way, and has done some good work, but he is unbalanced and impracticable, a sort of crank who could not be used, and so Wellman got rid of him at the earliest opportunity."[4]

All this was background noise to the year's main event, the presidential election. Theodore Roosevelt had already pledged not to seek what would practically be a third term. Wellman had been predicting since October 1905 that William Howard Taft would be the Republican nominee, but in December 1907 Wellman spread a rumor that Roosevelt would accept the nomination if it were "forced upon him."[5] The administration quickly denied this, but then Wellman revealed what he claimed was the game behind the third-term threat: the president was using it to force his Wall Street enemies to support Taft; the only way to keep Roosevelt out of the race was to back his handpicked successor as the lesser of two evils.[6]

At the Republican convention in June, Wellman proclaimed that Taft's nomination "fixes Theodore Roosevelt's place in history. This is the greatest triumph of his career," because "he has compelled the party to take his radicalism and stamp it with its unqualified approval and thus name it conservatism."[7]

Wellman also had been predicting for months that Taft's Democratic opponent would be William Jennings Bryan, whose candidacy would still be formidable despite two previous general election losses.[8] But if Wellman's readers expected him to attack the "Great Commoner," they were disappointed.

Wellman visited Bryan just before the Democratic National Convention in July. Bryan met him at the train station and drove him out to his farm on the western edge of Lincoln, Nebraska. He called his home, a redbrick mansion overlooking rolling countryside, Fairview. As an admirer of Thomas Jefferson, Bryan hoped Fairview would become a new Monticello for future generations of Democrats.[9]

Like many politicians Bryan had a strong memory for faces and names; he seemed to know everyone and exuded warmth and power. Wellman was obviously charmed—he was usually impressed with powerful men who treated him well—but he came to admire Bryan. Wellman told his

readers that Bryan was "one of the most remarkable men of our day." A man who formerly was "passionate but poor of judgment," he had "grown in poise and wisdom and judgment" and had "become almost ideal as a leader." After two electoral defeats, Bryan was once again "the undisputed leader of his party," and he had "regained his estate without the aid of wealth, or influence, or corporations, or organization." His enemies, Wellman wrote, "had everything with them except the people. Mr. Bryan had nothing except the people. And in the end . . . everything went the way the people wanted it to go."[10]

When a few days later Bryan was indeed nominated for the presidency, Wellman celebrated it as a triumph over the big-money interests of the Democratic Party.[11] Bryan, he said, no longer seemed like a radical. His progressive views were mainstream, and Bryan himself now claimed to a be a more legitimate heir than Taft to the legacy of Theodore Roosevelt.[12]

This isn't what one would expect from the unofficial mouthpiece of the last two Republican administrations. Wellman had recently written a glowing magazine profile of Taft, pronouncing him well suited for the presidency both by training and temperament. It was high praise but in substance not higher than his praise of Bryan.[13]

Wellman did not endorse Bryan, but he made it clear that he saw both nominees as Roosevelt-style Progressives, representatives of the best elements within their respective parties. Party allegiance pulled Wellman toward Taft, but his pet issues such as the tariff and banking pulled him toward Bryan. Wellman heartily approved of Bryan's call for bank deposit insurance, which Taft opposed, and was at least partly sympathetic to Bryan's well-known opposition to the gold standard.[14]

That year Wellman published a sixty-six-page book titled *The American Financial Union*, which sketched out his plan for reforming banking and monetary policy. Five years before the Federal Reserve Act, Wellman called for the creation of a federal agency to regulate banks, certify their soundness, and provide a more flexible money supply than what was possible through strict adherence to the gold standard. And twenty-five years before the Banking Act of 1933 created the Federal Deposit Insurance Corporation, Wellman called for mandatory insurance to protect deposits in case of bank failure. These ideas weren't original with Wellman, but

as with airships, he spread his gospel with the zeal of a new convert and with the self-confidence of an expert.

To Wellman, banking issues weren't a matter of Republicans versus Democrats so much as eastern financiers versus western agriculture. The East didn't understand the West—never had—and now with Bryan embracing both monetary and tariff reform, Wellman thought the Democrats had their best shot at the presidency since 1892.[15]

Wellman still predicted victory for Taft, but he thought the race would be closer than most people expected. On August 29 he wrote that "the most astute Republican leaders" feared only overconfidence and would welcome "a Republican scare" over Bryan's prospects.[16] Wellman soon provided that scare, making state-by-state predictions that gave Taft only a slim lead of 168 electoral votes to Bryan's 161, with 74 votes up for grabs. In the era before systematic opinion polling, such forecasting mostly involved Wellman's specialty of communicating with a carefully cultivated network of insiders and party contacts around the country. Up until the election, Wellman was practically the only major journalist to list Ohio and Indiana as leaning toward Bryan, and not until late in the campaign did he think New York was safe for Taft. Democratic papers eagerly reprinted these forecasts, usually omitting Wellman's consistent national prediction of a Taft victory. To a reader who only glanced at headlines of both Democratic and Republican papers, Wellman seemed to be calling the race for both sides.[17]

Some Republicans wondered just what Wellman was doing. The *Arizona Republican*, for example, tried to discredit his Ohio prediction by reminding readers that Wellman had also predicted that he would reach the North Pole, even though he "had not the slightest intention of finding the Pole. . . . It was known from the beginning that the balloon would make no more than a bald bluff of starting on its voyage."[18]

Wellman insisted that the Bryan scare was just what Republican managers had wanted, and by autumn the big-money campaign donations were rolling in for Taft. Wellman described Taft's now well-funded campaign as being run "like a great modern business enterprise," with workers even compiling a "card-index system for delegates and voters" in one of the earliest campaign databases.[19]

In an article titled "What It Costs to Elect a President," Wellman wrote of the enormous sums being spent on the campaign, but the article was not an exposé. Citing his long experience with politicians, Wellman called them "about the best lot of men we have," adding that "instead of making a man worse politics makes him better . . . you can never make a go of it unless you are straight square." But while the public felt that large campaign donors had undue influence over elections, Wellman insisted, "No presidential election in a dozen years has been changed an iota by the use of money. . . . It would be more accurate to say that the accumulation of a large campaign fund is a symptom of success instead of a cause."[20]

This breezy dismissal of the power of corporate money is at odds with Wellman's actual reporting. That fall he wrote of Republican managers in swing-state Ohio encouraging employers to pressure their workers to vote for Taft by threatening layoffs if Bryan was elected.[21] Writing from Indianapolis, Wellman said, "There are 40,000 votes that can be turned one way or the other with money. . . . Some of them can be 'hired' to bring in the voters on election day, in the Indiana style."[22] Nationally, he said, labor was "fighting for its life" as "the capitalistic class" tried to neutralize labor's political power.[23] To this end, as Election Day approached, money had been reportedly "pouring in upon the Republican national committee in a golden stream." A Democratic paper headlined Wellman's remarks as PROOF OF CORRUPTION.[24]

In the end Taft won handily, carrying all the states Wellman predicted he would win, plus Wellman's "doubtful" states of Ohio, Indiana, and New York. "Walter Wellman is now in the 'I told you so' class," the *Omaha Daily Bee* observed. "He predicted both ways and couldn't lose."[25]

It isn't clear to what degree Wellman may have been cooperating with Republican gamesmanship or engaging in his own. Perhaps he was pressured to write dismissively about the influence of big money. Perhaps he wrote that article to give himself cover for the rest of his reporting. Either way he seems to have grown dissatisfied with the partisan, for-profit press in which he had made his career. Speaking at the University of Missouri that winter, he called for the creation of an endowed newspaper, a "newspaper that would be wealthy enough to command the best talent in the country; a newspaper that would stand absolutely above all outside influence, and be absolutely neutral on all political questions." He suggested

that if Andrew Carnegie were to endow such a paper in Washington DC, it would be "the greatest monument to liberty ever established."[26] Whatever the problems with capitalism—and as a Progressive, Wellman saw plenty—he never lost faith in the power of great capitalists to solve them.

Wellman probably pitched the endowed newspaper idea to Carnegie himself, along with his proposal for another polar airship attempt. By August 1908 it was known that Wellman was making plans for a return to Danes Island the following year.[27] Among his other activities during the election year, Wellman published a booklet titled *To the Pole by Airship*, apparently intended for the press and potential donors; it detailed his plans and cited the endorsement of the National Geographic Society, the French Academy of Sciences, and others. Victor Lawson of the *Chicago Record-Herald* had granted him use of the airship and the equipment at Camp Wellman, but otherwise he wanted nothing more to do with the project. Wellman apparently made the rounds among his wealthy contacts; it was later rumored that both Carnegie and J. P. Morgan were among the donors anonymously supporting the 1909 expedition.[28]

The aerial world had changed during the year that Wellman focused on politics. In Germany Count Zeppelin's airships had become a national obsession. Unlike Wellman, who had launched his ship about as far from public view as possible, Zeppelin made his flights over German cities and the countryside. For most Germans their first sight of any type of flying craft was not a rickety aeroplane but a gray behemoth that was nearly the size of one of the Imperial Navy's new dreadnought battleships.[29]

On July 1, 1908, the LZ4 made a 240-mile round-trip flight to Zurich, Switzerland, and back. Zeppelin next attempted the twenty-four-hour endurance flight that the German military required as a precondition for purchasing an airship. On August 4 the LZ4 landed near the town of Echterdingen because of mechanical problems. During a storm the next day, the ship tore loose from its moorings, crashed into some trees, and burst into flames.[30]

Zeppelin assumed the dream was over. He had no money for a new airship and did not yet have a contract from the still-skeptical military. But he had underestimated the passion of the German people. Within days the public subscribed six million marks to build new zeppelins; the

response became known as the Miracle at Echterdingen. From then on Zeppelin was a national hero, and his namesake airship became a symbol of German pride.[31]

Wellman cited Zeppelin's success as proof of what he had been saying all along, and his predictions grew even bolder. Not only were airships suitable for exploration, but Zeppelin's achievement also "will assure the rapid building of aerial navies by the chief military powers." The airship "will prove to be an effective engine of war. She can make reconnaissances of an enemy's position, flying at an altitude giving her immunity from the enemy's guns. She cannot only gain invaluable information, but she can make attacks upon strategic points, such as cities, bridges and forts in the camps of hostile armies by dropping explosives down upon them."[32]

The idea of using an airship as a superweapon wasn't new. In 1894 Wellman had reported on predictions that "aerial destroyers" would soon make war obsolete, but in his own recent airship work he had expressed little interest in military uses until now.[33]

And there was something else: "Within a few years I expect to see the Atlantic Ocean crossed by an airship of the *Republique* or *America* type. In fact, the America can cross the Atlantic without much risk of accident with a little help from the winds."[34]

The year 1908 was also a major turning point in public awareness of the machines that were still sometimes confusingly called airships but were more commonly known as flying machines or aeroplanes. Ever since Santos-Dumont's first tentative hops in 1906, European aviators had been improving their designs; by early 1908 some were making flights of more than fifteen minutes. The secretive Wrights were far beyond that, but few people outside the United States gave their claims any credence. Finally, in August 1908, Wilbur Wright made his first public flights in France. Similar to a butterfly emerging unexpectedly from its chrysalis, Wright was suddenly transformed from a *bluffeur* to an international celebrity. European planes struggled through flat turns, but Wright astonished the crowd by banking through effortless figure eights. So obviously superior was the Wright flyer to all other aircraft that the brothers' primacy in aviation could no longer be denied.[35]

Orville Wright, meanwhile, traveled to Fort Myer, Virginia, to make a series of record-breaking demonstration flights for the U.S. Army. On

September 17 Orville was seriously injured and his passenger killed in a crash—the first airplane fatality. Wilbur continued breaking flight records for the rest of the year, setting a new endurance record with a flight of two hours and eighteen minutes on December 31.[36]

While some skeptics still believed that neither aeroplanes nor airships would amount to anything, the international public became enthusiastic for flight. Unlike the automobile, aeronautics had no immediate impact on daily life, but it seemed to herald a new era. Like the North Pole, flight was mainly of symbolic value, though many people believed it would soon become much more than that. In Paris alone, at least 350 different aeroplanes were under construction by the end of the year. Among them was a triplane designed and built by Melvin Vaniman. He made a few short hops in the metal tube–framed machine, said to be the first successful triplane, but he emerged a more committed airshipman. Aeroplanes were flashy, but only an airship could provide the range and payload for a great journey.[37]

Thus, Wellman's polar airship seemed less far-fetched in 1909 than it had only a few years earlier. And he would soon have competition. In November 1908 the Zeppelin company announced its intention to seek the North Pole in a specially built airship to be launched from northern Sweden. The announcement said the Germans had taken full advantage of Wellman's experience and were confident that a mighty German zeppelin could do what the French-style *America* had not. It wasn't clear how soon the Germans would be ready, but Wellman would have the polar skies to himself for probably no more than one more season.[38]

Robert Peary, meanwhile, had sailed north in the repaired *Roosevelt* on July 6, 1908, in preparation for a spring 1909 dash. Some newspapers speculated that Wellman might fly over the pole only to see the Stars and Stripes already planted there. If Peary made it, he would probably reach the pole before Wellman even arrived at Danes Island, although no one would know before next autumn.[39]

One more competitor was in the field, if he was still alive. Dr. Frederick Cook was a former companion of Peary's who in 1906 surprised the world with his claim to have led the first successful climb to the summit of Alaska's Mount McKinley (Denali). In August 1907 Cook was already in Greenland and surprised the world again by announcing that he planned to make a dash for the pole in the spring. As Wellman prepared for his

flight, Cook's whereabouts were still unknown. In November 1908 the *New York Times* rated the doctor's chance of rescue as "doubtful."[40]

Despite public enthusiasm for aeronautics, much of the press expressed doubts about Wellman's sincerity. He mostly tried to ignore the critics, but his 1909 press releases reveal a growing defensiveness masked as disdain. "We are in no hurry," he said on May 12.

> The people who are backing the expedition tell me to take advantage of good conditions if they present themselves; if not, to bide my time. There will be no fireworks and no catering to the good but foolish people who are like the old Romans in the arena who want to see a good Christian die; that is, if it can be prevented. If we strike good weather and meet with no accidents, we shall reach the pole this summer. If not, then we shall try again.[41]

While Wellman went to France, where Vaniman had been modifying the airship, Wellman's brother Arthur led the first group north to Danes Island, where Paul Bjørvig and another man had spent the winter (i.e., the last nine months) guarding Camp Wellman. With the *Frithjof*'s having sunk, Arthur rented another old tub, the *Arctic*, which barely made it through unseasonably bad ice and only because he prevented the skipper from turning back.

They steamed into Virgo Bay on June 18 to find disaster at Camp Wellman. Once again a storm had wrecked the airship hangar, jeopardizing this year's flight. And once again Bjørvig had been left all alone after the death of a comrade.[42]

20

Under the Ice, Over the Ice

Danes Island, Spitsbergen, 1908–1909

More than any other member of Wellman's team, Paul Bjørvig was a true polar man, an ishavsfarer from his youth, and now, at age fifty-two, a veteran of multiple winter camps. In 1898–99 he had passed the dark months in a freezing little hut with Bernt Bentsen and then with Bentsen's frozen corpse. He spent 1901–3 with a German Antarctic expedition aboard the ship *Gauss*, which was trapped in the ice for fourteen months. In 1906–7 he guarded Camp Wellman with only two other men—Felix Riesenberg and another man—and their dogs from the time of the ship's departure in September until its return the following June. Even when Bjørvig went back to his wife and large family, home was Tromsø, one of the world's northernmost settlements at 217 miles above the Arctic Circle.[1]

He had known tragedy. There was the loss of Bentsen, of course. After wintering on Danes Island in 1906–7, Bjørvig's first letter from home informed him that one of his grown sons was dead, lost in the ice of a Norwegian fjord while on a bear hunt. Two years later another son survived a shipwreck only to die after his injured foot was amputated.[2]

Now Bjørvig and a skipper named Knut Johnsen were wintering on Danes Island to ensure that everything was in order when Wellman returned to have another go at the North Pole. In all his years in the Far North, Bjørvig had never seen such a storm as the one that destroyed the airship hangar on December 26, 1908, carrying the roof a hundred yards away and reducing the frame to a mass of broken lumber.[3] But he and Johnsen were unharmed, and all remained well until May 19, when they went hunting on the ice at the edge of the bay. Crossing a glacier, Johnson fell through a crevasse into the water.

175

"Paul, help me!" he cried. But "it was surely 8 to 10 metres right down to him, smooth as a wall," Bjørvig said. He ran for the rope, but when he returned Johnson was gone.[4]

Bjørvig knew well the dangers of sea ice. "Had I walked a metre further to the side, we would have both been lost, and no one would have known what happened," he wrote.

"Again I am alone—far from home and humankind."[5] The days passed with no companion but the half-wild sled dogs, and no voices but their howling. Spring was slow in coming, and by June Bjørvig began to doubt that Wellman would come that year. There would be other ships and a way home before fall, but what Bjørvig didn't know was how many more weeks of solitude he would have to endure.

The *Arctic*, carrying Arthur Wellman, steamed into Virgo Bay on June 18. Soon the world knew, though it cared little, that another man had perished for the deadly dream of the North Pole. One newspaper said dryly that Wellman "has achieved a little local atmosphere through the death of a member of his party in an ice crevasse."[6] In purely practical terms the loss of the airship hangar was a bigger blow to the expedition. The Wellman brothers had anticipated this possibility—Arthur arrived with men and lumber—but the resulting delay would once again push *America*'s earliest departure late into the short season.[7]

It would happen without Paul Bjørvig in camp. Walter Wellman met him in Tromsø and encouraged him to come back for the summer, but Bjørvig refused.

"I have had enough sorrow from the Arctic," he wrote, though with his unfailing buoyancy of spirit he added, "but if a man has no sorrows, he has no joys."[8]

Wellman had another reason for worry, and this one came from back home. DAUGHTER RUNAWAY? "NO," SAYS MOTHER, read a front-page headline of the *Washington Times* on June 15. "Rumors of Stage Aspirations Are Denied by Mrs. Walter Wellman." Rita, second youngest of the Wellman daughters, was eighteen years old, fiercely intelligent, and utterly bored with conventional debutante life. It was said that she had run off to join a Philadelphia theater company as an actress. Newspapers across the country

soon printed photos of the explorer's "stunning" daughter, even as Mrs. Wellman insisted that Rita had only gone to visit friends.[9]

In fact, Rita had already been away from home for more than a year between the ages of sixteen and seventeen, first traveling to Europe with her adult sister Ruth in 1907 (including a side trip to Spitsbergen to visit their father) and then studying art with her sister Rae at the Pennsylvania Academy of the Fine Arts in Philadelphia.[10] The Wellman girls had grown up with increasing wealth and social prominence, moving into ever-more expensive houses, reading their names in the society columns, and enjoying European travel and education in the arts. Their father's frequent prolonged absences were part of the package—and so too was the baby half-brother they didn't yet know about.

In her own way, Rita was, like her father, deeply restless. Years later in an article about her friend and former Pennsylvania academy classmate Charles Demuth, by then a famous modernist painter, she wrote: "We were students together when we were very young. When we were very young, we were very old. We were all bored with life; knew everything there was to know, and only condescended to give our time and talents to painting because it seemed to our jaded spirits the one respectable calling left."[11]

Rita and Rae were said to be talented artists, though Rae was best known for her singing voice. Rita, though close to Demuth, felt outclassed by his burgeoning talent. She remembered the school in her typically acerbic way as "a nest of hornets, a den of wild beasts, a cave full of destroyers such as any art school is," but she observed that sometimes "it is the hornets and beasts and destroyers who help, the most. If you survive their onslaughts, both silly, pretentious and violently antagonistic, you at least know where you are, with only the next thing to find out, *who* you are."[12]

Rita and her father may have had many a deep conversation about metaphorical hornets' nests and finding out who you really are—or maybe they didn't. It isn't clear from their extant writings what sort of relationship they had. Rita remembered learning something about herself one day when a favorite art teacher was critiquing one of her drawings: "He looked up at me, quite kindly, and asked, 'Do you ever try to write stories?'"[13]

Rita's acting career seems to have been short lived, but her interest in the theater was genuine. Soon her dream was not to act in plays but to

write them, expressing all her complicated feelings about relationships and family life. The runaway episode was not the last time Rita Wellman would generate bigger headlines than her famous father would.

The second flight of the airship *America* began at 10:15 a.m. on August 15. Wellman had recently told *Popular Mechanics* magazine that he did not have "the slightest intention of permitting ourselves to be driven by public clamor or the fear of criticism into an action not warranted by circumstances and our own judgment."[14] Nevertheless, despite the *America*'s having an all-new car, redesigned rudder, and other modifications by Vaniman, Wellman set out for the North Pole at the first opportunity without even the pretense of a test flight.

Wellman had cobbled together funding for this year's expedition from a variety of sources. He publicly praised Victor Lawson of the *Chicago Record-Herald* for allowing him to use the airship again "free of charge," but this was a polite way of acknowledging that Lawson was no longer funding the project. The expedition now received little coverage in the *Record-Herald*.[15]

New to this year's crew were Vaniman's brother-in-law Louis Loud and a young Russian aristocrat named Nicholas Popov. Although known as a balloonist, Popov apparently secured his place on board by partly financing the expedition.[16] A planned fifth crew member, a young British airshipman named A. J. Corbitt, was excluded when Wellman decided to save weight.[17]

This time the wind was from the southwest, but until that morning it had been too strong to risk taking the balloon from the hangar. It was still blustery when they launched and dangerously so, as it turned out. In 1907 the ship *Express* had towed the *America* into Smeerenburg Sound, where it would have more room to maneuver, but this time—for reasons unknown—the crew cut the airship loose on shore. Just then a gust of wind lifted the ship, which barely cleared the hangar. No matter, they were airborne. Wellman stood at the wheel, Popov by his side. In the engine room, Vaniman and Loud started one of the motors.[18]

Wellman later wrote that in a light breeze, "I steered her several times around the strait . . . to learn if everything was in good order. All going well I headed her north."[19]

Fig. 15. The *America* in its hangar before the 1909 polar flight. From Wellman, *Aerial Age*, 200.

A *New York Times* report a week after the flight paints a different picture. The airship was flying low over a "narrow bay surrounded by high mountains, where the many cross currents of wind sent the craft in first one direction and then another." Wellman tried to exit by the east strait but was blown near the rocks.[20] Below, young Corbitt was riding in a small boat tethered to the airship, hoping to steady the *America* until it was well under way. But in the gusting wind, Corbitt's boat began skipping along so fast that he shouted to the men above to cast him off.[21]

The airship circled toward the western strait, where it was met with another blast of wind funneled between the mountains. Wellman circled again, commenting to Popov on the ship's good steering with its improved rudder. He headed northeast, passing 250 feet over a low corner of Smeerenburg Island, and at last saw nothing but open water between him and the ice pack.[22] Looking back, he saw the men at camp "waving their hats in excited glee and running for the hilltops, the better to see the airship as she moved toward the northern horizon."[23]

Riding a tailwind, they began making close to twenty-five knots. "To the east the icy mountains and huge glaciers of the Spitzbergen coast glistened in the sunlight," Wellman wrote. "To the north the ice-pack's white was looming in view. Far to the southwest our steamer, the *Arctic*, was headed our way, a dot on the waters, moving with such clumsy slowness compared with our ship of the air. Below us the dark green waters of the polar sea glided past, our equilibrator's lower end thirty or forty yards above them."[24]

"Equilibrator," a new word in Wellman's press dispatches this year, referred to the long, heavy tail that he had previously called the "serpent" or "sausage." The new word better described the tail's purpose—to maintain the airship's equilibrium of altitude—and sounded more scientific besides. But Wellman and his crew were hardly sober scientists as the land receded behind them. "So elated were we, one and all, that we hallooed to one another, and laughed, and cracked our jokes, Vaniman and Loud in the engine room smiling up at Popoff [*sic*] and me at the wheel."[25]

Wellman gave the helm to Popov and began making entries in the ship's log, noting the course, the distance, and the time. Vaniman came up from the engine room and smiled at Wellman, who shouted over the roar of the motors and propellers, "By George, we are started, anyway!"

"What's the course?" Vaniman asked.

"True north," Popov said. The Russian was elated to have the wheel and feel the ship steering easily under his control.[26]

Remembering the problems with the compass in 1907, Wellman climbed to the upper deck to the check the reserve compass, which hung where the motors' vibration would not disturb it. He stood briefly in the open air between the car and the rounded bulk of the gasbag. The green sea below was flecked with fields of ice, and they were nearly upon the edge of the pack, stretching white and endless before them. Finding their course was true, Wellman went below to record the data of their departure from the land "as the basis for our dead reckoning" over the featureless ice, which from the sky no longer looked like an impassible barrier to the North Pole.

"It is no wonder we were happy," he recalled.[27]

Unknown to the airship crew, the Norwegian ship *Farm* was cruising the northern coast of Spitsbergen as part of a topographical survey. The ship's ice pilot noticed a strange object in the sky.

"What the devil is that?" he called to the captain.[28]

Looking through his field glasses, Capt. Gunnar Isachsen recognized it as the airship he had heard about. Isachsen had little faith in airships but was impressed to see it moving so steadily and so fast. He and other men stood watching it until suddenly the *America* shot upward to about 6,000 feet and disappeared into the clouds.[29]

It was about noon. Wellman was in the car working on navigation when he cried, "My God! Look at that!"[30]

Through a window he had just seen something drop from the airship to the sea. It was the leather-skinned equilibrator, which had broken off only a few feet from the top.[31] Suddenly twelve hundred pounds lighter, the *America* rose rapidly. The air grew colder, and the men's ears began ringing with the change of altitude. Now they were in danger—if they weren't careful, the rising ship might burst like a toy balloon—and Wellman had a decision to make.

He left the bridge to talk with Vaniman in the engine room.[32] "Vaniman sang out to me, 'We'll have to fight our way back to Spitzbergen!' And

seeing the look on my face, he added, 'There is no help for it—you'll have to do it.'" And then "Vaniman jumped for the valve line and pulled it far down to let enough hydrogen out of the top of the balloon to prevent us going to still greater heights."[33]

Writing his narrative more than a year later, Wellman was still stung by accusations that he hadn't been serious about the journey and had seized the first excuse to turn back. We can hear his defensiveness as he describes himself with that "look on my face" and being scolded by Vaniman into turning the ship around, just as he had written of being forced by his men to ride the sledge after his injury in 1899.

"Instantly we all knew the voyage was at an end," he wrote, "that without the equilibrator the ship would soon become unmanageable."[34] That was questionable. The guide rope had a long history in long-distance ballooning, but not everyone used it; balloons were hardly unmanageable without it; and no other modern airship carried such a thing. Still it was Wellman's chosen method to extend his range. He needed the *America* to stay aloft longer than any balloon or airship had ever done, and to accomplish that he must avoid having to valve hydrogen (as Vaniman was now doing) every time the ship rose due to changing conditions.

Now he was heading north in a ship that he assumed had just lost much of its range, but how much was anyone's guess. Shorter range meant a greater chance of coming down on the ice far from home. In his narrative Wellman made light of the loss of provisions stuffed inside the equilibrator, saying they had plenty more on board, but the lost half ton represented a third of their total supply.[35] Wellman knew from experience how difficult it was to sledge over rotten summertime ice; if the airship failed they would need to pitch camp and wait out the winter darkness, which might last until June if they made it all the way to the pole. As there was little chance of finding game that far from land, they would be totally dependent on their supplies. Assuming they survived the winter, the lame, fifty-one-year-old Wellman would have to lead ten dogs and three inexperienced men south across the pack ice.

Would the Arctics never bring me anything but bad luck? And whilst Vaniman was working to stop our flight into the cloud I sat there

wondering if I had the right to take the lives of my crew in my hand by holding her head to the north, equilibrator or no equilibrator. My own life, yes; theirs, no. And in bitterness inexpressible, I told Popoff [*sic*] at the wheel to turn her around and steer for Spitzbergen.[36]

Even knowing that Wellman wrote this to answer his critics, I believe that he had been truly reluctant to turn back, though I suspect he had other reasons. He had devoted years of his life to this dream, faced mounting odds against raising support for a new expedition after yet another failure, and knew full well what his fellow journalists would do to him if he turned back while still in sight of land.[37]

As the *America* climbed, "the whole northern part of Spitzbergen spread out in one great frozen picture before our eyes, and I imagined that away in the east I could see Walden Island where the old *Ragnvald Jarl* had been crushed in the ice in 1894."[38] In such a reflective mood, there's a name that must have been on Wellman's mind but that, curiously, he fails to mention—Salomon Andrée.

Twelve years earlier, just as the balloon *Örnen* was floating north from this very coastline, its guide rope became unfastened and fell away. Thus, Andrée had already faced Wellman's dilemma; the similarities were eerie. Andrée chose to keep going but never returned.

On four previous expeditions, Wellman had come to grief before or soon after reaching the ice pack. One of the ironies of the 1909 flight is that once he decided to go home, the wind swept him north over the pack with ease.

"Then ensued a struggle which none of us engaged in it will ever forget," he wrote.[39] The wind was stronger at high altitude, and before they got the ship turned around, the Spitsbergen coast was fading in the distance, some sixty or seventy miles away. The *America* made headway against the wind only with difficulty and at times was blown backward. The men descended to where the wind was slower, but then the motor quit—probably from the airship being out of balance after the equilibrator fell off. At lower altitude the partially deflated gasbag sagged and lost shape, and the men worked the pumps to inflate the ballonets. Wellman ordered Vaniman to modify the retardateur (or ice anchor) as a substitute

equilibrator; since they would be flying home at low altitude, this four-hundred-pound weight might protect them against accidentally touching the ice. While Vaniman was working, the now-silent airship drifted steadily northward.[40]

They got the motor running again and headed southwest, but the improvised equilibrator kept catching on the jagged surface of the ice—just as it was designed to do. Popov and Wellman soon learned how to swing the airship around to get unstuck.[41]

As they made their way south, the men suddenly heard Popov screaming from the back of the car. The sound, Wellman wrote, was "unearthly . . . each of us felt sure that our comrade from Russia had lost his reason and become a jibbering maniac."[42] It turned out that Popov had gone to feed the dogs in their kennels, and the dogs, unsurprisingly, were confused and upset by their strange and noisy environment. One of the dogs had snapped at Popov, who had lost his temper and berated the whole pack in Russian.[43]

At last near the edge of the ice field, they met the *Farm* steaming toward them. Because of their balky motors, Wellman and Vaniman decided to let the ship tow them home, but as the wind grew stronger, it jerked the airship this way and that. They descended to the water's surface, hoping they would tow more easily there, but soon found themselves "wallowing in the trough of the sea."[44] Fearing the frail car would break up, Captain Isachsen sent his men to rescue the airship crew. He said that "as our boats approached the strange derelict we heard the frightful howling of the dogs as the waves dashed over the car of the airship."[45]

To their surprise, the boatmen found Wellman standing atop the car, lighting a cigar. He sat down for a smoke, shaded by a gasbag that still held the better part of 250,000 cubic feet of hydrogen, and calmly issued orders to unload the car.[46]

It took the boatmen several trips, each time approaching with care to avoid smashing into the car as it bobbed on the waves. Wellman was the last to abandon ship. But one mishap was to come, and it was nearly fatal.

The *America* arrived at Camp Wellman, having been towed ingloriously all the way from the edge of the ice pack. Corbitt climbed aboard to dismantle the engine, and Vaniman took a pickax to fourteen of the fuel

Fig. 16. Towed back to base by the Norwegian ship *Farm* after a flight over the polar ice on August 15, 1909. From Wellman, *Aerial Age*, 272.

tanks to lighten the load so they could beach the airship. Vaniman started at the bow and worked aft, not pausing to consider the consequences. As the bow grew lighter, the ship suddenly pointed nose up, and the remaining hydrogen surged into the nose of the gasbag. It all happened quickly. Suddenly the ship was rising. Everyone yelled for Corbitt to jump before it was too late. He fell twenty-five feet but landed in loose pebbles that broke his fall. At some point the gasbag separated from the car—by one account it was torn off by a mighty gust of wind—and rose into the sky.[47]

Corbitt remembered the thousands of squawking birds in the bay and how they fell silent as the giant gasbag rose a mile or more in the sky. Then it burst like a toy balloon—exactly what would have happened after the equilibrator fell off had the crew not opened the valve. The sound, like a cannon's shot, echoed from the mountains. As the three-ton rubberized envelope fell toward the bay, some of the sailors aboard the *Farm* thought it was going to hit them and jumped overboard, but as in 1906, the large falling object missed the ship.[48]

Thus ended the second flight of the *America*. "Had the ship not broken up while landing," Wellman said, "we would have tried another voyage this month with a new guide rope, notwithstanding one mishap following fast upon the heels of another."[49] He was still determined to try again.

Even the burst gasbag was "not seriously damaged" and was recovered for reuse. Once again Wellman left Danes Island in defeat, but he gave orders to expand the airship hangar. He and Vaniman intended to again enlarge the *America* and return in 1910 with a more powerful ship.[50]

His plans were about to change. Wellman already knew that he was one of three explorers currently trying to reach the North Pole. He was about to learn that he was the only one not claiming to have succeeded.

21

Nowhere Does His Story Ring True

Norway, Denmark, France, and the United States,
September–November 1909

A. J. Corbitt remembered Wellman's reaction to the telegram he received at the Arctic port of Bodø on September 1. They were southbound, and Corbitt stood next to Wellman at the ship's rail. Wellman tipped the messenger and said, "No reply."

"Not very good news, sir?" Corbitt asked.

"No," Wellman replied. "We shall not be going to Spitsbergen again next year. This wire from Bergen [Norway] tells me that Dr. Frederick A. Cook has found the North Pole."

"Well, at any rate he is an American."

"Yes, but he did *not* find the North Pole," Wellman insisted. "There will be so much controversy over this that there will be no more honor in even trying again."[1]

Corbitt's memory, more than fifty years later, is probably only partly accurate. Wellman later claimed to have disbelieved Cook from the start but remained determined to reach the pole himself.[2]

Cook's sudden reappearance created an international sensation. By then he had been all but given up for dead. Now suddenly he was not only alive but also claiming that he and two Inuit companions had reached the North Pole on April 21, 1908. Cook sold his story to the *New York Herald*, which printed the two-thousand-word dispatch under a triple-banner headline on September 2.[3]

Reading Cook's report, Wellman was certain it was fraudulent, or so he remembered later. Passing through Cristiania (Oslo) on September 4, reporters asked if Cook's story seemed credible. Wellman replied that it was possible, but "proofs must be supplied, which will be easy if Dr. Cook can produce exact observations which experts will verify."[4]

This was more provocative than it might seem. Up till then explorers had been taken at their word.[5] This ungracious demand for proof made Wellman sound like a jealous rival, especially when he insisted that Cook's claim would not change his own polar plans.

"The one thing that the world will listen to with least patience will be Wellman's comments on the achievement of Dr. Cook," said the *Salt Lake Herald*.[6]

But Wellman wasn't the only one to raise questions. It was astonishing that a three-man party should succeed—and on its first attempt!—where large and well-financed expeditions had failed repeatedly. Philip Gibbs, a young reporter from the London *Daily Chronicle*, met Cook in Copenhagen and almost immediately became suspicious. Learning that Cook had with him no journal or sextant observations, Gibbs asked how he could prove his story. Later Gibbs recalled how Cook replied with "a sudden violence of anger which startled me."

"You believed Nansen," Cook said, "and Amundsen, and Sverdrup. They had only their story to tell. Why don't you believe me?"[7]

Gibbs kept his suspicions to himself for the time being. Wellman, meanwhile, passed through Copenhagen while Cook was there, being feted by royalty and besieged by reporters and well-wishers. Returning from yet another failure, Wellman received little attention. And though he had time between trains and was only blocks from Cook's hotel, he left for Paris without paying his respects. Local papers attributed the snub to jealousy, but as Wellman was a lot less newsworthy than he had been, these reports didn't follow him home.[8]

Wellman was still in Paris on September 6 when Robert Peary stunned the world with his own telegram: STARS AND STRIPES NAILED TO THE POLE. PEARY.[9] A full-blown polar controversy followed in short order. After Cook gave a surprisingly brief and vague lecture in Copenhagen on September 7, Gibbs denounced him in print as a "fraud" and called his lecture a "fairy tale."[10] Peary telegrammed the *New York Times* a few days later, asserting that Cook "has not been at the pole on April 21st, 1908, or at any other time. He has simply handed the public a gold brick."[11]

Peary claimed to have proof of his accusation but was slow to produce it. In the interim Cook's defenders used Peary's account of his own journey against him. Peary's allies had been criticizing Cook for claiming

impossible daily distances across the rough ice, but it was soon pointed out that Peary's claims were even larger and that his narrative bore striking similarities to Cook's descriptions of ice and weather conditions along the way—exactly what one would expect if both men had reached the pole. By late September the growing public consensus was that both had succeeded.[12] Cook, after that first shaky speech in Copenhagen, thereafter bore himself with confidence and charm, acting the perfect gentleman and foil to the surly, sore-loser Peary. The facts may have been muddy, but the public knew which man *seemed* like a hero.[13]

Overshadowed in all this was Wellman's own announcement on September 8, two days after Peary's first telegram, that he had abandoned his North Pole plans. Wellman's attitude at this time can be gauged by his brother Arthur's comments to the *New York Tribune* on September 17. Arthur said Walter gave up because of Peary.

"Do you believe that Dr. Cook discovered the pole?" the reporter asked.

"I think that Dr. Cook thinks he discovered the pole," Arthur replied. "I believe Peary has discovered the pole. He is a man of great experience, and when he says he has discovered the pole I believe him."[14]

By the time Walter returned to the United States in mid-November, the public was growing impatient and wanted the controversy resolved. The game must have a winner. Peary's evidence against Cook turned out to be yet another unverified claim: Cook's Inuit companions told Peary's men that they had never been out of sight of land. This was quickly contradicted by Knud Rasmussen, a Greenlandic-Danish explorer who had interviewed members of the tribe to which Cook's companions belonged and who said they supported Cook's story. Peary's allies then tried to discredit Cook by producing an affidavit signed by one of Cook's companions from the Mount McKinley ascent who said they didn't actually reach the summit, but this was met with accusations that Peary's friends had paid the man to sign it.[15]

Cook and Peary both offered to submit their polar notebooks to independent experts for evaluation, Cook's to the University of Copenhagen and Peary's to the National Geographic Society. Both men were slow to follow through, however.[16]

As the feud unfolded, Wellman had plenty of time to decide whether to get involved. It wasn't so much a battle between men as between newspapers.

The *New York Herald*—still the city's most powerful paper, though losing ground to its rivals—staked its reputation on Cook. The *New York Times*, not a newcomer but still something of an underdog, had provided some of Peary's funding. Both companies strove to discredit their rival's polar mascot in what was now a high-stakes contest for readers and respectability. This was bigger than the North Pole. It was about money and power.[17]

Wellman made his move on November 23. A reception at the Naval Press Club of Washington occasioned the first meeting between Wellman and Peary since their awkward White House encounter three years earlier. Shaking Peary's hand, Wellman said, "I am glad to greet you as the only man who reached the North Pole."

Peary smiled, and the two new friends made plans to get together and chat about their experiences. A *New York Times* reporter was on hand to record the exchange.[18]

Cook already had the likes of Amundsen, Nansen, Ernest Shackleton, and Sverdrup on record expressing confidence in him; at this point Peary was no doubt grateful to have even controversial Wellman on his side.[19] And Wellman came with a built-in advantage: he knew how to attack a rival in print. The November 29 edition of the *New York Times* featured a long story headlined WELLMAN RIDDLES COOK'S NARRATIVE.

Cook, Wellman argued, claimed to have done things that experienced Arctic men knew to be impossible. With his usual passion for logistical calculations, Wellman walked the reader through the relevant figures of weights and distances. He showed that the main problem was that travelers of the ice pack had to bring food for the entire round-trip, as no game was available except near shore. The more food you brought, the farther you could go but the slower you'd travel, and men and dogs could only haul so much. A journey to the pole and back therefore required a large supply of provisions plus supporting parties to haul it at least part of the way. Cook's claim of making a round-trip of roughly fifteen hundred miles with three men, two sledges, and twenty-six dogs "never has been done, and it never can be done. No serious man would attempt it."

Peary's journey, by contrast, started closer to the pole and involved an army of support teams advancing supplies by relay, with fewer and fewer men moving to each succeeding stage—a remarkable feat of sledging, "but nothing miraculous or even surprising."

Wellman also found fault with Cook's narrative itself: "He is generally vague and indefinite, but like most men of his class, altogether too precise at the wrong place." Cook told of finding himself fourteen seconds of latitude shy of the pole and then carefully advancing the final fourteen hundred feet. This apparent diligence seemed calculated to impress the public, but anyone trained in celestial navigation knew that such a small difference lay within the sextant's margin of error, especially with a low sun and highly refracted light. "Nowhere does his story ring true," Wellman wrote. "It is always an approximation of reality, but never reality itself."

But the clincher was Cook's papers, which after many weeks of preparation were finally on their way to the University of Copenhagen for judgment. Wellman argued that a man of honor who found himself questioned would have turned over his records "instantly, the first hour." Cook's delay was itself evidence of dishonesty:

> The public should know that if Dr. Cook has any adequate records, they are dirty, greasy, grimy notebooks kept from day to day, poorly written, in places almost illegible, penned with frost-bitten fingers by a weary man . . . the original notes of all astronomical observations taken, with various corrections . . . every observation and computation coming in its proper place and fitting the story told of the journey and the dead-reckoning.
>
> Let it be thoroughly understood that such records are *always ready*. They are *complete and perfect the moment they are written*. They can be turned over to a scientific committee in two minutes as well as in two months—and much better. There is not a word or figure or letter to add to them. In fact, to add or erase or change is *exactly what must not be done* if they are to have value.[20]

Wellman then showed readers how to reverse-engineer the correct raw observations for any date and location "with a pencil and a nautical almanac." He believed that Cook had delayed to work with competent navigators and fill a notebook with this very thing. The Copenhagen judgment, which Wellman assumed would vindicate Cook, would therefore be worthless.

Though the *Times* editors praised Wellman's "considerable authority" and said his article "deserves most careful reading," many other papers

reacted as Wellman had feared.[21] His arguments were reprinted in truncated form, sometimes misrepresented or derided as simple jealousy. Said one paper: "It does not lie in the mouth Walter Wellman, braggart and bombast and the self-advertiser that he is, to charge Dr. Cook or anybody else with being an imposter when he claims to have discovered the North Pole. Wellman has shown himself about the biggest fake on record in connection with the North Pole discovery."[22] Or as another paper wryly put it, "If Walter Wellman says that Cook did not get to the Pole, he knows what he is talking about, for nobody has not gotten there any more than this same Wellman."[23]

Wellman was far from Cook's only critic, however, and when the doctor suddenly went missing and even his own attorney could do nothing but express embarrassment, Wellman found himself with plenty of company.[24] This opened him to a new line of criticism. "Wellman is a very shrewd fellow," said the *Salt Lake Herald*. "He didn't speak until he knew which way the jury was going to decide."[25]

But the jury that mattered—the council in Copenhagen—was still out. When it issued its verdict on December 21, Wellman's fears did not come to pass; the university rejected Cook's claim. And while over the years Cook's defenders have made much of the fact that the verdict was merely "not proven," individual members of the Danish committee were far more outspoken. Quoting *Literary Digest*:

> "His papers convict him of being a swindler," declares Commodore Gustav Holm, while Knud Rasmussen, the Arctic explorer who has championed Cook's cause from the first, describes his formally submitted proofs as "impudent," and "a most childish attempt at cheating," and Dr. [Ellis] Stromgren, president of the committee, characterizes his treatment of the university as "shameless." "We have been hoaxed," he adds, "by a man through whom we thought to honor a great nation."[26]

Wellman reveled in his vindication, saying that if "Cook had been anything other than a bungler," he would have invented a more plausible story and learned enough astronomy and navigation "to avoid making himself ridiculous."[27] On the lecture circuit the following January, Wellman added, "I wouldn't be in that man's shoes for all the money in the U.S."[28]

"The worst part about this Dr. Cook business is that it gives Walter Wellman a chance to say 'I told you so,'" groused William Jennings Bryan's *The Commoner*. The editors reverted to form after expressing the paper's high opinion of Wellman during the 1908 presidential campaign.[29]

The polar controversy was not over—it drags on to this day among Peary and Cook partisans—but from then on Cook was fighting a rearguard action, while Peary's own unproven claim received far less scrutiny. Like Cook, Peary made his final dash with no trained navigators besides himself. Peary sent the last man who could possibly contradict him back with the last support party when they were still 133 nautical miles short of the pole. Afterward Peary's daily mileage doubled, and it quadrupled on the return journey—but only until he was once again among men who could check his work. In between those times, Peary's five companions could only take their commander's word on faith.[30]

Others raised questions about this and other problems with Peary's story, but Wellman did not, nor did Wellman apply consistently one of his most damaging criticisms of Cook—the failure to promptly turn over his diary for independent verification.[31] Peary procrastinated too, made excuses, and then brought his papers not to a university or official body but to the National Geographic Society, which despite its official-sounding name was—as Wellman knew—a privately owned publishing business best known for its popular magazine. Wellman may not have known how superficial its committee was in examining Peary's diary, but he surely knew that the society was a sponsor of Peary's expedition—hardly a disinterested party—and that men on the committee were Peary's personal friends. Their verdict came a few weeks before the Copenhagen decision; not surprising, they certified Peary's claim. For the rest of his life Peary made sure that no one else examined the diary.[32]

Of Peary's machinations, Wellman said nothing. In his article for the *New York Times*, he called himself "a humble though not very lucky seeker for the pole," who "felt as one who had played in a large and fascinating game, and lost." He said his only purpose in exposing Cook was to do his duty "toward the establishment of truth and justice" and that "this is done without personal bias or interest, with nothing to gain, and perhaps with much criticism to endure on account of it."[33]

He was correct about the criticism, but whether Wellman had anything to gain was another matter. The North Pole was out of the question, but he still had an airship capable of long-distance flight. Soon Wellman was in contact with *New York Times* publisher Adolph Ochs, who had reason to be favorably disposed to him. Wellman had boasted in 1908 that "the *America* can cross the Atlantic without much risk of accident with a little help from the winds."[34] It was time to put those words to the test. Once more Wellman would try to convince powerful men to fund a journey that most people thought was impossible and that would be led by someone who was increasingly derided not merely as a failure—a man could live with that— but also as a fake and a coward, one who had boasted but had never dared to try. Andreé at least had had the courage to pursue his goal to the end.

As the year 1910 began, a man in Wellman's shoes might have wondered how many more chances he would have. Wellman being Wellman, he probably felt sure he needed only one more.

PART 4

The Atlantic Ocean, 1910–1912

22

Mr. Wellman's Unbusinesslike Charm

*Chicago, New York, and the White Nile River in
Egyptian Sudan, February–March 1910*

In Chicago Victor Lawson didn't see the small headline WELLMAN TO FLY
OVER SEA on the front page of the February 1, 1910, edition of the *New York
Times*. As a result, the *Chicago Record-Herald* publisher didn't know for
another two weeks that his famous employee was planning to fly across
the Atlantic Ocean in the airship in which Lawson owned a majority share.

The article said Wellman had recently sailed for Europe to make arrange-
ments and that the attempt was scheduled for July. It did not say who was
paying for the expedition. Lawson learned that and more after reading
a letter from W. C. Reick of the *New York Times*, which was sponsoring
the flight.

"I own three-fourths of the stock of the balloon company and am a
large creditor besides," Lawson telegrammed back on February 15, "and
yet your letter is the first information that has come to me of the present
enterprise. I shall have to cable for information. Will you please wire me
Wellman's address?"[1]

A year earlier Wellman had said that the *Record-Herald* had declined to
fund the 1909 expedition but had "turned over" the airship to him.[2] Law-
son, however, had only meant to loan the ship to Wellman for that year.
Lawson had no use for an airship but didn't like being taken for granted.

Wellman, by then on his way to Egypt, wrote back to explain: "It was in
November last I began talking with Mr. Reick about this proposed voyage
[meaning that he was already negotiating with the *Times* when his Cook
exposé appeared]. At that time I had very little idea it would ever be put
through. In December he told me you were content to have the thing go
on and either told me he had consulted you or I inferred he had, since

he knew your views. For that reason I did not confer with you directly, presuming you knew all about it."[3]

Lawson was skeptical and copied Wellman's letter into a telegram to Reick on February 28. From then on Lawson checked with Reick about everything Wellman told him. In his telegram Lawson also mentioned Wellman's assurance that Reick understood that the *Record-Herald* would share ownership of the expedition's exclusive news dispatches. Reick had said nothing about that, and now Lawson suspected that Wellman, in his eagerness to close a deal, had made no such demand.[4]

The whole expedition was now in jeopardy. Worse, Wellman now had to negotiate by long-distance cable from Africa. Word had reached him that Theodore Roosevelt was about to end his yearlong postpresidential safari and return to civilization. Wellman and other American reporters would soon be racing up the Nile in hopes of being the first to locate the former president. Everyone wanted to know how he would respond to news that President Taft, his handpicked successor, was beginning to infuriate Roosevelt's supporters with a series of unprogressive policy decisions.[5]

Lawson and Reick, meanwhile, were still at odds over the terms of the airship. "It is to be regretted that he [Wellman] could not have been more businesslike in his recent arrangement with you," Lawson wrote on March 4. "I have invested a great deal of money in Mr. Wellman's balloon enterprises and . . . I have had enough. If anybody else wants to take a flyer in the balloon (I almost said *my* balloon), God speed him in his flight but I do not want to participate." For the loan of the airship, Lawson demanded free of charge "all news value there may be used in the *Record-Herald*."[6]

But the *Times* didn't want to invest tens of thousands of dollars in a flight unless it retained exclusive rights to the resulting news stories. That was the whole game. Lawson cabled Wellman in Cairo, but the situation was still unresolved when Wellman set out on the Nile in a chartered boat. He lost contact with the outside world, knowing that he was facing a supreme embarrassment if the deal fell apart. Not only had the *Times* and other papers already announced the expedition, but also Vaniman was rebuilding the airship in Paris, incurring debts that Wellman didn't yet have the funding to pay and that neither Lawson nor Reick knew about.[7]

Somewhere above Khartoum on the White Nile, on March 11 Wellman's chartered boat met another boat coming downstream. Standing barefoot on the upper deck was a mustachioed, bespectacled man wearing a red shirt and pajamas. The man waved and smiled, "and when the smile revealed a brilliant row of much advertised teeth your correspondent knew his man. It was Roosevelt sure enough." Wellman, who probably had more experience chartering boats in remote places than all of his rival journalists combined, had beaten them all to the prize. Soon he was sitting down to breakfast with the former president.[8]

Roosevelt looked tanned and fit. He "ate six eggs and bunches of fried bacon for breakfast and declared that, after a year under the equatorial sun, he was fit for the fight of his life."[9]

Whether Roosevelt would involve himself in another political fight was exactly what the public wanted to know. A year into Taft's presidency, Progressives thought he was too deferential to his party's conservative leadership. And when Taft fired Chief Forester Gifford Pinchot, Roosevelt's closest ally in conservation, Progressives began to think of the president as a traitor.[10]

Roosevelt had followed the news during his safari and privately had deep concerns about Pinchot's firing. With Wellman, however, he was firm, at least for the record: "I have nothing to say and will have nothing to say on American or foreign politics . . . and I will give out no political interviews of any kind."[11]

That was clear enough, but Roosevelt didn't send Wellman away, either. Wellman accompanied him to Europe, where "the most talked-about man in the world" arrived to the adulation of a public who regarded "him as not a king, but something more than a king."[12]

This enthusiasm astonished Roosevelt, who had "schooled his mind to the belief that he had passed from the stage, had had his day, and that others had taken his place in the popular attention." Roosevelt was "surprised and delighted," but Wellman said this only showed that he had "his fair share of proper human vanity, and nothing more."[13]

But Wellman hinted at much more, though he was careful not to ascribe his own ideas to Roosevelt. As far as Wellman knew, Roosevelt had said nothing about seeking the presidency again. Wellman guessed

that Roosevelt felt he "should stay out of politics" but that "keeping still is the most arduous assignment in the world for him. . . . He loves to be in the thick of the fight. . . . He may intend one thing and by the stress of circumstances and the demands of his own nature be drawn into another before many months shall have passed."[14]

As for the circumstance that might draw Roosevelt in, "it is true that Mr. Roosevelt once made Mr. Taft President. That is known to all men, excepting, possibly, Mr. Taft himself. . . . There were reasons why he did it. Those reasons no longer exist."[15]

This was alarming news to Taft supporters but gave hope to Roosevelt partisans. As one paper put it, "Whatever may be said of Wellman as an Arctic explorer, he has long been noted as a correspondent who could size up a situation and who was almost startlingly accurate in making political forecasts. . . . The gist of his conclusions is that Roosevelt will neither oppose nor support Taft and that if the people want Roosevelt in 1912 they can have him."[16]

Back in New York and Chicago, negotiations concerning the airship dragged on, though Lawson was slowly giving way, reducing his demand from sharing equally in the news coverage to making sure that Reick didn't syndicate any of it to Lawson's Chicago rivals. Having learned that Wellman was already spending money, Lawson telegrammed him on March 25: "Your action assuming obligations without my knowledge and without completing arrangements with Reick unbusinesslike. You alone responsible resulting embarrassments."[17]

In the end, Lawson reluctantly agreed to partner with the *New York Times* and the *London Daily Telegraph* in jointly sponsoring the flight. Crossing the Atlantic Ocean by air was dime-novel stuff—or had been until recently. Now it hovered on the edge of possibility. The North Pole may have gone stale with repetition and controversy, but this goal was so fresh and of such epic proportions that even after Wellman's scheming was exposed, he had not only roped Lawson into it but two other major publishers besides. Lawson, however, was unimpressed with Wellman's offer to reimburse him if news revenue failed to cover expenses.

"That," he told a colleague, "is where the laugh comes in."[18]

23

The Funniest Damn Ship I Ever Joined

Atlantic City, New Jersey, July–August 1910

Under straw hats and parasols, tourists were the lifeblood of Atlantic City. All summer they flowed along the boardwalk and into hotels, shops, and restaurants. They sailed along the coast and crowded the beaches to swim in the surf while clothed in yards of soggy fabric. Evenings they walked out onto long piers that were little cities unto themselves, topped with spacious buildings dedicated to music and dancing and "children's carnivals, baby shows, cakewalks and moving picture exhibits."[1] The big ballroom at the end of Steel Pier was especially popular. "It's worth the walk out here just to see the hobble skirts dancing!" people said of the curiously narrow, form-fitting skirts that had become fashionable among young women.[2]

In keeping with the national aviation craze, in July the city hosted a ten-day Air Carnival at Bader Field, soon to be the city's first airport. Walter Brookins, a pilot from the Wright brothers' traveling exhibition team, celebrated his twenty-first birthday by coaxing his Flyer to a record altitude of 6,175 feet.[3] Wright rival Glenn Curtiss set an endurance record with a seventy-four-minute flight that covered more than fifty miles, and on another day Curtiss demonstrated aviation's military possibilities by "bombing" a yacht with oranges.[4]

Local businessmen were more interested in aviation as a source of tourism. Whatever was proved by Brookins's high flying or Curtiss's falling fruit, tourists loved it, and with that in mind, hotel owners paid for an airship hangar for Walter Wellman.[5]

By July the barnlike building was rising on the island's north end by Absecon Inlet. Two hundred fifty feet long, 80 feet wide, and 80 feet tall, the hangar stood near the end of the Boardwalk, its canvas front doors

Fig. 17. Funded by a group of local hotel owners, the Atlantic City airship hangar became a tourist attraction in its own right. From Wellman, *Aerial Age*, 312.

opening directly onto the beach. Once the newly expanded *America* and its hydrogen-generating apparatus arrived from Paris, Atlantic City would be home to "the first thoroughly equipped airship station in the United States."[6] Dr. Albert Zahm, secretary of the Aero Club of Washington (DC), was so enthused upon visiting the site later that year that he suggested calling it Airport. Like Wellman, Zahm was ahead of his time; that word wouldn't catch on for nearly another decade.[7]

To help the hotel owners recoup their investment, Wellman had agreed to open the hangar to paying visitors and to make test flights over the city.[8] He may have even suggested these things himself to help close the deal. As always, publicity was his only commodity.

Back in January, Wellman's premature announcement had received little attention after appearing once with no follow-up. But now the simultaneous July 9 announcement by the *New York Times*, the *Chicago Record-Herald*, and *London Daily Telegraph* proved to be the front end of a sustained media campaign.[9] The *New York Times* soon acknowledged that "majority opinion holds that the time is not yet ripe for success on such a trip, yet many maintain that with average luck the aviators have more than a sporting chance."[10] Should Wellman succeed, "the feat will crown the centuries old desire of man to govern the air."[11]

But the sponsoring newspapers stressed that they were "aiding the enterprise only as purchasers of the news of the expedition."[12] News of failure or death would be Wellman's responsibility. In London the *Telegraph* invoked the "dreams of Icarus." The editors had "been inclined to put off for another couple of decades" the hope of seeing such a feat attempted, but Wellman and Vaniman "have made up their minds to hurry up history. . . . If it succeeds it will be the greatest event in the intercourse between Europe and America since the voyage of Columbus."[13]

Wellman's career as an explorer was coming full circle. He started out in 1891 trying to locate Christopher Columbus's landing place. Now he would try to become a Columbus of the air. But it was no longer his enterprise alone. The *Telegraph* was correct in giving Wellman and Vaniman nearly equal billing. Unlike Peary, Wellman shared credit. And this was only fair now that the ever-changing *America* was mostly a Vaniman-designed airship filled with Vaniman's inventions.

While Wellman made arrangements in Atlantic City, Vaniman was back in Paris, supervising work on the airship. Though still known as the *America*, in many ways it was a new craft that incorporated remnants of the polar ship. Once again the gasbag was cut apart and expanded. The new rubberized fabric didn't match the old; the leather-colored airship now had a thick yellow band just forward of center, like a label around a cigar. Now 228 feet long and holding 345,000 cubic feet of gas, the airship was to carry an 80-horsepower motor for normal cruising and a 200-horsepower motor for bucking the wind. It would have a lifeboat and a Marconi wireless outfit to communicate with ships at sea, and it would drag a heavier equilibrator that comprised a chain of gasoline-filled metal cannisters.[14]

For much of the press, this Wellman project was one too many. The *Salt Lake Herald* repeated the canard that Wellman had "made several bluffs at the discovery of the North Pole by balloon" but "never attempted to leave the starting point."[15] The *Richmond Times-Dispatch* acknowledged that Wellman was "a good newspaperman" but cautioned readers "not to take Walter too seriously" as an aviator, predicting he would "make repairs and carry on preliminary experiments until the country gets tired of him and his plans." Even so, the idea was alluring:

Twenty years ago it would have seemed an idle dream, and a hundred years ago a man who proposed it would have been looked on as a maniac, but now, no one will regard it as anything more than a natural step in the forward movement of science. Twenty years from now it may be an every-day matter. The ocean will cease to be a barrier between the nations, and space will be no more.[16]

"Wellman should this time do all his flying first and his writing afterwards," said Iowa's *Ottumwa Tri-Weekly Courier*, "or some of the bird men who are now saying nothing, may beat him to it."[17] For once, Wellman seemed to agree.

"I don't want notoriety. I wish the newspapers would let my name alone," he told the *New York Times* with no apparent sense of irony. "I'm going to do a dangerous thing in a sane, level-headed way. . . . Time will only tell. We shall succeed if we can, but we are not afraid to try and fail and be sneered at."[18]

Wellman's critics were not having it. "Walter should not be too hard on the press," chided the *Daily Missoulian*, "for he has fattened on printer's ink."[19]

They were already behind schedule. In July Vaniman cabled from Paris, promising that he could have the *America* ready to fly in six days after his arrival in Atlantic City if only he could have two more weeks in Paris. Wellman gave him one week. They would finish the car and machinery in the new hangar under the gaze of paying visitors, who mostly held the view expressed in so many newspapers: "He needs to make good this time."[20]

Wellman had surely heard the news from Germany but said nothing to the press about it: on July 13 balloonist Oscar Erbslöh's airship had exploded in flight, killing all five aboard. It was the world's deadliest air disaster to date but not unbeatable. Wellman was planning for a crew of six.[21]

A native of West Australia, J. R. "Jack" Irwin had already had a taste of fame before signing on as the *America*'s wireless operator. He had been working at the Siasconset wireless station on Nantucket, Massachusetts, on January 23, 1909, when just before 4:00 a.m. he heard a weak CQD signal, the standard distress call that preceded the now-familiar SOS:

CQD CQD ATTENTION ALL STATIONS. DISTRESS. THE REPUBLIC
RAMMED BY UNKNOWN STEAMER 175 EAST OF AMBROSE LIGHT.
LAT 40.7, LON 70.

The RMS *Republic* was sixty miles away and crippled after being struck on its port side in a fog. The "unsinkable" ship with watertight bulkheads sank the next day but not before its fifteen hundred passengers were transferred to other ships that had received Irwin's relayed distress signal.

Wireless was several years old by then but still something of a novelty. The Siasconset station had been built by the *New York Herald* more for news than for safety, but the rescue provided both. This first major demonstration of wireless technology's usefulness in an emergency made international heroes of Irwin and the *Republic*'s wireless man, Jack Binns.[22] Though Zeppelin had been experimenting with an airborne wireless in Germany, Irwin would become the first wireless operator aboard an aerial vessel at sea.[23]

Wellman's plan was to install a lightweight wireless unit in the *America*'s lifeboat, which would hang beneath the car, thus keeping the "spark-gap" unit as far as possible from the gasbag. It would be powered by the airship motors, with a set of batteries as an auxiliary power source. Transmission range was only seventy miles, but Wellman intended to follow the steamship route toward London. Along the way Irwin would signal passing ships, which would then relay messages to and from shore stations. The airship crew would gain an added measure of safety; the sponsors would gain first dibs on the international front-page news that wireless dispatches from an airship at sea would generate. As long as the *America* stayed within the steamer track, the world would follow its progress hour by hour.[24]

Wellman needed an experienced navigator, and Irwin helped him find one by wiring his friend Murray Simon, a junior officer on the Atlantic liner RMS *Oceanic*.[25] Beginning with sailing ships, the Englishman had been a sailor for seventeen of his twenty-nine years. The *New York Times* reported that he "was so fascinated by the idea of flying across the ocean that he made a special trip to Atlantic City to ask Mr. Wellman to take him along as navigator. He pointed out the advantage of having a man who understood Atlantic conditions and winds, and Mr. Wellman accepted his offer."[26]

Colorful and opinionated, Simon was a hit with reporters. When the airship was inflated and the car attached, he said, "I dumped my gear in my bunk like any old whaler would, and I says to myself, as I looks over, this is the funniest damn ship I ever joined, and I joined a few since I've been fishin.'"[27]

With Vaniman's brother-in-law Louis Loud returning as assistant engineer, five of the planned six spots aboard the *America* were filled. Wellman said he was approached by three wealthy New Yorkers who offered $5,000 apiece for the opportunity, but Wellman turned them all down in favor of nineteen-year-old Fred Aubert, who first had to ask his mother's permission and who had nothing to offer but his enthusiasm and mechanical skills.[28] Personal connections may have been decisive. Wellman had known the Aubert family for years, and his youngest daughter, seventeen-year-old Rebekah, was Fred's sweetheart. "Beck" was "known to her friends as a girl of bravery and daring" and took a strong interest in her father's aerial work. To her great disappointment, she was unsuccessful in convincing her father to let her join the transatlantic airship crew. When this failed, she may have lobbied on Fred's behalf instead.[29]

Wellman said almost nothing in print about his family, and only a few of his personal letters survive, but the Wellman girls seem to have had a modern and independent streak. On September 3 Laura Wellman and three of her daughters drove an automobile, still a machine of questionable reliability, from their summer home in Gloucester, Massachusetts, to Atlantic City—or 370 miles on the barely improved dirt roads that passed for highways in 1910.[30] Adventurous journeys were becoming a Wellman family tradition.

Of the two remaining Wellman daughters, Rose was already in Atlantic City with her husband, LeRoy Chamberlin, who was serving as Walter's personal secretary. Nineteen-year-old Rita, who had run away a year earlier to join a theater company, was now studying in New York City and keeping company with a thirty-three-year-old stockbroker and tennis player named Edgar Leo. Rita didn't know it yet, but she was pregnant.[31]

All was not well in the Wellman family, though perhaps only Walter knew the secret of two other out-of-wedlock births. Even as he prepared to risk his life in the air, Wellman was playing a dangerous game at home. He had not one family but two, and both were in Atlantic City. A photo in Wellman's

Fig. 18. Penciled on the back of this photo are the words "Daddy Walter—My Boy and the Air Ship America—Atlantic City—October 1910." Walter Jr. was the son of Wellman's mistress Bergljot Bergersen. Smithsonian National Air and Space Museum (NASM 9A10732).

personal collection, taken in the Atlantic City hangar, shows him holding a little boy about two years old. Penciled on the back are the words: "Daddy Walter—My Boy and the Air Ship America—Atlantic City—October 1910."[32]

Walter Wellman Jr. had been born in Washington DC in 1908 to a twenty-six-year-old Norwegian woman named Bergljot Bergersen. Her second child by Wellman, Elsa, had been born earlier in 1910 in France.[33] Little is known about Wellman and Bergersen's relationship. Apparently Wellman's heartfelt remorse of 1899 had faded at least by 1907, the year of his first polar flight. But unlike his earlier mistress (and unlike any others he may have had over the years), Miss Bergersen and her children were not going away. As the photo indicates, Wellman didn't want her to, either.

24

The Airship, Bringer of Total War and Universal Peace

Osawatomie, Kansas, and Atlantic City, New Jersey, August–September 1910

While Wellman fussed over the details of his airship voyage and his complicated personal life, the political world he had once covered rolled on without him.

"Keeping still is the most arduous assignment in the world for him," Wellman had written of Theodore Roosevelt back in May, predicting that his volatile nature would soon draw him back into the thick of the fight.[1] On August 31 this prediction proved correct.

That day Roosevelt delivered a major speech titled "The New Nationalism" in Osawatomie, Kansas. He didn't name Taft directly, but listeners interpreted the speech as a denunciation of the current president and, perhaps, a promise of what to expect from a new Roosevelt administration.

Osawatomie was best known for its association with radical abolitionist John Brown, and something of Brown's warrior soul seemed to be marching on with Roosevelt's measured words. At least Republican leaders thought so.[2] If Roosevelt had made Wall Street interests uneasy before, he incensed them now.

He said, "The essence of any struggle for healthy liberty has always been, and must always be, to take from some one man or class of men the right to enjoy power, or wealth, or position, or immunity, which has not been earned by service to his or their fellows."[3]

Roosevelt said he supported the rights of property and did not oppose the accumulation of wealth, but the growing power of the capitalist class threatened the liberty of all. To provide a "square deal" for all citizens, corporate power had to be reined in.[4]

"There can be no effective control of corporations while their political activity remains. . . . It is necessary that laws should be passed to prohibit the use of corporate funds directly or indirectly for political purposes; it is still more necessary that such laws should be thoroughly enforced."[5]

Back in 1908 Wellman had denied that corporate money swayed elections, even while demonstrating that Republican leaders believed firmly that it did. Wellman may have been blindly inconsistent, or he may have been coy, but now Roosevelt openly denounced it as "one of the principal sources of corruption in our political affairs." He went further: "I believe that the officers, and, especially, the directors, of corporations should be held personally responsible when any corporation breaks the law."[6]

To further guard against dangerous concentrations of wealth, Roosevelt called for a graduated income tax and an inheritance tax on big fortunes, "properly safeguarded against evasion, and increasing rapidly in amount with the size of the estate."[7]

In Washington Taft was alarmed by the words of the man who had once been his close friend.[8] In Atlantic City Wellman was preoccupied. Back in May he had all but encouraged Roosevelt to challenge Taft in 1912. Now he wrote nothing for print except copy related to his upcoming flight. But Wellman hadn't forgotten the larger world or the progressive changes he desired for it. In fact, he was working on his own policy speech.

On September 15 in Atlantic City, Wellman addressed a group of prominent Pennsylvanians on the subject of war and peace, which, he insisted, was the main point of his attempt to fly across the ocean:

We believe that the airship will do more than any other single agency to bring about universal peace. War is barbaric, and should be obsolete. The way to make war impossible is to make it so destructive that all the world will at once see that it is suicide and crime to go to war.

Vaniman and I believe we know how to adapt airships to warfare in such a manner as to make armed conflict almost inconceivably terrible and ruinous. If we are right, a fleet of ten airships could not only destroy battleships, naval stations, fortresses, camps, bridges, arsenals, and strategic points, but could lay waste cities, strike terror to scores of millions of people, and overawe the most courageous and resourceful nation.

When it comes to war in the air, when great aerial fleets may devastate not only the high seas but the land and the centres of population, paralyze industry and annihilate wealth, there will be no more wars. That is what we aim at in our trans-Atlantic effort, to demonstrate the value of the plans which we shall soon afterward be prepared to submit to the principal governments.[9]

These claims were pretentious, but as usual Wellman reflected the spirit of the times. He had first written about aerial warfare and its potential to make war impossible in 1894, but even then he wasn't the first to predict it or to dream of building a superweapon so destructive that it would force nations to make peace.[10] Born of the Enlightenment, the idea had grown up with the industrial might of the United States and Europe.

After witnessing the first manned balloon flights in Paris in 1783, Benjamin Franklin wrote that "Convincing Sovereigns of the Folly of Wars may perhaps be one effect, since it will be impracticable for the most potent of them to guard his Dominions." Anticipating Wellman's calculations, Franklin estimated that "five thousand Balloons, capable of raising two Men each, could not cost more than Five ships of the line." No nation could afford to guard every part of its territory against "Ten Thousand Men descending from the Clouds."[11]

Robert Fulton, another American who was best remembered as the inventor of the first practical steamboat, spent years developing a series of experimental weapons that he promoted variously to the governments of France, Britain, and the United States. In 1797 he proposed to the French government a plan for a submarine he called the *Nautilus*, which for its time was a highly advanced forerunner of the modern naval submarine.[12] Though the *Nautilus* showed some promise in tests, Fulton soon dismantled it and turned his attention to "torpedoes," as anchored mines were then known. Moving to Britain in 1804, he worked as a paid consultant for the navy he had formerly promised to destroy, but British interest in his experiments ended in 1805 with Horatio Nelson's victory over the French at Trafalgar. Fulton returned to the United States, where he continued his torpedo experiments with a view toward arming the United States against the British. During the War of 1812 he designed the world's first steam-powered warship, the *Demologos*, to defend New York Harbor

against the Royal Navy, but both the war and Fulton's life ended before the ship saw any action.[13]

One could dismiss Fulton as an unprincipled mercenary or as a dreamer whose ideas outran his era's technological capacity, but in some ways he was a prototype of the industrial age weapons inventor. In his 1810 book *Torpedo War, and Submarine Explosions*, he articulated a rationale that was echoed by generations of writers and inventors.[14] The world, Fulton observed, was now menaced by modern offensive weapons that could "carry destruction to every harbor on earth." Since they were the result of science, could not science also destroy the fleets it had created "and give to the seas the liberty which shall secure perpetual peace between nations?"[15]

Fulton said he wasn't particular about which nation's fleet was destroyed first because his torpedoes "will be an effectual cure for so great an evil . . . [that] blowing up English ships of war, or French, or American, were there no other, and the men on shore, would be humane experiments of the first importance."[16] By making navies indefensible, Fulton would abolish them.

Similarly, in 1835 Alfred Lord Tennyson looked toward a future of aerial warfare while expressing hope for humanity in his poem "Locksley Hall," in which he wrote of "the nations' airy navies grappling in the central blue . . . / Till the war-drum throbb'd no longer, and the battle-flags were furl'd / In the Parliament of man, the Federation of the world."[17]

In 1891 dynamite inventor Alfred Nobel told Austrian countess and peace activist Bertha von Suttner, "Perhaps my factories will put an end to war sooner than your congresses: on the day that two army corps can mutually annihilate each other in a second, all civilised nations will surely recoil with horror and disband their troops."[18] By then Nobel was already thinking about his legacy. After his brother died in 1888, a French newspaper had mistakenly printed an obituary of Alfred. Headlined "The Merchant of Death Is Dead," it accused Nobel of becoming "rich by finding ways to kill more people faster than ever before."[19] With such condemnation in mind, Nobel made his remarks to the countess and later endowed his famous prizes.

By the time of Wellman's speech, bookstores and magazines had long carried a variety of science fiction stories describing future wars.[20] Some stories were meant to scare the American public into greater military spending; others, such as Mark Twain's *A Connecticut Yankee in King*

Arthur's Court (1889), are apocalyptic tales in which those who employ technological warfare are destroyed by it as well.

The dawning aerial age only heightened existing hopes and fears. In *The War in the Air* (1908), H. G. Wells describes an ever-expanding world war involving aeroplanes and airships, including a graphic account of an aerial bombardment of New York City. By the novel's end, civilization is in tatters, and survivors must relearn old-fashioned skills and scrape a living from the land. Jack London, meanwhile, stoked fears of a "yellow peril" in essays and a short story. His science fiction tale "The Unparalleled Invasion" appeared in *McClure's* in July 1910, while construction of Wellman's airship hangar was under way. In the story, an industrialized China floods the world with its teeming population until at last arises a hero, an American scientist who in 1976 arranges an aerial attack to exterminate the "yellow populace" with a new biological superweapon. Once the "sanitation of China" is complete, the land is resettled by white Westerners.

Thus, whatever Wellman's audience thought about his chances of crossing the ocean, his ideas about the military uses of airships were neither outlandish nor even surprising. With each new demonstration of aerial prowess, a feeling was growing that aviation—coupled with other new technologies—was about to change war into something unrecognizable, turning the entire world into a battlefield from which there would be no retreat.[21]

People responded to this in two ways. Some concluded that their nation must therefore gain the technological upper hand so as to dominate (and if necessary, exterminate) its rivals. Others followed Franklin and Fulton in thinking that technology's growing destructive power would be its own solution. Both camps promised an eventual, lasting peace. The first assumed that one nation or coalition would gain a permanent advantage and impose a hegemonic peace. The second looked to a permanent stalemate in which all sides could attack but none could successfully defend; the resulting peace would come from what a future generation would call mutual assured destruction. Unlike their Cold War counterparts, however, believers in stalemate assumed that the world's armies and navies would become useless and be dismantled.[22]

Wellman identified with the second camp, as it appealed not only to his internationalism but more importantly to his belief in the inevitability of

human progress, one he shared with many of the world's educated people. It's easy to see the intuitive appeal. Science and technology were manifestations of human progress; since advanced weaponry was the result of science, it too must be part of the march of progress. It cut against the narrative grain to think that science applied to warfare could set human civilization back or even end it entirely. The idea that human progress could be deeply ironic had not yet gained traction.

What was needed was a demonstration to convince the world of the growing folly of war. Would it require a destroyed fleet as Fulton predicted or an all-but-ruined civilization as Wells predicted? Or could this vital transformation in thought be prompted by a single, spectacular flight across the Atlantic Ocean?

Wellman hoped to demonstrate both the futility of conventional navies, which he foresaw could be destroyed by fleets of relatively inexpensive airships, and the vulnerability of nations—even the isolated United States, shielded by vast oceans—in the aerial age. The only sane policy necessitated that nations commit to peaceful means of resolving their differences. Ever the optimist, Wellman believed the world's great men would behave rationally once they knew the facts.

In their own ways, Wellman and Roosevelt each sought to redefine power and its relationship to the people—Roosevelt by subsuming capital to the greater public good and Wellman by using technology to make irrelevant the barbaric power of armies and navies. The nineteenth century had been a time of labor strife, growing nationalism, and ever-expanding armies; the twentieth brought hope for a new age of peace and enlightenment.

That was the dream, anyway, but Wellman's role in it depended on a successful flight. Without that, his speech would only make his unfulfilled plans sound even more grandiose and his failure even more liable to public ridicule.

25

The Aero-Not

Atlantic City, August–October 1910

Delays mounted through summer. The initial *New York Times* report on July 9 had said Wellman would depart during the "last part of August or early in September." Vaniman was more specific when he arrived in New York on August 1: "We will probably start on August 20 . . . we are not considering defeat." He added that they sought the English coast, "but I want to do more than that. I hope we will be able to land in London, thus making a real New York to London flight."[1]

Wellman usually hedged his statements by saying that he was not afraid to try and fail, but Vaniman's confidence bordered on arrogance. He boasted that the *America* would not condescend to race with Atlantic liners because "I believe we would outclass them."[2]

Colleagues remembered Vaniman as taciturn, hardworking, and self-centered, though possessing a sense of humor.[3] Wellman described his partner as unemotional, "seeming to live in his machines, a part of them, and as matter of fact as they."[4] When those machines were the topic of conversation, the childless Vaniman spoke of them like a proud parent.[5]

By the time the airship reached Atlantic City on August 8, Vaniman was already expressing frustration with delays, but he hoped to make up time with the French machinists he brought from Paris and begin trial flights the next week.[6] The gasbag was not even unpacked for another ten days, however, by which time test flights were rescheduled for ten days later.[7] On August 30 the *Times* reported that the gasbag was nearly three-fourths full and that a "serious attempt" to cross the ocean would be made within two weeks.[8] Through September the *Times* kept up a refrain of *next week* or the *next two weeks*.[9]

Filling the gasbag was the easy part. A thousand other details kept a hundred-man crew busy day and night.[10] The great hangar was complete by

August 18, and the gasbag was inflated with air and checked for leaks, and then filled with hydrogen and checked again. Every inch of the envelope's four thousand square yards of fabric had to be inspected; even pinprick holes were repaired.[11] Reporters marveled that "a diagram was made of each yard of cloth or section and each one numbered, and as the examination was made it was checked off like a huge globular checkerboard."[12]

Attaching the new car was equally painstaking; stress loads on the balloon fabric had to balance perfectly. The *Times* reported on August 19 that this would take several days, but it took a month.[13] Several major systems had to be assembled, tested, and installed: motors and new propellers; electric lights and speaking tubes for the car; a wireless receiver and transmitter; the equilibrator and the winch by which Loud would be lowered to retrieve fuel tanks; canvas covering and celluloid windows for the car, plus a coat of asbestos paint to keep sparks from the exhaust from setting it on fire; navigational instruments; a lifeboat stocked with provisions; and "two thousand wire joints to be tied with hemp string so they will not wear in two through the vibration of the airship."[14]

In late September Atlantic City hosted a convention of the Grand Army of the Republic, a fraternal organization for Union Army veterans of the Civil War. Many beribboned graybeards stopped in to observe Wellman's science fiction story come to life.

"To an old military man," said Gen. Daniel Sickles, who had lost a leg to a cannonball at Gettysburg, "nothing is so clear as the fact that it is often the most inconsequential item that determines the final success or failure."[15]

The airship was made up of thousands of such "inconsequential" items, all of which seemed to take longer to prepare than either Wellman or Vaniman anticipated. Determined not to be pushed up against the end of the season as in Spitsbergen, they seemed to forget that the *America* was once again a mostly brand-new ship filled with experimental technology.

By mid-September growing crowds came to gaze at the airship that required twelve thousand pounds of sandbags to hold it slightly above the hangar floor.[16] As in Spitsbergen the *America* was not entirely sheltered from the wind; on September 16 a forty-mile-per-hour gale made the ship wobble, bob, and strain at its ropes. Wellman left a team of watchmen on duty all night to prevent damage if they could.[17] The season was turning.

Strong winds were becoming more common, and by early October flocks of southbound geese passed overhead.[18]

The greatest weather risk would not be at mid-ocean. Away from land they could run before the wind if need be, and a westerly wind would carry them that much quicker to Europe. The real danger was being blown back upon the coast, where on land the equilibrator would catch like an anchor, holding the airship fast while the wind battered it down to the ground.

An even more humiliating risk was being wrecked by a gust of wind while exiting the hangar. On September 30 Wellman announced that a hundred local high school boys would serve as his ground crew. Without actually handling the airship, they were drilled on how to march it out of the hangar, swing it around to check the compass, and hold it while the equilibrator was attached at the water's edge. A hundred longshoremen had already tried out but had failed to develop as a team. Wellman reasoned that boys with high school military training were more likely to follow orders. Local lifeguards and boat captains would also assist. Vaniman warned that with any wind at all, the task "will be harder than holding ten thousand mad monkeys."[19]

Success would depend on the weather. The big 200-horsepower motor had not been completed in time; they would have to make do with two motors of 80 horsepower each. The first was a four-cylinder Lorraine-Dietrich engine, similar to the one they'd used last year; the second, a British-built eight-cylinder arranged in a new configuration known as an ENV, which was British slang for what the French called an *en vee* and what Americans would later call a v-8. The plan was to run one motor while cooling and servicing the other. But even both running at once wouldn't give them enough power or range to fight headwinds. They must launch only when they had several days of favorable winds ahead of them.[20] Wellman, naturally, had a high-tech plan to improve their odds of doing so.

Professor Willis Moore of the U.S. Weather Bureau had long published monthly North Atlantic wind forecasts based on reports from vessel masters.[21] Wellman studied Moore's records in detail while planning his trip, and Moore began wiring him daily bulletins from Washington as the *America* prepared for departure. Such a high-profile venture allowed Moore to demonstrate the value of adding wireless technology

to weather forecasting, and his office began gathering real-time updates from wireless-equipped ships at sea. Combined with meteorological data from land stations across the Northern Hemisphere, Moore compiled weather charts that were more comprehensive and current than anything previously possible.[22]

Newspapers criticized Wellman for planning to cross the ocean "in a vessel in which he dares not cross the boardwalk in a wind," but Wellman replied that "it would be about as fair to smite a steamship builder because he does not launch his vessel in the fiercest storm she is expected to weather after going to sea."[23] Still, as the early weeks of October passed, the public grew impatient as Wellman passed up calm days in Atlantic City because of telegrams from Washington.

"All Mr. Wellman wants of the weather is a dead calm around the hangar and a brisk west wind blowing everywhere else," said one sarcastic critic. "That's all he's been asking, and the dinged weather can't seem to get to it."[24]

Wellman trusted Moore's bulletins implicitly—more, apparently, than even some of his crew.

"Personally I'm very content to sit out the waiting period," Murray Simon told reporters in his working-class English brogue on October 1. "I know we're going to laugh last, for we're going to get across, and there you are."

But Simon's patience had its limits, as did his appreciation for Professor Moore's newfangled weather forecasting. By October 11 the *Times* reported that the crew had grown restless. Some members "who take their weather wisdom from the local skippers"—probably led by Simon, the group's only sailor—"insist that the ocean is already fit for eastward sailing."[25]

Wireless man Jack Irwin was hospitalized on October 5 after burning his foot with sulfuric acid from the hydrogen-making plant. Hearing a good weather report on October 12, Irwin left the hospital and limped into the hangar, where that afternoon Vaniman gave orders to clear away ballast and strip the netting from the top of the airship.[26] Irwin flashed goodbye messages to his fellow wireless operators along the coast . . . but then Wellman arrived and called it off, citing the weather.[27]

Rival papers had Wellman putting in an appearance at the hangar three hours after Vaniman had declared conditions perfect and "had pleaded over the telephone with Wellman to get out of bed and join them in the venture

at sea. The general public of the resort are beginning to look on the Wellman balloon and the Wellman declarations of intention as seashore jokes."[28]

There would probably be no test flights. Vaniman had already suggested publicly that they should skip them due to the risks involved in taking the ship out of the hangar and returning it. J. W. Salus, president of the local group supporting Wellman, released a statement on October 12 noting while their contract with Wellman called for trial flights, by which hotel owners might recover the $12,000 they had spent building the hangar, they would "cheerfully abrogate that clause" for the good of the expedition.[29]

Salus addressed one other thing in his statement. Rumors of unpaid debts and a "$2,000 sheriff's attachment" on the airship had been circulating for more than a month.[30] Salus called the rumors "wholly untrue," though he may have been speaking only of the Atlantic City group's finances and not those of Wellman himself.[31] Wellman's expenses had already outrun the money he had received from his newspaper sponsors, a difference he was making up out of his own pocket. A deal with *Hampton's Magazine*, announced on October 3, would pay him an undisclosed amount that was said to match what Peary received for his North Pole narrative, provided that Wellman actually made a flight. And if he did cross the Atlantic, publisher Benjamin Hampton predicted that Wellman could easily net $1 million in book rights and speaking fees in two or three years.[32]

All those speculative dollars were still only so much "hot air" (as newspapers were fond of saying of Wellman's hydrogen airship), and public doubt was festering into open ridicule. The *New Orleans Times-Democrat* dubbed Wellman the "aero-not," while another wag wrote:

"I will not fly," said Wellman,
"Because it looks like rain,
I'll wait until tomorrow
Before I try again."

"I will not fly," said Wellman,
"Because the wind's too strong,
If all is fair tomorrow
I'll rise and sail along."

"I will not fly," said Wellman,
"The day is much too calm,
I'll wait until tomorrow
With patience as my balm." Etc.[33]

Another reporter described Wellman's "Spartan regimen" in which the explorer rose from

his rough Louis XIV couch on the side of the Chalfonte [Hotel] that is entirely exposed to the uncouth and untamed ocean and ate the frugal but sustaining meal which wide experience at the wildest hotels along Broadway and other channels of travel has taught him is the best for adventurers. He rarely has more than steak, eggs, buckwheat cakes, potatoes, fruit, biscuits and coffee for breakfast.

A pause in training might be expected here, but Mr. Wellman is made of sterner stuff. He returned to his room, got his strength together, and when a newspaperman called up and asked "when the old gas-bag was going up," Mr. Wellman told him to go where a gas-bag would explode.[34]

Wellman claimed that the negative press didn't bother him, but it had never been this intense. Coast to coast he was denounced as a fraud, a fakir, the Dr. Cook of aviation. The *Los Angeles Herald* made what it thought was a cruel analogy by noting that Wellman "is again 'preparing' for his ocean balloon trip; and, it may be added, Nicola Tesla is still working on those electrical wonders announced in 1896 for early use."[35]

Wellman finally let his anger slip during an October 12 interview with the *New York Times*. He boasted that the "cowards who question motives and sincerity without knowing anything of the facts will neither hasten nor retard our departure a single moment," but he added, "we shall be bitterly disappointed if anything prevents our actual start within twenty-four hours."[36]

In his growing disdain, Wellman shared good company. In the fall of 1909, Wilbur Wright faced a New York crowd eager for him to fly his aeroplane despite inclement weather. Wright told a reporter: "These people who do not know me would not, in the nature of things, care particularly

if I should be hurt. They might even enjoy the excitement. Do you see those photographers? They would get better pictures if I should fall. No, I shall not fly until the wind is just right."[37]

One of Wellman's most prominent critics didn't accuse him of fakery or cowardice; instead, it did the opposite. In early October *Scientific American* ran an illustrated feature and follow-up editorial, saying that "one cannot but be impressed by the splendid equipment" and that the airship was "well designed for its tremendous task." Still, Wellman was about to attempt a three-thousand-mile flight when no airship had yet gone five hundred miles.[38]

"With the last doubt removed that Wellman is seriously attempting to make the passage of the Atlantic with his airship, we can only say that he and his associates are running a race against chance and accident, with the odds heavily against the dirigible," the editors wrote. Telling how last year's flight was ended by a broken equilibrator, they argued that this unexpected accident "shows the impossibility of guarding against every eventuality, and emphasizes the necessity of making thorough tests of an equipment in actual practice before starting on a hazardous venture."[39] The likelihood of failure due to lack of testing "can only be chargeable to inexcusable neglect; and it is just here, we think, that the chief peril of this most extraordinary undertaking lies."[40]

Wellman had no harsh words for *Scientific American*. When asked, he called it a fair statement of the challenges. As for the trip being foolhardy, Wellman said his answer would have to come from what he and his crew accomplished.[41]

By then Wellman was aware of a major issue not addressed in *Scientific American*. The airship was overweight by about four thousand pounds. So great was the *America's* lifting capacity that it would still rise under this added load, but to compensate it would have to carry only fifty-five hundred pounds of fuel instead of nine thousand. Now they desperately needed a tailwind, and Wellman became even more determined to wait for a good forecast, public impatience be damned.

"Probably it is possible to find mechanics and constructors who can take a rational engineering plan and carry it out pretty close to the schedule

of weight and cost, but I have never been fortunate enough to find one," he wrote later.[42]

He cited the lifeboat as an example. Custom built on the Isle of Wight, the boat's twenty-seven-foot hull was made of three layers of mahogany veneer and had watertight compartments fore and aft to make it "unsink-able." In flight it would carry the gasoline stove for cooking and the Marconi wireless set. Irwin would bring along a kite and antenna wire so he could keep broadcasting if they had to launch the boat. With thirty days' water and provisions, plus a mast, a sail, and even oars as a last resort, the lifeboat was designed to carry the crew into the busy Atlantic shipping lanes to await rescue.[43]

Wellman had stipulated that the boat was not to exceed a thousand pounds. The builder told him it weighed only eight hundred, but it tipped the scale in Atlantic City at twice that number.

But that was only part of the problem. Vaniman had supervised much of the work that spring while Wellman was chasing Theodore Roosevelt up the Nile. Wellman likened Vaniman to other mechanics in that he was "naturally more keen about strength than for adhering closely to a weight schedule"; but Wellman's own calculations may have been overly optimistic. Also he probably did business only with contractors who agreed up front to meet his short deadlines and low weights.[44] It wasn't that contractors deceived him, necessarily, about their ability to meet his requirements. They may simply have dealt with Wellman in the same way Wellman dealt with own his patrons—that is, declaring confidently that they would find a way to do what had never been done. Whether you were a contractor, explorer, or newspaper publisher, you had to promise more than you could deliver just to gain the attention of the people who controlled access to the object of your desire.

Wellman was soon vindicated in calling off the October 12 launch. He had received an updated weather bulletin in which Moore changed his forecast and warned of high winds from the east. This proved accurate. Had they launched, the *New York Times* told its readers the next day, the *America* would have been driven ashore in fifty-mile-per-hour winds, wrecking as soon as the equilibrator anchored on land.[45]

It would take at least a few more days for the weather to clear. A hurricane was forming off the coast of Cuba. "If it passes up the Atlantic Coast, out to sea," Wellman said, "we will try to jump out in front of it." With proper timing they could save fuel by riding the cyclone's clockwise rotation across the Atlantic.[46]

The next few days were filled with rumors and last-minute changes. Unwilling to trust their launch entirely to the hands of high school boys and lifeguards, Vaniman arranged to have teams of police officers and firemen join the ground crew. After all the negative press, this required some persuasion:

"Are you sure your balloon will ever go up?" asked the police chief. "My men would hardly relish a trip out there again only to be told that the weather did not look right."

"Well," replied Mr. Vaniman, who has taken in good part a great deal of chafing about the postponed departure, "there's a way you can get us off. All you've got to do is to let go after we get out of the shed once, and then we'll have to go. We'll be in your hands.... If you think we ought to go and you find us wanting to be switched back again—well, you see, it's what you do and not what we want that counts."[47]

That settled them. Vaniman would have his extra men, and as far as he and they were concerned, there would be no turning back once the airship was out of the hangar.

A seventh member was added to the airship crew on October 11. His name was Jean Jacon, a French mechanic who had worked as Vaniman's assistant for two years.[48] With growing concerns for the ship's weight, Wellman soon bumped Fred Aubert from the flight crew, preferring Jacon's greater experience. But Jacon suddenly quit the expedition, claiming that Wellman owed him $490 in back pay.[49] Young Aubert had his spot back just as the weather began clearing.

The *New York Times* said the rest of the crew "had their own suspicions" as to why the Frenchman suddenly "preferred the land to the air lane."[50] Other papers said Wellman was facing a "situation practically amounting to a mutiny," as the *Washington Times* put it, with Simon's threatening to leave the expedition or, in a different version, with Vaniman and Simon's

Fig. 19. The 1910 crew of the airship *America. Left to right:* Murray Simon, Walter Wellman, Melvin Vaniman, Fred Aubert, Jack Irwin, and Louis Loud. From *Literary Digest* 41, no. 18 (October 29, 1910): 732.

leading the crew in informing Wellman that they were departing with or without him.[51]

Laura Wellman soon dismissed the mutiny stories as "utterly silly," but even the *Times* acknowledged that Simon "had chafed perhaps more than any other member of the crew at the enforced delays of the last two weeks."[52] In fairness, reporters may have misread Simon. Though something of a hothead and prone to speaking his mind, he had served as an officer on an ocean liner; he knew how to take orders with which he disagreed.

Wellman still trusted him. He left Simon in charge at the hangar on the crucial night of October 14 after Wellman and Vaniman left for their hotel. Moore said the wind could die down by morning. It would be up to Simon to notify them early if conditions looked favorable.[53]

Wellman had written long ago of how the press and public had hounded Andrée into an ill-advised departure that amounted to virtual suicide. That night at the Hotel Chalfonte—with his wife and daughters present and with his lists, charts, and tables of figures—Wellman might have considered Andrée's words the day of his departure: "My companions insist on

starting, and as I have no absolutely valid reasons against it I shall agree to it, although with reluctance."[54]

The telephone rang at 4:20 a.m. It was Simon. The rain had stopped, and the wind was dying down.[55]

Vaniman arrived at the hangar before Wellman did. "We will never get anything like as perfect weather conditions for flight again," he said.[56] As dawn approached, the fog was heavy, but the air at last was still.

Wellman gave the order to prepare for departure, but the crew was already at work.[57] The press, the fund-raising, the rumors and criticism, the men's enthusiasm—all of this Wellman had been stirring up for months or for years, when counting the polar flights, and it had long since gained a momentum of its own. If he felt any hesitation about going through with the launch (and he never acknowledged any), it was almost beside the point. Stopping now was as unthinkable as stopping mid-ocean. The journey had begun long ago. This was only the next inevitable step.

26

It's Europe or Bust from This Minute On

Atlantic City, October 15, 1910

The papers didn't say which Wellman daughter drove the speeding automobile that delivered Walter to the hangar in the predawn darkness, but we can guess it was adventurous Rebekah. Her mother and sister Rose were in the car too. If the other three daughters arrived separately, it wasn't recorded.[1]

Onlookers made their way up the boardwalk in the gray light of a foggy morning. The *America* waited in the dark hangar, twelve and a half tons of metal, fuel, sandbags, and fabric floating "upon such an even balance that one could push the whole mass up or down with one hand."[2] A hundred men stood ready to walk the airship out of the hangar. Most of them were uniformed police, firemen, and lifeguards. Once the sandbags were untied, the ground crew would control a ship having excess lift (or "lifting force") equal to about four tons. Vaniman warned:

> Keep in mind that her lifting force as she is now weighed down is only 8,000 pounds. Your combined weight is 10,000 pounds, so don't let go in fright if a wind begins to make her dance. Stick to her. As soon as she clears the hangar, point her nose into the wind and then swing her to where the lifeboat will be waiting. When that is attached, march on again to the sea front and wait for the equilibrator.[3]

Thus, the whole mission—and what was left of Wellman's reputation—was literally in the hands of an amateur crew. If the men botched their work and wrecked the airship, or let go prematurely, Wellman would not make an Atlantic flight this year and probably not ever.

But the air was damp and still, and upon command the men guided the great ship effortlessly out to the waterfront to the cheers of the growing

crowd.[4] When the lifeboat was attached, there were handshakes all around, and Wellman hugged his family goodbye. Then he and his khaki-clad crew climbed into the boat—all but Vaniman—and up the rope ladder to the car, already weary from a lack of sleep and too many long days of anxiety and public criticism.

The crowd cheered again.

"Up and across!" onlookers shouted.

"Up for a trial," Wellman corrected, "and only if the going's good up and over."[5]

Vaniman, still on the ground and dressed in an old gray suit, was having none of it. "Not much you won't," he told Wellman. "There will be nothing doing right now but the trip all the way across. We have delayed too long already and the weather is too good to miss now. It's Europe or bust with us from this minute on."[6]

Vaniman suddenly ran a hundred yards back into the grass, far enough to see the *America* in full. After his varied career, at last he felt sure of his true calling, and it was this. His experience with both aeroplanes and dirigibles had taught him that dirigibles were the true airships of the future, at least for large tasks. His personal mission was to make it so. He stood for a full minute just looking at the airship—*his* airship, more than it was Wellman's, by now—then returned with tears in his eyes and climbed aboard to prolonged cheering.[7]

"We won't come back until we have had a try at Europe," he told his wife.[8]

But even Vaniman was not the last crew member to board. Ida Vaniman carried aboard the ship's mascot, a gray kitten known as Kiddo, and placed him in the car.[9] Wellman had already carried the first airship dogs in the two attempts to reach the North Pole. Now he would carry the first airship cat as he tried to cross the Atlantic.

Vaniman was right; this was no test flight. "Up for a trial" seems to have been Wellman's way of managing public perceptions in case a mechanical problem forced them back to shore. He admitted later that on that day he "had no great degree of confidence" in reaching Europe. He also conceded that making a trial flight would have been more prudent, but with "the season so far advanced and the stormy November hastening on, to stop for [a] trial would probably have meant no voyage whatever this

Fig. 20. Launch of the Atlantic flight, October 15, 1910. Fred Aubert stands on the rope ladder between the car and lifeboat while Wellman looks from the doorway. The man to Aubert's left appears to be Louis Loud. From *Scientific American* 103, no. 18 (October 29, 1910): 341.

year. And what would have happened then? Why, we should have been accused of being poseurs, and worse."[10]

For all his professed disdain of public opinion, Wellman believed there "was nothing for it under the circumstances, but to . . . stake our all, lives included, upon the single cast of the die. . . . We preferred our adventure, no matter what its outcome, and the criticism which might follow having it with an untested ship, to the more prudent method of preliminary trial trips, to be inevitably followed by criticism because there was no adventure at all."[11]

Vaniman was still in the lifeboat when he gave the order to let the ship up fifty feet to pick up the equilibrator. Carried by men marching in single file, the three-hundred-foot-long chain of gasoline tanks "looked like a Chinese dragon that sometimes winds a tortuous way through village parades and town processions."[12]

Determined to avoid last year's disaster, Vaniman had designed the new equilibrator for greater strength and durability. The metal tanks were

joined by steel cable, with oil-lubricated ball-and-socket couplings and felt pads at each joint. Even so, it sustained damage before the *America* was even under way. Crossing a seawall, one police officer dropped his end and punctured two tanks.[13]

"It's only a surplus store of gasoline anyhow," Vaniman called down from the lifeboat, "and salt water's almost as good as ballast."[14]

Vaniman knew better than that, and so did Wellman. They were already short of fuel unless they found a tailwind, but Van would allow nothing to stop them today. If only they could just get started, somehow they'd find a way to make it across.

With the order to "let go all," the men on shore dropped the lines, and the *America* rose, connected only by a towrope to the motor launch that would tow the airship away from the shore. But the airship didn't rise much; it was so heavy that only about a tenth of the equilibrator came up out of the water instead of half as Wellman had planned. It would have to do. The ship would grow lighter as its motors burned off fuel.[15]

Towed away from the shore, Wellman and the others looked down to see the crowd and hangar fade into the fog. Only the sound of cheering remained.

"'Now,' we said to ourselves," Simon wrote, "'let those landlubbers who are afraid of their own shadows and who like to criticise others, let the blighters go to blazes.'"[16]

On shore, reporters surrounded Laura Wellman and Ida Vaniman, both of whom played their appointed roles almost perfectly. Dry eyed, they expressed perfect confidence in the crew's safety and spoke cheerfully of their plans to meet their husbands in Europe. Mrs. Wellman let slip only the fear that something would force them to turn around: "I just dread to think of them coming back," she said.[17]

As the *America* rose into the air, only one crewmember expressed serious doubts about the wisdom of the expedition and did so with such a howl of fear and indignation that some of the men began to think that an airship was no place for a cat.[18]

Though still a kitten, Kiddo had already lived a life of danger. Billy Bonsall was Wellman's night watchman at the hangar. One night at the end of June, when work on the building had begun, Billy saw an automobile

drop a bundle in the road. He shouted, but the car sped away. Billy was unnerved at first to see the bundle twitching, but hearing faint meows he opened it to discover two gray kittens, who then came to live in the hangar. Dogs killed one of the kittens in August, but Kiddo took up residence in *America*'s car and became a favorite of the crew. They had planned for weeks to take him along.[19]

Kiddo had been asleep at the time of launch, indifferent to the cheering crowd. But once aloft, he began "rushing around the airship like a squirrel in a cage," as Simon put it.[20] Simon was at the wheel when Irwin shouted from lifeboat, "This cat is raising hell! I believe it's going mad!"

But when Irwin suggested leaving Kiddo behind, Simon—drawing on generations of sailor folklore—warned, "We must keep the cat at all costs. We can never have luck without a cat aboard."[21]

Thus, the first shipboard conference aboard the *America* concerned what to do with the cat. They were under tow; they had not started the motors yet, so it was still easy to talk. Vaniman, irritated, wanted Kiddo gone. The "momentous question" was referred to Wellman, his first command decision of the voyage.

"It all seemed rather trivial," Wellman recalled, and he told Vaniman to do as he pleased.[22] Without a thought for the history he was making, Vaniman ordered Irwin to send a wireless message back to LeRoy Chamberlin on shore before it was too late. Irwin dutifully tapped out the words exactly as Vaniman spoke them. It was the world's first wireless transmission from an aerial vessel to a shore station, a twentieth-century counterpoint to Samuel Morse's "What hath God wrought?"

ROY COME AND GET THIS GODDAM CAT.[23]

While Kiddo proclaimed his tidings of doom, Vaniman and the others formed sort of a reverse press gang, capturing the cat and stuffing him into a canvas bag. Unwilling to wait for LeRoy Chamberlin to find a boat and chase them down in the fog, Vaniman ordered Kiddo lowered by rope down toward the water's surface, where a boat carrying reporters was following them. Maybe they'd like to keep the cat as a souvenir, Vaniman reasoned. Simon recalled that they "could feel the rope vibrating and we knew that the cat was mad with rage all the time."[24]

Aboard the motorboat, the reporters had no idea what was in the bag. The next day the *Times* reported that a canvas bag, thought to contain messages, was thrown over just as the airship cut loose, but it wasn't recovered. The sea became so choppy that the boat had to turn around and head for shore. The last the reporters saw of the *America* was Vaniman in the lifeboat shouting orders to Loud and Aubert in the engine room to start the motors "and the dim outlines of Mr. Wellman seated on a cracker box in the car with Navigator Simon at the wheel."[25]

But the canvas bag wasn't lost. Once the crew saw that lowering the twitching bundle to the boat was, as one historian put it, "something like trying to thread a needle on a roller coaster," they pulled it back up.[26] Kiddo's mood had not improved.

Soon, however, the eight-cylinder motor roared to life and drowned out the cat's protestations. The *America* surged forward under its own power, "a real cruiser of the air," Wellman wrote proudly. "Down below through the fog we could see the equilibrator swimming along, for all the world like a great sea serpent, its head in the air, with a tortuous foamy wake."[27]

Simon took the first turn at the wheel. He was pleased to discover that it felt as if he were steering a ship in the water, except that he could sit down to steer.

Wellman remarked, "I'm happier now than I have been for the last four months."

Below in the lifeboat, Jack Irwin ignored his still-painful, acid-burned foot and joked "like a happy schoolboy."[28]

"All about me were radiant faces," Wellman wrote, "all save Kiddo's, it still a bit sour with strangeness; cats have no imagination, no ken of chemistry and human nature and the history of progress; no vanity in pioneering."[29] But Kiddo soon settled down, resigned at last to having been shanghaied by fools.[30]

27

Only a Question of Time

Atlantic City, New York City, and the
Long Island Coast, October 15, 1910

Back on shore, the motorboat returned with news that it wasn't clear whether the *America*'s motors were working. The airship might be helplessly adrift, or it might be making its way out to sea. No one knew what was happening on board; long voyages had always been shrouded in mystery for the people back home. But this one was already different.

In New York City a crowd was growing on Times Square, where passersby followed developments in close to real time via the *Times*'s electric press bulletin service. An early type of electric typewriter, the machine had been installed at the Times Building in July in time for the Jack Johnson–Jim Jeffries heavyweight championship fight. As news was received by telegraph, a clerk sitting at a special keyboard typed the bulletins, which were transmitted electrically to a machine that printed them in inch-and-half-high characters on a roll of paper visible through a window. The *Times* noted with pride that the *America* left Atlantic City at 8:03 a.m., and passersby on Broadway were reading about it only five minutes later. There was something intoxicating about instant news, especially when combined with a sensational event. By 9:00 a.m. the crowd was blocking the sidewalk, arguing with each other about Wellman's intentions.[1]

"They've been having a lot of fun with Wellman," one man said, "but I guess they will all eat crow now. He's making good." Not everyone agreed. This might be just another bluff. The next bulletin, or maybe the one after that, would tell the tale.[2]

Aboard the *America*, Jack Irwin sat in the lifeboat, straining to decipher dots and dashes over the engine noise. He was wearing the special

cotton-padded earphones that he and Ida Vaniman had designed while he was in the hospital.[3] They were meant to block out noise, but they could only do so much. At 10:20 a.m. they shut the motors down to allow Irwin to send a message to shore.[4] Irwin chuckled at a facetious message from one of his fellow wireless operators on shore: "So long, Jack Irwin . . . You're a goner." Then he sent a serious one of his own:

WE'RE GOING NORTHEAST BY EAST, STILL FOGGY, EVERYTHING FINE.

And it was this message, and not the earlier private one to LeRoy Chamberlin, that the *New York Times* credited as the first wireless message from an aircraft—plain but dignified.[5]

Messages were exchanged rapidly now, even after the motor was started up again. A little after eleven o'clock, Irwin sent one addressed to Laura Wellman and Ida Vaniman:

ALL GOING FINE. HEADED EAST-NORTHEAST. GOODBYE.—WELLMAN-VANIMAN.[6]

"Goodbye," as the two women explained—in case anyone missed the word's prearranged significance—meant that the *America* was definitely bound for Europe. This was no test flight.

"That's what I knew it was going to be all along," Laura Wellman said.[7]

Atlantic City and New York were fascinated by the flight itself, but they were equally enthralled with wireless communication. As word spread that messages had been received from Wellman at sea, three hours after his departure, the crowd swelled on Times Square, and the Atlantic City wireless station on Million Dollar Pier was "besieged for news."[8] Inside, Ida Vaniman, Laura Wellman, and some of the Wellman daughters heard each message directly from the wireless operator, who locked the door and took the telephone off the hook to block incoming calls.[9] Hour by hour the doubters and scoffers were gradually outnumbered. When at noon Atlantic City received warning that the Cuban hurricane was moving up the coast, people became alarmed at the thought of the brave crew facing the storm at sea.[10]

News spread among wireless-equipped ships across the North Atlantic. Irwin sometimes found his signals "jammed" by unrelated traffic from

ships with stronger transmitters than his own. The Atlantic City operator scolded one such offender:

SHUT UP YOU BLITHERING IDIOT. AN AIRSHIP'S ON THE LINE.[11]

Irwin's shipmates watched him with growing fascination. Here they were, cruising a hundred feet above the water, deep in fog and miles out to sea, while Irwin read them congratulatory messages fresh from shore. Even Vaniman, the most stoic of the group, had tears in his eyes.[12] Technology moved Van in a way that interaction with people did not.

In the lifeboat Irwin in his padded earphones was all smiles, with a cigarette dangling from his lips while he worked the wireless key and wrote in his log. "He sees a prospect of retirement from wireless work and a pretty rich job on the music hall stage," Simon reported. "He tells us we shall all be heroes, and just as soon as he gets back to land he will appear in the monologue describing the perils of the airship on the vast deep. We tell him to stop his nonsense or we will throw him overboard. Irwin responds that we can't do without him!"[13]

Beneath the carefree laughter lay the questions they had all been puzzling over for weeks. In Simon's words:

Will the balloon retain its gas, will the car be strong, how will the engines work, what sort of speed shall we make when the wind is against us, will the strength of the engines be sufficient to carry so big a craft along, will the equilibrator tug the life out of us, will the electric lighting prove satisfactory, or will it be so damaged by the vibration as to be useless; shall we have to work by torchlight and run the risk of being blown to bits in a big aerial explosion?[14]

The big eight-cylinder ENV was starting to run dangerously hot, and by 11:17 a.m. they had to shut it down. A few weeks earlier General Sickles had warned about little inconsequential items upon which a battle could turn, and now Vaniman, Loud, and Aubert discovered the tiniest of things in the motor's bearings—grains of sand blown in from the shore adjacent to the hangar.[15] That afternoon the ENV broke down entirely. Now it was up to the four-cylinder Lorraine-Dietrich to get them across the ocean.[16]

They lost wireless contact with the shore stations by 5:00 p.m. Persistent fog prevented Simon from making observations, leaving him with only a general idea of their location. In the cooling air the *America* sank closer to the waves, and the men poured out precious gasoline to lighten the ship. It galled Wellman to do so, but a lucky run of wind could still help them across.[17]

But an unlucky wind could wreck them. With so much of the equilibrator in the water, the amount of drag kept them from steering directly into the wind, which now threatened to sweep them onto the Long Island coast.[18]

Wellman called it the "night of many perils." The first was the wind itself. Simon "threw the helm as far as it would go" and tied it in place. He and Wellman called for more power, and Vaniman, Loud, and Aubert ran the Lorraine-Dietrich harder and kept it going hour after hour. Its exhaust pipe glowed red in the darkness and spewed a tail of sparks along the varnished cotton of the car, "up against the under part of the balloon itself, against the canvas rudder, and the ship's colors floating above the helm."[19]

This was the second peril. From the lifeboat Wellman watched the fireworks for several minutes, thinking all the while of "tons of volatile gasoline, half an acre of cotton," and 345,000 cubic feet of hydrogen.[20]

"Vaniman!" he shouted at last. "You must stop that motor at once!"

The propellers sputtered to a halt.

"What's the matter?" Vaniman called down from the engine room.

"Nothing but hellfire. We can't stand this. It's only a question of time when we blow up."

"It's been doing that all day," Vaniman said. "It looks lots worse than it is."

Wellman asked what could be done to stop the sparks.

"Nothing," Vaniman said.

"Nothing whatever?"

"Nothing except to stop running the motor altogether."

"And drift on the Long Island coast?"

"That's about the size of it."[21]

Wellman had a choice, but in his mind it was no choice at all, simply an unpleasant reality. "I had a particular horror of landing on Long Island," he wrote. "To leave Atlantic City for Europe and pull up some where near Montauk or Newport was not to be thought of. Even a holocaust seemed preferable to a fiasco."[22]

Wellman spent the next few hours watching the "fireworks" and calculating the odds of disaster. At some point Louis Loud climbed down from the engine room and looked up at the glowing spray of exhaust.

"Shit!" he said and sat down beside Wellman. "I don't mind what I can't see, but when I look at those globs of fire, I don't feel good." They sat in silence for a while, and then without another word Loud climbed back up into the car.[23]

Bound for Norfolk, Virginia, a four-masted schooner named the *Bullard* was running in a thick mist. Captain Sawyer was on deck about 8:00 p.m. when "the steady grind of an engine reached our ears, and we thought a steamer was close upon us."[24] Sawyer ran aft and tooted the foghorn while his sailors shouted to warn the approaching steamer's lookout.

They saw nothing but a light in the air, drawing nearer, and some of the men swore they heard voices. They all knew of Wellman, of course, but they had sailed from Boston without knowing of the *America*'s departure.[25]

"Then out of the darkness and mist shot a big aerial phantom," Sawyer reported. It was heading east, straight toward the ship, and only about a hundred feet above the water. The *Bullard*'s topmasts were 110 feet high.

"She came at us almost like the wind," the captain said.[26]

In the airship, Simon was at the wheel; Aubert, in the engine room. The others were in the lifeboat and saw topmasts under full sail. Loud recalled that they were "so near the water that the schooner's upper rigging would certainly have torn away the lifeboat with the four of us in it."[27]

Simon had been at the wheel all day and was getting tired.[28] Over the engine noise he heard a whistle from the speaking tube, then a voice: "Do you see that ship?" The *Bullard* was barely a hundred yards away.[29]

Wellman recalled ordering Vaniman to stop the motor, but when Vaniman climbed into the car, he ran forward toward Simon and said nothing to Aubert.[30] He made the right decision, as moving under power allowed Simon to steer.[31]

"I immediately jammed helm hard a-starboard and just cleared her, our bilge passing over her spanker," Simon wrote.[32] In layman's terms, the lower curve of the gasbag's left side passed over the schooner's rear-most sail. Several members of the *Bullard*'s crew said they "heard the airship scraping the topmasts as she veered off."[33]

Two sailors heard someone overhead shout "Clear the line!"—and just then the gasoline-filled equilibrator also barely missed the ship. A moment later, all that was visible was the faint glow of the airship's light.

The sailors couldn't know that the *America*'s electric lights were shut off. What they had seen was the airship's red-hot exhaust pipe.[34]

Making the most of its investment, the *New York Times* on October 16 announced Wellman's departure under the front-page headline, WELL-MAN OFF FOR EUROPE IN HIS AIRSHIP AMERICA, IN A HISTORY-MAKING VOYAGE UNDER AUSPICES OF THE TIMES.

Gone was the qualifier that the *Times* took no responsibility for the flight. An editorial crowed that Wellman had departed "to the shame of all his detractors." It went on to say that "nothing in the history of aeronautics is comparable with this courageous attempt. . . . The magnitude and difficulty of the feat he has undertaken fairly baffle the imagination, and no further proof is needed (if any was needed since the project was first made public) of his sincerity in undertaking it."[35]

For Laura Wellman the vindication was both more personal and more bitter: "For the newspapers which have been so cruel, I can take consolation in the fact that before they thought men could fly they hounded poor old Langley into his grave, and all France rang with denunciation of Wilbur Wright the morning he first took to the air." Ida Vaniman, meanwhile, reiterated her husband's hope "to rehabilitate the dirigible to the place from which aeroplanes have been crowding it."[36]

A major international aviation meet was under way at Belmont Park, New York, featuring the latest aeroplanes and many of the world's best-known pilots. The aviators were astonished that Wellman took off in a fog, something they would never do.[37]

Charlie Hamilton, one of the Wright brothers' popular pilots, had recently completed a round-trip flight from New York to Philadelphia. He noted that Wellman was "taking a big chance, but it will be a big thing even if he succeeds in reaching the Banks of Newfoundland. . . . I would not be tempted to make the attempt for a whole lot."[38]

Glenn Curtiss, the Wrights' main rival, also praised Wellman's courage but added that starting out without a "tryout flight must necessarily

lessen his chances." Curtiss thought Wellman's only hope of success was to be "caught in a storm and blown across, but I sincerely hope he will be successful."[39]

Nationwide, newspapers reported Wellman's departure with bold headlines, serious coverage, and even now and then a note of contrition.

"Walter Wellman is really off at last," said the *Washington (DC) Herald.* "Bon voyage! And we take it all back."[40]

28

The Queen of Spades

Nantucket Shoals, North Atlantic Ocean, October 16, 1910

Sunday morning came with gray light and fog. The *America* was still airborne, with its single working motor churning away and nothing but the sea in the crew's limited field of vision. Reading the water with a sailor's eye, Simon recognized shoal waters and tide rips in the waves; based on their rough log they must have been somewhere between Nantucket Island and the lightship at Nantucket Shoals. They even passed a small fishing smack, the crew of which later complained of nearly being smashed by the airship's monstrous tail.[1]

But the wind was blowing east–northeast, taking them out to sea. At last Vaniman could allow the motor to cool while they drifted broadside to the wind. After twenty hours at the wheel, Murray Simon was too tired even to climb into his hammock. He lay down beside the wheel and was soon fast asleep.[2]

Everyone was in a more cheerful mood, especially at 8:00 a.m. when Aubert cooked a hot breakfast of ham, eggs, and coffee in the lifeboat. Even Kiddo was in fine spirits while being hand-fed biscuits.[3] Irwin could hear clearly the Siasconset station on Nantucket Island—where he had famously received the *Republic*'s CQD—but didn't have enough battery power to make himself heard until later that morning when the *America* had apparently drifted closer.[4]

Siasconset: WHERE ARE YOU?

Irwin: HEAVEN ONLY KNOWS. DENSE FOG.

Even without the motor, they were making about twenty-five miles per hour east–northeast. Irwin wired that he thought he could hear the surf. Telephone calls went out across the island. Soon every lighthouse and lifesaving station on Nantucket was watching and listening, but the *America*

sailed by silently and invisibly.[5] In Wellman's words they had "escaped the humiliation of pulling up short on the coast of New England."[6]

"Now we were, indeed, out upon the great ocean," he wrote. Despite everything,

> we still had hopes, faint though they might have been, of reaching the European side. . . . Sound sense and reason told us that as we sailed hour after hour and league after league away from the continental shores toward the great central expanse of the ocean our chances of making a return to some land or picking up a ship in case of disaster must necessarily become smaller and smaller. But still it was a joy just to keep moving on.[7]

With one interview already in the morning papers, on Sunday afternoon Mrs. Wellman and Mrs. Vaniman spoke with the *New York Times* again, now more than one whole day into their husbands' flight. With no news, the women could only hope that all was well.

"I don't want to hear that he is coming back," Laura Wellman said. "I know it will crush his feelings too much, and yet I know also that if in his calm judgment he sees that it is not wise to push his journey further, he will not be afraid of any criticism that might be heaped upon him."[8]

Ida Vaniman said that she knew "all the details of the problems aboard the airship so intimately that I feel as if I were there myself, helping to fight them out. I know Mr. Vaniman did not sleep last night. I could feel it, but with an impulse so strong that it seemed almost telepathic. I ceased to worry about it at 12 o'clock to-day. 'There, now,' I said to myself, 'Melvin's asleep at last, and he knows the worst of his fight is over.'"[9]

The wind that carried the *America* out to sea also made the equilibrator leap from wave to wave, straining the airship's metal tubes and wires. All along one of the biggest uncertainties of the voyage was how the heavy tail would behave on rough seas. Wellman and Vaniman had admitted beforehand that they didn't know, though Vaniman was obviously proud of creating an altitude regulator that doubled as a reserve fuel supply. To retrieve fuel, Louis Loud could be lowered in a breeches buoy to retrieve

individual tanks. The only potential weakness was the airship itself. The equilibrator was attached to the steel-framed car, which was secured to the gasbag. Could it all withstand being tugged this way and that by a three-thousand-pound weight? They would find out.[10]

"The outlook is not so favorable, but we are keeping up the fight," Wellman had Irwin transmit at 11:00 a.m.[11]

Around noon, just as Ida Vaniman was feeling a sense of relief, a fifty-mile-per-hour gale struck the airship from the north. They started the motor and throttled up to full power to keep the airship pointed east.[12]

They lost contact with Siasconset before things got bad. Irwin heard the station responding to queries about the *America*: ALL'S WELL. GETTING ALONG FAMOUSLY. But he could no longer make himself heard.[13]

"Things commenced to look bad for us," Simon wrote. "All our hopes of getting across seem vanishing. The acting of the equilibrator and the increasing sea is something fierce, dragging us down until the seas touch the lifeboat at times, pulling and straining at the car until we expect the ship to go to pieces at any moment."[14] They jettisoned gasoline to stay above the waves.

Wellman said the equilibrator jumped "from wave to wave, fifty to eighty feet each leap," giving the airship a sickening rocking motion.[15] Everyone was worried, none more than Kiddo. "I never heard a cat make such a noise before," Simon wrote. Wrapping Kiddo in a blanket, Simon placed him in his hammock, where he lay quietly for the rest of the day.[16]

Launching the lifeboat was out of the question.[17] Whether they had realized it before or not, they saw now that the boat was fit only for fair-weather launch. If they cut loose while drifting broadside to the wind, the boat would roll sideways when it hit the waves. Even if they didn't capsize, the equilibrator would almost certainly strike them a moment later. Until the weather calmed, they needed to stay aloft if they could.[18]

"Once or twice the life boat nearly touched the crest of the waves," Wellman wrote, "if it had struck it would have been torn loose from its shackles, those of us in her would have been swamped or set adrift, while the members of the crew in the car overhead would have had no craft left in which to attempt an escape should opportunity offer. Several times we thought the end had come."[19]

The sea calmed somewhat by 2:00 p.m. "So Davy Jones will not get us just now," Simon wrote, and he began thinking about what he would do "if we get out of this alive."[20] At a shipboard conference about 3:00 p.m., the crew decided it was no longer possible to complete the crossing. Loud and Aubert began breaking up the ENV motor to throw it overboard piece by piece as needed.[21]

Someone now suggested that they take advantage of the relatively calm sea and launch the lifeboat. They had drifted near the transatlantic steamer lanes, where they were likely to be rescued, but the weather could change at any time. In the initial reports it wasn't clear who wanted to abandon ship; only months later did Wellman say it was Vaniman, a claim that the other men neither confirmed nor disputed.[22]

Wellman wanted to keep going. He reasoned that "if the wind should happen to change to the west again we might still make a run for the other side. . . . Vaniman and I discussed the matter for some time. He still insisted upon leaving the ship; I as strongly opposed it. The other members of the crew said nothing, though they overheard our conversation."[23]

We have only Wellman's testimony about what sounds like a heated argument. Rather than make a command decision, he put it to a vote. If there had been a good chance of crossing, "it would have been different," but with "the danger which confronted us, the possibility of getting away in safety now, I did not feel that I had the right as commander of the ship to order men still further to imperil their lives."[24]

But Wellman understood the politics of courage, just as he had when advising Evelyn Baldwin how to seek volunteers to winter in the stone hut in Franz Josef Land. Wellman called on the men one at a time, starting with Loud, then Simon, Irwin, Aubert, and finally Vaniman—surely an intentional sequence. In his writings Wellman frequently praises Loud for his courage, in one place calling him "as brave a man as ever trod the deck of an aerial cruiser."[25] Simon, another reckless soul, was a second sure vote. Once the fearless two spoke first—Loud: "Let's stick by the ship"; Simon: "I am with you for fighting it out"—Irwin would go along, as well as young Aubert, who wouldn't want to seem like a boy among men.[26] And then Vaniman would stand alone, outmaneuvered. It was as easy as guessing the outcome of a Senate vote or a cabinet debate. So it went.

"Boys, we are all together on this proposition," Vaniman said when his turn came.[27] Wellman called for bacon and eggs and hot coffee for all hands.

"I never wish to be shipmates with a better bunch," Simon wrote of the crew. "They are certainly stickers and there's nothing of the mollycoddle about any of them." He teased Aubert about "his little girl waiting for him in Atlantic City," meaning Rebekah Wellman. Aubert allowed he wouldn't mind being with her on some comfortable porch back at the hotel. Simon assured him that he stood a good chance.[28]

But not a guarantee. At 4:45 p.m., less than two hours after the meeting, Irwin's log contains this entry: "It's all up. Arranging to take boat. Serious problem. Calling CQD."[29]

Irwin and Vaniman were in the lifeboat when the airship took a sudden dive, nearly touching the waves. The two men scrambled into the car for safety, and pieces of the broken motor were thrown overboard. Irwin's wireless equipment was in the boat, so he had to climb back down to call for help. He had recently heard a ship with a strong signal, but his CQD went unanswered. The sea grew rough again, and Irwin found no one in range. As night fell and the gas contracted, his shipmates continued throwing away ENV parts just to stay airborne.[30]

The *America* was on its own. Family and friends received news of a severe electrical storm that struck Sable Island at 11:00 p.m. The island was along the airship's planned route and had a wireless station, but the storm was interfering with signals.[31] In fact, the *America* was drifting rapidly southward, away from shore stations and out of the transatlantic shipping lane.[32] Between 9:00 p.m. and 3:00 a.m. the wind and waves became so bad that the crew "wondered every minute when the ship would go to pieces," Simon wrote.[33]

Vaniman described floating barely five or six feet above the water and the next moment springing twenty or thirty feet in the air. "We knew what it meant to keep this up," he said.[34]

They knew at any moment they might have to lower the lifeboat in spite of the risks.[35] A man was always in the boat, watching the airship rise and fall.

"Three tanks up—two tanks up—now—she's going down! Overboard with something!"[36] And then gasoline, or cans of oil, or motor parts would

be hurled over the side until the ship rose to safety. Whenever they heard a noise that sounded like something breaking, Loud and Aubert scrambled forward and aft to investigate.

Wellman and Vaniman were still at odds. After midnight Wellman heard Vaniman order Loud and Aubert to take an ax and cut a hole in the main fuel reservoir.

"Against this I protested," Wellman wrote. By then the wind was driving them toward the Azores. With one good motor, with fuel, with a little luck, who's to say they couldn't make that famous stepping-stone of the mid-Atlantic?[37]

Vaniman said nothing to Wellman but recalled the order.[38] A little later the wind shifted again to the northeast, and then even the hope of reaching the Azores receded.

"This was the turning point of the voyage," Wellman wrote, though no one else described that night in those terms.[39] At last even Wellman had to admit that after nearly two days in the air, their goal was no longer Europe or any particular geographic point. Their goal was survival.

Several years earlier Wellman had written of how Theodore Roosevelt had given up a mid-level Washington position to risk everything "upon a single cast of the die." Now Wellman had in mind a new poem by Rudyard Kipling, "If," which includes the lines:

If you can make one heap of all your winnings
 And risk it on one turn of pitch-and-toss,
And lose, and start again at your beginnings
 And never breathe a word about your loss;
. .
Yours is the Earth and everything that's in it,
 And—which is more—you'll be a Man, my son.

Wellman took comfort in the poet's celebration of that same spirit, one that animated what some called a foolhardy voyage, but that night as he got a few hours' sleep, the game of chance haunting him was not pitch-and-toss but hearts, his favorite card game. In hearts the queen of spades is the one card that will ruin you if you get stuck with her, and in Wellman's dreams, she was always in his hand.[40]

29

A Sort of Bleeding to Death

North Atlantic Ocean, October 17, 1910

Wellman's flight continued to be front-page news across the United States and Europe. On Monday morning the *New York Times* pointed out that if the *America* was still airborne as of 9:13 p.m. the previous night, it had beaten Count Zeppelin's record thirty-seven-hour flight, and by that morning it had probably covered a quarter of the distance to London.

"The balloon has gone so far now . . . that the crossing of the Atlantic no longer seems impossible."[1]

The *Times* estimated that the airship should be in range of the wireless station at Cape Sable Island at the southernmost tip of Nova Scotia. If all was well, a message from Irwin might be relayed at any moment.

But morning passed to afternoon and then to evening with no word from the *America*. Twenty-five different Atlantic liners contacted Cape Sable that day, but none had heard from the airship.[2] Concern for the missing airmen grew despite assurances from Laura Wellman.

"It is just what we all expected," she told reporters on Monday, explaining that Mr. Wellman had anticipated losing touch temporarily with the steamship route at this stage of the journey.[3] Mrs. Wellman had played the role of explorer's wife perfectly for many years and was unwavering in her articulate expressions of confidence. Such a performance was a wifely duty, an expression of loyalty, but it didn't necessarily sway anyone's opinion about Wellman's safety. Once upon a time Lady Franklin had been adamant about her husband's well-being too, and she kept it up for years.

What was different about the wives' statements in 1910 was the speed with which they were called upon to make them, granting interviews within hours of their husbands' departure and daily ever since. In the 1840s the Franklin party was gone for three years before the first search

party was sent. In 1897 Andrée's failure to return before winter caused little stir. His last word came by carrier pigeon, and only after a year had passed, and then another, did concern mount and the hope of loved ones begin to fade into grief and acceptance of his loss.[4]

"Whatever Wellman's fate, if he should come to an untimely end it will be no carrier pigeon that brings the last message," the *Tacoma (WA) Times* observed. "It will be the wireless."[5]

And maybe that final message had come already. By Tuesday morning, thirty-six hours had passed since anyone had heard from Irwin. Across the North Atlantic every wireless-equipped steamer searched the airwaves in vain.[6]

Wellman was still reluctant to give up on the Azores. As conditions looked favorable at 3:00 a.m. Monday, he ordered the motor started up, but soon the wind picked up again. The airship's rudder wouldn't hold the airship on course. They shut down and drifted south toward Bermuda, saving their fuel for a final effort to reach land—any land.[7]

Morning dawned sunny for a change, but the fine weather was a mixed blessing. They began to rise quickly as the sun warmed the gasbag. Wellman shouted for Vaniman to open the valve, but in haste someone pulled the wrong cord, opening the air valve instead.[8] Now even lighter, the airship rose faster, topping out at 3,600 feet before they could bring the *America* down. Then it came down fast. The equilibrator "struck the water tail on, burying itself almost to the head," Simon wrote. "Then we bounced up like a rubber ball 500 feet. It began to look interesting. How the ship ever stood it I never could see."[9]

Wellman was frustrated, later calling the mistake "a stupid bit of work" that cost the *America* precious hydrogen.[10] Vaniman blamed the inexperience of the crew, saying, "There was too much that was brand new to all hands once we were up in the air." He wasn't startled when the ship began to rise. "I knew all I had to do was to ease off the valves until we ceased to rise and that then we'd swing beautifully back to lower levels," but "that sophistication was something no new men could be counted on to have."[11]

There was more to it. Vaniman wrote:

I used to go to sleep by the engines at such periods with just the tail of our equilibrator plashing through the waves. Then as the lifting force gained strength I would hear a little chugging like a door bell's ringing.

It was when the equilibrator had cleared the water until only the tip of the tail was hitting the wave crests.

The message that ran up the gasoline tanks was, "Vaniman, get on the job. She's clearing the water. Soon she'll be soaring to the moon if you don't mind the valve cords." And then I'd ease the valves a little, watch the tanks settle down one by one, and go to sleep again.[12]

A long-distance balloonist would have spotted the error: Vaniman corrected too late. Even a large balloon maintains a surprisingly delicate balance in the air. The slightest change of buoyancy sends it up or down, and momentum carries it beyond the new point of equilibrium, resulting in another correction. Novice balloonists rarely made long flights because they couldn't escape this yo-yo effect and found themselves constantly dropping ballast or venting hydrogen. This is what the equilibrator was meant to correct, but it still required a delicate hand. Making minor corrections as the ship began to rise or fall proved more efficient than making larger corrections later.[13]

And according to Wellman it wasn't some novice who pulled the wrong cord. It was Vaniman himself.[14] Of course, no one aboard was an expert balloonist or airshipman. Most of Vaniman's experience had been in tethered balloons. He and Wellman had made several free balloon flights with Frank Lahm in France, but this airship flight was only their third. And this was not the last time that morning they found themselves mistakenly in the clouds.[15]

It was a day of peace and foreboding. With little to do, the crew mostly stayed in the lifeboat, eating, smoking, and gazing up at the great streamlined bulk overhead or down at the airship's shadow on the water. They dreamed of the future: "There will be a fleet of aerial craft and we shall have been the pioneers," as Simon put it.[16] The sun, which played havoc with their altitude, was also a welcome change after days of fog, mist, and heavy seas. Vaniman's earlier description of sleeping beside the silent motor and tending the valves was framed by this one:

The tranquility of an airship voyage under clear skies is something no landsman can contemplate. When we had our motors turned off and were drifting with the wind, there was a peace to it all that was very beautiful and very rare. . . . It was glorious, cruising like that. It was something I would not match with any other sensation I ever have known.[17]

Simon remembered everyone "as happy as Larry on a picnic," including Kiddo.[18] "You must never cross the Atlantic in an airship without a cat," Simon wrote. "We have found our cat more useful to us than any barometer. He is sitting on the sail of the lifeboat now as I write washing his face in the sun, a pleasant picture of feline content. This cat has always indicated trouble well ahead. Two or three times when we thought we were 'all in' he gave most decided indications that he knew we should shortly be getting it in the neck."[19]

By wireless Irwin could hear Siasconset and Cape Cod calling him, but he didn't have enough power to reply. From the transmissions he learned of growing anxiety back home and of a pleasant weather forecast for the Banks of Newfoundland, where everyone presumed they were heading. Irwin also heard reports of the Cuban hurricane's progress up the coast, but no one on shore knew the *America* was now heading toward it.[20]

Simon calculated they were now 475 miles east of the Maryland coast.[21] Three-quarters of their gasoline was gone, but if the wind held and if they could stay airborne through the night, they might make Bermuda.[22] Even as they enjoyed the day, the crew discussed the inevitable end of their flight.

"We know the poor old *America* cannot keep afloat more than twenty-four hours at the outside," Simon wrote. "Our sudden flight aloft this morning cost us an immense amount of gas, and to an airship gas is lifeblood. The *America* airship will die from sheer exhaustion, a sort of bleeding to death, and before the last comes we must take to the boat."[23]

They faced this dilemma: They could lower the boat now and face the double risk of swamping from the sideways drift and being smashed by the three-thousand-pound metal chain, or they could try to ride out the night in the hope of making Bermuda the next day. The cold night air would make it difficult to stay aloft, meaning they might have to launch the boat anyway and maybe in worse weather.[24]

One idea was to send Loud down in the breeches buoy to cut away the equilibrator. This move would eliminate one of the biggest risks of launching the lifeboat, but the sudden loss of so much weight would send them shooting into the clouds, far higher than they'd gone before. Even if they didn't burst the gasbag, they'd come down fast, with "little in the way of ballast to lighten her and prevent her going plump into the sea, lifeboat and all," Wellman explained.[25]

There was one more possibility. Assuming they could hold their course until morning, they would cross the Bermuda–New York steamer route. This route was not well traveled; steamers often completed the forty-three-hour journey without hailing another ship.[26] But a packet was bound from Bermuda on Tuesday morning. With luck—a lot of luck, for their drift was perpendicular to the route—the ship would pass within their field of vision or at least come within Irwin's transmission range.[27]

Evening came cold and windy. As the airship sank, the crew prepared to abandon ship. As a last-ditch effort, they threw overboard everything they could spare, even extra food, until they rode a relatively safe fifty feet in the air. Wellman called another meeting, and, in Simon's words, "all voted to ride her to hell."[28]

Now it looked as if they'd make it till morning, when the sun would carry them through the next day either to Bermuda or to an evening launch of the boat.[29] Knowing this, they spent the evening together in the lifeboat, "smoking and spinning yarns," Simon wrote. "It is bright moonlight tonight, millions of stars are twinkling and the water below gleams like silver. Flying fish hover around our strange craft, and below big batches of gulf weed drift lazily by. . . . Aubert said he felt like going to church."[30]

They talked about friends who had come to see them off in Atlantic City, and they talked about women. They didn't discuss further what the next day might bring. Most of all they needed the weather to hold. If they struck the edge of the hurricane, things would go badly indeed. But there was nothing they could do about that. As the men talked, Wellman watched the barometer, and Simon watched the cat.[31]

30

CQD

North Atlantic Ocean, October 18, 1910

While the men slept, Wellman stayed on watch for most of the night as the *America* drifted under a full moon that shone brilliantly on the water. At 4:00 a.m. the wind shifted and began pushing them away from Bermuda (still about 300 miles away) and toward the U.S. coast (about 350 miles away).[1]

"I am not a fatalist, nor superstitious, nor anything of that sort," he wrote. But he was a born optimist who had "been in so many tight corners" that he felt sure that "we should get out of this one, sometime, somehow."[2]

The ship from Bermuda would solve everything, if only they could find it. Irwin had been monitoring the wireless into the night. At 1:00 a.m. he heard Cape Cod calling and wrote in his log, "It seems like home."[3] Then he went to sleep.

Wellman was getting sleepy himself. As he recalled later, while gazing into the darkness, "I saw a hundred steamers, some of them full electric lighted from stem to stern; trains of cars, rushing automobiles, tall buildings shining with lights. Then I shook myself, and saw nothing at all, only to drowse again."[4]

It was still dark, sometime after 4:30 a.m., when Wellman thought he saw lights in the distance. He thought his eyes were playing tricks on him again, but the lights remained, moving on the water.

"Why, there's a ship!" he called out. Simon saw it too, but the ship didn't see them and would soon steam past them.

Wellman ordered Vaniman to light a torch while Wellman rousted the rest of the crew. Vaniman doused a bundle of trash with gasoline, lit it, and lowered it from a wire.[5] Irwin called CQD on the wireless. Getting no response, he got out an electric blinker light and began signaling in flashes of Morse code.[6]

Fig. 21. The *America*'s thousand-mile voyage, October 15–18, 1910. From *Literary Digest* 41, no. 18 (October 29, 1910): 733.

The ship changed course. It was about a mile away when the ship responded with its own blinkers.

Ship: DO YOU WANT OUR ASSISTANCE?

Irwin: YES. COME AT ONCE. IN DISTRESS. WE ARE DRIFTING. NOT UNDER CONTROL.[7]

They didn't know if this was their packet from Bermuda, but Simon said it was British by the look of its rigging. He was sure it would stand by to help.[8]

The steamer's crew had some difficulty understanding the blinker signals, but they recognized the distress call and eventually understood Irwin

to say that he had a wireless. After establishing a connection, communication was easy. Irwin requested the ship, which he learned was the ss *Trent*, bound for New York, to stay with them until daylight.[9]

The captain and crew marveled at the airship off their port beam. It looked enormous in the moonlight.[10] Aboard the *America*, Simon wrote in his log that they held a "consultation as to whether to get out or hang on, as we were within an hour or two of the world's record for time in the air."[11] They knew that while they had already surpassed the duration of Zeppelin's longest motorized airship flight, they had done so by drifting much of the way, and they hadn't yet beaten the record duration for unpowered balloon flights.[12]

Wellman said nothing afterward about the desire for another record and who might have brought it up. He noted only that Simon had been reluctant to abandon ship, and Simon himself acknowledged that.

"The ship be blowed," Simon quoted himself as saying, "we can hang on for another twelve hours."[13] The airship's lone sailor said he was looking forward to a journey in the lifeboat.

"But that was instinct, not reason," Wellman wrote.[14] As it was, Wellman could only marvel at his good luck. The *Trent*'s usual route had been changed for this trip to allow it to call at Antilla, Cuba; on its normal schedule the ship would have missed the *America* entirely.[15] The wind, meanwhile, carried the airship at such a course and speed that it was at the right place at exactly the right time along that lonely steamer route.

"Had any one of these factors of chance failed or been shaded as much as 5 per cent, the strange meeting would never have occurred," Wellman acknowledged. "If we went on during that day and sunset came with the strong winds and heavy sea, the chances would be nine out of ten against us."[16]

They agreed to abandon ship; it was only a question of how. Simon wanted to launch the lifeboat and had an idea for how to do it without capsizing. Vaniman didn't trust the boat and proposed having the *Trent* come up underneath them so they could slide down a rope and onto the ship's deck.[17]

Simon alone thought this idea was insane, "and I am afraid that during the few minutes in which I urged my views I used more sailor language than I had used for years past."[18] But he convinced no one. With Irwin

and the *Trent* coordinating by wireless, the ship drew close enough for the two crews to shout to each other.[19]

"The problem of getting alongside her was entirely new to marine tactics," said Capt. C. E. Down of the *Trent*. Thinking of his ship's tall masts and smokestacks, he said that to "get close enough to catch a line presented the danger of hitting the car, smashing the machinery and gasoline tank, and setting the gasoline afire, thus putting the crew of the airship and those aboard the *Trent* in peril."[20]

Wellman also worried that the strain of tethering the ships might pull the *America* apart in midair before the men could safely exit. He worried too about the proximity of the *Trent*'s smokestacks to his hydrogen-filled gasbag. Looking down from the lifeboat, Wellman could see hundreds of passengers on deck, some with coats hastily thrown on over pajamas. Some were weeping and praying as they watched the crew struggle to save the airshipmen. Time and again they threw a line only to have it blown away before the *Trent*'s crew could secure it.[21]

Finally Irwin wired that they would launch the lifeboat after all. Vaniman started the motor to bring the airship into position, low off the *Trent*'s port bow. They climbed into the lifeboat and prepared to launch.[22]

Wellman, with his penchant for estimating odds, rated their chances of being struck by the equilibrator immediately after launch as all but certain and figured on "probably one chance in three that when the equilibrator struck us we should either be killed by the blow or be thrown into the rough sea rolling under us."[23]

They had another problem first. Unknown to the crew, an air supply pipe was out of place, and the air pump failed to fill a ballonet near the tail. Nose-heavy, hydrogen now rushed into the elevated tail, throwing the airship even further out of trim. They were in danger of nosing into the waves or having the boat and car tear away under a strain the airship had not been designed to withstand.[24]

Aubert was the first to realize what had happened. Without waiting for orders, he scrambled up into the car and along its now dangerously pitched walkway. He reset the faulty pipe and restarted the air-pump motor, burning his arm in the process, until the airship regained an even keel.[25]

At last they were all aboard the lifeboat—even Kiddo, who was shut inside one of the boat's airtight compartments—and ready for launch.

Fig. 22. The *America* as seen from the *Trent*, October 18, 1910, before the men took to the lifeboat. Library of Congress Prints and Photographs Division, George Grantham Bain Collection, LC-DIG-ggbain-08853.

To Wellman's amusement, it was Vaniman of all people who now worried the most about the cat's safety. Fearing Kiddo might suffocate, Vaniman insisted the others give him time to knock a hole in the bulkhead, even though Wellman thought "there must have been enough fresh air in that compartment to keep kitty going for at least a month!"[26]

With the airship now drifting broadside at about fifteen knots, they hoped to slow it down before launching the boat. Simon began to prepare the sea anchor, but Vaniman saw this as his own responsibility and perhaps was still angry at Simon for his profanity-laced critique of Van's proposal to slide down to the *Trent* on a rope. Vaniman snatched the sea anchor away, saying, "Think I can't tie a knot?"

According to Simon, Van tied a granny and threw the anchor overboard.[27]

Simon thought they could avoid swamping the boat by cutting away while still a few feet over the water. They would all have to lurch to one side to compensate for the momentum that would roll them the other way when they hit.[28] With Simon and Loud at the forward and aft shackles, Simon gave the order to release when they were still five feet in the air.[29]

They hit the water with a slap, rolling hard, and "we were jostled about like pebbles in a box," Wellman said.[30] Simon said the boat was "immediately

on beam ends"—at the point of capsizing—before righting.[31] The equilibrator was right behind them. A ton and a half of metal and gasoline came dancing on the waves and struck their port bow. It stove in one of the boat's air chambers, "nearly knocked Loud's head off" (Simon's words), struck Irwin, and threw Wellman partly overboard.[32]

As they pulled Wellman back into the boat, the dreaded equilibrator skipped away, and the derelict airship rose quickly into the sky. The boat had a six-inch hole above the waterline, and Loud—who, like Irwin, was not a good swimmer—was not seriously injured.[33] Now their only problem was the *Trent*, which was bearing down on them at fifteen knots and unable to stop.

For most of the crew, the journey's worst moments came next. Half drowned in spray, the men struggled to unship their oars as the lifeboat drifted in front of the *Trent*'s bow. Wellman said the ship's prow was rising "as high as a church"; Vaniman said it "looked like a mountain." Irwin was ready to jump overboard, hoping to swim clear of the ship's propellers. Then the ship slid past them, its wash throwing them clear while the passengers erupted in cheering. The ship's crew tried unsuccessfully to throw them a rope.

Months later Irwin told an audience, "As I think of it now it seems that I could have reached out my hand and touched her. These few moments were terrible."[34]

Only the stoic Loud and sailor Simon had little to say about this latest close call. As they wallowed in the heavy sea, waiting for the ship to circle back to them, Loud passed out cigarettes and Simon got out his pipe, grateful to smoke where there was no "chance of blowing up the whole business."[35] Vaniman became seasick and threw up over the side.

The *Trent* returned and again ran alongside the lifeboat. Someone on the ship's crew threw a rope. They all grabbed for it, but it ran burning through their fingers. A hitch in the rope wound around Wellman's hand and threatened to tear his fingers off or pull him overboard. Just as quickly he was free, though with a lacerated hand.[36]

It took three tries before they caught the rope and made it secure. At last they climbed up the ship's rope ladder to cheers and applause. They arrived haggard, wet, battered, and grateful.[37]

"That must have been our ninth escape from Davy Jones' locker," Simon told Wellman. "Told you it was a good thing to have a cat along—cats have nine lives!"[38] When the lifeboat was hoisted aboard, they opened Kiddo's air chamber and, as Simon put it, "found the damn cat curled up, sound asleep."[39]

"Every person with a pair of pajamas and a camera was on deck making pictures," the *New-York Tribune* reported. "There was a dearth of films and within an hour after daylight camera owners were offering $5 for a six film roll."[40] It wasn't just that an airship rescue at sea was unprecedented; it was also the thrill of the relatively new habit of recording one's experiences with cheap and easy-to-use cameras. The *Trent's* passengers would have more than just a story to tell.

Wellman might have marveled at this had he been anyone but the center of attention. But at the moment even the adoring crowd couldn't hold him as he worked his way toward the ship's bridge. He was eager to have one last look at his airship as the *America* drifted away to the southwest. Vaniman had tied the gas valves open in the hope that it would settle to the surface, fill with water, and sink quickly so as not to become a hazard to shipping.[41]

Standing beside Wellman on the bridge, Captain Down offered to save the airship despite the obvious difficulty of towing a sprawling mass of rubberized fabric. Wellman refused. The ship could never be used again, he said.[42] He and Vaniman had already been talking about its successor, which was going to be larger, faster, and outfitted with a different system of equilibration. At the time neither man expressed much sentimentality for the airship to which they had devoted years of their lives and in which they had lived their greatest adventures.[43]

In its various configurations the *America* had "brought us so much trouble in this world," Wellman later acknowledged.[44] And until only a few days earlier the big airship was widely considered to be little more than the oversized representation of Wellman's folly, the siren that lured a good man away from a life of responsibility and downward into a spiral of fanaticism and disgrace. But now, judging by the scene on deck, where his weary crewmen were posing for snapshots and flirting with young women, it appeared that despite its failure the *America* had at last made Wellman a hero. He would know for sure when he saw the newspapers.

Captain Down told reporters that when they last saw the airship on the horizon, it was drifting southwest with one end hanging in the water.[45] Wellman later described his last sight of the *America* differently: "Good old *America*, farewell. . . . In the years to come many aircraft will cross the Atlantic; and you will be honored as the ship that showed the way."[46]

In his memory, as he stood on the bridge, the ship was flying high, eight hundred feet above the water. Having come a thousand miles already, it vanished across the horizon, airborne still.[47]

31

You're All Right, Old Man!

Atlantic City and New York City, October–December 1910

President Taft was touring Ellis Island on Tuesday morning, October 18, when the conversation turned from immigration to the status of a certain world-famous airship, which was still missing as far as anyone on shore knew. Alarmed by what he heard, Taft ordered the island's naval office to wire the Treasury Department in Washington and ask if any revenue cutters were available to mount a search.[1]

The *New York Times* had been playing it two ways—on the one hand, stoking the public's sense of urgency regarding the *America's* crew with a dozen or more articles a day, and on the other hand, insisting calmly that "no news about them must be considered good news." Reminding its readers that the *America* by now had surely "broken all time records of air navigation," the *Times* defined success broadly by insisting that whether Wellman landed in Europe, in the Azores, or in Newfoundland, or even was picked up at sea, he and his crew had "done more as courageous and determined pioneers in the new science of air navigation than any of their competitors."[2]

The *Times* and its partners had a vested interest in burnishing Wellman's reputation, but other papers shared the enthusiasm even as uncertainty grew about the *America's* whereabouts. The *Philadelphia Ledger* said the flight "marks a new stage in the most modern of man's scientific conquests," while the *New York Press* called it "pioneering of the most brilliant kind," adding that the first man to cross the Atlantic in an airship would "go down to posterity in letters bigger than those in which the name of Peary is blazoned." Several papers made comparisons to Columbus, but the *Springfield (MA) Republican* outdid them all, praising Wellman's "preconceived audacity" as "Napoleonic." The writer added, "Should he actually cross the ocean, he would be capable of starting for

the moon. Should he reach the moon, he would start for Jupiter."[3] Even critics offered grudging praise, as when the *Los Angeles Herald* said that Wellman's "brave but foolhardy act" was "interesting as a sporting event."[4]

In such a media climate, Taft could not afford to seem indifferent to Wellman's fate. He soon learned that three ships were available, but word of the airship crew's rescue arrived before any revenue cutters were dispatched. And passersby on Times Square probably heard the news as quickly as the president did.[5]

Aboard the *Trent*, passengers in the dining room stood and "cheered wildly" as Wellman and his men, freshly bandaged and dressed in borrowed clothes, entered for breakfast.[6] The men signed autograph books and posed for pictures, and that evening Wellman delivered a speech to a rapt audience. The main difficulty lay in persuading the passengers not to stuff the cat with treats.[7] Talking with his men, Wellman reflected on his experiences of the past twelve months: a year ago flying above the Arctic Ocean, last spring meeting Roosevelt on the Nile, and now this.

"If that's not living a bit," he said, "I should like to know what is."[8]

Laura Wellman was in her hotel room in Atlantic City when the telephone rang just before luncheon. After listening to only part of the caller's message, she rushed into the adjoining room and told her son-in-law, LeRoy Chamberlin, to take the call. LeRoy did, no doubt with the "greatly agitated" Mrs. Wellman at his side. Soon a messenger boy brought a confirming telegram:

ON BOARD THE TRENT. AMERICA ABANDONED. ALL ARE SAFE AND WELL. WELLMAN.[9]

"Thank God for the good news," she said.[10] Reporters from the *New York Times* and other papers relayed the scene to the public. From then on the *Times* arranged everything, boasting the following day of chartering a fast launch to carry the Wellman and Vaniman families to meet the *Trent* in New York Harbor.[11] By then the families had arrived in the city and checked in at the Waldorf-Astoria.

In further interviews, the wives of the two leaders expressed delight in the rescue even while reiterating that they had never doubted a safe outcome. Both were disappointed by the loss of the *America*.

"I wonder how they could have parted with it," Ida Vaniman said. "I want ever so badly to know just what it was upset their plans and took them off their course. Then I'll know how Melvin will take it. He had planned things out so carefully."[12]

The *Trent* steamed into New York Harbor a little before noon on Wednesday, October 19, four days after the *America* departed Atlantic City. The *Times*'s chartered tug pulled alongside. Per regulations, the ship would stop first at quarantine for medical inspections before passengers would be allowed into the city. The first greetings were shouted through megaphones from one craft to another.[13]

Conspicuous on deck, Wellman and his men had changed back into their dirty khaki flight uniforms and aviator caps. The women noticed the injuries first: Wellman's arm in a sling, Loud's bruised forehead, and Aubert's bandaged hand. Vaniman held the cat.

"I hope it hasn't broken his heart to lose the balloon," Ida Vaniman said. The question was repeated through a megaphone.

"It hasn't," Vaniman called back.[14]

Mrs. Vaniman next called out to Wellman. A day earlier, after sending his initial terse telegram to his wife, he had composed a longer message for the *Times*. In it all mistakes and differences of opinion were forgotten in the euphoria of the moment.

"There was one thing in your dispatch that touched me to the heart," Ida said. "It was that reference to Melvin as 'the heroic Vaniman.'"

"And it came right out of the heart," Wellman called back. "I meant it, and it came right from here." And he pointed to his chest with his good hand.[15]

The *Times* men had come prepared, sending a stack of morning papers over to the *Trent*. They reported how the cheering passengers scooped them up to see their experiences validated in newsprint. Thus, the *Times* closed the loop with its coverage of the celebration it had orchestrated in honor of the news event that it had sponsored and promoted. Wellman

himself grabbed a paper and spent the next five minutes perusing it eagerly, only putting it down when he realized he was hiding his face from photographers.[16]

Wellman and his crew looked weary and far less excited about the proceedings than everyone around them.

"Are you going to try it again?" a reporter shouted to Wellman, who shrugged and replied in French: "Je ne sais pas" (I do not know).[17]

When told that his flight had turned public opinion in his favor, Wellman replied that he was glad to hear it, "but I became indifferent long ago to public opinion." Presumably he was still holding the newspaper as he spoke.

The *Trent*'s passengers, including the airship's crew, were released from quarantine a few hours later. Some entrepreneurial passengers sold their undeveloped film to eager newsmen; it was rumored that several people recouped their expenses for the trip to Cuba and Bermuda.[18] Other entrepreneurs sought out the adventurers themselves. "Scores of theatrical agents armed with blank contracts" awaited the airship crew.

"Wellman will be seized and hauled about like a bargain counter clerk if the impatient attitude of the agents is any indication," the United Press reported. "Every member of the crew will be bid for and one agent has been instructed to secure even the cat."[19]

Reporters took notes on family reunions. Meanwhile, Ida Vaniman hung on her husband's arm, and her elderly mother stood weeping with one arm around her son, Louis, and the other around her son-in-law, Melvin.

Laura Wellman embraced Walter and kissed him on both cheeks.[20] It's safe to say that Bergljot Bergersen, Walter Jr., and baby Elsa were not present on the *Times*'s tug. It is not known if they were even in the city at that time.

The tug began a triumphal procession up the harbor to Forty-Second Street, serenaded by shrieking whistles from passing ships and cheered by passengers lining the deck rails. The Staten Island ferryboat passed them while listing badly as its passengers crowded one side of the deck for a better view.[21]

"You're all right, old man! It was only blamed hard luck that stopped you!" one man called from the ferry, but by now Wellman had no reason to curse his luck. When they reached the Forty-Second Street wharf, the

Fig. 23. Melvin Vaniman (*left*) next to his wife, Ida; other family members; and Kiddo, the cat, aboard the *Trent* in New York Harbor, October 19, 1910. Library of Congress Prints and Photographs Division, George Grantham Bain Collection, LC-DIG-ggbain-08771.

police had to clear a path for his party to reach the waiting taxicabs for the crosstown ride to a reception at the Times Building. The rival *New-York Tribune* noted that the city's reception of Wellman "was the biggest greeting since Theodore Roosevelt's arrival, but was nothing compared with that prepared for Dr. Cook."[22]

Wellman spent the next day greeting a long line of well-wishers at his Waldorf suite. Telegrams and letters of congratulations began to arrive from noteworthy figures such as Theodore Roosevelt, Robert Peary, and even Frederick Cook. Across the United States and Europe, most newspapers shared the view of the *Washington Times*'s lede: "Wellman has made good. The world must take off its hat to him."[23] Wellman had not become a new Columbus, but some papers in London and several in the United States suggested that he was just as daring.[24] Attending the American Music Hall later that week, the performance was interrupted when the Wellman party entered the stage box, and the cheering lasted for several minutes.[25] Visiting Atlantic City the next day, Wellman and

Vaniman were met at the train station by two military companies and a brass band as their escort to the Hotel Chalfonte.[26]

It didn't matter that the expedition was technically a failure. "The very fact that such an effort was seriously made is in itself a victory," said journalist James A. Edgerton in a syndicated article. "For eighteen carat, standard weight, bonded and guaranteed nerve . . . Wellman's attempt to fly over the Atlantic in a balloon has put all the other exhibitions in the also ran class."[27]

Although Wellman's courage and sincerity were now almost universally recognized, that didn't mean that everyone approved of his voyage. *Engineering Magazine* considered the project so technically unsound and foolhardy as to be "utterly reprehensible" and compared it to a dangerous circus stunt.[28] The *New-York Tribune* questioned "the moral responsibility of the newspapers which for advertising purposes encouraged Wellman to incur risks so accurately foreseen," noting that the sponsoring papers would have been condemned if the crew had been lost and "are not less blameworthy because of the rescue in which they had no part."[29]

Others disapproved of Wellman's stage-managed triumphal entry into New York and the new style of public heroism that it represented. One *Trent* passenger groused to reporters about the way the airship crew had enjoyed the attention while signing autographs and posing for pictures. "The whole thing savors so much of mock heroism and fake advertising that it seemed ridiculous to me," he said.[30]

Of course there was nothing "mock" or "fake" about the *America's* three-day flight or the dangers it entailed. Something else about the scene rang false to this man, and "mock heroism" was the handiest expression he found to label it. One could have less pejoratively called it the New Heroism, the public perception of heroism that was deliberately and almost instantly magnified by intensive press coverage. New Heroism moved at lightning speed, bursting into print with worldwide banner headlines. It fed upon itself, as a significant amount of a New Hero's press coverage was about all the other press coverage, which in turn validated even more coverage. And because reports of New Heroism sold newspapers and thus helped the papers sell advertising, it had itself become a commodity.

Newspapers such as the *Chicago Record-Herald* and *New York Times* recognized it when they sponsored Wellman's expeditions.

But no one used the term "New Hero." Instead, as people thought more about the modern aspects of fame in a mass media–driven culture, eventually they settled on an old word that acquired new connotations as the century progressed—"celebrity."

Wellman tried to manage his new fame carefully. He had been famous for years but not like this. He was no longer a nationally known conduit to the great men; now he was a great man himself—or a great circus performer, depending on one's opinion. With an eye on his dignity, he declined offers to lecture on the vaudeville stage and arranged a joint lecture tour with Vaniman at more respectable venues.[31] He had already arranged to write about his voyage for *Hampton's Magazine*; he soon had a book deal as well.[32]

Celebrity brought attention and the opportunity to make money, but traditional fame brought gravitas, which is what Wellman sought most of all. He knew his flight had touched something in the public imagination. It represented a promise of a new technological world at a time when such a world was still more promising than frightening. Edwin Davies Schoonmaker tried to capture this in his poem "The Sailing of the 'America,'" which invoked the name of the world's greatest ocean liner in its opening lines: "What will the *Lusitania* say to thee, / Bold voyager of the wandering ocean sail." It went on to promise that

Millions will see new glory in the moon:
"Wellman to-night is gleaming on his way."
Or tremble with the swishing of the grass:
"Wellman to-night is miles upon the sea."[33]

Literary Digest called the first part of the poem "grave and impressive," for this was still an age in which great deeds inspired solemn verses in the epic style. Wellman surely appreciated the effort. He had spoken often of the poetry of the deed, seeing adventure as inspiration even if it has no practical value. Like the *America*, however, the poem failed to complete its journey. The *Digest* complained that in the latter stanzas "the author's inspiration has left him, and we fancy that we can hear the squeak of his pen."[34]

A more enjoyable poem appeared in the *New-York Tribune* one day after the rescue, but Wellman was not its hero.

THE CAT THAT FLEW WITH WELLMAN

Let Tabitha and Thomas Cat
Whose home is in a Harlem flat,
Meow and purr most gently at
The cat that flew with Wellman.

It is an honor when a man
Tries the Atlantic pond to span,
But is no greater honor than
The cat's that flew with Wellman.

But how could Wellman hope to fly
Across the ocean's billow high
Without some mice to satisfy
The cat that flew with Wellman?

The reason for the failure seems
A lack of rats in midair streams:
The ocean's vessels grant its dreams—
The cat that flew with Wellman.

Wellman might gain the airy track
Without the pains of seasick's rack,
But cats! 'Tis known that cats come back!
That's why one flew with Wellman.[35]

Kiddo, now renamed Trent, had become the darling of the voyage. People wanted to look at the cat, pet him, feed him, or buy him, and there were rumored plots afoot to steal him. The Vanimans kept Trent locked in their rooms at the Waldorf-Astoria, though he was briefly displayed in the window of Gimbels department store on Herald Square.[36] Years later

Simon told of pushing through the crowd to see his old friend reclining on plush cushions in a gilded cage.

"Hello, Kiddo," Simon said, but the cat turned his back on his former shipmate. Simon joked as he remembered that day, "*Nouveau riche!* He came up in the world too fast."[37]

Public obsession with the cat was so intense that it provoked a *New York Times* editorial wondering why, when so many people didn't care all that much for cats (at least compared to affection for "the noble dog"), such attention was given to this lucky feline. The editors concluded that it was for two reasons: a cat was comically out of place on an airship—"the incongruous and the grotesque are always interesting"—and it reflected nobly on the crew that even in their hour of danger they did not "forget the one passenger who made the desperate voyage by compulsion."[38]

The *Chicago Tribune* put it in a lighter vein: "We can fully understand why Wellman and his companions embarked on a voyage which for foolhardiness exceeds anything in the history of human recklessness; but what gets us is how a perfectly sane cat ever consented to go."[39]

Wellman didn't seem to mind any of this, but perhaps he had second thoughts when, at the pinnacle of his fame, the expedition made the cover of the January 1911 issue of *Hampton's Magazine*. Only one crew member was pictured, and it was not Wellman. He had been upstaged by "The Good Luck Cat."[40]

Fame is like that, especially the new, lightning-speed, wirelessly transmitted, banner headline fame. You spend years trying to accomplish some great thing, telling yourself through all the difficult toil that you're only trying to serve the public, but—if they notice at all—they are almost certain to miss your point and focus on something that to you was only an afterthought. For all the talk about aeronautics, science, and discovery, few people actually cared about those things except to the degree that they made them feel something beyond what Wellman called "the humdrum money grubbing and . . . routine though admirable round of quiet duty doing."[41]

Wellman had long understood this aspect of human nature. It was how he funded his expeditions. Now Vaniman, too, was beginning to make use of it. Though Simon seems to have been fondest of Kiddo, after

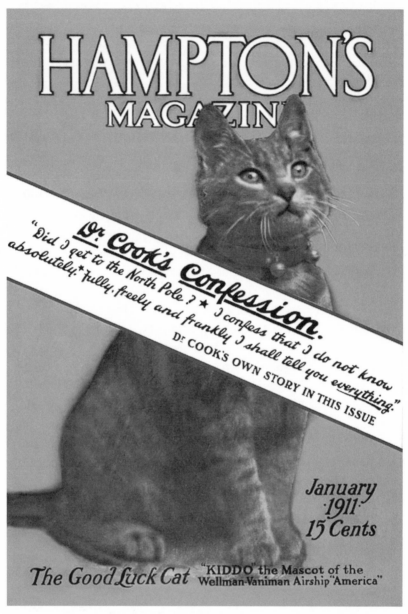

Fig. 24. Kiddo upstaged Wellman and Vaniman for a spot on the cover of *Hampton's*. A purported "confession" by Dr. Frederick Cook in the same issue upstaged everyone. *Hampton's*, January 1911.

the rescue it was Vaniman who was photographed holding the cat, who renamed him, and who took him home.[42] Why his sudden affection for the cat, when not long ago he had stuffed it in a canvas bag and thrown it overboard at the end of a rope?

Vaniman seems to have recognized Kiddo's publicity value. He considered giving the cat to the *New York Times* as a souvenir but kept him instead as a mascot for his next airship.

Wellman was giving mixed signals about another voyage, but Vaniman was already fund-raising. Within a day of arriving in New York, he wired Wellman's patron Joseph Salus in Atlantic City. Salus said Vaniman "told me that if they had the thing to do over again they would win out."[43] Speaking with reporters, Vaniman played up the accomplishments of the flight and said that "if I had the money I would begin on a bigger, stronger and better airship to-morrow."[44] He was so enthusiastic that the *New York Times* commented on "the obsession which inevitably will drive him out over the ocean . . . until he either loses his life in the attempt to reach Europe or succeeds in getting there by his chosen route."[45]

Though Wellman was undecided, reporters noticed that he spoke mainly of "we" and not "I." He insisted, "Mr. Vaniman and I are partners, not only in the present attempt, but in any future venture of the sort."[46]

If Wellman was to make a second attempt at the Atlantic, he needed Vaniman. But it was no longer clear that the reverse was true.

32

New Dreams for the Aerial Age

New York City, Atlantic City, and Akron, Ohio, 1911

"Personally I have simply got to go on building airships," Vaniman said a few days after the voyage. "That's what I have started in to do. It's all the road there is open to me."[1] He said little about Wellman except to deny reports of "friction" between Wellman and the crew, claiming everyone had gotten along.[2]

Wellman praised Vaniman repeatedly in his magazine narrative, which was published in two installments in the December 1910 and January 1911 issues of *Hampton's Magazine*. But something changed between the appearance of the second *Hampton's* piece on December 16 and the publication of Wellman's memoir, *The Aerial Age*, a month later.[3] The book's account of the Atlantic flight is nearly identical to the *Hampton's* version except for a few added explanations and a markedly different attitude toward the *America's* chief engineer. Most praise of Vaniman is either omitted or broadened to the engineers generally; mistakes or disagreements formerly attributed vaguely to unnamed crew members are now pointed at Vaniman.

Wellman betrayed no anger. He knew the subtle ways of cutting someone in print. Writing, for example, of how the airship exceeded its weight specifications, he explained how this had occurred while he was away on the Nile and Vaniman was in charge of construction. Wellman uses backhanded praise:

> Though not an engineer in the true sense, [Vaniman] is a clever mechanic and foreman, and had done the best he could under the discouraging circumstances. Being compelled to build hurriedly, perhaps it is not surprising that he was not as careful about the weights as

he should have been, and as he probably would have been under other and more favorable conditions, though, like all mechanics executing the designs and working to the calculations of another, he is naturally more keen about strength than for adhering closely to a weight schedule.[4]

"Executing the designs . . . of another" was grossly unfair, but Vaniman never responded directly. His public posture was simply to ignore Wellman and to continue raising money for a transatlantic airship of his own. The first report that Vaniman was in Atlantic City arranging for financial backing appeared on December 19, right about the time Wellman's second article for *Hampton's* was hitting the newsstands.[5] We don't know what drove the men apart in late 1910. Perhaps Vaniman was eager to move ahead while Wellman dithered. Perhaps Wellman was willing, but Vaniman realized that he no longer needed to share either the glory or the decision-making. Whatever happened, Wellman took it badly.[6]

He had good reason to be ambivalent about another flight. He knew how lucky he had been, not only to escape death, but also to recover his honor after it seemed irretrievably lost. It's one thing to rise from obscurity, quite another to come back from scandal and, most difficult of all, to recover from being a national joke. Wellman would not forget either the applause or the mockery that preceded it.

"All my life I have been writing for the people," he wrote in the opening pages of *The Aerial Age*. "To please, to inform, to help educate, to win the approval of the people, is, I admit, the very breath of life in my nostrils."[7]

He no longer trusted the people's judgment, as his earlier complaints about the impatient public made clear. And if he needed further evidence of the dark side of celebrity, it came with the death of pilot Ralph Johnstone on November 17, 1910. As an exhibition pilot for the Wright brothers, the thirty-year-old had become one of America's most famous pilots by setting altitude records. He and fellow Wright pilot Arch Hoxey were known as the "heavenly twins," spurring each other toward ever-greater deeds of airmanship. Then Johnstone was killed in a crash in Denver. "Scarcely had he hit the ground," the Associated Press reported, "when sensation-mad brutes, both men and women, swarmed over the wreckage fighting with one another for souvenirs." They even pulled off the dead

aviator's gloves and yanked a bloody sliver of wood from his body. In the grandstands, the band hired for the event never ceased playing, and Johnstone's broken body was driven off the field to the cheerful strains of the "Grizzly Bear Rag."[8]

Once again Wellman sought the attention of men of power but not for another adventure. In the final chapter of *The Aerial Age* he wrote, "As these pages go to press I am submitting to the Congress of the United States a proposal that our government take an advanced step toward utilization of aerial navigation in time of war. It would not be proper for me to state here all that I am suggesting to the government."[9]

But he was happy to outline his plans for his readers. Denying any pecuniary interest, he said he was offering his proposal at no charge. The basic idea was that the United States was "an isolated power" whose policy "is one of peace. We are not likely to cross the seas to attack an enemy."[10] America's primary military concern, then, was coastal defense, which presented a growing challenge in an era of ever-larger battleships and nascent airpower. Despite his lack of military background, Wellman believed that his airship experience made him uniquely qualified to advise the nation's leaders on defense in the aerial age.[11]

He proposed that the traditional navy would become the nation's second line of defense behind a new "Aerial Coast Defense Fleet" comprising motor balloons and aeroplanes stationed along both coasts. A fleet of fast, long-range airships would provide reconnaissance by cruising a thousand to fifteen hundred miles offshore and reporting home by wireless. They would not engage an enemy, but Wellman's plan also included a fleet of aerial battleships, "composed primarily of motor-balloons but with many aeroplanes fitted to the combination," that would engage enemy ships by bombing them from the air. As an added disincentive to potential enemies, Wellman called for some of the airships to be large enough to cross the Atlantic while "carrying explosives and means of using them against the enemy which cannot be here disclosed."[12]

All of this rested on an as-yet-untested claim: "It is my belief that I know how to build and equip an aerial battleship which shall have at least an equal chance in deadly combat with a ten million dollar monster

of steel down in the seas below."[13] Even if such an aerial fleet sustained heavy losses, its cost would be far less in dollars and men than a comparable naval force. And with that thought Wellman closed his memoir, looking not toward the past or his many real-life adventures but toward an imaginary future in which he hoped to secure world peace by developing weapons that would make traditional armies and navies obsolete.

Nothing came of this proposal. Neither Congress nor U.S. military leaders were ready to embrace aeronautics on a large scale, and their reluctance applied even to the more fashionable aeroplane. Development of military aeronautics in Europe, where questions of warfare had a greater urgency, greatly outpaced that in the United States. Still, Wellman's proposal was within the mainstream of American public opinion. A 1909 *McClure's* article had predicted that the recent success of German zeppelins "means the end of armies within the next ten years."[14] Few commentators would go that far, but by 1910 the press was giving serious consideration to aerial warfare, weighing the aeroplane's cheapness and maneuverability against the airship's superior range and payload.[15] The technology was evolving so rapidly that it was hard to say where it would all lead. Germany inaugurated the world's first passenger airship service in June 1910. On November 14 of that year, American civilian pilot Eugene Ely launched his plane from a wooden platform atop an armored cruiser, and using a primitive tailhook apparatus, he landed on a similar platform on another ship on January 18, 1911. In December 1910 a Paris aviation exhibition included biplanes mounted with small machine guns.[16]

Even in Russia, infamous for its hidebound approach to military matters, former Wellman crew member Nicholas Popov learned to fly a Wright aeroplane and successfully demonstrated it to the war minister. Badly injured in a crash in 1910, Popov recovered and taught many Russian officers to fly. In 1912 he offered his services to the Bulgarian army during the First Balkan War, the first war to include aerial bombardment by aeroplanes and airships. Flying reconnaissance over besieged Adrianople, Turkey, on October 30, Popov became one of the world's first military pilots to be killed in combat when he was shot down by shrapnel.[17]

Watching all of this, Wellman did not return to Washington and did not resume his position with the *Chicago Record-Herald*; instead, he set himself

up as a transportation engineer and consultant in New York. Among his proposals was a plan to relieve the city's subway congestion with trains of twenty to thirty cars each, with multiple entrances and correspondingly longer platforms.[18] Otherwise, he kept out of the public eye, prompting a squib from an unfriendly newspaper on May 18, 1911: "A Chicago newspaper paragrapher paused the other day to inquire what ever had become of Walter Wellman and he got no reply. Has any one here seen Walter since the explosion of his last gas bag?"[19]

Vaniman didn't seek newspaper funding for his airship. He approached city leaders instead. In February a syndicate of Cincinnati men pledged $70,000 for an airship to be named after their city.[20] The deal fell through, but in June Vaniman announced that Frank Seiberling, president of the Goodyear Tire and Rubber Company, was going to finance the project. Seiberling provided the money out of his own pocket, but the gasbag was to be manufactured to Vaniman's specifications at the Goodyear plant in Akron, Ohio.[21] Unlike the French-built *America*, the *Akron* would be the first world-class airship built entirely in the United States. It is sometimes credited as the prototype Goodyear blimp. This isn't technically true, as airship aficionados make much of the distinction between nonrigid blimps (a word not yet coined in 1911) and semirigid pressure ships stiffened by a keel. Like the *America*, the *Akron* was the latter type.[22] Also, the company neither designed nor owned the ship. Even so, its manufacture represented Goodyear's entry into the lighter-than-air business; within a year the company was using pictures of the *Akron* to advertise its new line of Goodyear Balloons and Aeroplane Accessories.[23]

Said to be longer than a New York City block and wider than Broadway, the *Akron* was sleeker in appearance than the *America*, being slightly narrower and thirty feet longer and holding more hydrogen—some 400,000 cubic feet to the *America*'s 345,000.[24] The *Akron*'s car was also longer than its predecessor's but was similarly built over a tubular gasoline tank. It would carry five tons of gasoline (as originally intended for the *America*) and would have two 100-horsepower motors and one of 80 horsepower, plus a 17-horsepower utility motor to fill the ballonets and power a dynamo for electric lights and wireless telegraph. The propellers were set

on swivels to provide thrust at any angle, helping the ship rise or fall as desired. Fore and aft adjustable stabilizing planes would also help point the ship up or down.[25]

Safety improvements included a more powerful wireless, giving Jack Irwin a range of five hundred miles, and a swivel attachment for the lifeboat so the crew wouldn't have to launch it broadside if the engines failed. Vaniman also selected stronger fabric than that used in previous airships; he felt the added precaution against a pressure burst was worth the additional weight. One persistent risk apparently couldn't be prevented, but he made the best of it and designed a cookstove to fit over an exhaust pipe, where it would be heated by conduction. If they couldn't help running red hot, they could at least enjoy fried eggs and bacon.[26]

One of the most important new features was the improved equilibrator. As before, it was a chain of metal tanks strung on cables, but this time the tanks were designed to scoop up seawater. By using the swiveling propellers and stabilizing planes, Vaniman hoped to drive the ship down to sea-level as needed. The metal tanks had openings near the top and would fill with water as they dragged along the surface. Once filled, the chain of tanks would be raised and stored in the car. The water could then easily be dumped as needed to lighten the ship. Not only would this avoid the strain of dragging a heavy tail in rough seas, but the "hydrolevator," as Vaniman called it, would allow the *Akron* to fly higher than the *America* had. Early in the voyage the airship would cruise at two hundred to a thousand feet altitude and higher as fuel burned off.[27]

The *Akron* would have yet another means of controlling altitude. In ordering stronger fabric, Vaniman was thinking beyond the ordinary fluctuations of pressure. He wanted to use internal pressure to control the airship's altitude without venting precious hydrogen. The *Akron*'s air-filled ballonets would now serve a second purpose beyond maintaining the gasbag's shape: By overfilling them with the air pump, Vaniman not only could prevent the hydrogen from expanding in warm weather but also could compress it at will by reducing the gasbag's volume. The ship's displacement would remain steady, but because air has fourteen times the weight of hydrogen, the ballonets could make the ship heavier or lighter. Vaniman, in other words, was going to use air as ballast.[28]

He had to be careful. Higher pressure meant more strain on fabric and seams. The gasbag would have the usual safety measures—pressure gauges for the crew to monitor, plus safety valves designed to open automatically at a given pressure. But mostly Vaniman trusted the new fabric, the composition of which he and Goodyear kept to themselves. The envelope would have multiple layers of it and triple-sewn seams, and he designed it to withstand eight times the pressure he planned to impose on it.[29]

In all by autumn 1911 Vaniman could be proud of his achievements thus far. Not only was the *Akron* a more advanced airship than the *America*, but with its launch he believed that the United States would have an original design that was a true rival to any European airship. It may have started as Wellman's dream, but now Vaniman was poised to fulfill it.

33

The Most Perilous Element of All

Atlantic City, October 1911–July 1912

Even before closing the deal with Seiberling in June, Vaniman had signed an agreement with Atlantic City businessmen for a series of trial flights in preparation for the Atlantic voyage. He would receive $2,500 for each flight.[1] He promised an October launch, but as usual, everything took longer than expected. By late October he still wasn't ready and refused to rush his preparations. Feeling that the men had been too panicky on last year's voyage, he trained this year's crew by making them sleep in the lifeboat with the motors running.[2] And while the *Akron* didn't receive nearly the press coverage that the *America* had, either positive or negative, the U.S. Navy took the airship seriously enough to assign a fast scout cruiser to follow it across the ocean.[3]

Besides Vaniman, two members from the *America* crew returned—Jack Irwin and Louis Loud. Murray Simon had gone back to the White Star Line, and Fred Aubert's mother told reporters that her only son would never go up in another airship if she had anything to say about it.[4] And with the March 12 announcement of his engagement to Rebekah Wellman, Aubert had other reasons to avoid working with Vaniman.[5]

The *Akron* made its first test flight on November 4, with Vaniman and five crewmen, plus Trent (aka Kiddo) the cat. Three hundred feet above the crowded streets of Atlantic City, the airship cruised past the cheering spectators "at express train speed and was perfectly controlled."[6] Experimenting with the air pump, Vaniman practiced making the ship rise and descend by means of air pressure alone.[7]

The ship ran into trouble several miles outside the city when one of the air-filled ballonets leaked air into the hydrogen-filled gasbag. The resulting uneven distribution of gas and air made the ship lighter at the stern, which rose fifty feet higher than the bow. As the crew rushed to

Fig. 25. Vaniman's airship *Akron* in Atlantic City, 1912. Library of Congress Prints and Photographs Division, Ernest L. Jones Collection, LC-USZ62–68851.

redistribute sandbags to trim the ship, Vaniman accidentally dropped one on a main engine radiator pipe, knocking it loose. They had to shut off the motor. Already running heavy, the airship sank without engine power and nosed into the waves with its tail sticking up in the air. Though not badly damaged, a dredge had to tow it back to the hangar.[8]

Vaniman declared himself well pleased with the airship, but soon he had to bow to reality and the advancing season. The *Akron* was simply not ready. The Atlantic flight was postponed until 1912. Such a delay probably would have scuttled the *America*'s flight, but Vaniman was still riding a wave of public goodwill. Sieberling's money would still be there next year, and the Atlantic City men would gladly pay for more crowd-pleasing test flights.[9]

Criticism was muted. "There is a growing feeling that Aviator Vaniman should either proceed to aviate across the ocean or take a job as a street car conductor," a Nebraska paper complained, but mostly he was allowed to repair his airship in peace.[10]

In April Vaniman announced he was nearly ready for another test flight. He didn't mention the departure of the two remaining men from

the *America*.[11] Louis Loud had quietly departed for reasons unknown, but Jack Irwin made no secret of his reason for taking as a job as a wireless operator aboard a steamship. "There's less chance of meeting trouble," he told reporters when his ship docked in Honolulu.[12]

Vaniman's troubles continued when the *Akron* finally made its second flight on June 1. This time one of the swiveling propellers broke when it got tangled in a rope. A thousand feet high, the airship "listed and wobbled down to the water," once again plunging partly beneath the waves.[13] When a gust of wind then lifted the airship five hundred feet in the air, spectators thrilled to see Calvin Vaniman (Melvin's younger brother) climb out on the propeller strut to untangle the rope. Heroics aside, the day ended with another boat rescue and another return to the hangar for repairs.[14] Adding to the frustration, the mishap was reported alongside news of Count Zeppelin's 450-mile trip across Germany in his latest airship, averaging an impressive 43 miles per hour.[15]

Though busy with test flights and troubleshooting, Vaniman was already looking beyond the European shore and beyond the *Akron*'s limitations. "We are on the eve of the epoch of air travel," he wrote in the May issue of the *Aero Club of America Bulletin*, promising it would be "safer and more economical than travel has ever been before in the world's history."[16]

He would achieve this with an airship built of a fabric of fine steel wire that he was developing. Far stronger than what was in the *Akron*, this non-elastic steel fabric would be coated inside the envelope with "a jellylike substance that prevents all escape of the hydrogen gas." Too strong to burst from overpressure, it would be safe as a ship's hull and would require no ballast other than the air pumped into its ballonets, or "collapsible ballast tanks," as Vaniman now called them. In all atmospheric conditions, the airship would rise and fall only as air was added or subtracted upon the captain's orders.[17]

The article was illustrated with photos of the cabin of the Zeppelin LZ10 *Schwaben*, the world's first commercially successful passenger aircraft, but Vaniman compared his proposed airship not to a zeppelin but to the ocean liner RMS *Olympic*. Currently it was the world's largest ship and, presumably, the standard of safe ocean travel.[18]

This was an ironic comparison by the time it appeared in print. It's likely that Vaniman's original manuscript named not the *Olympic* but its slightly larger sister ship, the brand-new *Titanic*, and that a copy editor changed the name after the latter sank on April 15. But the irony remained. Like the *Titanic*, the *Olympic* carried an insufficient number of lifeboats. Facing public outcry, White Star Line officials purchased secondhand collapsible lifeboats and kept the liner in service. In late April, 284 of the ship's firemen went on strike, protesting that the collapsibles were unseaworthy. White Star officials brought in strikebreakers, but the sailors complained that the new firemen were untrained and dangerous. While still at port, fifty-four sailors walked off the ship and were immediately charged with mutiny.[19]

This wasn't the impression Vaniman sought to convey when he boasted, with Wellman-esque enthusiasm, of "a new epoch, creating its own desires, its own delights, its own unbounded experiences, and its own necessities."[20] His proposed airship would be an oceangoing liner in its own right. At 525 feet long, it would be larger even than the latest zeppelins and contain forty cabins, eight staterooms, a kitchen, dining rooms, a drawing room, a smoking room, promenades, and four bathrooms, and carry enough fuel for a 4,000-mile journey.[21] He did not use the by-now ridiculed word "unsinkable" but wrote that air travel would "give mankind his largest delight and greatest safety in what would appear to one as the most perilous element of all."[22]

The July 2 flight was to be the final tune-up before the Atlantic attempt. Despite the 6:15 a.m. departure, a large crowd came out as before to watch the *Akron* be put through its paces over Brigantine Beach. The ship rose, making wide circles, and kept rising in the bright sunshine, up and up to 2,500 feet.[23]

After about twenty minutes in the air, the *Akron*'s nose and adjustable propellers began pointing downward. It appeared as if the crew was trying to bring the ship down or at least prevent it from rising still higher.[24]

Suddenly the gasbag split open near the stern. The airship hung in the air a moment, and then, collapsing, it plunged stern first toward the water a half mile below. Most of the gasbag tore away from the car, which plunged end first before swinging nearly horizontal right before hitting the shallow

water of Absecon Inlet. The gasbag followed, coming to rest on the waves a short distance away. Soon it floated up the channel with the tide.[25]

It was reported later that Ida Vaniman had had a premonition of her husband's death early that morning.[26] She and three other crewmen's wives watched from the porch of a cottage near the hangar, with many interminable seconds during the half-mile fall in which to consider the nonsurvivability of the coming impact. The new widows were soon reported to be "suffering from nervous prostration" and in the care of physicians.[27] It took several days to recover all the bodies.

Many newspapers reported that the airship had "exploded," implying fire. Some eyewitnesses reported seeing smoke and even flames, but Goodyear's investigation of the wreckage found no evidence of fire. The smoke had simply been engine emissions typical of early gasoline motors.[28] The envelope had ruptured, but why?

The Goodyear report considered several possibilities. The year-old fabric retained nearly its original strength and gas tightness. Though unlikely, a wooden propeller could have struck a rope or another object, breaking off and then slicing open the gasbag. More likely the envelope burst from overpressure, perhaps due to Vaniman's ballonet-pumping experiments. The report noted that while the *Akron* carried an automatic safety valve from a reputable French company, Vaniman had "provided it with extra springs since the previous flight, which did not allow it to open fully." Even Ida Vaniman considered the safety valve the culprit.[29]

Goodyear, however, thought the most likely cause was something that no one had yet considered—the ropes that held the car to the envelope. Though having ample strength under normal conditions,

> they had been tightened up much beyond their usual allowance. We have it from two of the mechanics that these ropes had been breaking frequently when simply standing in the shed. If two or more happened to break at once, the others would speedily follow suit, thus throwing all the strain on the bottom fabric, tearing it open and ripping the whole bag from the car.[30]

If this was the cause, then Vaniman was killed not by the risk that had so disturbed Wellman and Riesenberg back in 1907 (the hydrogen

carburetor) and not by the risks that Vaniman himself had considered carefully and worked to avoid (the strain of the equilibrator and the chance of a pressure burst). Instead, he and his crew were felled by something he apparently had deemed inconsequential.

The Goodyear report reached no final conclusion, however, because it was impossible to say at which spot the gasbag had ruptured. Too much of it went missing immediately after the crash, as souvenir hunters in fishing boats took it away piece by piece.[31]

Melvin Vaniman had spent much of his aeronautical career in Walter Wellman's shadow. At last he had emerged with his own identity, his own airship, his own crew—and then in death he again shared the headlines with another famous aviator. In Massachusetts less than twenty-four hours before the *Akron* disaster, pilot Harriet Quimby and a passenger fell to their deaths after her Bleriot monoplane pitched forward in flight. The thirty-seven-year-old Quimby—journalist, theater critic, and screenwriter, iconic in her purple aviation costume—was the first woman to fly the English Channel and now became the first American woman killed in a plane crash.[32] Vaniman's accident earned the distinction of the WORLD'S GREAT-EST TRAGEDY OF THE AIR, according to a headline.[33] The *Akron's* death toll equaled that of the German airship *Erbslöh*, which also burst in flight two years earlier after emerging suddenly from fog into bright sunshine.[34]

"The sport of flying continues to be one more fitted for daredevils than for ordinary human beings," one newspaper observed. The writer calculated the year's aviation death toll at forty-six—"compared with seventy-three during all of 1911"—and reminded readers that 1912 was "still young."[35]

"When will this craze end!" said another paper. "The announcements of fatalities from aeroplanes have come with a sickening regularity which make us all shudder to hear. And yet the end seems nowhere in sight."[36]

Vaniman himself was criticized by some experts who believed, as Dr. Paul F. Gans said to the *New-York Tribune*, that "Vaniman had not, through study or practice, acquired sufficient knowledge" to build an airship that would meet an engineer's approval. Echoing Wellman in *The Aerial Age*, some dismissed Vaniman as a clever mechanic who lacked the knowledge or caution of a trained engineer. "Mr. Vaniman was a bold man," Gans concluded, "who built his airship solely on his nerve."[37]

"It seems tragical," *Scientific American* added, "that Vaniman, who has displayed exceptional ingenuity in many details, should have fallen a victim to neglect of proven facts."[38]

Other than Ida Vaniman, the widows of the $18-a-week crew members now faced destitution. Local people organized benefits to raise a relief fund. One affair charged admission to see Trent the cat—apparently not aboard the *Akron* that day but still a celebrity—along with recovered airship wreckage.[39]

Reporters also sought out Wellman for comment. "Melvin Vaniman was one of the bravest and most resourceful men I have ever known," he said, praising Vaniman's "valor, his persistency, his marvelous ingenuity as a mechanic." Wellman added that he "seemed destined to do great things."[40]

If Wellman harbored any bitterness toward his former partner, he did not show it. But he was careful to draw a distinction between Vaniman the man and Vaniman's airship dreams:

> The gas-buoyant airship is extra hazardous; it suffers sharp physical limitations; it is improbable the problem of true air navigation can ever be solved with it as the instrument. . . . Regardless of its permanent value as a step of progress, he had set his heart upon crossing the Atlantic by airship. With life and time, I think he would have achieved it.[41]

Now a year and a half removed from his final voyage, and past any hope of having his aerial navy proposal adopted, Wellman looked at aeronautics with the clear eyes of a man who has no personal stake in the outcome. Addressing aviation's rising death rate in an article for the *New York Sun*, he said that "flight cannot be stopped: the wheels of progress once set in motion, they roll on forever. It is in the blood of man to conquer the air, and he will go on till he does it, no matter how long it takes or how great the cost."[42]

Noble sentiment aside, he acknowledged that much of aeronautics had become "a vaudeville of the air in the name of science. . . . One of the most beautiful of man's endeavors to conquer nature is thus degenerated into a sort of Roman Coliseum . . . if we analyze ourselves frankly, danger is the fascination; the possibility of tragedy is the magnet which draws the multitude."[43]

Wellman deplored the waste of life in exhibition flights, though he still felt that aeroplanes could be useful in war. Airships, he believed, had a legitimate role in war and exploration, even if they were fundamentally too dangerous for passenger travel. But airship development should no longer rely on private funds as he and Vaniman had done. The costs and risks were too great. "Under Government control, with ample resources, scientific design and the best execution, the dirigible should be brought to its highest perfection as a war instrument with little or no loss of life." Wellman knew something about the pressure to cut corners, and he had his own ideas concerning the cause of the *Akron*'s demise. With government funding such as the Zeppelin company received in Germany, "considerations of cost would not lead to the use of inferior cloth in making the balloon."[44]

It was time, he said, for "more science and less sensationalism." These words could just as easily be invoked about Wellman's own career as an explorer and aeronaut, but what other means did he have? He was not a millionaire or a man with scientific credentials. He was a journalist. Sensationalism had been the only commodity he could trade for a chance to do the impossible. If at times his expeditions seemed little more than "advertising schemes," it was because he paid for his dreams by becoming a merchant of dreams. In this way his closing words about Vaniman could just as well have been about himself: "Vaniman the enthusiast and dreamer had to do the best he could with resources at his command, and he did well."[45]

Wellman said one other thing of note in that article, though it seemed to pass unnoticed, tucked away in the middle of a paragraph. He still defended the polar expeditions and believed that the Atlantic crossing was *possible* with current technology, if someone cared to risk it. But he was standing apart from it now, out of the glare of publicity, and no longer chasing redemption across a storm-tossed ocean.

"To cross the Atlantic by airship," he wrote, "is not and never was a rational proposal."[46]

Epilogue

New York City, 1912–1934

"I do not care for marriage as it exists today," Rita Wellman told journalist Jane Dixon in 1920. "It is so banal, don't you think?"

Dixon, who was best known for covering prizefights, called this the "first bomb exploded by the girlish writer in the abbreviated black frock and the very French shoes."[1]

Rita's famous father had always tried to maintain a conservative image even when promoting the most hazardous expedition. Now famous in her own right, the twenty-nine-year-old playwright and novelist delighted in subverting social conventions. Her plays and stories were filled with unhappy relationships and artistic young women struggling against the constraints of matrimony and motherhood.[2]

Rita was, in fact, married. Though she wrote mostly under her maiden name, legally she was Mrs. Edgar Leo, wife of a New York stockbroker and mother of a nine-year-old. Her daughter, Meta, had been conceived out-of-wedlock during the summer when the world's eyes (and scorn) were directed toward her father's airship hangar in Atlantic City. The woman who had once run away to join a theater company now found herself trapped in domestic life, even after having a novel published and a play produced on Broadway.[3]

"There is nothing in the world so stale as habit," she said, arguing that husbands and wives should maintain separate homes and not always dine together. She went further: "It is the sheerest folly for a man to marry any sort of creative woman—a writer, for example, or an artist or an actress."

"And your husband?" Dixon asked. "Does he agree with you on this point?"

Rita flashed a mischievous smile. "'My husband?' said the revolutionary, rippling into laughter. 'Oh, gracious—he is used to me!'"[4]

Fig. 26. Rita Wellman (Mrs. Edgar Leo) with her daughter, Meta, in 1916, a few years before Rita became famous as a playwright and novelist. Library of Congress Prints and Photographs Division, Arnold Genthe Collection, LC-DIG-agc-7a15372.

The following year Rita sold her rare book collection for nearly $19,000 and used the money to start an independent life, living abroad for as long as a year at a time while leaving Meta in her father's care. Though Rita and Edgar did not divorce, eventually they maintained separate residences even when Rita was in New York.[5]

Of all the Wellman daughters, Rita seems to have been the most like her father, seeking attention and adventure and growing restless between long absences from family. But an absentee father was acceptable in a way that an absentee mother was not. Rita did not speak publicly about her daughter, and journalists seemed unaware that the daring Miss Wellman was also a mother.

Rita told Jane Dixon that she knew only two married couples who were completely happy. She didn't say so, but her parents were not among them. Walter and Laura had split up sometime before the 1920 census, by which time Walter was living in Manhattan with Bergljot and their three children: Walter Jr., age twelve; Elsa, ten; and Francis, four. Laura also lived in Manhattan, sharing an apartment with her eldest daughter, Ruth, now a librarian with the New York Public Library, and Ruth's companion Isabella Doughty. Laura listed her marital status as "widowed."[6]

Rita's fame had eclipsed that of her father despite Walter's having published books in 1916 and 1918. Following Roosevelt's 1912 Bull Moose campaign, in which the former president ruined his old friend Taft but lost to Woodrow Wilson, Wellman for several years wrote only occasional articles before beginning his final political crusade during World War I. Two years into the bloodiest war the world had yet seen, he published a small volume with the incongruous title *The German Republic*. Germany was not, of course, a republic, and when the book appeared in mid-1916 it was difficult to imagine how a nation so fanatically devoted to the kaiser and the Fatherland ever could be.

In a way that would have seemed treasonous only a year later when the United States entered the war, Wellman begins his book by praising Germany for "the finest example of national patriotism and unity recorded in all the pages of history."[7] But he was no supporter of the kaiser's army; he was simply using his usual tactic of sympathizing with the group he was about to criticize. He follows with an impassioned indictment of German militarism written from the imagined perspective of the German people at the war's end. In Wellman's view Germany's defeat was inevitable, but in his narrative the war ends not with the Allies' conquest but with a sudden armistice.[8] Months of fruitless negotiation are followed by an apparent miracle, the rising force of a "great awakening" among the German people, who now realize that their beloved military, which they saw as existing for

national defense, is for the aristocracy a means to "maintain the power of caste in the state."[9]

In the end, Wellman writes, Germany accepts responsibility for the war but with qualifications. They are not to be blamed more than other great European nations for "permitting survival of the spirit of tribalism, armed nationalism."[10] The Germans recognize that their country became a menace because the people didn't control their own foreign policy; henceforth, the "power to make war must be wholly in the hands of those who are to bear the heat and burden of the war."[11] And the world must recognize that lasting peace will only come from an end to militarism itself, with universal disarmament and the arbitration of international disputes by a "Supreme Court of the World."[12]

Over the next few years Wellman's newspaper columns continued to develop his ideas and publicize those of others who were calling for a League of Nations.[13] He completed his next book, *The Force Supreme*, as the Second Battle of the Marne was ending in early August 1918; it was published just after the November 11 armistice.[14] In the book Wellman argues that the proper goal of the struggle isn't just to "make the world safe for democracy" as American war propaganda had it. If the Allied nations sought only to punish Germany, as Wellman feared, they would merely set the stage for the next war. He continues,

> If the world is not only to conquer Germany but become the gaoler of that great tribe, subjugate it and then keep it in subjugation with the old system of physical force, the world must make up its mind to be a vast military machine for many generations. For the moment vigilance nods, the iron grip is in the slightest relaxed, would come the fierce uprising to drive out the invader.[15]

And then Germany would look east toward Russia, which lay like "a flock of sheep in a rich pasture."[16]

"In the Germany of the future," Wellman explains, "there is to be no nation, nothing but an army."

> What once passed for a nation will be mere servants . . . for the military dynasty. Even motherhood is to be sin-dicated, made doubly efficient in its mission of breeding kanonfoder!

For the first time in history a great industrial nation is to be permanently mobilised into a purely military organism. Every German and every German's work are to be bound to the chariot wheels of the god of war. The doctrine that the individual exists for the state is to be carried to its super-extreme. There are to be no more citizens, no more individuals, only pieces of mechanism.

The final aim of this great mechanical state is war . . . upon all who dare try to block its way to world supremacy.[17]

Against this scenario Wellman offers a vision of a world in which rogue nations are controlled without warfare. "Every industrial nation is in effect a mail order establishment," he writes, dependent upon the world's transportation and communications infrastructure, international credit, and the willingness of other nations to trade with it.[18] That was the point of control. The solution was not to build some international military force capable of keeping everyone in line—that option would carry its own risks—but the nations should commit to disarmament and exclude from trade any nation that sought to rearm itself. Wellman was among those who believed that sanctions, not war, were the way of the future.

Drawing on his western frontier background, Wellman's book compares the process to a community that suppresses crime by means of a vigilance committee,

then learned the only way to keep it suppressed is to forbid the criminals to carry weapons, after that has learned the only way to make sure no criminal carries a weapon is to take weapons away from everybody, and learned finally the only way to keep weapons out of every one's hands is to make a community in which no one needs a weapon, thinks of carrying one, *or could stay and earn a livelihood if he did carry one.*[19]

In this work Wellman did not propose developing aerial navies or any kind of technological superweapon. He was done with that. Even the potential for industrial-scale devastation, he and the rest of the world now knew, did not prevent nations from going to war. Only a change of thinking could accomplish that. Throughout his career Wellman had believed in human progress not only in technology but in human relations as well.

Amid violent strikes and their suppression, amid wars and rumors of war, he had always looked to what he believed was the gradual growth of human enlightenment. One had to be an optimist to view the world as Wellman did—just as one had to be an optimist to attempt to fly to the North Pole or across the Atlantic Ocean—and it was in keeping with everything Wellman had ever believed that, as Europe lay in ruins and revolution, with millions of dead and millions more thirsting for revenge, he could write: "For the first time in history, there is a wellnigh universal concept that a wrong to one people is a wrong to the community of peoples."[20]

"An injury to one is the concern of all," was how Big Bill Haywood had put it, though Wellman had probably forgotten that. What mattered was the idea itself, and more than technology, he believed, ideas would change the world.[21]

WE MAKE HISTORY FASTER THAN GRANDPA DID, read a syndicated headline from August 1919. Old-timers, the article said, used to compare present and past by telling of pioneer days or the Civil War, but now "any adult can recall a period so radically different from this that it seems like another age. . . . There are debutantes who remember how Walter Wellman was laughed at for proposing to fly over the ocean!"[22]

British airmen John Alcock and Arthur Brown made the first nonstop transatlantic flight on June 14–15, 1919, flying an overloaded Vickers Vimy bomber from St. John's, Newfoundland, to County Galway, Ireland, in fewer than sixteen hours. Less than a month later, the British airship *R-34*, based on the design of a captured German zeppelin, made the first east–west aerial crossing and the first Atlantic crossing by airship. By prearrangement the *R-34* carried a piece of canvas that Murray Simon had cut from the car of the *America* before abandoning ship in 1910.[23]

It seemed like another age indeed when the world held its breath waiting for news of the *America*. After Alcock and Brown's flight, a *New-York Tribune* reporter visited Wellman at his home and found "an elderly, quiet gentleman living on Washington Heights who is conclusive proof that New York City and the rest of the world has a twenty-four-hour memory or less." Together the reporter and the sixty-year-old Wellman pored over news clippings that were already "a bit yellowed around the edges" and talked of the old days so that the reporter could rehash the story for readers who had forgotten it.[24]

Wellman no longer saw much future in airships. When in 1925 the USS *Shenandoah* (ZR-1) was torn apart in a storm over Ohio, resulting in the deaths of fourteen of its forty-three-man crew, Wellman complained that the U.S. Navy was wasting money and lives on a technology that had already proved useless in war and was too hazardous for commercial use.[25]

But exploration was still the one thing that Wellman had always said could justify an airship's inherent risks. On May 12, 1926, the airship *Norge* (Norway) passed over the North Pole on a nonstop flight from Spitsbergen to Alaska. At 672,000 cubic feet, it was twice the size of the *America*, and with three 250-horsepower engines it had far greater power, with a cruising speed of 50 miles per hour.[26] The *Norge* shared one bit of irony with Wellman's airship, however; just as the *America* had been built in France, the *Norge* was built in Italy. Norwegian Roald Amundsen and American Lincoln Ellsworth headed the expedition, but Italian airshipman Umberto Nobile designed, built, and piloted the airship.

Wellman claimed vindication for himself and the other "pioneers," but his vicarious triumph may have been even greater than he thought.[27] Before the *Norge*, three expeditions claimed to have reached the North Pole: Cook in 1908, Peary in 1909, and aviator Richard Evelyn Byrd Jr. in 1926, only days before the *Norge* departed. Though each of these men still has his partisans, historians have shredded all three's polar claims. Wellman participated in the preliminary debunking of Cook's story, and subsequent research has further discredited Cook. Many holes in Peary's account were apparent to skeptics in Wellman's day, but Peary's papers were unavailable to scholars until the National Geographic Society finally released them in 1987. Most historians now think not only that Peary failed to reach the pole but also that most of the earlier achievements on which his reputation was based were also false or exaggerated. Finally, Byrd's account suffers from the same basic problem as Cook's and Peary's: his mileage and fuel numbers are implausible. And when Byrd's original erasure-filled flight log was finally released in 1996, it was found to contain two sets of sextant readings, with one set having been erased and covered over with significantly different numbers.[28]

It appears, then, that the first people to reach the North Pole—and certainly the first with a verified claim—did so in an airship, just as Wellman had predicted two decades earlier.

As for the first attempt by air, no one knew what had become of S. A. Andrée and his two companions. They had simply been swallowed up by the vastness of the Arctic Ocean. For all anyone knew, they might have been first to the pole but died before they could tell anyone. In 1930 Andrée's final camp was discovered on the barely accessible White Island (Kvitøya) east of Spitsbergen. The men's diaries and the undeveloped film in their camera told their story. After floating, bouncing, and dragging 295 miles in three days, the balloon refused to rise. They dragged sledges back to White Island by early October, but there the diaries end abruptly. The men's bodies—one buried in haste—were found dead in camp. Their exact cause of death remains uncertain.[29]

None of Wellman's former associates ever made it to the North Pole, though Evelyn Baldwin tried for years to raise money for a new expedition after the failure of the 1901 Baldwin-Ziegler North Pole Expedition.[30] One member of the 1910 crew, however, eventually crossed the Atlantic in an airship. In May 1936 Cdr. Murray Simon, still proud of his association with Wellman and the *America*, was among the passengers on the maiden transatlantic voyage of that greatest of airships, Germany's *Hindenburg* (LZ129).[31]

Simon was not aboard the *Hindenburg* the following year when it burst into flames while landing at Lakehurst, New Jersey, killing thirty-six people. Vaniman's *Akron* had been New Jersey's first airship disaster and the *Hindenburg* its last, but neither was its deadliest. On April 4, 1933, the 785-foot-long uss *Akron* (zrs-4) went down in a thunderstorm off the Jersey coast, killing all but three of the seventy-six men aboard and resulting in the world's worst airship disaster. The second *Akron* crashed soon after passing over Barnegat Light, New Jersey, about thirty miles up the coast from where the first *Akron* had burst near Atlantic City.[32]

Ida Vaniman and her brother Louis Loud returned home to Illinois. When Atlantic City issued a special postal cachet in 1935 to commemorate the twenty-fifth anniversary of the *America*'s flight, Loud wrote in to identify himself as a proud survivor of the crew. He and his sister were still living in Springfield.[33]

Jack Irwin, who spent some time lecturing on the vaudeville stage after the 1910 Atlantic flight, married an actress in 1911. He went west after he

left Vaniman's employment the following year, but his wife refused to come along. "I suspect she cared more for the stage than for me," he said.[34] Irwin went on to a career in the U.S. Army Signal Corps, rising to the rank of colonel before he was killed in action in World War II.[35]

From the 1906–7 expedition, Felix Riesenberg later became a prolific author. As noted previously, in 1922 he wrote *Standard Seamanship for the Merchant Service*, a common textbook for a generation of seamen, before turning to novels and movie screenplays. He died in 1939.[36]

And Paul Bjørvig, Wellman's beloved, bear-chasing "wild man" who experienced so much tragedy in the Far North, lived to become a respected elder seaman in his native Tromsø. He died in 1932 at age seventy-five and lies beneath a lovely marble monument carved to resemble a polar bear climbing over a block of ice. Above his name is the word *Ishavsfarer* (Arctic sailor, literally Ice Sea-farer), both a job description and a title of honor.[37]

One can imagine such a gravestone for Walter Wellman, though perhaps topped with an airship rather than a polar bear. But as far as I know he has none, and the final disposition of his ashes is likewise unknown. Perhaps like Felix Riesenberg's, they were scattered at sea.[38]

Though at the peak of his career Wellman was among the nation's highest-paid journalists, in his later years he had to rely on the support of friends. For a few years in the early 1920s, he received financial assistance from *New York Times* publisher Adolph Ochs.[39] In 1926 Wellman was arrested and jailed for an unpaid debt of $280.[40] Calling the situation "too sad a spectacle to be endured," banker and amateur explorer H. Murray Jacoby paid the debt to release Wellman the next day.[41]

Wellman managed to keep his and Bergljot's family in their Washington Heights apartment for the rest of his life, even into the dark years of the Great Depression. Not everyone in his first family was so fortunate. Financial worries led to the suicide of Rita's estranged husband, Edgar Leo, who shot himself in his apartment on September 9, 1930. He was discovered next to a stack of unpaid bills and a slip of paper bearing Rita's name and telephone number.[42] She continued writing, turning mostly to art criticism. Their daughter, Meta, became an artist with a taste for travel; she moved to England and married in 1937.[43]

Fig. 27. A Walter Wellman press photo from 1926, the year he was briefly jailed for an unpaid debt of $280. Author's collection.

By 1932 the Depression caught up to Rae Wellman Warner, the middle Wellman daughter. She and her husband fell on hard times in California and at last were forced to hitchhike from Los Angeles to San Jose. Afterward her husband said they split up, thinking they'd get along better apart; Rae said they had a suicide pact. She gave a false name when taken to a

hospital after slashing her wrists and poisoning herself, but her identity was soon found out. The story went coast to coast. WOULD-BE SUICIDE WELLMAN'S DAUGHTER, read a *New York Times* headline on June 19.

"We are white collar people," the trained operatic singer told the *Oakland Tribune*, "and there doesn't seem to be any place in the world for white collar people when they get down and out."[44] Rae recovered and eventually lived in San Francisco with her sister Rebekah, who by then was divorced from Fred Aubert. The women shared a house and took in boarders.[45]

Things were better with Rose Wellman Chamberlin and her husband, LeRoy, to whom Vaniman had once sent a wireless message about a certain "goddam cat." The Chamberlins became prosperous citizens in Waterford, Virginia, and part of the Wellman family gathered around them: Laura, later Rita, and, if only for burial, Ruth.[46]

Still living with his second family in New York, Walter Wellman died of liver cancer on February 1, 1934. Newspapers hailed him as a "pioneer," remembering his airship flights, especially his final one, more than his journalism.[47]

Though still widely recognized at the time of his death, Wellman's name faded with the passage of time, as names tend to do. Pieces of his story became colorful anecdotes in various histories of aeronautics, polar exploration, or Progressive era politics. Few historians have dealt with him at length.[48] The most damning critique comes not from a historian but from a fellow explorer, Fridtjof Nansen, who, in his 1920 book *En ferd til Spitsbergen* (A journey to Spitsbergen), describes Wellman as

> a strange man who demonstrates how one may, with the help of the great art of advertising, keep the world's newspapers' attention year after year without having one single thing of interest to report. It's simply a matter of knowing what sort of material the newspapers crave in order to satisfy the world's spiritual needs—and in this area the man was truly great.[49]

Nansen, of course, had enjoyed the patient beneficence of his nation's government as he spent years preparing his experimental ship, the *Fram*. Wellman had no such luxury when it came to funding. A newspaperman, he played the only game he knew, and he both thrived and suffered within

its limitations. As for his skills in the field, he was never going to be a Nansen or Amundsen—or a Wright or a Santos-Dumont for that matter—but under other circumstances he might have been a Count Zeppelin, providing vision and charismatic leadership for some great national effort.

But in many ways the criticism of Wellman as an explorer or an aeronaut misses the point. Nansen was correct in identifying Wellman's field of greatness, even if Nansen disapproved and considered him a humbug. Quoting Nansen's words in a 2007 scholarly article about Wellman, Jan Anders Diesen and Neil Fulton suggest that "Wellman probably deserves greater space in the history of the media than in the history of polar exploration."[50]

That suggestion has informed this book, in which I've tried to give equal play both to the events themselves and to the way in which those events were curated and packaged for mass media consumption. Wellman's career defies easy categorization not only because of the many different roles he played—explorer, political operative, aeronaut, pitchman, journalist, reformer, celebrity, and social and technological visionary—but also because the individual roles became blurred, one spilling over into another in a way that seems oddly familiar to the twenty-first-century reader. Wellman existed within a new cultural space of the amplified feedback loop of modern mass media, and this area—not the Arctic or the air—was his primary field of exploration. Wellman was not simply the progeny of Elisha Kent Kane, who spun a failed expedition into national heroism by way of a best-selling book, or of James Gordon Bennett Jr., who sold newspapers by sending journalist Henry Stanley to look for David Livingstone in Africa; he was also the forerunner of all those who use mass media to give the public the vicarious thrill of exploration. We can imagine a twenty-first-century Wellman taking a leave of absence from cable news political coverage to film his attempted trip to Mars as a reality show. For better or for worse, he was a man for our times.

Wellman had been all but forgotten by 1961 when Edward Mabley published an article titled "Wild Ride of the Gas Bag Sailors" in *True* magazine. Mabley, who as a boy witnessed the launch of the *America* in Atlantic City, soon received letters from Murray Simon and Fred Aubert, from A. J. Corbitt from the 1909 crew, and from Wellman's grandson Wellman Chamberlin. Mabley corresponded with or visited each of these men

and used their information to expand the article into his 1969 book, *The Motor Balloon "America."* Though based mostly on newspapers, the book's eyewitness sources made it the final Wellman narrative informed by living memory.[51]

Several years later the Walt Disney Company began work on a motion picture based on Ian Cameron's 1961 novel *The Lost Ones*, which was set in 1960 and involved a helicopter journey in search of a legendary Arctic island that was still inhabited by Vikings. In Disney's hands the year changed to 1907, and the helicopter became a *Lebaudy*-style airship. The movie was released in 1974 as *The Island at the Top of the World*. At the time I thought it was the best movie ever made, and I spent hours building crude airships from Legos and flying them through the Arctic mists toward imaginary islands.

The movie's glory had faded by the time I watched it on video many years later, but I still think the producers were wise to trade the helicopter for an airship and to choose a more romantic year. But until I heard of Wellman, I had no idea that the polar airship was based on reality. Someone involved with the movie knew about Wellman, perhaps from Mabley's book.

But that wasn't how the movie was promoted. Posters promised "Adventure Beyond Imagination," and the theatrical trailer boasted that the story was "in the Walt Disney Jules Verne tradition." Wellman in his day was often seen as a Jules Verne character come to life and was once falsely accused of plagiarizing the French novelist to create his airship narrative.

It seems appropriate, then, that someone should borrow from Wellman's real life to make a Jules Verne–style movie. This, at last, brings his story full circle. Wellman was active at a moment in history when his plans passed from science fiction to possibility to obsolescence in the space of a few years. In the end, he probably knew he would not be long remembered, but perhaps he would take pleasure at finding his own echo in an imaginary story, a part of himself transformed into an ancient myth from the dawn of the aerial age.

NOTES

Abbreviations

CRH *Chicago Record-Herald*

NASM National Air & Space Museum Archives

NYT *New York Times*

Prologue

1. "Wellman Off for Europe in His Airship America," NYT, October 16, 1910.

2. "Wellman Starts for Europe," *New-York Tribune*, October 16, 1910.

3. "Wellman Starts for Europe," *New-York Tribune*, October 16, 1910.

4. "Problems of First Transatlantic Balloon Trip," NYT, July 10, 1910; and "Getting Ready to Fly Oversea in a Balloon," NYT, August 7, 1910. Capelotti discusses earlier modifications of the *America* in *Wellman Polar Airship Expeditions*, 60–70, 92.

5. "Wellman Flying over Sea, Off for Europe in Airship," *Washington (DC) Times*, October 15, 1910.

6. "Wellman Off for Europe in His Airship America," NYT, October 16, 1910.

1. In Search of Christopher Columbus

1. "His First Sea Voyage," *Capital City Courier* (Lincoln NE), July 18, 1891.

2. "His First Sea Voyage," *Capital City Courier* (Lincoln NE), July 18, 1891.

3. "His First Sea Voyage," *Capital City Courier* (Lincoln NE), July 18, 1891.

4. "His First Sea Voyage," *Capital City Courier* (Lincoln NE), July 18, 1891.

5. "Columbus' First Landing," *Evening Star* (Washington DC), June 4, 1891.

6. Wellman, *Descendants of Thomas Wellman*, 500. Wellman was actually born in nearby Concord, but as an adult he always claimed Mentor as his hometown.

7. "Lake County Mini-Profiles—the Story of Walter Wellman," Local Lore, *News-Herald* (Willoughby OH), October 7, 2013, http://wwwnews-heraldcom.blogspot.com/2013/10/lake-county-mini-profiles-story-of.html.

8. Sherard, *Civil War Veterans*, 37.

9. Mabley, *Motor Balloon "America,"* 16; and "Walter Wellman," *Wichita (KS) Daily Eagle*, April 5, 1894.

10. "Death Record," *Omaha Bee*, October 9, 1902.

11. Old Settlers Association, *Old Settlers' History*, 67.

12. "Walter Wellman," *Wichita (KS) Daily Eagle*, April 5, 1894.

13. *Centennial Sketch of Clay County*, 4. Copies of the *Sutton (NE) Times* are no longer extant. See also Hinel, *Story of Clay County*, 39. For the patent inside, see Kjaer, *Productivity of Labor*, 150.

14. "Nebraska in Brief," *Columbus (NE) Journal*, December 29, 1909 (reprint of December 1879 article from *York [NE] Republican*).

15. "Walter Wellman Won," *Pullman (WA) Herald*, August 10, 1894 (reprint of undated *New York Herald* article).

16. "Walter Wellman," *Wichita (KS) Daily Eagle*, April 5, 1894.

17. "The Young Editor of the Repository," *Stark County (OH) Democrat*, August 14, 1879.

18. "Lake County Mini-Profiles."

19. "Wellman's Case," *Canton (OH) Repository*, October 8, 1881.

20. "Wellman's Case," *Canton (OH) Repository*, October 8, 1881; and "The Penny Paper Plot," *Cincinnati Daily Gazette*, October 12, 1881.

21. "The Penny Paper Plot," *Cincinnati Daily Gazette*, October 12, 1881.

22. "Personal Mention," *Stark County (OH) Democrat*, November 24, 1881; and "The End of Wellman's Case," *Canton (OH) Repository*, December 20, 1881.

23. "Scripps Card," *Cincinnati Penny Post*, September 1, 1883.

24. Scripps, *History of the Scripps Concern*, 161–63.

25. Scripps, *History of the Scripps Concern*, 161–63.

26. "Local Laconics," *Stark County (OH) Democrat*, March 9, 1882.

27. Cohill, *Spin on the Past*, 11.

28. Editorial, *Eaton (OH) Democrat*, August 30, 1883; and editorial, *Spirit of Democracy* (Eaton OH), July 31, 1883.

29. "Criminal Libel," *Cleveland Leader*, May 19, 1883; "Libel Suit," *Canton (OH) Repository*, June 6, 1883; editorial, *Democratic Northwest* (Napoleon OH), November 29, 1883; and "Akron Daily News Dead," *Cincinnati Commercial Gazette*, July 25, 1883.

30. Cohill, *Spin on the Past*, 8.

31. "More Manufactories," *Summit County (Akron OH) Beacon*, August 15, 1883.

32. "Council Proceedings," *Stark County (OH) Democrat*, January 2, 1884.

33. Mabley, *Motor-Balloon "America,"* 16.

34. Walter Wellman, "Girls at the Capital," *Austin Weekly Statesman*, January 29, 1891. Wellman was said to be a believer in women's rights. See "Fun Makers," *Canton (OH) Repository*, April 20, 1886.

35. "Where Columbus Landed," *Wichita Daily Eagle*, July 31, 1891.

36. "Where Columbus Landed," *Wichita Daily Eagle*, July 31, 1891.

37. "Where Columbus Landed," *Wichita Daily Eagle*, July 31, 1891; and van der Krogt and van der Krogt, "Chicago Monument."

38. "Where Columbus Landed," *Sunday Herald and Weekly National Intelligencer* (Washington DC), July 5, 1891.

39. Redway, "First Landfall of Columbus," 179–92.

40. "Columbus' First Landing," *Evening Star* (Washington DC), June 4, 1891.

2. Arctic Enthusiasm

1. Walter Wellman, "Omens of Trouble," *Roanoke (VA) Times*, January 6, 1894.
2. Letter from Walter Wellman to his family, April 26, 1894, Wellman NASM.
3. "Saturday's Twenty-Page Star," *Evening Star* (Washington DC), February 23, 1894.
4. Berton, *Arctic Grail*, 333.
5. Berton, *Arctic Grail*, 18–19.
6. Berton, *Arctic Grail*, 331. See also Rondeau, "Wrecks of Franklin's Ships," 1–3.
7. Berton, *Arctic Grail*, 337–38.
8. Berton, *Arctic Grail*, 151.
9. Berton, *Arctic Grail*, 268.
10. Berton, *Arctic Grail*, 151.
11. Robinson, *Coldest Crucible*, 31.
12. Robinson, *Coldest Crucible*, 34–35.
13. Robinson, *Coldest Crucible*, 43–44.
14. Robinson, *Coldest Crucible*, 45–48.
15. Berton, *Arctic Grail*, 303; and Robinson, *Coldest Crucible*, 48–54.
16. Mill, "Race to the North Pole," 147.
17. Mill, "Race to the North Pole," 150–55.
18. Mill, "Race to the North Pole," 147.
19. Walter Wellman, "To the North Pole," *Evening Star* (Washington DC), February 24, 1894.
20. Walter Wellman, "To the North Pole," *Evening Star* (Washington DC), February 24, 1894.
21. At that time the Svalbard archipelago was usually known by the name of its largest island, Spitsbergen, a practice I will follow throughout.
22. Berton, *Arctic Grail*, 97–98.
23. Berton, *Arctic Grail*, 98–100.
24. Berton, *Arctic Grail*, 100–101.
25. Walter Wellman, "Fish at the Fair," *Bismarck Weekly Tribune*, June 23, 1893.
26. Capelotti, *Greatest Show in the Arctic*, 29–33.
27. Walter Wellman, "To the North Pole," *Evening Star* (Washington DC), February 24, 1894.
28. Waldo, "Aluminum in the United States," in Minet, *Production of Aluminum*, 243–44.
29. Waldo, "Aluminum in the United States," in Minet, *Production of Aluminum*, 243–44.
30. Walter Wellman, "To the North Pole," *Evening Star* (Washington DC), February 24, 1894.

3. A Dog Show and the Seven Islands

1. Walter Wellman, "Dogs for the Pole," *Evening Star* (Washington DC), May 5, 1894.
2. Walter Wellman, "Dogs for the Pole," *Evening Star* (Washington DC), May 5, 1894.
3. Walter Wellman, "Dogs for the Pole," *Evening Star* (Washington DC), May 5, 1894.

4. Walter Wellman, "Dogs for the Pole," *Evening Star* (Washington DC), May 5, 1894; and "To the North Pole," *Evening Star* (Washington DC), February 24, 1894.

5. Evelyn Baldwin, Wellman's second-in-command in his 1898–99 expedition, wrote in his diary that "Mr. Wellman had said that Norwegians were better than Eskimos to assist in the work [of reaching the North Pole] and therefore the Expedition had" gone to Franz-Josef Land. See Baldwin, *Franz Josef Land Archipelago*, 109. An 1898 newspaper report said Wellman used Norwegians because "experience has proved to him that Norwegians are much more hardy, understand traveling through the frozen zone in all its technical details quite as well as the Eskimos, and have vastly greater courage, intelligence and persistence." See "The Pole Is His Mecca," *Saint Paul Globe*, May 29, 1898, 19.

6. "The Pole Is His Mecca," *Saint Paul Globe*, May 29, 1898, 19.

7. Walter Wellman, "His Dogs in Norway," *Evening Star* (Washington DC), May 26, 1894.

8. Walter Wellman, "Bound for the Pole," *Evening Star* (Washington DC), June 2, 1894; and Walter Wellman, "Wellman Ice Bound," *Evening Star* (Washington DC), September 29, 1894.

9. Wellman, "Bound for the Pole," *Evening Star* (Washington DC), June 2, 1894.

10. "News from Wellman," *Anaconda (MT) Standard*, July 20, 1894. (July 19 dispatch from Tromsø, reporting a May 10 dispatch from Danes Island that Wellman had sent with the captain of the yacht *Sadie*.)

11. Walter Wellman, "Pullman a Success," *Springfield (OH) Globe-Republic*, December 5, 1886.

12. "The Wellman Expedition," *Los Angeles Herald*, July 15, 1894. It reports a cable dispatch from Tromsø expressing fears for Wellman's safety.

13. "Lost in the Ice," *San Francisco Call*, July 25, 1894; and Associated Press, "Is Wellman's Party Lost?," *New York World*, July 24, 1894.

14. "The Wellman Party," *Evening Star* (Washington DC), July 24, 1894.

15. Walter Wellman, "Ramming through the Ice," *Evening Star* (Washington DC), September 22, 1894.

16. Walter Wellman, "Ramming through the Ice," *Evening Star* (Washington DC), September 22, 1894.

17. Walter Wellman, "Ramming through the Ice," *Evening Star* (Washington DC), September 22, 1894.

18. Wellman, "Wellman Ice Bound," *Evening Star* (Washington DC), September 29, 1894.

19. Walter Wellman, "They Pressed On," *Evening Star* (Washington DC), October 20, 1894. Henry Wemyss Feilden, a British military officer and naturalist who was aboard the ship that discovered Øyen on Danes Island, said Norwegian seal and walrus hunters in the area told him the *Jarl* was old, underpowered, and unsuited for the polar ice. See Capelotti, *Greatest Show in the Arctic*, 45.

20. Walter Wellman, "Wellman in the Ice," *Evening Star* (Washington DC), September 22, 1894; and Wellman, "Wellman Ice Bound," *Evening Star* (Washington DC), September 29, 1894.

21. P. J. Capelotti devotes a part of *By Airship to the North Pole* to Wellman's veracity (129–61). In two instances he was "able to match [Wellman's] words against his archaeology" and found not only that the all-steel airship car Wellman boasted about in his 1906 reports was actually a flimsy thing built mostly of wood but also that Wellman was correct, and not just making an excuse, when he claimed in 1907 that substandard iron filings had resulted in a poorer quality of hydrogen for his airship.

22. "Paul Bjørvig."

23. Walter Wellman, "Leaving the Jarl," *Evening Star* (Washington DC), October 6, 1894.

24. Walter Wellman, "Leaving the Jarl," *Evening Star* (Washington DC), October 6, 1894.

25. Walter Wellman, "Leaving the Jarl," *Evening Star* (Washington DC), October 6, 1894.

26. Walter Wellman, "Leaving the Jarl," *Evening Star* (Washington DC), October 6, 1894.

27. Walter Wellman, "Leaving the Jarl," *Evening Star* (Washington DC), October 6, 1894.

28. Wellman, "They Pressed On," *Evening Star* (Washington DC), October 20, 1894.

29. Wellman, "They Pressed On," *Evening Star* (Washington DC), October 20, 1894.

4. Shipwrecked at the Hotel White Bear

1. Walter Wellman, "Arctic Travel," *Evening Star* (Washington DC), October 27, 1894; and Walter Wellman, "They Pressed On," *Evening Star* (Washington DC), October 20, 1894.

2. Godoy, "'Cocaine for Snowblindness.'"

3. Wellman, "They Pressed On," *Evening Star* (Washington DC), October 20, 1894.

4. Wellman, "They Pressed On," *Evening Star* (Washington DC), October 20, 1894.

5. Wellman, "Arctic Travel," *Evening Star* (Washington DC), October 27, 1894.

6. Wellman, "They Pressed On," *Evening Star* (Washington DC), October 20, 1894.

7. Wellman, "They Pressed On," *Evening Star* (Washington DC), October 20, 1894.

8. Wellman, "Sledging toward the Pole," 410. Robert Peary, for example, took enough dogs on his 1909 polar expedition "to allow for the loss of sixty per cent" (Peary, *North Pole*, 202). See also Nickerson, *Harnessed to the Pole*, for a book-length study of the treatment of sledge dogs during this period.

9. Wellman, "Arctic Travel," *Evening Star* (Washington DC), October 27, 1894.

10. Wellman, *Aerial Age*, 28.

11. Walter Wellman, "The Ice King Wins," *Evening Star* (Washington DC), November 3, 1894.

12. Walter Wellman, "The Ice King Wins," *Evening Star* (Washington DC), November 3, 1894.

13. Walter Wellman, "The Ice King Wins," *Evening Star* (Washington DC), November 3, 1894.

14. Walter Wellman, "The Ice King Wins," *Evening Star* (Washington DC), November 3, 1894. North Rep Island is also known as Nordre Repøya.

15. Walter Wellman, "The Ice King Wins," *Evening Star* (Washington DC), November 3, 1894.

16. Letter from Walter Wellman to Arthur Wellman, August 20, 1894, Wellman NASM.

17. See Capelotti, *Greatest Show in the Arctic*, 48.

18. Wellman, *Aerial Age*, 27. Platen Island, also known as Platenhalvøya, the northeastern part of Prins Oscars Land. Wellman had already said that the area was not well mapped, and during this expedition he named some geographical points that, as it turned out, others had already named.

19. Wellman, *Aerial Age*, 30–31.

20. Walter Wellman, "Toil and Peril" *Evening Star* (Washington DC), November 10, 1894.

21. Walter Wellman, "Home at Last," *Evening Star* (Washington DC), November 17, 1894.

22. Walter Wellman, "Home at Last," *Evening Star* (Washington DC), November 17, 1894.

23. "Wellman Talks," *Evening Star* (Washington DC), September 29, 1894. Henry Wemyss Feilden, who found Øyen on Danes Island, thought the supplies at Wellman's camp would have been inadequate if the expedition had to winter there. See Capelotti, *Greatest Show in the Arctic*, 45.

24. Wellman, "Wellman in the Ice," *Evening Star* (Washington DC), September 22, 1894; and Wellman, "Fighting the Ice," *Evening Star* (Washington DC), August 15, 1894.

25. Wellman, *Aerial Age*, 21–22.

26. Editorial, *New York Sun*, September 9, 1894; and "Wellman Will Try Again," *New-York Tribune*, September 28, 1894.

27. Walter Wellman, "De Bausset's Designs," *Springfield (OH) Daily Republic*, June 18, 1887.

28. Wellman, *Aerial Age*, 36.

29. Letter from Walter Wellman to Arthur Wellman, August 20, 1894, Wellman NASM.

30. Wellman, *Aerial Age*, 37.

31. Wellman, *Aerial Age*, 37.

5. The President Cannot Be Stampeded

1. Walter Wellman, "Delay of Mr. M'Kinley," *Houston (TX) Daily Post*, November 18, 1897.

2. "It Cannot Be Done," *Saint Paul (MN) Globe*, November 17, 1897, 4; and editorial, *Rock Island (IL) Argus*, April 16, 1898.

3. Gould, "William McKinley."

4. Reprinted as "Intervention Coming," *Kansas City (MO) Journal*, March 5, 1898.

5. Walter Wellman, "Touching the Fact of Responsibility," *Scranton (PA) Tribune*, February 23, 1898.

6. Walter Wellman, "Mines at Havana," *Kansas City (MO) Journal*, February 25, 1898.

7. Walter Wellman, "Mines at Havana," *Kansas City (MO) Journal*, February 25, 1898.

8. Walter Wellman, "No Immediate Danger of War," *Kansas City (MO) Journal*, February 27, 1898.

9. Walter Wellman, "Spain Preparing for War," *Kansas City (MO) Journal*, February 27, 1898.

10. Walter Wellman, "Says Intervention Is Certain," *Rock Island (IL) Argus*, March 3, 1898.

11. Walter Wellman, "War Cloud Lifting," *Kansas City (MO) Journal*, March 16, 1898.

12. Walter Wellman, "President's Plan of Cuban Intervention," *Scranton (PA) Tribune*, March 26, 1898.

13. Walter Wellman, "Cuban Annexation," *Copper Country (Calumet MI) Evening News*, April 16, 1898.

14. Gould, "William McKinley."

15. The cause of the explosion is still disputed by historians.

16. Walter Wellman, "Where Corruption Flourishes," *Freeland (PA) Tribune*, May 9, 1898.

17. Editorial, *Daily Ardmoreite* (Ardmore OK), May 29, 1898; editorial, *Sioux City Times*, reprinted in *Omaha Daily Bee*, May 14, 1898; and regarding Wellman's plans, see letter from Walter Wellman to Arthur Wellman, July 10, 1897, Wellman NASM.

6. Like Opening a Grave

1. Letter from Walter Wellman to Arthur Wellman, July 1, 1898, Wellman NASM. Wellman figured that he could at least catch a ride back to Norway with any ship that happened to be in the area (and pay later), as he had done in 1894 in Spitsbergen. But fewer ships visited Franz Josef Land, and there was no guarantee one would come in 1899. See also Capelotti, *Greatest Show in the Arctic*, 67, 174–76.

2. Wellman, "On the Way to the North Pole," 533.

3. Barr, *Franz Josef Land*, 8–11.

4. "Wellman Is in Washington," *Washington (DC) Times*, September 29, 1894.

5. Barr, *Franz Josef Land*, 68–69.

6. Capelotti, *Greatest Show in the Arctic*, 63–64.

7. Andrée, *Andrée's Story*, 43.

8. Andrée, *Andrée's Story*, 43.

9. Wilkinson, *Ice Balloon*, 16.

10. "Who First Suggested," *Aeronautical Journal*, 20; and Wilkinson, *Ice Balloon*, 36–39.

11. "Who First Suggested," *Aeronautical Journal*, 20; and Wilkinson, *Ice Balloon*, 36–39.

12. Crouch, *Eagle Aloft*, 465–69.

13. Wise, *System of Aeronautics*, 271–96.

14. Wise, *System of Aeronautics*, 271–96.

15. Wise, *System of Aeronautics*, 95–97.

16. Bacon, *Dominion of the Air*, 6–7, 109–10.

17. Bacon, *Dominion of the Air*, 6–7, 109–10.

18. Andrée, *Andrée's Story*, 21–24.

19. Andrée, *Andrée's Story*, 34–35.

20. Wilkinson, *Ice Balloon*, 24–25.

21. Andrée, *Andrée's Story*, 37–39.

22. Hempleman-Adams, *At the Mercy*, 82–83.

23. Andrée, *Andrée's Story*, 54–55.

24. Hempleman-Adams, *At the Mercy*, 158.

25. Andrée, *Andrée's Story*, 75–76.

26. Wellman, "Where Is Andrée?," 422–26; and Baldwin, *Franz Josef Land Archipelago*, 29.

27. Riesenberg, *Living Again*, 133–34. A Wellman crew member in 1906–7, Riesenberg heard the story at that time from Bjørvig, who presumably also told it to Wellman in 1898. Wellman tells a similar story in *Aerial Age* (1911) that he attributes to unnamed men present at Andrée's departure.

28. Wellman, "On the Way," 533.

29. Wellman, "On the Way," 533. According to Baldwin, the party continued to hold out hope for at least a few days longer. See Baldwin, *Franz Josef Land Archipelago*, 34–38.

30. Wellman, *Aerial Age*, 38–39.

31. Wellman, *Aerial Age*, 38–39.

7. Tell Them What It Was Like for Us

1. Wellman, "Arctic Day and Night," 556.

2. Wellman, "Arctic Day and Night," 556.

3. Wellman, "Arctic Day and Night," 556.

4. "Walter Wellman's Polar Trip," NYT, August 25, 1897.

5. Letter from Walter Wellman to His Family, August 1, 1898, Wellman NASM, Box 1, Folder 9. Spelling has been standardized; Wellman often used many abbreviations.

6. Letter from Walter Wellman to His Daughters, August 2, 1898, Wellman NASM, Box 1, Folder 10.

7. Letter from Walter Wellman to Arthur Wellman, July 1, 1898, Wellman NASM.

8. Letter from Walter Wellman to Arthur Wellman, August 2, 1898, Wellman NASM.

9. Wellman, "Wellman Polar Expedition," 482; and Barr, *Franz Josef Land*, 77, 110.

10. Wellman, "Wellman Polar Expedition," 481, 486–89.

11. Letter from Walter Wellman to His Family, August 1, 1898, Wellman NASM.

12. Letter from Walter Wellman to Arthur Wellman, August 2, 1898, Wellman NASM.

13. Gore, "Wellman Polar Expedition," 267.

14. Baldwin, *Franz Josef Land Archipelago*, 3. See also Capelotti, "Historical Geography of an Archipelago of Polar Explorers," 15.

15. Baldwin, *Franz Josef Land Archipelago*, 3.

16. Wellman and Baldwin first corresponded in 1894. Capelotti, *Greatest Show in the Arctic*, 54.

17. Cather, *World and the Parish*, 833. Willa Cather may have met Baldwin in Washington in 1898, when she interviewed Wellman and wrote Associated Press reports about the upcoming expedition.

18. Baldwin, *Franz Josef Land Archipelago*, 13, 127.

19. Baldwin, *Franz Josef Land Archipelago*, 45, 130.

20. Baldwin, *Franz Josef Land Archipelago*, 48.

21. Baldwin, *Franz Josef Land Archipelago*, 130.

22. "Aluminum Boats," *Turner County (Hurley SD) Herald*, October 17, 1895. The metal "could be easily crumbled in one's hand."

23. Westerdahl, "Sewn Boats of the North," 33–62.

24. Baldwin, *Franz Josef Land Archipelago*, 50, 54, 153.

25. Baldwin, *Franz Josef Land Archipelago*, 134.

26. Baldwin, *Franz Josef Land Archipelago*, 136.

27. Baldwin, *Franz Josef Land Archipelago*, 136.

28. Baldwin, *Franz Josef Land Archipelago*, 60.

29. Baldwin, *Franz Josef Land Archipelago*, 144.

30. Baldwin, *Franz Josef Land Archipelago*, 145.

31. Baldwin, *Franz Josef Land Archipelago*, 149.

32. Bjørvig, *Norwegian Bravado*, 6. P. J. Capelotti discusses Bjørvig's diary and his relationships with Bentsen and Baldwin in *Greatest Show in the Arctic*, 139–62, 179–83.

33. Baldwin, *Franz Josef Land Archipelago*, 81.

34. Wellman, "Arctic Day and Night," 560.

35. Baldwin, *Franz Josef Land Archipelago*, 87, 90–94.

36. On August 4 Wellman had warned Baldwin to "avoid glacier-crossing if possible." Baldwin, *Franz Josef Land Archipelago*, 128.

37. Baldwin, *Franz Josef Land Archipelago*, 95–98; and Barr, *Franz Josef Land*, 78.

38. Baldwin, *Franz Josef Land Archipelago*, 100–101.

39. Baldwin, *Franz Josef Land Archipelago*, 136.

40. Bjørvig, *Norwegian Bravado*, 11.

41. Bjørvig, *Norwegian Bravado*, 8–10.

42. Bjørvig, *Norwegian Bravado*, 10.

43. Baldwin, *Franz Josef Land Archipelago*, 108; and Nansen, *Farthest North*, 80, 101, 254.

44. Baldwin, *Franz Josef Land Archipelago*, 106.

45. Baldwin, *Franz Josef Land Archipelago*, 106.

46. Baldwin, *Franz Josef Land Archipelago*, 111.

47. Baldwin, *Franz Josef Land Archipelago*, 108.

48. Baldwin, *Franz Josef Land Archipelago*, 109.

49. Baldwin, *Franz Josef Land Archipelago*, 110, 114.

50. Baldwin, *Franz Josef Land Archipelago*, 116, 149.

51. Bjørvig, *Norwegian Bravado*, 10.

52. Bjørvig, *Norwegian Bravado*, 10–13; and Barr, *Franz Josef Land*, 78.

53. Baldwin, *Franz Josef Land Archipelago*, 116–24.

54. Bjørvig, *Norwegian Bravado*, 10.

55. Bjørvig, *Norwegian Bravado*, 11.

56. Bjørvig, *Norwegian Bravado*, 12–13.

57. Bjørvig, *Norwegian Bravado*, 14.

58. Bjørvig, *Norwegian Bravado*, 13.

59. Bjørvig, *Norwegian Bravado*, 17.

8. The Strenuous Life

1. Baldwin, *Franz Josef Land Archipelago*, 156.

2. P. J. Capelotti interprets this passing of letters not as a means of privacy but as evidence that the two men were barely on speaking terms. Capelotti, *Greatest Show in the Arctic*, 177.

3. Wellman, "Race for the North Pole," 322.

4. Wellman, "Wellman Polar Expedition," 492–93.

5. Wellman, *Aerial Age*, 150.

6. Wellman, "Race for the North Pole," 322; and Wellman, "Wellman Polar Expedition," 495, 497–98.

7. Riesenberg, *Living Again*, 135–36.

8. Wellman, "Mystery of the Great White North," 11.

9. Letter from Walter Wellman to Arthur Wellman, February 15, 1899, Wellman NASM, Box 1, Folder 18. In "Mystery of the Great White North," Wellman commented on the failure of a recent Baldwin-led Arctic expedition. He noted that Baldwin was charged with "a fatal inability to command the respect or confidence of his men. Probably the fault was his only in part, but as the responsible leader he must be judged by results."

10. Baldwin, *Franz Josef Land Archipelago*, 156–58.

11. Walter Wellman to Arthur Wellman, February 15, 1899, Wellman NASM, Box 1, Folder 18.

12. Letter from Walter Wellman to Emma and Arthur Wellman, December 31, 1898, Wellman NASM, Box 1, Folder 12.

13. Walter Wellman to Arthur Wellman, February 15, 1899, Wellman NASM, Box 1, Folder 18.

14. Walter Wellman to Emma and Arthur Wellman, December 31, 1898, Wellman NASM, Box 1, Folder 12.

15. Walter Wellman to Arthur Wellman, February 15, 1899, Wellman NASM, Box 1, Folder 18.

16. Wellman, "Race for the North Pole," 324; and Wellman, "Wellman Polar Expedition," 498.

17. Wellman, "Race for the North Pole," 324.

18. Bjørvig, *Norwegian Bravado*, 22–23.

19. Wellman, "Race for the North Pole," 324.

20. Wellman, "Wellman Polar Expedition," 499.

21. Wellman, "Wellman Polar Expedition," 499.

22. Wellman, "Race for the North Pole," 326.

23. In "Race for the North Pole," Wellman described a "one-man sleeping-bag, empty. . . . Just beyond, within arm's reach, lay a similar bag" (326). Bjørvig, however, wrote, "It is pretty miserable to lie together with a dead man. It was cold enough while he was alive to lie in the sleeping bag, and it feels a lot worse now he lies there dead." Bjørvig, *Norwegian Bravado*, 17.

24. Bjørvig, *Norwegian Bravado*, 16.

25. Bjørvig, *Norwegian Bravado*, 17–18.

26. Bjørvig, *Norwegian Bravado*, 21.

27. Wellman, "Race for the North Pole," 326; and Wellman, "Wellman Polar Expedition," 499.

28. Wellman, "Race for the North Pole," 327.

29. Wellman, "Race for the North Pole," 322.

30. Wellman, "Wellman Polar Expedition," 491.

31. Barr, *Franz Josef Land*, 79.

32. Wellman, "Race for the North Pole," 318.

33. Wellman, "Race for the North Pole," 327.

34. Wellman, "Sledging toward the Pole," 412.

35. Wellman, "Race for the North Pole," 327.

36. Bjørvig, *Norwegian Bravado*, 25.

37. Wellman, "Wellman Polar Expedition," 500.

38. Wellman, "Race for the North Pole," 327.

39. Wellman, "Sledging toward the Pole," 405; and Bjørvig, *Norwegian Bravado*, 25–26.

40. Wellman, "Sledging toward the Pole," 405–6; and Bjørvig, *Norwegian Bravado*, 26.

41. Wellman, "Sledging toward the Pole," 405–6; and Bjørvig, *Norwegian Bravado*, 26.

42. Wellman, *Aerial Age*, 112.

43. Wellman, *Aerial Age*, 112. In "Walter Wellman Reaches New York," *San Francisco Call*, October 9, 1899, Wellman is quoted as saying he walked on for eight days after his injury; in 1911 in his *The Aerial Age*, he said he continued two or three days after the icequake.

44. Capelotti, *Greatest Show in the Arctic*, 189–90.

45. Wellman, "Wellman Polar Expedition," 500.

46. Wellman, *Aerial Age*, 115.

47. See Capelotti, "E. B. Baldwin."

48. See Capelotti, "E. B. Baldwin."

49. Roosevelt, *Strenuous Life*, 1, 21.

50. See Rotundo, *American Manhood*, 222–46.

51. Quoted in Rotundo, *American Manhood*, 226.

52. Baldwin, "Meteorological Observations," 516; and "Wellman at Tromsoe," *Washington (DC) Times*, August 18, 1899.

53. Editorial, *Willmar (MN) Tribune*, November 1, 1899.

54. "Heroism of Polar Exploration," *Princeton (MN) Union*, October 26, 1899.

55. Wellman, "Sledging toward the Pole," 406–7.

56. Wellman, "Sledging toward the Pole," 406–7.

57. "Walter Wellman Reaches New York," *San Francisco Call*, October 9, 1899.

9. The People Are Barely Able to Exist

1. Morris, *Theodore Rex*, 79.

2. Morris, *Theodore Rex*, 78–79, 97; and "Can It Be Possible?," *Commoner* (Lincoln NE), April 18, 1902.

3. Goodwin, *Bully Pulpit*, 228, 280–81.

4. "Chief Justice Fuller," *Aberdeen (SD) Daily News*, December 31, 1889.

5. Letter from Walter Wellman to George B. Cortelyou, May 9, 1902, Roosevelt Papers. The connection seems to have been *Collier's Weekly*; both Bryan and Wellman wrote for the magazine.

6. "Isn't It Time for Somebody to Speak?," *Bee* (Earlington KY), July 31, 1902.

7. Letter from Theodore Roosevelt to Walter Wellman, April 5, 1902, Roosevelt Papers.

8. "'Duty' vs. Ambition," *Commoner* (Lincoln NE), May 2, 1902. Roosevelt did not fire Miles, who reached mandatory retirement age in 1903, though the president eventually outmaneuvered him and eliminated him as a political threat.

9. Letter from Walter Wellman to Theodore Roosevelt, April 18, 1902, Roosevelt Papers.

10. "Is Roosevelt Sincere?," *Commoner* (Lincoln NE), July 25, 1902.

11. Phelan, *Divided Loyalties*, 2–5.

12. Phelan, *Divided Loyalties*, 6–8.

13. Phelan, *Divided Loyalties*, 22–23.

14. Phelan, *Divided Loyalties*, 30–32.

15. Phelan, *Divided Loyalties*, 41, 45, 63.

16. Phelan, *Divided Loyalties*, 32–33, 38.

17. Phelan, *Divided Loyalties*, 95.

18. Phelan, *Divided Loyalties*, 102.

19. Phelan, *Divided Loyalties*, 123.

20. "Senator Hanna to Meet Vanderbilt," *Minneapolis Journal*, June 3, 1902.

21. Grossman, "Coal Strike of 1902."

22. Phelan, *Divided Loyalties*, 160.

23. "Coal Strike Hearings," 773.

24. Wright, "Report to the President," 1150–51, 1155–56, 1162–63.

25. Wright, "Report to the President," 1177.

26. Wright, "Report to the President," 1212.

27. "The Coal Strike," *Commoner* (Lincoln NE), June 13, 1902.

28. "The Coal Barons' Side of the Case," *Rock Island (IL) Argus*, June 17, 1902.

29. Quoted in "Violence in the Coal Strike," 857.

30. Phelan, *Divided Loyalties*, 163–66.

31. Jones, *Autobiography of Mother Jones*, 26–27.

32. Phelan, *Divided Loyalties*, 176.

33. Wellman, *Fairmont Coal Region*.

34. Walter Wellman, "Judge Jackson's Defining of Law," CRH, August 2, 1902.

35. Walter Wellman, "Jackson Known as 'Iron Judge,'" CRH, August 3, 1902, 47.

36. Walter Wellman, "Jackson Known as 'Iron Judge,'" CRH, August 3, 1902, 47.

37. Walter Wellman, "No Desire to Strike," CRH, August 6, 1902.

38. Walter Wellman, "Treat Miners Right," CRH, August 8, 1902.

39. Walter Wellman, "Treat Miners Right," CRH, August 8, 1902.

10. With Johnny D'Mitch

1. "Evidence Not Lacking," *Commoner* (Lincoln NE), August 8, 1902.

2. Walter Wellman, "What Has Become of Wright's Report?," CRH, August 15, 1902.

3. Associated Press, "Wright's Report on Coal Strike," *Richmond (VA) Times*, September 4, 1902.

4. Wright, "Report to the President," 1165–66.

5. Phelan, *Divided Loyalties*, 180.

6. Phelan, *Divided Loyalties*, 182–83.

7. Theodore Roosevelt to Winthrop Murray Crane, October 22, 1902, quoted in Grossman, "Coal Strike of 1902."

8. Phelan, *Divided Loyalties*, 183.

9. Walter Wellman, "Morgan Backs up Roosevelt," CRH, October 2, 1902. Publisher H. H. Kohlsaat, formerly of the *Chicago Record-Herald*, suggested to Roosevelt on October 2 that he meet with Wellman, saying he had "valuable information" and was close to Mitchell. Telegram from Herman Henry Kohlsaat to Theodore Roosevelt, October 2, 1902, Roosevelt Papers.

10. Wellman, "Morgan Backs up Roosevelt."

11. Walter Wellman, "The Barons' 'Amazing Effrontery,'" CRH, October 4, 1902.

12. Walter Wellman, "The Barons' 'Amazing Effrontery,'" CRH, October 4, 1902; and Phelan, *Divided Loyalties*, 184.

13. Wellman, "Inside History," 6.

14. Phelan, *Divided Loyalties*, 184.

15. Grossman, "Coal Strike of 1902"; and Walter Wellman, "Mark Hanna Right for Once," CRH, October 3, 1902.

16. Walter Wellman, "An Inquiry Likely," CRH, October 6, 1902; Note regarding George B. Cortelyou, Dr. Shaw, and Mr. Wellman, October 7, 1902, Roosevelt Papers; and Morris, *Theodore Rex*, 623n165.

17. Walter Wellman, "A Possible Ground," CRH, October 8, 1902.

18. "Napoleon of Labor," *Aberdeen (wy) Herald*, October 13, 1902.

19. Phelan, *Divided Loyalties*, 185; and Goodwin, *Bully Pulpit*, 317–18.

20. "Roosevelt Chagrined at Miscarriage of His Plans to Settle Strike," *Houston Daily Post*, October 11, 1902; and "Coal Strike Situation," 484.

21. Walter Wellman, "Concessions to the Miners," CRH, October 11, 1902.

22. "Coal Strike Situation," 484.

23. "Miners Deliberating over Operators' Plan," NYT, October 15, 1902; Walter Wellman, "How It Was Done," CRH, October 14, 1902; Grossman, "Coal Strike of 1902"; and Phelan, *Divided Loyalties*, 185.

24. Phelan, *Divided Loyalties*, 186.

25. Grossman, "Coal Strike of 1902"; and Phelan, *Divided Loyalties*, 186.

26. Walter Wellman, "Mitchell Will Accept It," CRH, October 15, 1902.

27. Telephone message from Walter Wellman, October 14, 1902; Walter Wellman note, October 15, 1902; telegrams from Walter Wellman to George Bruce Cortelyou and to Colonial Montgomery, October 16, 1902; and long-distance telephone from Wilkes-Barre PA, 11:30 a.m., October 16, 1902—all from Roosevelt Papers.

28. "Hangs in a Balance," *Seattle Star*, October 15, 1902.

29. "Mitchell Is Here," *Evening Star* (Washington DC), October 15, 1902.

30. By long-distance telephone from Walter Wellman, October 16, 1902, Roosevelt Papers.

31. Walter Wellman, "Joy Reigns in the Coal Region," CRH, October 17, 1902.

32. Phelan, *Divided Loyalties*, 198.

33. Walter Wellman, "The Question of Unionization," CRH, October 24, 1902; and Phelan, *Divided Loyalties*, ix.

34. Wellman, "Inside History of the Great Coal Strike," 6. Before it appeared in *Collier's* magazine, publisher Robert J. Collier first proposed it to Roosevelt, who replied that "I should particularly like to have Mr. Wellman write such an article as you suggest." Letter from Theodore Roosevelt to Robert J. Collier, October 19, 1902, Roosevelt Papers.

35. Wellman, "Settlement of the Coal Strike," 552.

36. Wellman, "Settlement of the Coal Strike," 552.

37. Quoted in Phelan, *Divided Loyalties*, 187.

38. Reprinted as "The Mining Horrors," *Yellowstone Monitor* (Glendive MT), July 22, 1909.

11. This Crime against Organized Labor

1. Walter Wellman, "Either Hanging or Exile for Colorado Unionists," *New York Herald*, August 10, 1904.

2. Walter Wellman, "Either Hanging or Exile for Colorado Unionists," *New York Herald*, August 10, 1904.

3. Walter Wellman, "Either Hanging or Exile for Colorado Unionists," *New York Herald*, August 10, 1904. See also Wright, *Report on Labor Disturbances*, 247.

4. "The Social World," *Evening Star* (Washington DC), September 10, 1904.

5. Good summaries of the situation in Colorado are Baker, "Reign of Lawlessness"; and Wright, *Report on Labor Disturbances*.

6. Phelan, *Divided Loyalties*, 212–20.

7. Wright, *Report on Labor Disturbances*, 112–66.

8. Wright, *Report on Labor Disturbances*, 51–67; and Baker, "Reign of Lawlessness," 52–53.

9. Baker, "Reign of Lawlessness," 53.

10. "Hearst's Bid for Presidency," CRH, January 11, 1904.

11. "Wellman's Story Was Written under Orders," *Labor World*, April 9, 1904.

12. "'Mother' Jones Assails President," *New York Herald*, August 8, 1904. See also "Catching the 'Labor Vote,'" 410.

13. Morris, *Theodore Rex*, 339–40.

14. "The Political Outlook," *Havre (MT) Herald*, July 6, 1904.

15. Walter Wellman, "Either Hanging or Exile for Colorado Unionists," *New York Herald*, August 10, 1904.

16. Walter Wellman, "Labor Seeks Control of Colorado's Government," *New York Herald*, August 11, 1904.

17. Walter Wellman, "Labor Seeks Control of Colorado's Government," *New York Herald*, August 11, 1904.

18. Walter Wellman, "Labor Seeks Control of Colorado's Government," *New York Herald*, August 11, 1904.

19. Walter Wellman, "Labor Seeks Control of Colorado's Government," *New York Herald*, August 11, 1904.

20. Walter Wellman, "Labor Seeks Control of Colorado's Government," *New York Herald*, August 11, 1904.

21. Walter Wellman, "General Bell's Tale of the Colorado Mine War," *New York Herald*, August 13, 1904.

22. "Roosevelt in Danger," *New-York Tribune*, September 27, 1900; and "Friends of Bryan Make Assault on Roosevelt at Victor, Colorado," *San Francisco Call*, September 27, 1900.

23. Carlson, *Roughneck*, 62.

24. Walter Wellman, "General Bell's Tale of the Colorado Mine War," *New York Herald*, August 13, 1904.

25. Walter Wellman, "General Bell's Tale of the Colorado Mine War," *New York Herald*, August 13, 1904." See also Carlson, *Roughneck*, 62.

26. Carlson, *Roughneck*, 63.

27. Carlson, *Roughneck*, 75–77.

28. Walter Wellman, "Colorado's Governor Says He Was Forced into War," *New York Herald*, August 12, 1904, 6.

29. Carlson, *Roughneck*, 71.

30. Baker, "Reign of Lawlessness," 43–57.

31. Wellman, *Walter Wellman's Indictment*, 1–2.

32. Wellman, *Walter Wellman's Indictment*, 10; Baker, "Reign of Lawlessness," 53; and Wright, *Report on Labor Disturbances*, 65.

33. Carlson, *Roughneck*, 65.

34. Wellman, *Walter Wellman's Indictment*, 13.

35. Baker, "Reign of Lawlessness," 50–51.

36. Wellman, *Walter Wellman's Indictment*, 6.

37. Wellman, *Walter Wellman's Indictment*, 12–13; and Walter Wellman, "Either Hanging or Exile for Colorado Unionists," *New York Herald*, August 10, 1904.

38. Baker, "Reign of Lawlessness," 49.

39. Baker, "Right to Work," 323–36.

40. Baker, "Reign of Lawlessness," 46.

41. "Walter Wellman on Colorado," *Labor World* (Duluth MN), August 20, 1904; "Wellman Has Flunked on Colorado Story," *Labor World* (Duluth MN), September 17, 1904; and "Walter Wellman Taken to Task for Colorado Mine War Letters," *Rock Island (IL) Argus*, October 11, 1904.

42. Wellman, *Walter Wellman's Indictment*, 1.

43. Walter Wellman, "Republican Victory Is Fully Assured," CRH, November 7, 1904.

44. Theodore Roosevelt to Victor Lawson, December 9, 1904, Wellman LOC.

45. Quoted in Dennis, *Victor Lawson*, 302–3.

12. Motor Sledges and Airships

1. Wellman, *Aerial Age*, 119.

2. "Sure of Reaching Pole," *New-York Tribune*, December 13, 1903.

3. See also "Walter Wellman Has a Plan," *Omaha Daily Bee*, December 13, 1903.

4. Wellman, *Aerial Age*, 19.

5. "Something New under the Sun," 125; and *History of Jo Daviess County*, 477.

6. "Steam Logging Sleigh," 13.

7. "Call for a Motor Driven Sleigh," 90.

8. See, for example, "Horseless Sleigh," 18; "Over Ice and Snow," *Evening Star* (Washington DC), October 2, 1897; "Automobile Sleigh Used in Canada," *St. Paul (MN) Globe*, May 6, 1900; and editorial, *Alexandria (VA) Gazette*, March 26, 1901.

9. Stockton, "Great Stone of Sardis," 582, 585. In an even more futuristic aside, the author added that in 1941 a Swiss mountaineer scaled vertical rock faces with a motor sledge that had suckers on the wheels.

10. "Will Make an Attempt," *Republican News Item* (Laport PA), March 15, 1900; Hitchcock, *Two Women in the Klondike*; and biographical sketch of Hitchcock in "The Iceland Influence," *New-York Tribune*, February 24, 1901.

11. "To the North Pole by Automobile," 805; and "Will Explore Polar Regions in an Automobile," *Cook County Herald* (Grand Marais MN), September 20, 1902.

12. Francis, "Bernier, Joseph-Elzéar."

13. Examples of Santa Claus and automobiles: "Santa Claus' New Automobile," *Seattle Star*, December 19, 1901; Myra Goodwin Plantz, "Uncle John's Xmas," *Monroe City (MO) Democrat*, December 11, 1902; editorial, *Norfolk (NE) Weekly News-Journal*, December 12, 1902; and "The 20th Century Boy," *Bourbon News* (Paris KY), December 23, 1902. Regarding the motor sleigh fad: "Bells Ring Merrily," *Evening Star* (Washington DC), January 30, 1902; "Now the Motor Sleigh," *Anadarko (OK) Daily Democrat*, April 2, 1902; "Peary Might Use It," *Camden (TN) Chronicle*, May 9, 1902; editorial, *New-York Tribune*, December 27, 1904; and "Sleighing in Automobiles Now the Very Latest Society Recreation," *New York Evening World*, December 27, 1904.

14. "In an Air-Bag to the Pole?," 196.

15. Wellman, *Aerial Age*, 119–25.

16. Wellman, *Aerial Age*, 120, 124.

17. Wellman, *Aerial Age*, 123–24.

18. I have been unable to locate this pamphlet, but it is reviewed in "Municipal Transport Problems," 680–82. Wellman's motor sledge proposal is not extant, but I've made inferences about his sales pitch and supporting materials based on what he later published regarding his polar airship plans.

19. "Must Look after His Laurels," *Evening Star* (Washington DC), July 9, 1905.

20. "Return Journeys of the Navigable Balloon," 34; and "Wind Forces Overcome in the Experiments," 49–53.

21. Santos-Dumont, *My Airships*, 355.

22. D'Orcy, *D'Orcy's Airship Manual*, 82.

23. "Must Look after His Laurels," *Evening Star* (Washington DC), July 9, 1905; and "French War Officers Test New Dirigible Balloon," *San Francisco Call*, July 9, 1905.

24. Scott, *Hague Peace Conferences*, 2:153.

25. "Airships in War," *New-York Tribune*, October 19, 1905.

26. "Dirigible Balloon Bombs Fort," *Washington (DC) Times*, October 29, 1905.

27. "Airship in Military Service," *New-York Tribune*, October 29, 1905.

28. "World Affairs as Seen by Observers Abroad," *New-York Tribune*, November 12, 1905.

29. Crouch, *Bishop's Boys*, 297–300.

30. "Aerial Torpedoes Fell with Effect," *Washington (DC) Times*, November 19, 1905; and Wellman, "Polar Airship," 211.

31. "Wellman to Seek North Pole in Largest Airship Ever Built," CRH, December 31, 1905.

32. "Wellman to Seek North Pole in Largest Airship Ever Built," CRH, December 31, 1905. In his announcement Wellman claimed to have spent "many months" consulting with "scores of eminent experts." In *Aerial Age* (124–25), he said he began after hearing of the *Lebaudy*'s success while at the Portsmouth Peace Conference "in the autumn of 1905" (the conference was held in August). Because he remembered the season as autumn, he may have been thinking of the *Lebaudy*'s more highly publicized October flights.

33. "Walter Wellman on Future Modes of Travel," *Duluth (MN) News-Tribune*, May 7, 1893. Promoting his first polar expedition the following year, Wellman said dog sleds were the only means to the pole until "airships take the place of marine vessels." See Walter Wellman, "To the North Pole," *Evening Star* (Washington DC), February 24, 1894.

34. Wellman, "Long Distance Balloon Racing," 209.

35. "Walter Wellman," *Valentine (NE) Democrat*, January 18, 1906, and other papers; and quoted in "Another 'Dash for the Pole,'" 87. The CRH reported varied reactions: "Beveridge Praises Quest of Wellman," January 1, 1906; "Praise for Pole Hunt," January 3, 1906; and "Stirred by Pole Hunt," January 6, 1906.

36. "Wellman to Seek North Pole in Largest Airship Ever Built," CRH, December 31, 1905; "First Step in Trip of Wellman to Pole," CRH, January 5, 1906; "France Lends Aid to Wellman," *San Francisco Call*, January 15, 1906; "Walter Wellman's Expedition," 205; and Wellman, *Aerial Age*, 126–27.

37. Wellman, "American Life Insurance on Trial," 458–68; "Mr. Wellman's Plan," *Salt Lake Herald* (Salt Lake City UT), July 16, 1905; "Taft and Bryan as Next Leaders," CRH, October 23, 1905; and "Taft Not a Candidate," NYT, October 26, 1905. Wellman also sent unsolicited advice to Roosevelt during the Portsmouth negotiations. See Walter Wellman, "Peace Agreement," August 21, 1905, Roosevelt Papers.

38. "Wellman to Seek North Pole in Largest Airship Ever Built," CRH, December 31, 1905.

39. Arthur, "Walter Wellman," 317.

40. See, for example, "The Press Club," *Critic* (Washington DC), February 7, 1891; "News of the Capital," *Los Angeles Herald*, June 17, 1891; "In Social Circles," *Evening Star* (Washington DC), December 31, 1891; "Mr. Wellman to Go Abroad," *Evening Star* (Washington DC), January 1, 1894; and "At the Gridiron Roast," *Helena (MT) Independent*, February 12, 1894.

41. Arthur, "Walter Wellman," 318.

42. Arthur, "Walter Wellman," 318.

43. Mabley, *Motor Balloon "America,"* 36.

44. Wellman, *Aerial Age*, 9–11.

45. Walter Wellman, "Luck of Roosevelt," CRH, July 25, 1903. Perhaps seeking deniability in case the article offended the president, Wellman frames the sketch as an article-length quotation from an unnamed speaker in a discussion "the other night at an uptown [New York City] club."

46. Walter Wellman, "Roosevelt Gags Cabinet Officers," CRH, October 20, 1905.

13. The Scheme Was Crazy Enough

1. "First Step in Trip of Wellman to Pole," CRH, January 5, 1906; and "Musical Mention," *Evening Star* (Washington DC), January 14, 1906, 13.

2. "Mr. Wellman's Venture," *New-York Tribune*, February 22, 1906.

3. "Mr. Wellman's Venture," *New-York Tribune*, February 22, 1906; "Plans Trip to the Pole," *Omaha Daily Bee*, December 31, 1905; and Wellman, *Aerial Age*, 124–25.

4. "Aerial Torpedoes Fell with Effect," *Washington (DC) Times*, November 19, 1905.

5. Wellman, "Long Distance Balloon Racing."

6. Wellman, *Aerial Age*, 163–64; and Wellman, "Polar Airship," 211–12.

7. Wellman, "Polar Airship," 211–12.

8. "Plans Trip to the Pole," *Omaha Daily Bee*, December 31, 1905.

9. Wellman, "Polar Airship," 213.

10. Wellman, "Polar Airship," 213. Wellman said a fast ship would need 14,000 pounds of fuel; a slow ship would carry 5,500 pounds (p. 208). He gave somewhat different figures the following year to make the same point in "By Airship," 196.

11. Wellman, "Polar Airship," 223.

12. Wellman, "Polar Airship," 216. The anchor (*retardateur*) was a steel cable with spikes, designed to hold the airship steady in a 10- to 12-mile-per-hour headwind and slow it down in a stronger wind. It was thought that this would place less stress on the airship than an anchor that would hold it more firmly in place.

13. Wellman, "Polar Airship," 224.

14. Wellman addressed the question of how he could "speak with so much confidence of the speed of an airship that has never been tried in air" in his article, "Will the 'America' Fly to the Pole?," 234. In short, he said such estimates were commonly made for ships before construction and that by now enough airships had been built to make similar (albeit less precise) estimates.

15. "How to Fly to the North Pole," *New York Sun*, March 24, 1906. The NYT on March 24 printed what seems to be a garbled report of this speech. The NYT has Wellman saying that the distance to the pole was 1,200 miles when in fact that was his figure for the round-trip distance (in nautical miles). Based on this misunderstanding, the reporter mistakenly thought the round-trip exceeded the airship's range and even quoted Wellman as saying, "You perhaps may ask how I am

going to get back, as the airship will not carry enough fuel to come entirely home by it. Well, I am now having built in Paris and America two experimental motor sledges." The quotation is probably inaccurate, as it contradicts not only the *Sun's* report of the speech but also Wellman's other published statements.

16. "Wellman Here," *New-York Tribune*, March 11, 1906; "Wellman's Arctic Plans," *New-York Tribune*, March 24, 1906; "Can Reach North Pole, Says Walter Wellman," *NYT*, March 24, 1906; and "Mr. Wellman in Paris," *Evening Star* (Washington DC), May 21, 1906.

17. "Wellman's Expedition to the North Pole in an Air Ship," *Spokane (WA) Press*, April 16, 1906.

18. "Walter Wellman's Expedition," 207.

19. Riesenberg, *Living Again*, 118–19.

20. Riesenberg, *Living Again*, 120–21.

21. Riesenberg, *Living Again*, 121.

22. Riesenberg, *Living Again*, 121–22.

23. Riesenberg, *Living Again*, 123–26. Riesenberg writes that they departed July 4, but it was June 15 according to Wellman in *CRH*, July 2, 1906.

24. "The Riesenberg Saying," Fort Schuyler Maritime Alumni Association, Inc., http://www.fsmaa.org/the-riesenberg-saying/, accessed January 5, 2017.

25. Riesenberg, *Living Again*, 126–27.

26. "Wellman Off for Norway," *Evening Star* (Washington DC), June 15, 1906.

27. "Will Reach the Pole by Airship—Wellman," *NYT*, April 24, 1906; and "Huge Balloon for Wellman Quest," *Minneapolis Journal*, May 21, 1906.

28. *Evening Star* (Washington DC), March 18, 1906, 23. In early 1907 the *America* was inflated inside the cavernous Galerie des Machines on the Exposition Universelle grounds in Paris, just as the *Lebaudy* had been several years earlier. See Wellman, "Will the 'America' Fly?," 232.

29. "Wellman Off for Norway," *Evening Star* (Washington DC), June 15, 1906. Regarding the delay from labor strikes, see "Wellman Motors a Success," *NYT*, June 12, 1906; and Wellman, *Aerial Age*, 147.

30. "Wellman's Old Mother Bids Him Farewell," *Washington (DC) Times*, April 12, 1906.

31. "Wellman's Good-Bye," *Arizona Republican (Phoenix)*, April 13, 1906.

14. The Airship Station on Virgo Bay

1. British Film Institute, "Walter Wellman at Virgo Harbor." See also Diesen and Fulton, "Wellman's 1906 Polar Expedition," 76–85.

2. Riesenberg, *Living Again*, 127–28.

3. Riesenberg, *Living Again*, 129. See also Capelotti, Van Dyk, and Caillez, "Strange Interlude at Virgohamna," 69.

4. Riesenberg, *Living Again*, 129.

5. Riesenberg, *Living Again*, 130–31.

6. Riesenberg, *Living Again*, 131.

7. Diesen and Fulton, "Wellman's 1906 Polar Expedition," 79–80. Only one of these films, an eight-minute short attributed to the Charles Urban Trading Company, is extant and is now in the British National Film and Television Archives. A segment of this film is on YouTube.

8. Capelotti, Van Dyk, and Caillez, "Strange Interlude at Virgohamna," 73.

9. Capelotti, Van Dyk, and Caillez, "Strange Interlude at Virgohamna," 73.

10. Capelotti, Van Dyk, and Caillez, "Strange Interlude at Virgohamna," 73–74. See also Riesenberg, *Living Again*, 161.

11. Robinson, *Coldest Crucible*, 118–22.

12. "Wireless Telegraphy," *Hopkinsville Kentuckian*, September 8, 1899. Reprint of undated *Chicago Record* article.

13. "Wireless Telegraphy Experiments," 162.

14. Baker, "Marconi's Achievement," 291. Emphasis in the original.

15. "Wireless to the Pole?," *New York Sun*, April 4, 1906; and "Polar Airship Trip All Arranged For," NYT, May 6, 1906.

16. "Wellman to Roosevelt," NYT, July 24, 1906.

17. Wellman, *Aerial Age*, 137–38.

18. Riesenberg, *Living Again*, 132.

19. Fayant, "Fools and Their Money," 9–11. DeForest's successor company, the United Wireless Telegraph Company, was formed later in 1906 and engaged in fraudulent stock promotion. Until its bankruptcy in 1912, it was the largest wireless company in the United States.

20. "Wellman Polar Expedition," 712; Wellman, *Aerial Age*, 153–54; and Capelotti, Van Dyk, and Caillez, "Strange Interlude in Virgohamna," 70–71.

21. "DARE Interview." The auxiliary informant was an unidentified African American male who spoke of his work as an automobile mechanic and specifically his work on a modified Indian motorcycle for a Walter Wellman polar expedition. The Indian may have looked like the "Car for Climbing the North Pole" shown in the *Deseret Evening News* (Salt Lake City UT), June 23, 1906, and in other papers.

22. Riesenberg, *Living Again*, 132–33; and Wellman, *Aerial Age*, 133. See also Capelotti, Van Dyk, and Caillez, "Strange Interlude at Virgohamna," 66, 69.

23. Wellman, *Aerial Age*, 132.

24. "How to Fly to the North Pole," *New York Sun*, March 24, 1906.

25. Nansen, "Future North Polar Exploration," 299. Wellman made a similar point when announcing the expedition in the CRH, December 31, 1905.

26. "Wellman Labors in Light of Midnight Sun," CRH, July 2, 1906; Wellman, "Polar Airship," 208, 212; and Wellman, *Aerial Age*, 130.

27. Capelotti, *By Airship to the North Pole*, 131–43. Capelotti conducted an archaeological investigation at Danes Island in 1993. There he identified the 1906 car where it lay abandoned, describing it as "a meager thing, ill constructed and hopelessly ill-suited to the polar environment" (143).

28. D'Orcy, *D'Orcy's Airship Manual*, 179; and Wellman, "Polar Airship," 208–11.

29. D'Orcy, *D'Orcy's Airship Manual*, 179; and Wellman, "Polar Airship," 208–11.
30. Wellman, *Aerial Age*, 155.
31. Wellman, "By Airship," 196; and Riesenberg, *Living Again*, 133.
32. "Is Wellman in Earnest?," 434–35. On the two-year project, see "Walter Wellman's Expedition," 207; *Evening Star* (Washington DC), June 3, 1906; *Albuquerque Morning Journal*, March 7, 1906 (interview with Hersey); and *New-York Tribune*, March 11, 1906.

15. Wellman vs. Peary

1. Bryce, *Cook & Peary*, 14–19.
2. Bryce, *Cook & Peary*, 20–21.
3. Bryce, *Cook & Peary*, 22.
4. Peary, *Nearest the Pole*, 202.
5. "Sverdrup and Peary," *New-York Tribune*, January 6, 1898.
6. "Stealing Peary's Ideas," *New York Sun*, February 13, 1898.
7. Bryce, *Cook & Peary*, 211–12.
8. Bryce, *Cook & Peary*, 231.
9. Bryce, *Cook & Peary*, 231.
10. Bryce, *Cook & Peary*, 265, 1024n5.
11. "Fears for Safety of Peary after Year in Arctic Zone," *Washington (DC) Times*, July 6, 1906.
12. *Topeka (KS) State Journal*, July 7, 1906.
13. Riffenburgh, *Myth of the Explorer*, 169.
14. Bryce, *Cook & Peary*, 233.
15. Riffenburgh, *Myth of the Explorer*, 163–64; and "Amundsen, Discoverer of the Northwest Passage, Brings Storm-Tossed Gjoa into Port," *San Francisco Call*, October 20, 1906.
16. Riffenburgh, *Myth of the Explorer*, 163–64; and "Amundsen, Discoverer of the Northwest Passage, Brings Storm-Tossed Gjoa into Port," *San Francisco Call*, October 20, 1906.
17. "Walter Wellman Accused of Filching Polar Plan," *Washington (DC) Times*, November 3, 1906. Verne wrote stories about the North Pole (*Adventures of Captain Hatteras*), airships and flying machines (*Robur the Conqueror*), and balloons (*Five Weeks in a Balloon*, *A Drama in the Air*, and *The Mysterious Island*) but nothing approximating Wellman's plan.
18. "Wellman Is Still Sure of Reaching the Pole," *NYT*, November 18, 1906.
19. "No Airships for Peary," *NYT*, November 26, 1906.
20. "Peary Sees the President," *NYT*, December 2, 1906; and "About People and Social Incidents," *New-York Tribune*, December 2, 1906.
21. "Arctic Explorers," *National Tribune* (Washington DC), December 6, 1906.
22. "Wellman Takes a Shot at Commander Peary," *NYT*, December 7, 1906.
23. "Says Peary Is No Aeronaut," *Washington (DC) Herald*, April 4, 1907.
24. "Pres. Grants Peary New Leave," *Washington (DC) Times*, April 10, 1907.

25. Reprinted as "Rival Explorers Scoff at Each Other's Plans to Reach Pole," *San Francisco Call*, May 5, 1907.

16. Balloons, Aeroplanes

1. *Pacific Commercial Advertiser* (Honolulu), February 26, 1901, reprinted in Tierney, *Melvin Vaniman*, 12–14.
2. *Pacific Commercial Advertiser* (Honolulu), February 26, 1901, reprinted in Tierney, *Melvin Vaniman*, 12–14.
3. *Pacific Commercial Advertiser* (Honolulu), February 26, 1901, reprinted in Tierney, *Melvin Vaniman*, 12–14.
4. *Pacific Commercial Advertiser* (Honolulu), February 26, 1901, reprinted in Tierney, *Melvin Vaniman*, 12–14.
5. *Pacific Commercial Advertiser* (Honolulu), February 26, 1901, reprinted in Tierney, *Melvin Vaniman*, 12–14.
6. Tierney, *Melvin Vaniman*, 11–12; *Vaniman Panorama*; and Margot Pitkin, "The Crow's-Eye View," *Sydney (AU) Daily Telegraph*, n.d., Newspaper Source, EBSCOhost.
7. Tierney, *Melvin Vaniman*, 11–12; *Vaniman Panorama*; and Margot Pitkin, "The Crow's-Eye View," *Sydney (AU) Daily Telegraph*, n.d., Newspaper Source, EBSCOhost.
8. Russell, "Melvin Vaniman—Aerial Adventurer," 17.
9. Kenney, *Canton's Pioneers in Flight*, 10–13.
10. Kenney, *Canton's Pioneers in Flight*, 10–13.
11. Kenney, *Canton's Pioneers in Flight*, 10–13.
12. Crouch, *Bishop's Boys*, 307.
13. "Record-Herald's North Polar Expedition by Wellman," *Albuquerque Evening Citizen*, February 27, 1906, in which a local aeronaut translates news from the January issue of the French publication *L'Aerophile*; and Tierney, *Melvin Vaniman*, 29.
14. "Aerial Navigation," *Evening Star* (Washington DC), April 8, 1906.
15. For example, "To the North Pole by Airship," *Aberdeen (WA) Herald*, March 1, 1906.
16. Crouch, *Bishop's Boys*, 315.
17. See "Brothers Wright and Their Flying-Machine," 833. Summarizing recent press coverage, the *Literary Digest* referred to "the Wright brothers, whose aeroplane has been so widely heralded as the first practical solution of the problem of aviation—the first machine heavier than air, to fly with a human passenger."
18. "Santos-Dumont's Aeroplane," 755.
19. Crouch, *Bishop's Boys*, 167–69, 317.
20. Wellman, *Aerial Age*, 168.
21. Wellman, "Will the 'America' Fly," 241–42; and *Aerial Age*, 169. Vaniman later said that the idea for the airship's fuel tank "backbone" was his own, having come to him in a dream. "Vaniman's Career One of Adventure," *NYT*, October 5, 1910.
22. Wellman, *Aerial Age*, 237.
23. Wellman, *Aerial Age*, 243.

24. Wellman, "Will the 'America' Fly," 239–40.

25. Wellman, "Will the 'America' Fly," 245; and Wellman, *Aerial Age*, 169.

17. Go? Of Course

1. Riesenberg, *Living Again*, 192–93.

2. Riesenberg, *Living Again*, 192–93.

3. Wellman, *Aerial Age*, 171.

4. Wellman, *Aerial Age*, 171; and Riesenberg, *Living Again*, 192.

5. Riesenberg, *Living Again*, 193–95.

6. Riesenberg, *Living Again*, 193–95.

7. "Pres. Grants Peary New Leave," *Washington (DC) Times*, April 10, 1907; and "Peary Will Try Again," *Evening Star* (Washington DC), April 11, 1907.

8. See, for example, editorial, *Columbus (NE) Journal*, May 8, 1907.

9. "Lack of $60,000 May Balk Peary," *Chicago Daily Tribune*, April 29, 1907; Officer and Page, *Fabulous Kingdom*, 145; and Riffenburgh, *Myth of the Explorer*, 171.

10. "Peary at Lenox, Consulting M. K. Jesup Concerning Funds for His Expedition," *NYT*, June 23, 1907.

11. "Peary Starts Soon," *New-York Tribune*, July 14, 1907.

12. "No Dash to Pole This Year—Peary," *NYT*, August 11, 1907.

13. Wellman, "Polar Airship," 218–23.

14. Earth System Research Laboratory, "NOAA Solar Calculator."

15. Riesenberg, *Living Again*, 163–64.

16. Riesenberg, *Living Again*, 163–64.

17. "Airship in Arctic," *Bisbee (AZ) Daily Review*, December 10, 1907. This syndicated article is Vaniman's account of the *America*'s first flight on September 2. He does not elaborate on the nature of the "experiments" with kites.

18. Riesenberg, *Living Again*, 164; and for the time of sunrise, see Earth System Research Laboratory, "NOAA Solar Calculator."

19. Wellman, *Aerial Age*, 174.

20. On Hersey's illness, "Wellman's Balloon Fell on Glacier," *NYT*, September 14, 1907.

21. Riesenberg, *Living Again*, 165.

22. The following narrative of *America*'s September 2, 1907, flight is based on "Mr. Wellman's Effort," *New-York Tribune*, September 15, 1907 (reprint of Wellman's dispatch to the *Berlin Lokal Anzeiger*); Wellman, *Aerial Age*, 172–78; Vaniman's account in "Airship in Arctic," *Bisbee (AZ) Daily Review*, December 10, 1907; and Reisenberg, *Living Again*, 166–71.

23. National Centers for Environmental Information, "Historical Magnetic Declination" (accessed January 3, 2016).

24. Wellman, "Will the 'America' Fly," 242–43.

25. Wellman, "Will the 'America' Fly," 243.

18. Lost in a Snowstorm

1. Unless otherwise noted, the following narrative of *America*'s September 2, 1907, flight is based on "Mr. Wellman's Effort," *New-York Tribune*, September 15, 1907 (reprint of Wellman's dispatch to the *Berlin Lokal Anzeiger*); Wellman, *Aerial Age*, 172–78; Vaniman's account in "Airship in Arctic," *Bisbee (AZ) Daily Review*, December 10, 1907; and Reisenberg, *Living Again*, 166–71.

2. *TopoSvalbard*.

3. Wellman said in his 1907 dispatch that they traveled about fifteen miles; in *Aerial Age* he said thirty-five. This may be more than just the growth of a tale. The first figure is a reasonable estimate of the sailing distance from Virgo Bay to Fowl Bay, and the second is a plausible flying distance if the *America* went a few miles beyond the northernmost islands before being swept south past Cloven Cliff (Klovningen), plus a few loops and meanders as the airship fought the wind. Of course, the second number sounds better. My account of the 1907 flight differs from P. J. Capelotti's map in *Wellman Polar Airship Expeditions* (17–18); he has the airship turning around before exiting Smeerenburg Sound and landing on Fowl Point Glacier (Fuglepyntbreen). One important reason is that I'm relying on Riesenberg's account in *Living Again*. Both Wellman and Vaniman identified their landing site as a glacier in "Foul [sic] Bay," known in Norwegian as Fuglefjorden (bird fjord). Riesenberg later wrote that they landed on "Foul Glacier," which might be taken to mean Fowl Point Glacier (Fuglepyntbreen), as there is no Fowl Glacier and the glacier debouching into Fowl Bay is called Svitjodbreen. The *America* passed Fowl Point on its way north, but its small glacier is set well back from the waters of Smeerenburg Sound and doesn't match Riesenberg's description of a "wide amphitheater." Also the *America* would not have been likely to drift there from Klovningen in winds from the north to northwest. See Helgeland, "Fuglefjorden (Svalbard)."

4. On flight duration, Vaniman said they were in the air two hours and fifteen minutes; Wellman said three hours, fifteen minutes; and Reisenberg, four and a half hours.

5. "Mr. Wellman's Effort," *New-York Tribune*, September 15, 1907 (reprint of Wellman's dispatch to the *Berlin Lokal Anzeiger*).

6. "Wellman May Not Go Again," *NYT*, September 16, 1907.

7. Capelotti, *By Airship to the North Pole*, 81–82.

8. See, for example, "Wellman Abandons North Pole Flight," *Washington (DC) Times*, September 10, 1907; "Loses His Airship," *Evening Star* (Washington DC), September 13, 1907; and "Wellman Explains," *New York Sun*, September 17, 1907.

9. "Mr. Wellman's Successful Failure," 431–32.

10. Quoted in "Hot Air Explorations," *Free Press* (Hays KS), November 9, 1907.

11. "Walter Wellman," *Los Angeles Herald*, August 31, 1907.

12. "Wellman Expedition," *Los Angeles Herald*, September 15, 1907.

13. Wellman, *Aerial Age*, 178.

14. "Wellman's Steamer Lost," *NYT*, October 11, 1907; and Reisenberg, *Living Again*, 172.

15. Riesenberg, *Living Again*, 171.

16. "Foreign News," *New-York Tribune*, September 22, 1907.

19. Campaigns and Dollars

1. "Calls It an Arctic Bluff," *Washington Post*, May 10, 1908; and "Wellman Sues Paper," *Spokane Press*, October 14, 1908. Newspapers usually spelled the name Liwenthal.
2. "Wellman Files Suit," *Washington (DC) Herald*, May 27, 1908; "Wellman Sues Paris Paper," *NYT*, November 25, 1908; and "The Court Record," *Evening Star* (Washington DC), November 5, 1909.
3. "Calls It an Arctic Bluff," *Washington Post*, May 10, 1908.
4. "Calls It an Arctic Bluff," *Washington Post*, May 10, 1908; and "Wellman Sues Paper," *Spokane Press*, October 14, 1908.
5. "Mr. Wellman Disavowed," *Arizona Republican (Phoenix)*, December 18, 1907.
6. Walter Wellman, "Wall Street for Taft to Block a Third Term," *CRH*, December 10, 1907.
7. Walter Wellman, "Taft the Candidate," *CRH*, June 19, 1908.
8. Walter Wellman, "Bryan against Roosevelt in the Next Campaign," *CRH*, December 10, 1907.
9. Winkelman, "Fairview," 144.
10. Walter Wellman, "Bryan Trying to Reunite Party and Is Playing No Favorites," *CRH*, July 2, 1908.
11. Walter Wellman, "People with Bryan in Spite of Money," *CRH*, July 4, 1908.
12. Goodwin, *Bully Pulpit*, 552.
13. Wellman, "Taft, Trained to Be President," 675–81.
14. "Walter Wellman Sounds a Warning," *Commoner* (Lincoln NE), April 17, 1908; and "Guaranteed Banks," *Commoner* (Lincoln NE), September 4, 1908.
15. Walter Wellman, "Greatest Get Together Convention of the Party," *Rock Island (IL) Argus*, July 6, 1908. The term "West" still included what today is called the Midwest.
16. Walter Wellman, "Taft Sure Winner; Apathy Only Peril," *CRH*, August 29, 1908.
17. Bryan's paper, *Commoner* (Lincoln NE), reported election forecasts favorable to Bryan. On September 25, 1908, it reprinted the *New York Herald*'s predictions, listing Indiana and New York as "doubtful" and Ohio as Republican but potentially a "surprise state." The October 9 *Commoner* said that N. O. Messenger, political writer for the *Washington (DC) Star*, had called Indiana for Bryan and Ohio doubtful. Examples of Democratic papers selectively quoting Wellman's predictions or noting enthusiasm of other Democratic papers for Wellman: *Williams (AZ) News*, September 26, 1908; *Commoner* (Lincoln NE), October 9, 1908; *Daily Democrat* (Anadarko OK), October 19, 1908; and *Rock Island (IL) Argus*, October 28, 1908. Wellman finally calls New York for Taft in *CRH*, October 30, 1908.
18. "Interesting Reading," *Arizona Republican (Phoenix)*, October 21, 1908.
19. Walter Wellman, "The Management of the Taft Campaign," 432–38.
20. Walter Wellman, "What It Costs to Elect a President," *San Francisco Call*, November 1, 1908.
21. "Difficult to Bulldoze Them This Year," *Commoner* (Lincoln NE), October 23, 1908.
22. "Walter Wellman's Statement," *Commoner* (Lincoln NE), November 6, 1908.

23. Walter Wellman, "Money Is Pouring in to Defeat Bryan while Labor Is Fighting for Its Very Life," *Rock Island (IL) Argus*, October 29, 1908

24. "Proof of Corruption," *Salt Lake Herald*, November 3, 1908.

25. Editorial, *Omaha Daily Bee*, November 8, 1908.

26. "Higher Journalism Standards Urged," *University Missourian* (Columbia), February 23, 1909.

27. "1909 the Year for Wellman?," *New York Sun*, August 13, 1908.

28. Mabley, *Motor Balloon "America,"* 32, 35.

29. Robinson, *Giants in the Sky*, 36–41.

30. Robinson, *Giants in the Sky*, 36–41.

31. Robinson, *Giants in the Sky*, 36–41.

32. "Predicts an Airship Trip across the Atlantic," *Fulton County News* (McConnellsburg PA), August 13, 1908.

33. "Aerial Destroyers: Prediction that War Will Soon Be Impossible," *Idaho Statesman* (Boise), March 1, 1894.

34. "Predicts an Airship Trip across the Atlantic," *Fulton County News* (McConnellsburg PA), August 13, 1908.

35. Crouch, *Bishop's Boys*, 349, 368, 375.

36. Crouch, *Bishop's Boys*, 349, 368, 375.

37. "Aviation Declared a Failure," 549; "Future of Sky-Sailing," 973–74; "Flying as an Art," 196–97; and "Aeroplanes and Motors," 81–82.

38. "Zeppelin Will Try for the North Pole," *Albuquerque (NM) Daily Citizen*, November 17, 1908.

39. "Peary's Persistence," 75.

40. "A Lost Explorer and His Chance of Rescue," *NYT*, November 8, 1908.

41. "Walter Wellman Leaves for Third Attempt to Fly to the North Pole," *Rock Island (IL) Argus*, May 12, 1909.

42. Wellman, *Aerial Age*, 182.

20. Under the Ice, Over the Ice

1. Bjørvig, *Norwegian Bravado*, 34.

2. Bjørvig, *Norwegian Bravado*, 34.

3. "Wellman's Balloon House Is Wrecked," *NYT*, June 28, 1909; Wellman, *Aerial Age*, 183; and Bjørvig, *Norwegian Bravado*, 43.

4. Bjørvig, *Norwegian Bravado*, 46. See also "Wellman's Balloon House Is Wrecked," *NYT*, June 28, 1909.

5. Bjørvig, *Norwegian Bravado*, 47.

6. Editorial, *Paducah (KY) Evening Sun*, June 29, 1909.

7. "Wellman's Balloon House Is Wrecked," *NYT*, June 28, 1909.

8. Bjørvig, *Norwegian Bravado*, 48.

9. "Mrs. Wellman Denies Rumor," *Washington (DC) Herald*, June 16, 1909; "Rita Wellman Is Runaway," *Columbus (GA) Daily Enquirer*, June 17, 1909; and "Will Try the Stage," *Spokane Daily Chronicle*, June 25, 1909.

10. "Social Doings at Seaside," *Washington (DC) Times*, August 16, 1907; "Wellman Home, Explaining," NYT, November 22, 1907; and "In the Social World," *Washington (DC) Herald*, June 5, 1908.

11. Wellman, "Pen Portraits," in Kellner, *Letters of Charles Demuth*, 167–68.

12. Wellman, "Pen Portraits," in Kellner, *Letters of Charles Demuth*, 167–68.

13. Wellman, "Pen Portraits," in Kellner, *Letters of Charles Demuth*, 167–68.

14. "Wellman May Attempt Flight," 203.

15. Wellman, *Aerial Age*, 182. See also Capelotti, *Wellman Polar Airship Expeditions*, 43–55.

16. Mabley, *Motor Balloon "America,"* 34.

17. Grierson, *Challenge to the Poles*, 45.

18. "Balloon Wreck Ends Polar Trip," NYT, August 22, 1909.

19. Wellman, *Aerial Age*, 185.

20. "Balloon Wreck Ends Polar Trip," NYT, August 22, 1909.

21. Grierson, *Challenge to the Poles*, 45.

22. "Balloon Wreck Ends Polar Trip," NYT, August 22, 1909.

23. Wellman, *Aerial Age*, 186.

24. Wellman, *Aerial Age*, 186.

25. Wellman, *Aerial Age*, 186–87.

26. "Balloon Wreck Ends Polar Trip," NYT, August 22, 1909.

27. Wellman, *Aerial Age*, 186.

28. "Balloon Wreck Ends Polar Trip," NYT, August 22, 1909.

29. "Balloon Wreck Ends Polar Trip," NYT, August 22, 1909.

30. "Balloon Wreck Ends Polar Trip," NYT, August 22, 1909.

31. What caused the equilibrator to break? Wellman told the *New York Times* (August 22, 1909) upon his return that it was "of the same material, weight, and workmanship as the one so severely tested on the trial trip two years ago" and that the "cause was a weak spot in the leather, undetected and unsuspected." However, Riesenberg, who was not there but who followed the events with interest, wrote that that it was same leather serpent as before and had deteriorated in storage (*Living Again*, 176). Writing in 1911 Wellman seems to indicate the same thing in *Aerial Age* (185): "Again we carried the leather equilibrator which had been so severely tested in the flight of 1907." One can imagine him, cobbling together funding from multiple sources, trying to save money by reusing an ice-battered piece of the 1907 ship and then covering up this decision after it proved unwise. Or maybe not. A 1909 photo that Corbitt provided for Mabley's book *Motor Balloon "America"* (35) shows Popov riveting rows of metal scales onto a long strip of

leather, said to be the equilibrator. To me it looks more like the preparation of a new object than the repair of an old one.

Author John Grierson, who interviewed Corbitt for his 1964 book *Challenge to the Poles*, concluded the equilibrator was unsuited for dragging over the ice. He wrote that the airship reached the pack "with results which might have been foreseen," that the leather serpent "started to oscillate violently from side to side like a long flailing whip," and that it broke after an hour of this strain (45–46). Neither Popov nor Wellman said anything about this; both indicated the flight had been smooth until the equilibrator broke, which Wellman said happened just short of the pack (*Aerial Age*, 187). See comments on Grierson in note 37 of this chapter.

32. Wellman, *Aerial Age*, 187.
33. Wellman, *Aerial Age*, 188.
34. Wellman, *Aerial Age*, 188.
35. "Wellman's Airship," *Evening Star* (Washington DC), June 16, 1912.
36. Wellman, *Aerial Age*, 189.
37. John Grierson says Corbitt told him another version of events in the 1960s. Corbitt was not aboard the airship but was with the crew immediately after the flight. He said Wellman was unperturbed by the loss of the equilibrator but that Loud panicked as the airship shot upward. In Grierson's words, Loud "pulled the release for the top gas valve and refused to let go. The *America* sank until she hit the ice with a bump . . . [and] two of the steel petrol tanks in the hull of the nacelle were stove in" (*Challenge to the Poles*, 46). Capelotti cites this version of events in *By Airship to the North Pole* (87). However, it contradicts Vaniman: "I tugged at the gas valve till I dared to let no more out, and then I found we had ceased to rise" ("Vaniman's Career One of Adventure," *NYT*, October 5, 1910). It is also inconsistent with Wellman's and Popov's description of a slow, controlled descent; with Wellman's claim that Vaniman controlled the valve; and with Wellman's consistent praise of Loud's courage (see Wellman, *Aerial Age*, 185, for example). Corbitt apparently didn't tell this story to Edward Mabley, who interviewed him for his 1969 book, *Motor Balloon "America."* Mabley attributes other details to Corbitt but writes that the crew let out gas a little at a time and came down slowly (39). Grierson's Wellman narrative confuses many details of the 1907 and 1909 flights; whatever Corbitt told him, it's not clear that he got it straight.
38. Wellman, *Aerial Age*, 189–90.
39. Wellman, *Aerial Age*, 189–90.
40. "Balloon Wreck Ends Polar Trip," *NYT*, August 22, 1909; and Wellman, *Aerial Age*, 190.
41. Wellman, *Aerial Age*, 190.
42. Wellman, *Aerial Age*, 191.
43. Wellman, *Aerial Age*, 191.
44. Wellman, *Aerial Age*, 191.
45. "Balloon Wreck Ends Polar Trip," *NYT*, August 22, 1909; and Wellman, *Aerial Age*, 190.

46. "Balloon Wreck Ends Polar Trip," *NYT*, August 22, 1909; and Wellman, *Aerial Age*, 190.

47. Mabley, *Motor Balloon "America,"* 40–41; and Grierson, *Challenge to the Poles*, 46.

48. Mabley, *Motor Balloon "America,"* 40–41; and Grierson, *Challenge to the Poles*, 46.

49. "Balloon Wreck Ends Polar Trip," *NYT*, August 22, 1909; and Wellman, *Aerial Age*, 190.

50. Wellman, *Aerial Age*, 193.

21. Nowhere Does His Story Ring True

1. Mabley, *Motor Balloon "America,"* 42.

2. Wellman, *Aerial Age*, 197.

3. "The North Pole Is Discovered by Dr. Frederick A. Cook, Who Cables to the Herald an Exclusive Account of How He Set the American Flag on the World's Top," *New York Herald*, September 2, 1909.

4. "Wellman Not to Be Balked," *Evening Star* (Washington DC), September 5, 1909.

5. Wellman tacitly acknowledged this in a later anti-Cook article in which he argued that personal character was the most reliable criterion for the acceptance of any explorer's claim. "Wellman Riddles Cook's Narrative," *NYT*, November 29, 1909.

6. "Any Way, Wellman Didn't," *Salt Lake Herald*, September 4, 1909.

7. Gibbs, "Adventures of a Reporter," 482–83, quoted in Bryce, *Cook & Peary*, 357.

8. Wellman, *Aerial Age*, 198.

9. "Peary Sends in Report that American Flag Is Nailed to North Pole," *Evening Star* (Washington DC), September 6, 1909.

10. Philip Gibbs, "Cook's Bewildered Story of Retreat," *NYT*, September 8, 1909.

11. "Peary Denounces Cook," *NYT*, September 11, 1909.

12. "Polar Discovery and Controversy," 417–19.

13. "Cook-Peary Cudgels," 459–61.

14. "Quit When He Heard from Peary," *New-York Tribune*, September 18, 1909.

15. "Peary's 'Proofs,'" 659–61. The accusation of payment was confirmed years later. See Bryce, *Cook & Peary*, 443–44.

16. Bryce, *Cook & Peary*, 448–49, 458.

17. Riffenburgh, *Myth of the Explorer*, 1–5, 172–90.

18. "Peary Meets Wellman," *NYT*, November 24, 1909.

19. "Cook-Peary Cudgels," 460.

20. "Wellman Riddles Cook's Narrative," *NYT*, November 29, 1909. Emphasis in the original.

21. "Topics of the Times" and "The Plight of Dr. Cook," *NYT*, November 30, 1909.

22. Editorial, *Gold Leaf* (Henderson NC), December 2, 1909.

23. *Charleston News and Courier*, quoted in "Topics in Brief," 1122.

24. "Chill for Dr. Cook," *New-York Tribune*, November 30, 1909.

25. Editorial, *Salt Lake Herald*, November 30, 1909.

26. "Repudiation of Cook," 1.

27. "Did Cook Plan to Make a Million?," *NYT*, December 25, 1909.

28. "One More Slap at Dr. Cook," *Spokane Press*, January 9, 1910.

29. Editorial, *Commoner* (Lincoln NE), December 31, 1909.

30. Bryce, *Cook & Peary*, 378–80.

31. Bryce, *Cook & Peary*, 861.

32. Bryce, *Cook & Peary*, 447–50, 876–81.

33. "Wellman Riddles Cook's Narrative," NYT, November 29, 1909.

34. "Predicts an Airship Trip across the Atlantic," *Fulton County News* (McConnellsburg PA), August 13, 1908.

22. Mr. Wellman's Unbusinesslike Charm

1. Dennis, *Victor Lawson*, 305.

2. "Wellman to Try Again," NYT, May 4, 1909: "The owners of the Chicago Record-Herald have turned over to Mr. Wellman, free of charge, the airship, plant, buildings and machinery of Mr. Wellman's former enterprise."

3. Dennis, *Victor Lawson*, 306.

4. Dennis, *Victor Lawson*, 306–7.

5. "In a Nutshell," *Commoner* (Lincoln NE), February 4, 1910; and "Khartoum as Mecca," *Washington (DC) Times*, March 11, 1910.

6. Dennis, *Victor Lawson*, 306–7.

7. Dennis, *Victor Lawson*, 306–7; and Wellman, *Aerial Age*, 257.

8. Walter Wellman, "Roosevelt Is the Picture of Health," CRH, March 14, 1910.

9. Walter Wellman, "Roosevelt Is the Picture of Health," CRH, March 14, 1910.

10. Goodwin, *Bully Pulpit*, 12, 115–16.

11. "Roosevelt Is the Picture of Health," CRH, March 14, 1910.

12. Wellman, "Home-Coming of Roosevelt," 555–56.

13. Wellman, "Home-Coming of Roosevelt," 556.

14. Wellman, "Home-Coming of Roosevelt," 559.

15. Wellman, "Home-Coming of Roosevelt," 560.

16. James A. Edgerton, "Run of the News in Washington," *Wenatchee (WA) Daily World*, June 7, 1910 (syndicated article).

17. Dennis, *Victor Lawson*, 307.

18. Dennis, *Victor Lawson*, 307.

23. The Funniest Damn Ship

1. "Atlantic City," *New-York Tribune*, August 7, 1910.

2. "Atlantic City," *New-York Tribune*, July 31, 1910.

3. "Brookins Tells of Amazing Climb," *Evening Star* (Washington DC), July 11, 1910.

4. "Aeroplane in Warfare," *New-York Tribune*, July 13, 1910.

5. "Wellman Airship Is Nearly Ready," NYT, August 30, 1910.

6. "Think Wellman Can Win," NYT, July 10, 1910.

7. Rovner, "Melvin Vaniman," 20. Atlantic City still boasts of being the place where the word "airport" was coined; however, the connection is not to Wellman but to Bader Field, site of the 1910 air carnival, that began regularly serving both land-based planes and seaplanes in 1911. Though it was not the first functioning

airport, it became the first to be so described when in 1919 a newspaper writer dubbed it an "air-port." But the expression was not entirely new even when Zahm used it; during a visit to the United States in 1902, Santos-Dumont predicted that New York City would become "the great air port of the world." See Hoffman, *Wings of Madness*, 183.

8. "Wellman Is Confident," *NYT*, August 8, 1910.

9. "By Airship across Ocean," *NYT*, July 9, 1910.

10. "Think That Balloon Can Cross Atlantic," *NYT*, July 10, 1910.

11. "Problems of First Transatlantic Flight," *NYT*, July 10, 1910.

12. "By Airship across Ocean," *NYT*, July 9, 1910.

13. Quoted in "Think That Balloon Can Cross Atlantic," *NYT*, July 10, 1910.

14. "A Flight by Airship across the Atlantic Ocean," *NYT*, July 9, 1910.

15. "Wellman Again," *Salt Lake Herald*, July 10, 1910.

16. "Walter Again," *Richmond (VA) Times-Dispatch*, July 11, 1910.

17. Editorial, *Ottumwa (IA) Tri-Weekly Courier*, July 12, 1910.

18. "Wellman on His Plans," *NYT*, July 23, 1910.

19. "Wellman," *Daily Missoulian* (MT), August 4, 1910.

20. Wellman, *Aerial Age*, 260; and editorial, *Owingsville (KY) Outlook*, July 14, 1910.

21. "A Flight by Airship across the Atlantic Ocean," *NYT*, July 9, 1910.

22. "Personnel of the Crew," *NYT*, October 16, 1910; and Dilks, "Jack Irwin."

23. "Wireless Telegraphy in Aerial Navigation," *Washington (DC) Times*, April 14, 1907.

24. "Airship to Test Wireless," *New-York Tribune*, August 19, 1910.

25. Mabley, *Motor Balloon "America,"* 46.

26. "Personnel of the Crew," *NYT*, October 16, 1910.

27. "Wellman Off for Europe in His Airship America," *NYT*, October 16, 1910.

28. "Six in Wellman's Crew," *NYT*, September 7, 1910.

29. "Thinks Balloonists Will Have Success," *Washington (DC) Times*, October 16, 1910.

30. "Atlantic City," *New-York Tribune*, September 4, 1910; and "Wellman Balloon Is Almost Ready," *Richmond (VA) Times-Dispatch*, September 5, 1910.

31. "In the Social World," *Washington (DC) Herald*, October 28, 1910, 5; and Rita W. Leo in *U.S. Federal Census*, 1920. Meta Leo was born May 19, 1911. See also New York Passenger Lists, 1820–1957, S.S. *Britannic*, sailing from Liverpool, September 8, 1934, at Ancestry.com.

32. Smithsonian National Air and Space Museum, Walter and Arthur Wellman Collection, NASM-9A10732.

33. Walter Wellman in *U.S. Federal Census*, 1920.

24. Bringer of War and Peace

1. Wellman, "Homecoming of Roosevelt," 559.

2. Goodwin, *Bully Pulpit*, 643.

3. Roosevelt, *New Nationalism*, 10.

4. Roosevelt, *New Nationalism*, 11.

5. Roosevelt, *New Nationalism*, 13.

6. Roosevelt, *New Nationalism*, 14.

7. Roosevelt, *New Nationalism*, 18.

8. Goodwin, *Bully Pulpit*, 643.

9. "Wellman's Aim in His Ocean Flight," NYT, September 16, 1910.

10. "Aerial Destroyers: Prediction that War Will Soon Be Impossible," *Idaho Statesman* (Boise), March 1, 1894.

11. Quoted in Franklin, *War Stars*, 81.

12. The first military submarine was the acorn-shaped, hand-powered *Turtle*, built in 1775 and used against the British Royal Navy during the Revolutionary War.

13. Franklin, *War Stars*, 12–16.

14. Franklin, *War Stars*, 15–16.

15. Franklin, *War Stars*, 15.

16. Franklin, *War Stars*, 16.

17. Written in 1835, the poem was not published until 1842.

18. Tägil, "Alfred Nobel's Thoughts."

19. Quoted in Ellen Johnson Sirleaf, "Alfred Nobel's Legacy to Women," NYT, December 13, 2011.

20. Franklin, *War Stars*, 20–22.

21. See, for example: "How Aerial Engines of War Will Devastate the Seas," *Washington (DC) Times*, April 21, 1907; "Flying Machines for the Army"; and "What a War between the Great Powers."

22. For examples of peace predictions, see Dienstbach and MacMechen, "Aerial Battleship," 343–54; and "Future Wars Will Be Fought in Air," NYT, September 29, 1907. Examples of calls for preparedness: "Says United States Is Far behind in Aerial Navigation," *Los Angeles Herald*, October 07, 1907; "Aeroplane Invasion of England"; and "Germany's Aerial Campaign." See also Franklin, *War Stars*, 20–22.

25. The Aero-Not

1. "Vaniman Arrives for Atlantic Flight," NYT, August 1, 1910.

2. "Vaniman Arrives for Atlantic Flight," NYT, August 1, 1910.

3. Mabley, *Motor Balloon "America,"* 24; and Riesenberg, *Living Again*, 191.

4. Wellman, *Aerial Age*, 288.

5. See, for example, "Vaniman Confident Flight Can Be Made," NYT, October 20, 1910.

6. "Begin Work on Balloon," NYT, August 9, 1910.

7. "Wellman Inspects Balloon," NYT, August 21, 1910.

8. "Wellman Airship Is Nearly Ready," NYT, August 30, 1910.

9. See NYT for the following dates in September 1910: 7, 11, 16, 17, and 21.

10. "Wellman Airship Is Nearly Ready," NYT, August 30, 1910.

11. Wellman, *Aerial Age*, 223.

12. "Atlantic City," *New-York Tribune*, September 4, 1910.

13. "Wellman Fears Coast Winds," NYT, September 21, 1910.

14. "Wellman Engines Get First Try-Out," *NYT*, September 26, 1910. See also "Wellman's Aim in His Ocean Flight," *NYT*, September 16, 1910; and "Wellman's Plans for Ocean Flight Perils," *NYT*, September 28, 1910.

15. "Wellman Engines Get First Try-Out," *NYT*, September 26, 1910.

16. "Wellman Airship Is Safely Launched," *NYT*, September 25, 1910; and "Wellman's Flier Ready for the Air," *NYT*, September 27, 1910.

17. "Wellman Airship in Danger," *NYT*, September 17, 1910.

18. "Wellman Airship Met Weather Crisis," *NYT*, October 4, 1910.

19. "School Boy Handlers for Wellman Flier," *NYT*, September 30, 1910.

20. "Times Sends News to Waiting Wives," *NYT*, October 19, 1910; and Mabley, *Motor Balloon "America,"* 51.

21. Wellman, *Aerial Age*, 234.

22. "Wellman Explains Why He Didn't Sail," *NYT*, October 14, 1910; and Wellman, *Aerial Age*, 427.

23. "Flying against Chance," *NYT*, October 6, 1910.

24. Quoted in Mabley, *Motor Balloon "America,"* 65.

25. "Wellman Waiting to Start," *NYT*, October 11, 1910.

26. "Airship's Wireless Man to Hospital," *NYT*, October 6, 1910, 4; and "Wellman Plans to Start Today," *NYT*, October 12, 1910.

27. "Wellman Plans to Start Today," *NYT*, October 12, 1910; and "New Storm Wind Stops Wellman," *NYT*, October 13, 1910.

28. "Wellman Refuses to Fly," *Marion (OH) Daily Mirror*, October 13, 1910. See also "Wellman in Delay," *Washington (DC) Herald*, October 13, 1910.

29. "Airship's Tail Got Ready," *NYT*, October 9, 1910, 2; and "Wellman Plans to Start Today," *NYT*, October 12, 1910. See also "School Boy Handers for Wellman Flier," *NYT*, September 30, 1910.

30. Editorial, *Seattle Star*, September 10, 1910.

31. "Wellman Plans to Start Today," *NYT*, October 12, 1910.

32. "Carrier Pigeons for Wellman Flyer," *NYT*, October 3, 1910.

33. Quoted in editorial, *Donaldsonville (LA) Chief*, October 1, 1910; and Mabley, *Motor Balloon "America,"* 61.

34. Quoted in Mabley, *Motor Balloon "America,"* 63–65.

35. Editorial, *Los Angeles Herald*, October 7, 1910.

36. "Wellman Plans to Start Today," *NYT*, October 12, 1910.

37. "'Directness' of Wilbur Wright," 601.

38. "Proposed Transatlantic Airship Fight," 259.

39. "Proposed Transatlantic Airship Fight," 259.

40. "Running a Race with Chance," 270.

41. "Test New Propellers for Wellman Flier," *NYT*, October 7, 1910.

42. Wellman, *Aerial Age*, 256.

43. Wellman, *Aerial Age*, 267–68. The lifeboat is preserved at the National Air and Space Museum. See Crouch, "In the Museum."

44. Wellman, *Aerial Age*, 258.

45. "New Storm Wind Stops Wellman," NYT, October 13, 1910.

46. "Wellman Explains Why He Didn't Sail," NYT, October 14, 1910.

47. "Wellman Explains Why He Didn't Sail," NYT, October 14, 1910.

48. "Wellman Waiting to Start," NYT, October 11, 1910.

49. "Wellman Flying over Sea, Off for Europe in Airship," *Washington (DC) Times*, October 15, 1910.

50. "Wellman Off for Europe in His Airship America," NYT, October 16, 1910.

51. "Wellman Flying over Sea, Off for Europe in Airship," *Washington (DC) Times*, October 15, 1910; and "Giant Balloon Blazing Trail across Ocean," *Richmond (VA) Times-Dispatch*, October 16, 1910. The *Times-Dispatch* article is inaccurate in many details, such as Vaniman's spending the night in the hangar or Wellman's phoning the police and fire departments, so it's probably not to be entirely trusted in its report of a near mutiny. Clearly both Vaniman and Simon were frustrated, though, and other sources report Simon's threat to resign.

52. "Wellman Unjustly Assailed, Says Wife," NYT, October 17, 1910; and "Wellman Off for Europe in His Airship America," NYT, October 16, 1910.

53. "Wellman Prepares Again for a Start," NYT, October 15, 1910.

54. Andrée, *Andrée's Story*, 54.

55. "How the Start Was Made," NYT, October 16, 1910.

56. "Wellman Flying over Sea, Off for Europe in Airship," *Washington (DC) Times*, October 15, 1910.

57. "How the Start Was Made," NYT, October 16, 1910.

26. It's Europe or Bust

1. "Wellman Starts for Europe," *New-York Tribune*, October 16, 1910.

2. Wellman, *Aerial Age*, 280.

3. "Wellman Off for Europe in His Airship America," NYT, October 16, 1910; and "Vaniman Arrives for Atlantic Flight," NYT, August 1, 1910.

4. "Vaniman Confident Flight Can Be Made," NYT, October 20, 1910; Wellman, *Aerial Age*, 278; and "Wellman Flying over Sea, Off for Europe in Airship," *Washington (DC) Times*, October 15, 1910.

5. "Wellman Off for Europe in His Airship America," NYT, October 16, 1910.

6. "Achievement of a Century, Wellman Off in a Balloon," *Marion (OH) Daily Mirror*, October 15, 1910. See also "Wellman Starts for Europe," *New-York Tribune*, October 16, 1910, which tells a similar story with different dialogue.

7. "Wellman Off for Europe in His Airship America," NYT, October 16, 1910; "Wellman Starts for Europe," *New-York Tribune*, October 16, 1910; and "Wellman Unjustly Assailed, Says Wife," NYT, October 17, 1910.

8. "Wellman Starts for Europe," *New-York Tribune*, October 16, 1910.

9. "Wellman Flying over Sea, Off for Europe in Airship," *Washington (DC) Times*, October 15, 1910.

10. "Wellman Tells of His Record Airship Voyage," *NYT*, October 20, 1910.

11. "Wellman Tells of His Record Airship Voyage," *NYT*, October 20, 1910.

12. "Wellman Off for Europe in His Airship America," *NYT*, October 16, 1910; and "Wellman Flying over Sea, Off for Europe in Airship," *Washington (DC) Times*, October 15, 1910.

13. "Wellman Off for Europe in His Airship America," *NYT*, October 16, 1910.

14. "Wellman Off for Europe in His Airship America," *NYT*, October 16, 1910.

15. Wellman, *Aerial Age*, 281–82.

16. Wellman, *Aerial Age*, 336.

17. "Wellman Off for Europe in His Airship America," *NYT*, October 16, 1910.

18. Wellman, *Aerial Age*, 283.

19. "Wellman to Lecture, Refuses Vaudeville," *NYT*, October 22, 1910, citing LeRoy Chamberlin; and "Carrier Pigeons for Wellman Flyer," *NYT*, October 3, 1910.

20. Wellman, *Aerial Age*, 339.

21. Wellman, *Aerial Age*, 339.

22. Wellman, *Aerial Age*, 283–84.

23. Mabley, *Motor Balloon "America,"* 68. This apparently was Simon's story to Mabley. It is recorded nowhere else.

24. Wellman, *Aerial Age*, 339; and "The America's Log," *NYT*, October 20, 1910.

25. "Wellman Off for Europe in His Airship America," *NYT*, October 16, 1910.

26. Mabley, *Motor Balloon "America,"* 68.

27. Wellman, *Aerial Age*, 285.

28. Wellman, *Aerial Age*, 340.

29. Wellman, *Aerial Age*, 286.

30. Wellman, *Aerial Age*, 339–40.

27. Only a Question of Time

1. "News to Crowd by Electric Bulletins," *NYT*, October 16, 1910; and "Bulletins Printed by Unseen Hands," *NYT*, July 2, 1910.

2. "News to Crowd by Electric Bulletins," *NYT*, October 16, 1910; and "Bulletins Printed by Unseen Hands," *NYT*, July 2, 1910.

3. "All Atlantic City Eager for Messages," *NYT*, October 16, 1910.

4. Wellman, *Aerial Age*, 341.

5. "Wellman Off for Europe in His Airship America," *NYT*, October 16, 1910; and Wellman, *Aerial Age*, 287.

6. "Wellman Starts for Europe," *New-York Tribune*, October 16, 1910.

7. "All Atlantic City Eager for Messages," *NYT*, October 16, 1910.

8. "All Atlantic City Eager for Messages," *NYT*, October 16, 1910.

9. "Wellman Starts for Europe," *New-York Tribune*, October 16, 1910.

10. "All Atlantic City Eager for Messages," *NYT*, October 16, 1910.

11. "The America's Log," *NYT*, October 20, 1910.

12. Wellman, *Aerial Age*, 288.

13. Wellman, *Aerial Age*, 342–43.

14. Wellman, *Aerial Age*, 343–44.

15. Wellman, *Aerial Age*, 344–45.

16. "Wellman Tells of His Record Airship Voyage," NYT, October 20, 1910; and Wellman, *Aerial Age*, 290, 345–46.

17. Wellman, *Aerial Age*, 291–92.

18. Wellman, *Aerial Age*, 292–93.

19. Wellman, *Aerial Age*, 293.

20. Wellman, "Thousand Mile Voyage," 9.

21. Wellman, "Thousand Mile Voyage," 9. Afterward Vaniman told *Scientific American* that he was not aware of the sparks until nightfall, but he said the ship was so wet from fog there was no chance of fire. Apparently he felt there was no risk of a hydrogen leak. "Chief Engineer Vaniman," 334.

22. Wellman, *Aerial Age*, 302.

23. Wellman, *Aerial Age*, 295.

24. Wellman, *Aerial Age*, 298.

25. Wellman, *Aerial Age*, 298.

26. Wellman, *Aerial Age*, 299.

27. "Loud Tells of the Trip," NYT, October 20, 1910.

28. "The America's Log," NYT, October 20, 1910.

29. Wellman, *Aerial Age*, 346.

30. Wellman, *Aerial Age*, 297.

31. Mabley, *Motor Balloon "America,"* 72.

32. Wellman, *Aerial Age*, 346.

33. Wellman, *Aerial Age*, 300.

34. Wellman, *Aerial Age*, 300.

35. "Wellman's Flight," NYT, October 16, 1910.

36. "Wellman Starts for Europe," *New-York Tribune*, October 16, 1910.

37. "Aviators Praise Wellman's Daring," NYT, October 16, 1910.

38. "Aviators Praise Wellman's Daring," NYT, October 16, 1910.

39. "Aviators Praise Wellman's Daring," NYT, October 16, 1910.

40. Editorial, *Washington (DC) Herald*, October 16, 1910, 4.

28. The Queen of Spades

1. "Dodged the Equilibrator," NYT, October 22, 1910; and "Loud Tells of Trip," NYT, October 20, 1910.

2. "The America's Log," NYT, October 20, 1910.

3. Wellman, *Aerial Age*, 349.

4. Wellman, *Aerial Age*, 378.

5. "Heard Nantucket Surf," NYT, October 17, 1910; and "Wellman's Wireless Messages to the Times," NYT, October 17, 1910.

6. Wellman, *Aerial Age*, 302.

7. "Wellman Tells of His Record Airship Voyage," *NYT*, October 20, 1910.

8. "Wellman Unjustly Assailed, Says Wife," *NYT*, October 17, 1910.

9. "Wellman Unjustly Assailed, Says Wife," *NYT*, October 17, 1910.

10. Vaniman said later that he had hoped his swiveling propellers would allow the engines to raise the ship and pull the equilibrator out of the water when needed, but the swivels had some mechanical problem that kept him from adjusting their angle. See "Story of the Wellman Ocean Air Trip," 340.

11. "Wellman's Wireless Messages to the Times," *NYT*, October 17, 1910.

12. "The America's Log," *NYT*, October 20, 1910; and "Monday Night the Worst," *NYT*, October 20, 1910. After the flight, Aubert recalled the gale striking after they lost contact with land, or not until 12:45 p.m., but Simon had it in his log as noon.

13. Wellman, *Aerial Age*, 349–50.

14. Wellman, *Aerial Age*, 349.

15. Wellman, *Aerial Age*, 305.

16. Wellman, *Aerial Age*, 350; and "The America's Log," *NYT*, October 20, 1910.

17. Wellman, *Aerial Age*, 306.

18. "The America's Log," *NYT*, October 20, 1910.

19. Wellman, *Aerial Age*, 403–4.

20. Wellman, *Aerial Age*, 350.

21. Wellman, *Aerial Age*, 350.

22. Simon and Loud also mention a vote in their narratives, but they report only that it was unanimous in favor of staying with the airship. See Wellman, *Aerial Age*, 351; and "Loud Tells of the Trip," *NYT*, October 20, 1910. Vaniman later said that he alone had not feared that the airship would be pulled apart ("Chief Engineer Vaniman," 334). In a speech to the Aeronautical Society he placed more emphasis on the difficulty of keeping the airship aloft and the amount of fuel that was jettisoned (Vaniman, "Voyage of the America," 199). If Wellman's story is correct, in other words, it seems that Vaniman's main worry was not the integrity of his airship but the prospect of taking to the lifeboat far from the shipping lanes.

23. Wellman, *Aerial Age*, 307.

24. Wellman, *Aerial Age*, 307.

25. Wellman, *Aerial Age*, 295.

26. "Wellman Tells of His Record Airship Voyage," *NYT*, October 20, 1910.

27. "Wellman Tells of His Record Airship Voyage," *NYT*, October 20, 1910.

28. Wellman, *Aerial Age*, 350.

29. Wellman, *Aerial Age*, 378–79.

30. "Jack Irwin Tells of Wireless Work," *NYT*, October 20, 1910; and Wellman, *Aerial Age*, 350.

31. "Storm at Sable Island," *NYT*, October 17, 1910.

32. Wellman, *Aerial Age*, 350.

33. See also "Wellman Tells of His Record Airship Voyage," *NYT*, October 20, 1910.

34. Vaniman, "Voyage of the America," 199.

35. "The America's Log," *NYT*, October 20, 1910.

36. Wellman, *Aerial Age*, 313.

37. Wellman, *Aerial Age*, 314.

38. Wellman, *Aerial Age*, 314.

39. Wellman, *Aerial Age*, 315.

40. "Wellman Tells of His Record Airship Voyage," *NYT*, October 20, 1910.

29. A Sort of Bleeding to Death

1. "Wellman's Voyage," "Wind-Driven Craft Far away on Ocean," and "Zeppelin's Flight Probably Beaten"—all in *NYT*, October 17, 1910.

2. "No Word from the Balloon to Ship or Station," *NYT*, October 18, 1910; "Wireless Sweeping Seas," *NYT*, October 18, 1910; and "Cannot Locate Wellman Party," *Marion (OH) Daily Mirror*, October 18, 1910.

3. "Mrs. Wellman Not Alarmed," *NYT*, October 18, 1910.

4. Berton, *Arctic Grail*, 154–57; and Wilkinson, *Ice Balloon*, 154–65.

5. "Andree's Last Word Carried by Pigeon; Will Wellman's Come by the Wireless?," *Tacoma (WA) Times*, October 17, 1910.

6. "Wireless Sweeping Seas," *NYT*, October 18, 1910; and "Siasconset without News," *NYT*, October 18, 1910.

7. "Wellman and Crew Rescued at Sea," *NYT*, October 19, 1910; and "Loud Tells of the Trip," *NYT*, October 20, 1910.

8. Wellman, *Aerial Age*, 319.

9. "The America's Log," *NYT*, October 20, 1910.

10. Wellman, *Aerial Age*, 319.

11. "Vaniman Confident Flight Can Be Made," *NYT*, October 20, 1910.

12. "Vaniman Confident Flight Can Be Made," *NYT*, October 20, 1910.

13. Rolt, *Aeronauts*, 77–78; and Wise, *System of Aeronautics*, 95–96.

14. Wellman, *Aerial Age*, 320.

15. Wellman, *Aerial Age*, 379.

16. Wellman, *Aerial Age*, 354.

17. "Vaniman Confident Flight Can Be Made," *NYT*, October 20, 1910.

18. "The America's Log," *NYT*, October 20, 1910.

19. Wellman, *Aerial Age*, 356.

20. Wellman, *Aerial Age*, 354; and "Jack Irwin Tells of Wireless Work," *NYT*, October 20, 1910.

21. Mabley, *Motor Balloon "America,"* 78.

22. Wellman, *Aerial Age*, 354; and "Loud Tells of the Trip," *NYT*, October 20, 1910.

23. Wellman, *Aerial Age*, 355.

24. Wellman, *Aerial Age*, 318–19.

25. Wellman, *Aerial Age*, 319.

26. "Chance Put Rescuer in Wellman's Path," *NYT*, October 19, 1910.

27. "Wellman Tells of His Record Airship Voyage," *NYT*, October 20, 1910.

28. "The America's Log," *NYT*, October 20, 1910.

29. Wellman, *Aerial Age*, 358.

30. Wellman, *Aerial Age*, 358.

31. Wellman, *Aerial Age*, 316–23.

30. CQD

1. "Wellman Tells of His Record Airship Voyage," *NYT*, October 20, 1910, 4.

2. Wellman, *Aerial Age*, 322.

3. "Jack Irwin Tells of Wireless Work," *NYT*, October 20, 1910.

4. Wellman, *Aerial Age*, 323.

5. "The America's Log," *NYT*, October 20, 1910; "Trent Brings Home the Rescued Airmen," *NYT*, October 20, 1910; and Wellman, *Aerial Age*, 324, 361.

6. Wellman, *Aerial Age*, 380.

7. "Jack Irwin Tells of Wireless Work," *NYT*, October 20, 1910.

8. Wellman, *Aerial Age*, 362.

9. Wellman, *Aerial Age*, 381.

10. "Trent Brings Home the Rescued Airmen," *NYT*, October 20, 1910.

11. "The America's Log," *NYT*, October 20, 1910.

12. "The America's Log," *NYT*, October 20, 1910; and "Wellman Gets Two Records," *NYT*, October 19, 1910.

13. Wellman, *Aerial Age*, 361.

14. Wellman, *Aerial Age*, 325.

15. "Chance Put Rescuer in Wellman's Path," *NYT*, October 19, 1910.

16. "Wellman Tells of His Record Airship Voyage," *NYT*, October 20, 1910.

17. Wellman, *Aerial Age*, 362.

18. Wellman, *Aerial Age*, 362.

19. "Sighted America at 5 A.M.," *NYT*, October 19, 1910.

20. "Sighted America at 5 A.M.," *NYT*, October 19, 1910.

21. Wellman, *Aerial Age*, 326; "Wellman and Crew Rescued at Sea," *NYT*, October 19, 1910; "Sighted America at 5 A.M.," *NYT*, October 19, 1910; and "Loud Tells of the Trip," *NYT*, October 20, 1910.

22. Wellman, *Aerial Age*, 382.

23. "Wellman Tells of His Record Airship Voyage," *NYT*, October 20, 1910.

24. Wellman, *Aerial Age*, 327; and "Monday Night the Worst," *NYT*, October 20, 1910.

25. Wellman, *Aerial Age*, 327; and "Monday Night the Worst," *NYT*, October 20, 1910.

26. Wellman, *Aerial Age*, 327.

27. Mabley, *Motor Balloon "America,"* 82.

28. "The America's Log."

29. Loud said Vaniman gave the order; Wellman and Simon said it was Simon. "Wellman and Crew Rescued at Sea," *NYT*, October 19, 1910.

30. "Wellman Tells of His Record Airship Voyage," *NYT*, October 20, 1910.

31. "The America's Log."

32. "The America's Log"; and "Loud Tells of Trip," *NYT*, October 20, 1910.

33. Wellman, *Aerial Age*, 329.

34. Wellman, *Aerial Age*, 331, 364, 382; and Vaniman, "Voyage of the America," 199. See also "Monday Night the Worst," *NYT*, October 20, 1910 (Aubert's narrative); and "Jack Irwin Enjoyed Airship Trip, Will Try It Again with Vaniman," *Tacoma (WA) Times*, March 30, 1911.

35. Wellman, *Aerial Age*, 364–65, 382.

36. Wellman, *Aerial Age*, 331–32.

37. Wellman, *Aerial Age*, 333, 382.

38. Wellman, *Aerial Age*, 333.

39. "The America's Log," *NYT*, October 20, 1910.

40. "Crew of Abandoned Dirigible Arrives," *New-York Tribune*, October 20, 1910.

41. "Trent Brings Home the Rescued Airmen," *NYT*, October 20, 1910.

42. "Trent Brings Home the Rescued Airmen," *NYT*, October 20, 1910.

43. "Wellman Tells of His Record Airship Voyage," *NYT*, October 20, 1910; and "Trent Brings Home the Rescued Airmen," *NYT*, October 20, 1910.

44. Wellman, *Aerial Age*, 333.

45. "Trent Brings Home the Rescued Airmen," *NYT*, October 20, 1910.

46. Wellman, *Aerial Age*, 334.

47. Wellman, *Aerial Age*, 333; and "The America's Log," *NYT*, October 20, 1910.

31. You're All Right, Old Man!

1. "Graphic Stories of Wellman's Rescue," *New-York Tribune*, October 19, 1910. Administered by the Treasury Department, the U.S. Revenue Cutter Service handled offshore search and rescue until its 1915 merger with the U.S. Life-Saving Service to form the U.S. Coast Guard.

2. "Wellman and His Airship," *NYT*, October 18, 1910.

3. Quoted in "Comment on Wellman's Trip," *NYT*, October 18, 1910.

4. "Wellman's Trip," *Los Angeles Herald*, October 18, 1910.

5. "Graphic Stories of Wellman's Rescue," *New-York Tribune*, October 19, 1910.

6. "Graphic Stories of Wellman's Rescue," *New-York Tribune*, October 19, 1910.

7. "Will Try Again," *Alexandria (VA) Gazette*, October 19, 1910; and "Trent Brings Homes the Rescued Airmen," *NYT*, October 20, 1910.

8. Wellman, *Aerial Age*, 366.

9. "Atlantic City Excited," *NYT*, October 19, 1910.

10. "Mrs. Wellman Pleased," *Evening Times* (Grand Forks ND), October 18, 1910.

11. "Times Sends News to Waiting Wives," *NYT*, October 19, 1910.

12. "Times Sends News to Waiting Wives," *NYT*, October 19, 1910.

13. "Met by the Times Tug," *NYT*, October 20, 1910.

14. "Met by the Times Tug," *NYT*, October 20, 1910.

15. "Met by the Times Tug," *NYT*, October 20, 1910.

16. "Crew of Abandoned Dirigible Arrives," *New-York Tribune*, October 20, 1910.

17. "Crew of Abandoned Dirigible Arrives," *New-York Tribune*, October 20, 1910.

18. "Crew of Abandoned Dirigible Arrives," *New-York Tribune*, October 20, 1910.

19. United Press, "Wellman's Cat to Go on the Stage," *Tacoma (WA) Times*, October 19, 1910.

20. "Walter Wellman Abandons Airship," *Herald and News* (Newberry SC), October 21, 1910.

21. "Crew of Abandoned Dirigible Arrives," *New-York Tribune*, October 20, 1910.

22. "Crew of Abandoned Dirigible Arrives," *New-York Tribune*, October 20, 1910.

23. "Wellman Makes a Remarkable Flight," *Washington (DC) Times*, October 19, 1910. See also "Wellman Has Made Good," *NYT*, October 21, 1910; "Day Long Crowd at Wellman's Door," *NYT*, October 21, 1910; "Congratulations from Peary," *NYT*, October 22, 1910; Mabley, *Motor Balloon "America,"* 90; and "Doc. Cook Says That Wellman Is Great," *Spokane Press*, November 1, 1910.

24. "English Praise for Wellman," *Chanute (KS) Times*, October 28, 1910. See, for example, "History of 400 Years Ago Recalled in Air Voyage!," *Abbeville (SC) Press and Banner*, October 26, 1910.

25. "Wellman Attends Music Hall," *New-York Tribune*, October 22, 1910.

26. "Wellman Ovation at Atlantic City," *NYT*, October 23, 1910.

27. "Wellman's Trip Proved Grit, Although He Missed His Goal," *New Ulm (MN) Review*, October 26, 1910.

28. "Engineering View," 977–78.

29. "Wellman's Failure," *New-York Tribune*, October 19, 1910.

30. "Displeased One Passenger," *New-York Tribune*, October 20, 1910.

31. "Wellman to Lecture, Refuses Vaudeville," *NYT*, October 22, 1910; and "Wellman's Lecture Plans," *NYT*, November 12, 1910. Irwin, Loud, and Aubert lectured in vaudeville theaters, with Wellman's approval.

32. "Carrier Pigeons for Wellman Flyer," *NYT*, October 3, 1910; and "Walter Wellman on the Future of Aerial Navigation," *NYT* (magazine section), February 5, 1911.

33. "Current Poetry," 888.

34. "Current Poetry," 888.

35. "The Talk of the Day," *New-York Tribune*, October 19, 1910.

36. "Wellman to Lecture, Refuses Vaudeville," *NYT*, October 22, 1910; and "Will Try Another Flight to Europe, Says Wellman," *Washington (DC) Times*, October 19, 1910.

37. Mabley, *Motor-Balloon "America,"* 90.

38. "Topics of the Times: A Strange Place for a Cat," *NYT*, October 20, 1910.

39. Quoted in "Wellman Has Made Good," *NYT*, October 21, 1910.

40. See photo on page 266.

41. Wellman, *Aerial Age*, 10.

42. "Will Try to Cross Ocean in Balloon," *Richmond (VA) Times-Dispatch*, June 11, 1911.

43. "Funds Are Secured for Another Trial," *Washington (DC) Times*, October 19, 1910.

44. "Crew of Abandoned Dirigible Arrives," *New-York Tribune*, October 20, 1910. See also "Vaniman Confident Flight Can Be Made," *NYT*, October 20, 1910.

45. "Topics of the Times: An Adventure in All Its Aspects," *NYT*, October 21, 1910. Arthur Wellman's wife was reported to have said the same about Walter. See "Sister-in-Law of Wellman in Tacoma," *Tacoma (WA) Times*, October 20, 1910.

46. "Crew of Abandoned Dirigible Arrives," *New-York Tribune*, October 20, 1910.

32. New Dreams for the Aerial Age

1. "Vaniman Confident Flight Can Be Made," *NYT*, October 20, 1910.

2. "Crew of Abandoned Dirigible Arrives," *New-York Tribune*, October 20, 1910.

3. Frederick Cook's "confession" in the same issue received great publicity starting December 16. See United Press, "Cook Says Life in the Far North Makes a Person 'See Things,'" *Tacoma (WA) Times*, December 16, 1910. The first ads for *Aerial Age* started appearing in papers on January 18, 1911. See, for example, *Forest Republican* (Tionesta PA), January 18, 1911.

4. Wellman, *Aerial Age*, 257–58.

5. "Planning Trip over Ocean," *New-York Tribune*, December 19, 1910.

6. Vaniman finally acknowledged Wellman's noninvolvement on July 25, 1911. "Wellman Gives up Trip," *Richmond (VA) Times Dispatch*, July 26, 1911.

7. Wellman, *Aerial Age*, 11.

8. "Johnstone, Wing Crippled, Drops 500 Feet; Killed," *Los Angeles Herald*, November 18, 1910.

9. Wellman, *Aerial Age*, 441–42.

10. Wellman, *Aerial Age*, 443–44.

11. Wellman, *Aerial Age*, 448.

12. Wellman, *Aerial Age*, 447.

13. Wellman, *Aerial Age*, 448.

14. Dienstbach and MacMechen, "Aerial Battleship," 343.

15. See, for example, "Aeroplane and Dirigible in War," 16–17; and "Aeroplane or Dirigible in War?," 434–35.

16. "Ely Flies in Fog from Ship to Land," *NYT*, November 15, 1910; "Flies to Warship Then Back Again," *NYT*, January 18, 1911; and "Cannon on an Aeroplane," 250.

17. "Use of Aeroplanes," 402–403; "Nicholas Popoff," 110; and "Aviators and Bulgarians," *NYT*, November 3, 1912, 2. The world's first airplane pilot to be shot down was 2nd Lt. Piero Manzini on August 25, 1912, during the Italo-Turkish War. Flying a reconnaissance mission in Libya, Manzini died after his plane was brought down by Turkish rifle fire.

18. "Cure for Rush Hour Jam," *NYT*, July 2, 1911. A later version of his plan called for ten-car local trains and fifteen-car express trains. See Walter Wellman, "Multiple Entrances to Relieve Subway Crush," *New York Sun*, July 14, 1912.

19. Editorial, *Ottumwa (IA) Tri-Weekly Courier*, May 18, 1911.

20. "Vaniman Gets Fund for European Trip," *Marion (OH) Daily Mirror*, February 8, 1911; and "Vaniman Asks Chance to Try Cross-Ocean Flight," *Washington (DC) Times*, February 27, 1911.

21. "To Back Cross-Sea Flight," *NYT*, June 12, 1911.

22. As are the latest generation of Goodyear-owned Zeppelin NT airships.

23. Goodyear Tire and Rubber Co., "Wonderful Future for Ballooning," 25.

24. "Filling a 400,000 Cubic-foot Balloon," 316.

25. "Vaniman-Seiberling Transatlantic Expedition," 366–67.

26. "Vaniman-Seiberling Transatlantic Expedition," 366–67.

27. Goodyear Tire and Rubber Co., "Causes of the Akron Disaster," 28–29.

28. Goodyear Tire and Rubber Co., "Causes of the Akron Disaster," 28–29.

29. Goodyear Tire and Rubber Co., "Causes of the Akron Disaster," 28–29.

33. The Most Perilous Element of All

1. "Ready to Cross Ocean," *Washington (DC) Herald*, May 9, 1911.

2. "Another Attempt to Fly across the Atlantic," *Ocala (FL) Evening Star*, October 20, 1911.

3. "Navy to Follow Vaniman Balloon," *Richmond (VA) Times-Dispatch*, October 31, 1911.

4. "Ban on Airships," *Washington (DC) Herald*, October 26, 1910.

5. "Heroine of Aviation Romance," *Washington (DC) Herald*, March 12, 1911.

6. "Vaniman Makes Trial Trip in New Dirigible," *Calumet (MI) News*, November 4, 1911.

7. "Destruction of the Airship 'Akron,'" 28–29.

8. "No Flight for Ten Days," *New-York Tribune*, November 6, 1911.

9. "Vaniman Puts Off Trans-Atlantic Flight," *Washington (DC) Times*, November 9, 1911; and "Vaniman Gives Up Plan to Cross Sea in Airship," *Rock Island (IL) Argus*, November 6, 1911.

10. Editorial, *Norfolk (NE) Weekly News*, November 24, 1911.

11. "Dirigible Rebuilt to Fly across Atlantic," *San Francisco Call*, April 3, 1912.

12. "Wellman's Wireless Operator Is Here in the Hilonian," *Hawaiian Star* (Honolulu), April 30, 1912.

13. Associated Press, "Vaniman Met Accident in Dirigible," *Bryan (TX) Daily Eagle*, June 1, 1912.

14. "Vaniman Airship Falls into Sea, Saved by Youth," *New York Evening World*, June 1, 1912.

15. "Zeppelin Speeds His New Dirigible on 450 Mile Trip," *New York Evening World*, June 1, 1912.

16. Vaniman, "New Dirigible," 9.

17. Vaniman, "New Dirigible," 10.

18. Vaniman, "New Dirigible," 10–11.

19. "Firemen Strike; Olympic Held," *NYT*, April 25, 1912; "Olympic Strikers Make New Demand," *NYT*, April 26, 1912; and "Free Olympic Mutineers," *NYT*, May 5, 1912.

20. Vaniman, "New Dirigible," 11.

21. In *Aerial Age* (410–31), Wellman proposed an airship of even greater dimensions—656 long and with a gas volume of 2.1 million cubic feet. The ship would be only a little larger than the British airship R34, which made a successful round-trip crossing of the Atlantic in 1919. Germany had zeppelins capable of such a trip

a few years earlier. Reality quickly exceeded many of Wellman's and Vaniman's far-fetched aerial dreams.

22. Vaniman, "New Dirigible," 9–11.

23. Goodyear Tire and Rubber Co., "Causes of the Akron Disaster," 30. Eyewitness accounts differed in many details; this represents a summary of the points of agreement. See also "Vaniman Killed with Four Men Aloft in Airship," *NYT*, July 2, 1912; "Vaniman and Four Aides Killed When Airship Explodes," *Washington (DC) Times*, July 2, 1912; "Vaniman Ship Burst in Air; Five Killed," *Evening World* (NY), July 2, 1912; and "Five Killed When Dirigible Bursts," *New-York Tribune*, July 3, 1912.

24. Goodyear Tire and Rubber Co., "Causes of the Akron Disaster," 30.

25. Goodyear Tire and Rubber Co., "Causes of the Akron Disaster," 30.

26. "Aviation Tragedies; 5 Die," *Honolulu Star Bulletin*, July 2, 1912.

27. "Vaniman and Crew Killed," *Chateaugay (NY) Record*, July 5, 1912.

28. Goodyear Tire and Rubber Co., "Causes of the Akron Disaster," 30.

29. Goodyear Tire and Rubber Co., "Causes of the Akron Disaster," 31; and "Two Bodies of Vaniman Balloon Victims Recovered," *Washington (DC) Times*, July 3, 1912.

30. Goodyear Tire and Rubber Co., "Causes of the Akron Disaster," 31.

31. Goodyear Tire and Rubber Co., "Causes of the Akron Disaster," 30–31.

32. "Miss Quimby Dies in Airship Fall," *NYT*, July 2, 1912; and "Miss Quimby's Great Feats," *NYT*, July 2, 1912.

33. Associated Press, "World's Greatest Tragedy of the Air," *Bryan (TX) Daily Eagle*, July 2, 1912.

34. Forlanini, "Causes of Accidents," 157.

35. "The Vaniman Tragedy," *Calumet (MI) News*, July 3, 1912.

36. Editorial, *Yale Expositor* (St. Clair County MI), July 4, 1912.

37. "Vaniman's Lack," *New-York Tribune*, July 4, 1912.

38. "Fate of Vaniman," 50.

39. "Dead Airship Crew Left Needy Families," *NYT*, July 4, 1912; and "Walter Gest's Body Found," *New York Sun*, July 11, 1912.

40. "Dead Airship Crew Left Needy Families," *NYT*, July 4, 1912.

41. "Dead Airship Crew Left Needy Families," *NYT*, July 4, 1912.

42. Walter Wellman, "Walter Wellman Tells of Risks Fliers Face," *New York Sun*, July 7, 1912, section 4, 1, 3.

43. Walter Wellman, "Walter Wellman Tells of Risks Fliers Face," *New York Sun*, July 7, 1912, section 4, 1, 3.

44. Walter Wellman, "Walter Wellman Tells of Risks Fliers Face," *New York Sun*, July 7, 1912, section 4, 1, 3.

45. Walter Wellman, "Walter Wellman Tells of Risks Fliers Face," *New York Sun*, July 7, 1912, section 4, 1, 3.

46. Walter Wellman, "Walter Wellman Tells of Risks Fliers Face," *New York Sun*, July 7, 1912, section 4, 1, 3.

Epilogue

1. Jane Dixon, "Novelist Calls Marriage Banal," *Milwaukee Journal*, April 22, 1920 (syndicated by Evening Telegram, New York Herald Co.).

2. Barlow, *Women Writers*, 89–92.

3. Meta's date of birth is confirmed by various shipping manifests, such as the "List of United States Citizens" aboard the ss *Samaria* when it sailed from Liverpool on August 3, 1929 (Ancestry.com, "New York, Passenger Lists"). Traveling with her father, Edgar Leo, Meta was listed as having been born May 19, 1911, in New York City. On October 29, 1910, the *Washington (DC) Herald*'s In the Social World column reported that Rita Wellman "has been studying in New York for some time" and would live with her family that winter in their apartment in the city. A passport application signed by Rita on June 13, 1924, contains a statement (not written in her hand) that she was "married November 1910" (Ancestry.com, "U.S. Passport Applications."). Rita's play *The Gentile Wife* premiered at the Vanderbilt Theatre on December 24, 1918. Her first novel, *The Wings of Desire*, was published in 1919.

4. Jane Dixon, "Novelist Calls Marriage Banal," *Milwaukee Journal*, April 22, 1920.

5. "Library Brings $18,881," NYT, October 27, 1921; Rita Wellman Leo, passport issued June 18, 1924, Ancestry.com; and "Broker Ends Life by Shot," NYT, September 9, 1930.

6. See *U.S. Federal Census*, 1920. In the 1930 census Laura Wellman listed her marital status as "married," though she never remarried. I have not found records confirming that Walter and Laura divorced or that Walter and Bergljot ever married. Ruth and Isabella lived and traveled together for many years.

7. Wellman, *German Republic*, 9.

8. Wellman, *German Republic*, 27.

9. Wellman, *German Republic*, 37, 88.

10. Wellman, *German Republic*, 143.

11. Wellman, *German Republic*, 165.

12. Wellman, *German Republic*, 165.

13. See, for example, "World War to Be Help to Humanity," *Lynden (WA) Tribune*, August 30, 1917; Walter Wellman, "Society of the World's Nations to Thwart the Power of Prussia," NYT, March 3, 1918; Walter Wellman, "Make Kaiser Stop by Trade Threat," NYT, March 17, 1918; and "Calls War Boycott American Weapon," NYT, April 12, 1918.

14. Wellman, *Force Supreme*, xi–xii.

15. Wellman, *Force Supreme*, 36.

16. Wellman, *Force Supreme*, 120–21.

17. Wellman, *Force Supreme*, 36.

18. Wellman, *Force Supreme*, 97.

19. Wellman, *Force Supreme*, 124. Emphasis in the original.

20. Wellman, *Force Supreme*, 75.

21. Wellman felt so strongly about these ideas, including the League of Nations, that in 1920 the lifelong Republican endorsed the Democratic ticket of James M. Cox and Franklin D. Roosevelt for president and vice president. After President Warren Harding's death in 1923, Wellman and a few others claimed that the late president had secretly favored U.S. membership in the league and had only opposed it for political reasons. Wellman even claimed that Harding had told him privately two months before his death that he was planning to call a peace congress in 1924. See "Wellman Declares for Cox and League," *NYT*, October 31, 1920; "Harding Planned a Peace Congress," *NYT*, August 27, 1923; and "Asserts Harding Favored League," *NYT*, September 3, 1923.

22. "We Make History Faster than Grandpa Did," *Washington (DC) Herald*, August 18, 1919, and other papers.

23. "R-34 Starts at Midnight, Flies over City," *New-York Tribune*, July 10, 1919.

24. "How It Felt to Try the Atlantic in 1910," *New-York Tribune*, June 22, 1919, Section 7:5.

25. Walter Wellman, "Sees No Future for Gas Airships," *NYT*, September 11, 1925.

26. Grierson, *Challenge to the Poles*, 100.

27. "Wellman Attempts Message to Amundsen," *NYT*, May 13, 1926.

28. Among the most influential books about Robert Peary are Dennis Rawlins's *Peary at the North Pole* and Wally Herbert's *The Noose of Laurels*. Both conclude that Peary falsified his claim; Herbert did so after examining Peary's long-unavailable 1909 diary. Robert M. Bryce, in *Cook & Peary*, examines both explorers' claims with special emphasis on Cook's papers and concludes that Cook and Peary lied. Rawlins examines Byrd's claim in "Byrd's Heroic 1926 Flight."

 Not everyone is convinced, but the defenders seem to be fighting a rearguard action. Writing about Cook and Peary for the *New York Times*, John Tierney argues that "the 'discovery' of the North Pole may qualify as the most successful fraud in modern science, as well as the longest-running case study of a psychological phenomenon called 'motivated reasoning.'" See "A Clash of Polar Frauds and Those Who Believe Them," *NYT*, September 7, 2009.

29. See Andrée, *Andrée's Story*; and Wilkinson, *Ice Balloon*.

30. Capelotti, Introduction, in Baldwin, *Franz Josef Land Archipelago*, 23–25.

31. "Wellman Survivor Hails Air Conquest," *NYT*, May 10, 1936.

32. Robinson and Keller, *"Up Ship!,"* 185–86.

33. "Wellman Flight Survivor Found Living in Illinois," *New York Herald Tribune*, November 1, 1935. Clipping in Wellman LOC file.

34. "Jack Irwin Divorced; Wife, an Actress, Wouldn't Come West," *Seattle Star*, May 5, 1915.

35. Dilks, "What Happened?"

36. "Felix Riesenberg, Sea Author, Dies," *NYT*, November 19, 1939.

37. "Paul Bjørvig." For photos of Bjørvig's grave, see "Polar Bear Tomb," My Little Norway (blog), December 4, 2011, http://mylittlenorway.com/2011/04/polar-bear-tomb/.

38. Capelotti, "Historical Geography of an Archipelago of Polar Explorers." Wellman's body was cremated at the Fresh Pond Crematory in Middle Village, New York.

"New York, New York City Municipal Deaths, 1795–1949," *FamilySearch* database, https://familysearch.org/ark:/61903/1:1:2wkn-63q, accessed December 12, 2015.

39. Adolph S. Ochs Papers.

40. "Wellman Pursued by His Old Ill Luck," *NYT*, July 20, 1926.

41. "Banker Sends Check to Release Wellman," *NYT*, July 21, 1926. Jacoby later became U.S. ambassador to Abyssinia (Ethiopia) and an expert on Latin American affairs.

42. "Broker Ends Life by Shot," *NYT*, September 9, 1930.

43. Meta Leo, Passenger List, S.S. *American Merchant*, arrived in London, July 29, 1935, Ancestry.com; and "England and Wales, Civil Registration Marriage Index," Ancestry.com, 362.

44. "Would Be Suicide Found to be Prominent Woman," *San Jose Evening News*, June 18, 1932.

45. *U.S. Federal Census*, 1940.

46. Virts, "My Waterford Virginia Years." Photos of the Wellman graves at Fairfax Friends Cemetery in Waterford, Virginia, are at findgrave.com, searchable by name or memorial number: Laura Wellman (#31813071), Ruth Wellman (#31813074), Rose Chamberlin (#90548223), and Rita Wellman (#90548332).

47. "Wellman, Pioneer in Air Feats, Dies," *NYT*, February 1, 1934.

48. Wellman has received the most scholarly attention from P. J. Capelotti, who writes critically of his polar expeditions in several articles and parts of three books: his *By Airship to the North Pole* and *Greatest Show in the Arctic* and Baldwin's *Franz Josef Land Archipelago*. Michael F. Robinson, in *Coldest Crucible*, devotes a chapter (107–32) to comparing Wellman and Peary and the very different public images the two men cultivated regarding their use of modern technology. A few articles cited elsewhere in this book deal with specific aspects of some of Wellman's expeditions.

49. Translated and quoted in Diesen and Fulton, "Wellman's 1906 Polar Expedition," 76–85.

50. Diesen and Fulton, "Wellman's 1906 Polar Expedition," 79.

51. Mabley, *Motor Balloon "America,"* 8–9.

BIBLIOGRAPHY

Wellman was a newspaperman, and online databases of historical newspa-
pers provided an invaluable resource for this project: the National Endowment
for the Humanities and the Library of Congress's Chronicling America data-
base (chroniclingamerica.loc.gov); the newspaper archive at Genealogy Bank
(genealogybank.com); the New York Times Article Archive (http://query.nytimes.com
/search/sitesearch/); and Fulton History (fultonhistory.com). These databases enabled
me not only to find Wellman's many articles but also to gauge the range of press reac-
tions to his writings and adventures. Newspaper sources are cited in the notes.

Archives and Manuscripts

Adolph S. Ochs Papers, 1853–2006. New York Times Company Records. New York
Public Library Archives and Manuscripts. Series II. Subjects, b.56 f.12–16, Wellman
and Vaniman, 1909–1910, 1921, 1924–1925. archives.nypl.org/mss/17781#c206339.

Theodore Roosevelt Papers. Library of Congress Manuscript Division. www
.theodorerooseveltcenter.org. Theodore Roosevelt Digital Library. Dickinson
State University.

E. W. Scripps Papers, 1868-1926. Mahn Center for Archives & Special Collections,
Ohio University Libraries. http://media.library.ohiou.edu/cdm/landingpage
/collection/scripps.

Walter Wellman Collection, DS0-2577-3487. Library of Congress, Washington DC
(Wellman LOC).

Walter and Arthur Wellman Collection, Acc. No. 2004-0007. National Air & Space
Museum Archives, Chantilly VA (Wellman NASM).

Published Works

"Aeroplane and Dirigible in War." Literary Digest 41 (July 2, 1910): 16–17.

"An Aeroplane Invasion of England," Literary Digest 39 (August 7, 1909): 193.

"Aeroplane or Dirigible in War?" Literary Digest 41 (September 17, 1910): 434–35.

"Aeroplanes and Motors at the First Paris Aeronautical Salon." Scientific American 100
(January 23, 1909): 81–82.

Ancestry.com. "England and Wales, Civil Registration Marriage Index, 1916–2005."
Provo UT: Ancestry.com Operations, 2010.

———. "New York, Passenger Lists, 1820-1957." Provo UT: Ancestry.com Operations, 2010.

———. "U.S. Passport Applications, 1795-1925." Lehi UT: Ancestry.com Operations, 2007.

Andrée, S. A. *Andrée's Story: The Complete Record of His Polar Flight, 1897: From the Diaries and Journals of S. A. Andrée, Nils Strindberg, and K. Frænkel, Found on White Island in the Summer of 1930 and Edited by the Swedish Society for Anthropology and Geography.* Translated by Edward Adams-Ray. New York: Viking, 1930.

"Another 'Dash for the Pole' in a Balloon." Science and Invention. *Literary Digest* 32, no. 3 (January 20, 1906): 87–88.

Arthur, Charles W. "Walter Wellman: Who Plans to Reach the North Pole in an Airship." *The World To-Day* 10, no. 3 (March 1906): 316–19.

"Aviation Declared a Failure." *Literary Digest* 37 (October 17, 1908): 549.

Bacon, J. M. *The Dominion of the Air: The Story of Aerial Navigation.* Philadelphia: David McKay, 1903.

Baker, Ray Stannard. "Marconi's Achievement: Telegraphing across the Ocean without Wires." *McClure's Magazine* 18, no. 4 (February 1902): 291–99.

———. "The Reign of Lawlessness: Anarchy and Despotism in Colorado." *McClure's Magazine* 23 (1904): 53.

———. "The Right to Work: The Story of the Non-Striking Miners." *McClure's Magazine* 20 (1903): 323–36.

Baldwin, Evelyn B. *The Franz Josef Land Archipelago: E. B. Baldwin's Journal of the Wellman Polar Expedition, 1898-1899.* Edited by P. J. Capelotti. Jefferson NC: McFarland, 2004.

———. "The Meteorological Observations of the Second Wellman Expedition." *National Geographic Magazine* 10, no. 12 (December 1899): 512–16.

Barlow, Judith E., ed. *Women Writers of the Provincetown Players: A Collection of Short Works.* Albany NY: State University of New York Press, 2009.

Barr, Susan, ed. *Franz Josef Land.* Oslo: Norsk Polarinstitutt, 1995.

Berton, Pierre. *The Arctic Grail: The Quest for the Northwest Passage and the North Pole, 1818–1909.* New York: Viking, 1988.

Bjørvig, Paul. *Norwegian Bravado: Diaries from Franz Josef's Land and Danes Island.* Translated by Sue Nichols. Skien, Norway: Vågemot Miniforlag, 2004.

British Film Institute. "Walter Wellman at Virgo Harbor, Danes Island, Svalbard, 1906." PSUAbingtonAnthy (Penn State Abington Archaeology). Accessed November 28, 2015. https://www.youtube.com/watch?v=7vKEfkpV1es.

"The Brothers Wright and Their Flying-Machine." Science and Invention. *Literary Digest* 32 (June 2, 1906): 833.

Bryce, Robert M. *Cook & Peary: The Polar Controversy, Resolved.* Mechanicsburg PA: Stackpole Books, 1997.

"Call for a Motor Driven Sleigh." *Scientific American* 75 (February 8, 1896): 90.

"A Cannon on an Aeroplane." *Literary Digest* 42 (February 11, 1911): 250.

Capelotti, P. J. *By Airship to the North Pole: An Archaeology of Human Exploration.* New Brunswick NJ: Rutgers University Press, 1999.

———. "E. B. Baldwin and the American-Norwegian Discovery and Exploration of Graham Bell Island, 1899." *Polar Research* 25 (2006): 155–71.

———. *The Greatest Show in the Arctic: The American Exploration of Franz Josef Land, 1898–1905*. Norman: University of Oklahoma Press, 2016.

———. "The Historical Geography of an Archipelago of Polar Explorers." Septentrio Conference Series, No. 3 (2015). In *Proceedings of a Workshop on the Historic Place Names of Franz Josef Land*. Tromsø, Norway: Septentrio Academic Publishing, 2015). DOI: http://dx.doi.org/10.7557/5.3579.

———. *The Wellman Polar Airship Expeditions at Virgohamna, Danskøya, Svalbard: A Study in Aerospace Archaeology*. Meddelelser no. 145. Oslo: Norsk Polarinstitutt, 1997. http://hdl.handle.net/11250/173030.

Capelotti, P. J., Herman Van Dyk, and Jean-Claude Caillez. "Strange Interlude at Virgohamna, Danskøya, Svalbard, 1906: The Merkelig Mann, the Engineer and the Spy." *Polar Research* 26 (2007): 64–75.

Carlson, Peter. *Roughneck: The Life and Times of Big Bill Haywood*. New York: Norton, 1983.

"Catching the 'Labor Vote.'" *Literary Digest* 29 (October 1, 1904): 410.

Cather, Willa,. *The World and the Parish: Willa Cather's Articles and Reviews, 1893–1902*. Vol. 2. Edited by William Martin Curtin. Lincoln: University of Nebraska Press, 1970.

The Centennial Sketch of Clay County, Nebraska. Sutton NE: E. H. White, 1876. Reprint by Clay County Sun, Clay Center NE, n.d.

"Chief Engineer Vaniman on the Airship Cruise." *Scientific American* 103, no. 18 (October 29, 1910): 334.

"The Coal Strike Hearings." *Public Opinion* 33 (December 18, 1902): 772–73.

"The Coal Strike Situation." *Public Opinion* 33 (October 16, 1902): 484–85.

Cohill, Michael C. *A Spin on the Past: The Origin Story of the Modern American Toy Industry, as It Occurred in Akron, Ohio, Including the Story of S. C. Dyke and the First Mass-Produced Toy—Clay Marbles*. Edited by Carol L. Robinson. Ravenna OH: Hounding Productions, 2001.

"The Cook-Peary Cudgels." *Literary Digest* 39 (September 25, 1909): 459–61.

Crouch, Tom D. *The Bishop's Boys: A Life of Wilbur and Orville Wright*. New York: Norton, 1989.

———. *The Eagle Aloft: Two Centuries of the Balloon in America*. Washington DC: Smithsonian Institution Press, 1983.

———. "In the Museum: Dangerous Crossing." *Air & Space Magazine*, November 2010. http://www.airspacemag.com/history-of-flight/in-the-museum-dangerous -crossing-58604113/.

"Current Poetry." *Literary Digest* 41 (November 12, 1910): 888.

"DARE Interview: Black man of unknown age and education from Washington, D.C.; recorded in 1966." *Dictionary of American Regional English*. Digitized by American Languages project, University of Wisconsin–Madison. Accessed November 21, 2015. http://csumc.wisc.edu/AmericanLanguages/search_english.php?county=&state=dc.

Dennis, Charles. *Victor Lawson: His Time and His Work*. Chicago: University of Chicago Press, 1935.

"Destruction of the Airship 'Akron': Vaniman's Career and Tragic End." *Scientific American* 107 (July 13, 1912): 28–29.

Dienstbach, Carl, and T. R. MacMechen. "The Aerial Battleship." *McClure's Magazine* 33, no. 4 (August 1909): 343–54.

Diesen, Jan Anders, and Neil Fulton. "Wellman's 1906 Polar Expedition: The Subject of Numerous Newspaper Stories and One Obscure Film." *Polar Research* 26 (2007): 76–85.

Dilks, John. "Jack Irwin, Marconi Wireless Man." *QST*, August 2010. http://www.naval -airships.org/resources/Documents/vintage.radio.0810.pdf.

———. "What Happened after the Rescue?" *QST*, January 2011. http://www.naval -airships.org/resources/Documents/vintage.radio.0111.pdf.

"The 'Directness' of Wilbur Wright." *Literary Digest* 40 (March 26, 1910): 601.

D'Orcy, Ladislas. *D'Orcy's Airship Manual: An International Register of Airships with a Compendium of the Airship's Elementary Mechanics*. New York: Century, 1917.

Earth System Research Laboratory. "NOAA Solar Calculator." Boulder: Global Monitoring Division, National Oceanic and Atmospheric Administration. http://www .esrl.noaa.gov/gmd/grad/solcalc/. Accessed January 10, 2016.

"Engineering View of the Wellman Failure." *Literary Digest* 41 (November 26, 1910): 977–78.

"The Fate of Vaniman." *Scientific American* 107 (July 13, 1912): 50.

Fayant, Frank. "Fools and Their Money." *Success Magazine*, January 1907, 9–11.

"Filling a 400,000 Cubic-Foot Balloon: Hydrogen-Generating Plant for Vaniman's Transatlantic Expedition." *Scientific American* 105 (October 7, 1911): 316.

"Flying as an Art." *Literary Digest* 39 (August 7, 1909): 196–97.

"Flying Machines for the Army." *Literary Digest* 36 (January 4, 1908): 8.

Forlanini, Enrico. "Causes of Accidents with Airships." *Journal of the Military Service Institution of the United States* 55 (1914): 157–62.

Francis, Daniel. "Bernier, Joseph-Elzéar." *The Canadian Encyclopedia*. Toronto: Historica Canada. http://www.thecanadianencyclopedia.ca/en/article/joseph-elzear -bernier/. Accessed November 11, 2015.

Franklin, H. Bruce. *War Stars: The Superweapon and the American Imagination*. New York: Oxford University Press, 1988.

"The Future of Sky-Sailing." *Literary Digest* 37 (December 26, 1908): 973–74.

"Germany's Aerial Campaign." *Literary Digest* 40 (May 21, 1910): 1024.

Gibbs, Philip. "Adventures of a Reporter." *World's Work*, March 1923, 482–83.

Godoy, Martha. "'Cocaine for Snowblindness': What Polar Explorers Packed for First Aid." *Shots: Health News from NPR*. National Public Radio, September 28, 2012. http://www.npr.org/sections/health-shots/2012/09/27/161881513/cocaine-for -snowblindness-what-polar-explorers-packed-for-first-aid.

Goodwin, Doris Kearns. *The Bully Pulpit: Theodore Roosevelt, William Howard Taft, and the Golden Age of Journalism*. New York: Simon and Schuster, 2013.

Goodyear Tire and Rubber Co. "The Causes of the Akron Disaster and Lessons Drawn from It." *Aero Club of America Bulletin* 1, no. 8 (September 1912): 30–31.

———. "A Wonderful Future for Ballooning." Advertisement. *Aeronautics* 11 (July 1912): 25.

Gore, J. Howard. "The Wellman Polar Expedition." *National Geographic Magazine* 10, no. 7 (July 1899): 267–68.

Gould, Lewis L. "William McKinley: Impact and Legacy." U.S. Presidents. Charlottesville: Miller Center, University of Virginia. http://millercenter.org/president/mckinley/essays/biography/9. Accessed June 1, 2015.

Grierson, John. *Challenge to the Poles: Highlights of Arctic and Antarctic Aviation.* Hamden CT: Archon, 1964.

Grossman, Jonathan. "The Coal Strike of 1902: Turning Point in U.S. Policy." U.S. Department of Labor, Washington DC. http://www.dol.gov/dol/aboutdol/history/coalstrike.htm. Accessed August 11, 2015. Article originally appeared in the *Monthly Labor Review*, October 1975.

Helgeland, Conrad. "Placenames: Fuglefjorden (Svalbard)." Norwegian Polar Data Centre, Norsk Polarinstitutt, 2002. http://placenames.npolar.no/stadnamn/Fuglefjorden?lang=en.

Hempleman-Adams, David. *At the Mercy of the Winds.* London: Bantam, 2001.

Herbert, Wally. *The Noose of Laurels: Robert E. Peary and the Race to the North Pole.* New York: Atheneum, 1989.

Hinel, Bill, ed. *The Story of Clay County.* Sutton NE: King Newspapers, n.d.

The History of Jo Daviess County, Illinois. Chicago: H. F. Kett, 1878.

Hitchcock, Mary E. *Two Women in the Klondike: The Story of a Journey to the Gold-Fields of Alaska.* New York: G. P. Putnam's Sons, 1899.

Hoffman, Paul. *Wings of Madness: Alberto Santos-Dumont and the Invention of Flight.* New York: Theia, 2003.

"Horseless Sleigh." *Industrial World and Iron Worker* (Chicago) 47, no. 24 (December 10, 1896): 18.

"In an Air-Bag to the Pole?" Science and Invention. *Literary Digest* 29 (August 13, 1904): 196.

"Is Wellman in Earnest?" *Literary Digest* 33 (September 29, 1906): 434–35.

Jones, Mary Harris. *Autobiography of Mother Jones.* Mineola NY: Dover, 2004. Originally published in 1925 by Charles H. Kerr.

Kenney, Kimberley A. *Canton's Pioneers in Flight.* Charleston SC: Arcadia Publishing, 2007.

Kjaer, Swen. *Productivity of Labor in Newspaper Printing.* Washington DC: U.S. Government Printing Office, 1929.

Mabley, Edward. *The Motor Balloon "America."* Battleboro VT: Stephen Greene Press, 1969.

Mill, Hugh Robert. "The Race to the North Pole: The Expeditions of Nansen and Jackson." *McClure's Magazine* 1, no. 2 (July 1893): 147–55.

Morris, Edmund. *Theodore Rex.* New York: Modern Library, 2001.

"Mr. Wellman's Successful Failure." *Literary Digest* 35 (September 28, 1907): 431–32.

"Municipal Transport Problems: A Discussion of Rapid Transit in New York City with Propositions for Their Improvement." *Engineering Magazine* 27 (July 1904): 680–82.

Nansen, Fridtjof. *Farthest North: Being a Record of a Voyage of Exploration of the Ship Fram, 1893–96, and of a Fifteen Months' Sleigh Journey by Dr. Nansen and Lieut. Johansen.* Vol. 1. New York: Harper, 1898.

———. "Future North Polar Exploration." *McClure's Magazine* 10, no. 4 (February 1898): 293–305.

National Centers for Environmental Information. National Oceanic and Atmospheric Administration. US Department of Commerce. "Historical Magnetic Declination." Accessed January 3, 2016. http://maps.ngdc.noaa.gov/viewers /historical_declination/.

"New York, New York City Municipal Deaths, 1795–1949." *FamilySearch* database. Accessed December 12, 2015. https://familysearch.org/ark:/61903/1:1:2wkn-63q.

"Nicholas Popoff First to Fall in War." *Aero and Hydro: America's Aviation Weekly,* November 9, 1912, 110.

Nickerson, Sheila. *Harnessed to the Pole: Sledge Dogs in Service to American Explorers of the Arctic, 1853–1909.* Fairbanks: University of Alaska Press, 2014.

Officer, Charles, and Jake Page. *A Fabulous Kingdom: The Exploration of the Arctic.* Oxford: Oxford University Press, 2012.

Old Settlers' Association. *Old Settlers' History of York County and Individual Biographies.* York NE: Old Settler's Association, 1913. https://archive.org/details /oldsettlershisto00olds.

"Paul Bjørvig." *Norsk Polarhistorie* (Norwegian Polar Institute, Tromsø County Council, and University of Tromsø). http://www.polarhistorie.no/personer/Bjorvig %2C%20paul. Accessed January 18, 2016.

Peary, Robert E. *Nearest the Pole: A Narrative of the Polar Expedition of the Peary Arctic Club in the S.S. Roosevelt, 1905–1906.* London: Hutchinson, 1907.

———. *The North Pole: Its Discovery in 1909 under the Auspices of the Peary Arctic Club.* 2nd ed. New York: Frederick A. Stokes, 1910.

"Peary's Persistence." *Literary Digest* 37 (July 18, 1908): 75.

"Peary's 'Proofs.'" *Literary Digest* 39 (October 23, 1909): 659–61.

Phelan, Craig. *Divided Loyalties: The Public and Private Life of Labor Leader John Mitchell.* Albany: State University of New York Press, 1994.

"Polar Discovery and Controversy." *Literary Digest* 39 (September 18, 1909): 417–19.

"Proposed Transatlantic Airship Fight." *Scientific American* 103 (October 1, 1910): 259–68.

Rawlins, Dennis. "Byrd's Heroic 1926 Flight & Its Faked Last Leg: How Byrd's Hare Lost to Amundsen's Tortoise." *DIO* 10 (January 2000): 9–106.

———. *Peary at the North Pole: Fact or Fiction?* Washington DC: Robert B. Luce, 1973.

Redway, Jacques W. "The First Landfall of Columbus." *National Geographic Magazine* 6 (December 29, 1894): 179–92.

"The Repudiation of Cook." Topics of the Day. *Literary Digest* 40 (January 1, 1910): 1.

"The Return Journeys of the Navigable Balloon, 'La France,'" *Aeronautical Journal* 5, no. 2 (April 1901): 34.

Riesenberg, Felix. *Living Again: An Autobiography*. London: Methuen, 1938.

Riffenburgh, Beau. *The Myth of the Explorer: The Press, Sensationalism, and Geographical Discovery*. Oxford University Press, 1993.

Robinson, Douglas H. *Giants in the Sky: A History of the Rigid Airship*. Seattle: University of Washington Press, 1973.

Robinson, Douglas H., and Charles L. Keller. *"Up Ship!": U.S. Navy Rigid Airship, 1919–1935*. Annapolis MD: Naval Institute Press, 1982.

Robinson, Michael F. *The Coldest Crucible: Arctic Exploration and American Culture*. Chicago: University of Chicago Press, 2006.

Rolt, L. T. C. *The Aeronauts: A History of Ballooning, 1783–1903*. New York: Walker, 1966.

Rondeau, Robin M. "The Wrecks of Franklin's Ships *Erebus* and *Terror*; Their Likely Location and the Cause of Failure of Previous Search Expeditions." *The Journal of the Hakluyt Society*, March 2010, 1–11. http://www.hakluyt.com/pdf/Rondeau_Franklin.pdf.

Roosevelt, Theodore. *The New Nationalism*. New York: The Outlook Company, 1910.

———. *The Strenuous Life: Essays and Addresses*. New York: Century, 1901.

Rotundo, E. Anthony. *American Manhood: Transformations in Masculinity from the Revolution to the Modern Era*. New York: Basic Books, 1993.

Rovner, Adam. "Melvin Vaniman: Forgotten Pioneer Aviator." *American History* 41, no. 1 (April 2006): 20.

"Running a Race with Chance." *Scientific American* 103 (October 8, 1910): 270.

Russell, Isaac. "Melvin Vaniman—Aerial Adventurer." *Collier's* 48, no. 9 (November 25, 1911): 17.

Rydmark, Dag. "En mislykket polarferd" (A failed polar expedition). *Norsk Polarhistorie* (Norwegian Polar Institute, Tromsø County Council, and University of Tromsø). http://www.polarhistorie.no/artikler/2008/en%20mislykket%20polarferd. Accessed July 7, 2015.

Santos-Dumont, Alberto. *My Airships*. New York: Century, 1904.

"Santos-Dumont's Aeroplane." Science and Invention. *Literary Digest* 33 (November 24, 1906): 755.

Scott, James Brown. *The Hague Peace Conferences of 1899 and 1907: A Series of Lectures Delivered before the Johns Hopkins University in the Year 1908*. Vol. 2, *Documents*. Baltimore: The Johns Hopkins Press, 1909.

Scripps, E[dward]. W[illis]. *History of the Scripps Concern*. Edited by Gilson Gardner. Unpublished manuscript, n.d. In E. W. Scripps Papers, Series 4, Box 07, Folder 02. http://media.library.ohiou.edu/cdm/compoundobject/collection/scripps/id/8929/rec/1.

Sherard, Gerald E. *Civil War Veterans, York County, Nebraska*. n.d., Knoxville TN.

"Something New under the Sun." *Mechanics' Magazine, and Journal of the Mechanics' Institute* 7, no. 2 (February 1836): 125.

"A Steam Logging Sleigh." *The Wood Worker* (Indianapolis IN) 8, no. 1 (March 1889): 13.

Stockton, Frank R. "The Great Stone of Sardis." *Harper's New Monthly Magazine* 95 (September 1897): 570–85.

"Story of the Wellman Ocean Air Trip." *Scientific American* 103 (October 29, 1910): 340–53.

Tägil, Sven. "Alfred Nobel's Thoughts about War and Peace." Nobelprize.org, November 20, 1998. http://www.nobelprize.org/alfred_nobel/biographical/articles/tagil/.

Tierney, Alan. *Melvin Vaniman (1866–1912): A Biographical Note.* Goulburn NSW, Australia: A. Tierney, 2000.

"To the North Pole by Automobile." *Literary Digest* 24 (June 14, 1902): 805.

"Topics in Brief." *Literary Digest* 39 (December 18, 1909), 1122.

TopoSvalbard. Norwegian Polar Institute. Accessed January 9, 2016. http://toposvalbard.npolar.no/.

U.S. Federal Census Collection. Provo UT: Ancestry.com Operations, Inc. http://search.ancestry.com/search/group/usfedcen.

"The Use of Aeroplanes in Actual Warfare." *Scientific American* 107, no. 19 (November 9, 1912): 402–3.

Van der Krogt, René, and Peter van der Krogt. "Chicago Monument, San Salvador Island, East Beach, 1891." *Columbus Monuments Pages.* Accessed February 2, 2015. http://www.vanderkrogt.net/statues/object.php?webpage=co&record=bs004.

Vaniman, Melvin. "The New Dirigible—Its Great Possibilities." *Aero Club of America Bulletin* 1, no. 4 (May 1912): 9–11.

———. "The Voyage of the America." *Aeronautics* 7 (December 1910): 199.

Vaniman Panorama. Exhibit catalog. State Library of New South Wales, Sydney, Australia, 2009.

"Vaniman-Seiberling Transatlantic Expedition." *Scientific American* 105 (October 21, 1911): 366–67.

"Violence in the Coal Strike." *Literary Digest* 24 (June 28, 1902): 857–58.

"Virginia, Find A Grave Index, 1607–2012." Provo UT: Ancestry.com Operations, Inc., 2012.

Virts, William Benton. "My Waterford Virginia Years in the Thirties." *The History of Waterford, Virginia* (Waterford Foundation). http://www.waterfordhistory.org/history/waterford-1930s.htm.

Waldo, Leonard. "Aluminum in the United States." In *The Production of Aluminum and Its Industrial Use,* edited by Adolphe Minet, 243–44. Translated by Leonard Waldo. New York: John Wiley and Sons, 1905.

"Walter Wellman's Expedition to the North Pole." *National Geographic Magazine* 17, no. 4 (April 1906): 205–7.

"Wellman May Attempt Flight to Pole in August." *Popular Mechanics* 12 (August 1909): 203.

Wellman, Joshua Wyman. *Descendants of Thomas Wellman of Lynn, Massachusetts.* Boston: Arthur Holbrook Wellman, 1918.

Wellman, Rita. "Pen Portraits: Charles Demuth, Artist." In *Letters of Charles Demuth, American Artist, 1883–1935*, edited by Bruce Kellner, 167–68. Philadelphia: Temple University Press, 2000.

Wellman, Walter. *The Aerial Age.* New York: A. R. Keller, 1911.

——. *The American Financial Union: Suggestions for Unifying the Banks, the Business and the Government of the United States in a Scientific and Symmetrical System.* Washington DC: Press of Judd & Detweiler, 1908.

——. "American Life Insurance on Trial." *American Monthly Review of Reviews* 32 (1905): 458–68.

——. "An Arctic Day and Night." *McClure's Magazine* 14, no. 6 (April 1900): 555–63.

——. "By Airship to the North Pole." *McClure's Magazine* 29, no. 2 (June 1907): 189–200.

——. *Fairmont Coal Region: A Treatise.* Chicago, 1902. Reprint from the *Chicago Record-Herald.*

——. *The Force Supreme.* New York: George H. Doran, 1918.

——. *The German Republic.* New York: E. P. Dutton, 1916.

——. "The Home-Coming of Roosevelt." *American Review of Reviews* 41, no. 5 (May 1910): 555–60.

——. "The Inside History of the Great Coal Strike." *Collier's* 30, no. 3 (October 18, 1902): 6–7.

——. "Long Distance Balloon Racing." *McClure's Magazine* 17, no. 3 (July 1901): 203–14.

——. "The Management of the Taft Campaign." *American Review of Reviews* 38, no. 4 (October 1908): 432–38.

——. "The Mystery of the Great White North." *Collier's* 30, no. 2 (October 11, 1902): 10–11.

——. "On the Way to the North Pole: The Wellman Polar Expedition." *The Century* 57, no.4 (February 1899): 531–37.

——. "The Polar Airship." *National Geographic Magazine* 17 (April 1906): 208–28.

——. "Race for the North Pole." *McClure's Magazine* 14, no. 4 (February 1900): 318–28.

——. "The Settlement of the Coal Strike." *American Monthly Review of Reviews* 26 (November 1902): 552–55.

——. "Sledging toward the Pole." *McClure's Magazine* 14, no. 5 (March 1900): 405–14.

——. "Taft, Trained to Be President." *American Review of Reviews* 37 (June 1908): 675–81.

——. "The Thousand Mile Voyage of the Airship 'America.'" *Hampton's Magazine* 25, no. 12 (December 1910): 733–47.

——. "The Thousand Mile Voyage of the Airship 'America.'" *Hampton's Magazine* 26, no.1 (January 1911): 3–16.

——. *Walter Wellman's Indictment of Moyer, Haywood and the Western Federation of Miners.* Pamphlet, n.p., 1904.

——. "The Wellman Polar Expedition." *National Geographic Magazine* 10, no.12 (December 1899): 481–505.

——. "Where Is Andrée?" *McClure's Magazine* 10, no. 5 (March 1898): 422–26.

———. "Will the 'America' Fly to the Pole?" *McClure's Magazine* 29, no. 3 (July 1907): 229–45.

"The Wellman Polar Expedition." *National Geographic Magazine* 10, no. 9 (September 1899): 361–62.

"The Wellman Polar Expedition." *National Geographic Magazine* 10, no. 12 (December 1899): 481–505.

Westerdahl, Christer. "Sewn Boats of the North: A Preliminary Catalogue with Introductory Comments." *The International Journal of Nautical Archaeology and Underwater Exploration* 14, no. 1 (1985): 33–62. http://www.sewboat.narod.ru /partl/partl.htm.

"What a War between the Great Powers Would Mean." *American Review of Reviews* 39, no. 5 (May 1909): 613–14.

"Who First Suggested Arctic Exploration by Balloon?" *Aeronautical Journal* 1, no. 4 (October 1897): 20.

Wilkinson, Alec. *The Ice Balloon: S. A. Andrée and the Heroic Age of Exploration.* New York: Knopf, 2011.

"The Wind Forces Overcome in the Experiments of M. Santos Dumont with His Navigable Balloon in Paris 1901." *Aeronautical Journal* 7, no. 3 (July 1903): 49–53.

Winkelman, Phyllis H. "Fairview: Home of William Jennings Bryan." *Nebraska History* 55 (1974): 142–56.

"Wireless Telegraphy Experiments from a Balloon." *Aeronautical Journal* 4, no. 3 (October 1900): 162.

Wise, John. *A System of Aeronautics, Comprehending Its Earliest Investigations, and Modern Practice and Art.* Philadelphia: Joseph A. Speel, 1850.

Wright, Carroll D. *A Report on Labor Disturbances in the State of Colorado: From 1880 to 1904, Inclusive, with Correspondence Relating Thereto.* Washington DC: Government Printing Office, 1905.

———. "Report to the President on Anthracite Coal Strike." *Bulletin of the Department of Labor,* 43 (November 1902): 1147–1324.

INDEX

Page numbers in italic indicate illustrations.
"WW" refers to Walter Wellman.

Arctic Ocean (*continued*)
32–36, 136–37, 190–91; WW airship flights over, 158–62, 178–84. *See also* Andrée, Salomon August: polar balloon expedition of

Atlantic City NJ: air carnival in, 201; and "airport" word origin, 202, 326n7; airship hangar in, xv, xvi, 201, *202*, 204; and *Akron* airship, 267, 269, 275, *276*; and *America* airship, xv–xviii, 201–2, 218, 225–28; Grand Army of the Republic in, 215; Hotel Chalfonte in, xv, 219, 223, 258, 262; police and fire departments of, xvi, 222, 225, 228; summer tourist season in, 201; WW aerial warfare speech in, 209–10; WW and Vaniman triumphal return to, 261–62; wireless station in, 232–33

Atlantic Ocean: aerial crossing proposals for, xviii, 46, 172, 200–204, 213, 267, 288; weather forecasting for, 216–17, 221, 223. *See also* Wellman, Walter: expeditions

Aubert, Fred: bravery of, 252, 259; conversations of, 242, 248; correspondence of, 294; flight duties of, 223, 230, 233, 234, 235, 238, 241, 243, 333n12; hired by WW, 206, 222, 227; and Rebekah Wellman, 206, 242, 293; vaudeville lectures of, 337n31

aviation. *See* aeroplanes; airships

Azores, 243, 245, 257

Bacon, Rev. J. M., 130
Bader Field, Atlantic City NJ, 201, 326n7
Baer, George, 84, 89–90
Bahamas, 3–4, 11–12
Baker, Ray Stannard, 102–4, 130
Baldwin, Evelyn Briggs: background of, 55, 304nn16–17; on Baldwin-Ziegler North Pole Expedition, 290; in Franz Josef Land with WW, *44*, 54–61,

63–65, 68, 72, 304n29; leadership style of, 56–57, 59–60, 64–65, 306n9

balloonists: Frank S. Lahm, 144, 246; John Wise, 46; Louis Godard, 116, 124; Melvin Vaniman, 143–44, 246; Nicholas Popov, 178; Oscar Erbslöh, 204; Rev. J. M. Bacon, 130; Salomon August Andrée, 45–49, 55, 113, 125, 183, 290; WW, 144, 246

balloons: Fridtjof Nansen's opinion of, 132; guide ropes of, 46–47, 182, 246; landing risks of, 161–62; long-distance flight of, 46–47, 115, 119–20, 132, 246, 251; in Paris balloon race (1901), 115–16; Robert Peary's opinion of, 139; in warfare, 113–14, 210; WW 1894 investigation of, 37–38, 11. *See also* balloonists

banking: WW's reform proposal for, 168–69. *See also* Morgan, John Pierpont

bears. *See* polar bears

Bell, Alexander Graham, 72

Bell, Sherman, 99–104

Bentsen, Bernt, *44*, 55, 59–62, 66–68, 175

Bergersen, Bergljot, 207, 260, 285, 291, 341n6

Bermuda, 245, 247, 248, 249, 250, 260

Bernier, Joseph-Elzéar, 110–11

bituminous coal, 82, 85

Bjørvig, Paul: career and family of, 29, 175, 291; deaths of companions of, 61–62, 66–68, 174, 306n23; in Franz Josef Land (1898–99), *44*, 55, 57–62, 66–68, 70, 72; grave of, 291; as *ishavsfarer*, 29, 291; in Spitsbergen (1894), 29–30; in Spitsbergen (1906–7), 123; in Spitsbergen (1908–9), 174–76; testimony about S. A. Andrée by, 49, 303n27

Boardwalk, Atlantic City, xv, 201, 217, 225

Bottelfsen, Johan, 26, 28, 29, 31–32, 35–36

Brookins, Walter, 201

polar balloon research in, 37. *See also* airships: Zeppelin airships; Zeppelin, Ferdinand von

Gibbs, Philip, 188

Giffard, Henri, 113

glaciers, 58, 135–36, 161–63, 166, 175–76, 305n36

Godard, Louis, 115, 116, 124, 133, 146

gold standard, 14, 168

Goodyear Tire and Rubber Company, 272, 274, 279–80

Gottberg, Otto von, 128–29

Graham Bell Land, Franz Josef Land, 52, 72

Grand Army of the Republic, 215, 291–93

Great Depression, 291

Greely, Adolphus, 47, 136

Greenland, 20, 24, 55, 73, 135–38, 173, 189

Grierson, John, 324n31, 324n37

Grinnell Arctic expeditions, 1850–51 and 1853–56, 19–20

Gulf Stream, 23, 44

guide rope. *See* balloons: guide ropes of; equilibrator

Hague Convention of 1899, 113

Hall Island, Franz Josef Land, 52, 56

Hamilton, Charlie, 236

Hampton's Magazine, 218, 263, 265, 266, 268–69

hangar, airship: at Atlantic City, xv–xvi, 201, *202*, 204, 214–15, 218, 225, 229; at Danes Island, 122, 125, *126*, 131–32, 150, *151*, 174–76, *179*, 186

Hanna, Mark, 83, 92

Harding, Warren, 342n21

Harmsworth House, 63, 72

Haywood, William "Big Bill," 95, 99–100, 101–4, 288

Hearst, William Randolph, 40, 98

Hersey, Henry, 122, *147*, 153, 166–67

Hofma, Edward, *44*, 64–65

Holmes, Oliver Wendell, Jr., 73

Honolulu HI, 142–43, 277

Hotel Chalfonte, Atlantic City, xv, 219, 223, 262

Hoxey, Arch, 269

hurricane during WW Atlantic flight, xv, 222, 236, 247, 248

hydrolevator, 273

ice anchor. *See* retardateur

ice pack. *See* Arctic Ocean

icequake, 69–71, *71*, 73–74

Independence Bay, Greenland, 136

Independence Depot CO, 96, 99, 101

Indian motorcycle, 132, 316n21

Industrial Workers of the World, 103

International Geographical Union, 45, 47–48

Inuits (Eskimos), 18–19, 20, 24–25, 129, 136, 140, 187, 189, 300n5

Irwin, Jack (J. R.): background and early fame of, 204–5; later life of, 290–91; with Vaniman airship *Akron*, 273, 275, 277; vaudeville appearances of, 233, 290, 337n31

—as *America* (1910) crew member: abandoning airship, 254; CQD to *Trent*, 249–52; equipment of, 205, 221; hospitalization of, 217; in-flight transmissions on day one, xviii, 229, 230, 231–33; in-flight transmissions on day two, 238, 240, 242; in-flight transmissions on day three, 244, 245, 247, 248; before launch, 223; and vote against abandoning ship, 241

Isachsen, Gunnar, 181, 184

ishavsfarer (Arctic sailor). *See* Bjørvig, Paul

The Island at the Top of the World, 295

Jackson, Frederick, 20, 45, 49

Jackson, John Jay, Jr., 86–87, 104

Jacoby, H. Murray, 291, 343n41

Jacon, Jean, 222

Johansen, Hjalmar, 45, 125

Johnsen, Knut, 175–76

Johnstone, Ralph, 269–70

Jones, Mary Harris "Mother," 83, 85–86, 95, 98

journalism, 5, 39–40, 44, 40–42. *See also* exploration: press criticism of; exploration: press promotion of; Wellman, Walter: journalistic style of

Kane, Elisha Kent, 19–20, 135, 138, 294

Kiddo the cat (Trent): aboard airship *Akron*, 275; as "barometer," 247; becoming *America's* mascot, xviii, 226; and behavior during Atlantic flight, 229–30, 238, 240, 247, 252–53, 255; as celebrity, *261*, 264–66, *275*; discovered near hangar, 228–29; exhibited after Vaniman's death, 281; and "goddam cat" wireless message, 229; Vaniman's sudden regard for, 253, 259, 265–67

Kipling, Rudyard, 243

Kohlsaat, H. H., 37–38, 309n9

labor strikes: during 1890s, 14, 26–27; 1902 anthracite coal, 81–86, 89–95; and Colorado Labor Wars (1903–04), 96–104; by firemen of RMS *Olympic* (1912), 278; Parisian, and *America* delay (1906), 124

Lahm, Frank S., 144, 145, 246

Lake, Carson, 8–9

Lapp boat, 56

Lawson, Victor, 104–5, 110, 112, 164, 171, 178, 197–98, 200

League of Nations, 286, 342n21

Leo, Edgar, 206, 283–84, 291

Leo, Meta, 283, *284*, 291, 327n31

Leo, Rita. *See* Wellman, Rita

Liege, Belgium, 24

lifeboat of airships *America* (1910) and *Akron*: on airship *Akron*, 273–75; attached to *America*, 225–26, 227, 253; crew living in, 231–32, 234, 238, 240, 242, 246, 248; features of, xviii, 203, 205, 221; launch of, 251–55; at National Air and Space Museum, 329n43; near-miss of ship's masts by, 235; risk of launching, 240, 241, 248, 333n22

Lincoln NE, 167

Liwentaal, Alexandre, 128–29, 131, 166–67

London, England, 45, 47–48, 165, 188, 205, 214, 244, 261

London, Jack, 212

London Daily Telegraph, 200, 202, 203

Long, John Davis, 41

Long Island NY, 234

Lorraine-Dietrich engine. *See under* engines

Los Angeles Herald, 164–65, 219, 258

Loud, Louis: as *Akron* (1911) crew member, 275, 277; as *America* (1909) crew member, 178, 180; courage of, 241, 324n37; later years of, 290

—as *America* (1910) crew member: 206, 223, 227; engine room duties of, 230, 233, 234, 235, 241, 243; equilibrator duties of, 215, 239, 248; and fear of explosion, 235; injured during lifeboat launch, 253–54, 259; vaudeville lectures of, 337n31; and vote not to abandon airship, 241, 333n22

Mabley, Edward, 294–95

Marconi, Guglielmo, 130. *See also* wireless telegraphy

masculinity, changing views of, 72–73, 130

McClelland, Thomas, 101

McClintock, Francis L., 17–18

McClintock Island, Franz Josef Land, 51